Caracals may use their long ears to communicate.

NATIONAL GEOGRAPHIC

KIDS

ALMANAC 2010

NATIONAL GEOGRAPHIC

WASHINGTON, D.C.

National Geographic Children's Books gratefully acknowledges the following people for their help with the *National Geographic Kids Almanac 2010*.

Curtis Malarkey, Julie Segal, and Cheryl Zook of the National Geographic Explorers program; Truly Herbert, National Geographic Communications; and Chuck Errig of Random House

Your World 2010

Dr. Bryan Wallace, Science Advisor, Sea Turtle Flagship Program, Center for Applied Biodiversity Science, Conservation International

Chris Sloan, NATIONAL GEOGRAPHIC magazine

Awesome Adventure

Jen Bloomer, Media Relations Manager, The National Aquarium in Baltimore

Dereck and Beverly Joubert, National Geographic Explorers-in-Residence

Amazing Animals

Dr. Thomas R. Holtz, Jr., Senior Lecturer, Vertebrate Paleontology, Department of Geology, University of Maryland

Dr. Luke Hunter, Executive Director, Panthera

"Dino" Don Lessem, President, Exhibits Rex

Kathy B. Maher, Research Editor, NATIONAL GEOGRAPHIC magazine

Kathleen Martin, Canadian Sea Turtle Network

Barbara Nielsen, Polar Bears International

Andy Prince, Austin Zoo

Julia Thorson, translator, Paris, France

Dr. Sylvia Earle, National Geographic Explorer-in-Residence

Culture Connection

Dr. Wade Davis, National Geographic Explorer-in-Residence

Deirdre Mullervy, Managing Editor, Gallaudet University Press

Geography Rocks

Dr. Mary Kent, Demographer, Population Reference Bureau

Dr. Walt Meier, National Snow and Ice Data Center

Dr. Richard W. Reynolds, NOAA's National Climatic Data Center

United States Census Bureau, Public Help Desk

Dr. Spencer Wells, National Geographic Explorer-in-Residence

Glynnis Breen, National Geographic Special Projects

Going Green

Eric J. Bohn, Math Teacher, Santa Rosa High School

Stephen David Harris, Professional Engineer, Industry Consulting

Dr. Carl Haub, Demographer, Population Reference Bureau

Cid Simões and Paola Segura, National Geographic Emerging Explorers

History Happens

Dr. Gregory Geddes, Lecturer, Department of History, State University of New York, College at Plattsburgh

Dr. Robert D. Johnston, Associate Professor and Director of the Teaching of History Program, University of Illinois at Chicago

Dr. Fredrik Hiebert, National Geographic Visiting Fellow

Wonders of Nature

Anatta, NOAA Public Affairs Officer

Douglas H. Chadwick, wildlife biologist and contributor to NATIONAL GEOGRAPHIC magazine

Drew Hardesty, Forecaster, Utah Avalanche Center

Dr. Robert Ballard, National Geographic Explorer-in-Residence

Super Science

Tim Appenzeller, Executive Editor, NATIONAL GEOGRAPHIC magazine

Dr. José de Ondarza, Associate Professor, Department of Biological Sciences, State University of New York, College at Plattsburgh

Lesley B. Rogers, Assistant Managing Editor, NATIONAL GEOGRAPHIC magazine

Abigail A. Tipton, Director of Research, NATIONAL GEOGRAPHIC magazine

Erin Vintinner, Biodiversity Specialist, Center for Biodiversity and Conservation at the American Museum of Natural History

Barbara L. Wyckoff, Research Editor, NATIONAL GEOGRAPHIC magazine

Dr. Enric Sala, National Geographic Visiting Fellow

Special thanks to NATIONAL GEOGRAPHIC KIDS magazine Senior Editor Robin Terry, Design Director Jonathan Halling, and the entire NG KIDS magazine staff.

Contents

Your World 2010

8

Awesome Adventure

18

Amazing Animals

38

Culture Connection

112

Geography Rocks

144

Going Green

218

History Happens

240

Wonders of Nature

270

Super Science

298

COOL CLICK

Throughout the almanac, our virtual pet, Zipper, indicates cool click Web links to help you find out more.

Your World
2010

Got any plans for February 12–28, 2010?
Maybe you should try checking out the 2010 Winter
Olympics being held in Vancouver, Canada.
(See p. 267 for more about the Olympic Games.)

Barack Obama
Becomes First African-American U.S. President

Even though they live in the White House—Malia and Sasha are regular kids who go to school, have slumber parties, and love the Jonas Brothers!

PRESIDENT BARACK OBAMA'S INAUGURATION was the big event of 2009. A huge crowd—almost two million people—showed up in Washington, D.C., to see the country's first African-American President take the oath of office. Now, he and his family have settled into the White House at 1600 Pennsylvania Avenue. His wife, Michelle, is the first African-American First Lady, and their daughters Malia and Sasha are the first young kids living in the White House in more than ten years. As a result, a new playground has been added to the White House grounds!

President Obama campaigned on a platform of change, and he's already made many. For instance, during his first two months in office, he signed legislation that will help make it easier for people to get the pay they deserve from jobs—regardless of their gender, race, or age.

So what's in store for the President in 2010? One big goal is to end the combat mission in Iraq.

PANDA HOME GETS EXTREME MAKEOVER

A surveyor measures a courtyard that was destroyed by an earthquake in southwest China's Yunnan Province.

WHEN A DEVASTATING EARTHQUAKE hit central China in May 2008, there were some unlikely victims: pandas. Sixty-three captive pandas living at the Wolong Nature Reserve lost their home. Although all but two of the pandas survived, their home was badly damaged, and the pandas had to be temporarily relocated.

The Chinese government has pledged money to help reconstruct and expand Wolong, which will make it the world's largest panda breeding and research facility. This safe new home will go a long way toward protecting this endangered species.

The Secret Language of Dolphins

Here's a conversation worth talking about: A mother dolphin chats with her baby ... over the telephone! The special call was made in an aquarium in Hawai'i, where the mother and her two-year-old calf swam in separate tanks connected by an under-water audio link. The two dolphins began squawking and chirping to each other—distinctive dolphin chatter.

Hey! You guys want to chase some boats?

CRACKING THE CODE

"It seemed clear that they knew who they were talking with," says Don White of Project Delphis, a conservation effort to save wild dolphins. "Information was passing back and forth pretty quickly." But what were they saying? That's what scientists are trying to find out by studying the secret language of wild and captive dolphins all over the world. They haven't completely cracked the code yet, but they're listening ... and learning.

Really Wild PETS

WHEN PEOPLE THINK ABOUT OWNING PETS, most think of dogs and cats. But how about a cross between a domestic cat and an African wild cat called a serval? It's a real pet called a savannah cat! No wonder exotic pets—a cross between a domestic animal and a wild animal—are becoming more and more popular.

But not everyone thinks exotic pets are a good idea. These pets may need special medical care and unusual food. Their behavior can also be different from traditional pets, so they may need extra training and patience. But they certainly are cute!

The savannah cat

What's HOT

snowboarding

cast of iCarly

Here, Max!

Shrek

Taylor Swift

SPORTS
The X Games' viewership averages almost a million households each night! Don't miss gold medal snowboarder Shaun White at the Winter X Games from January 28 to 31, 2010.

PETS Five Hot Pet Names
1. Max   2. Sam   3. Lady   4. Bear   5. Shadow

MUSIC
Teen country sensation Taylor Swift headlined her first tour in 2009, hitting 50 cities. Look for her in your town in 2010.

MOVIES Five Hot Films in 2010
1. *Toy Story 3*   2. *The Chronicles of Narnia: The Dawn Treader*
3. *Harry Potter and the Deathly Hallows: Part One*   4. *Ramona and Beezus*
5. *Shrek Goes Fourth*

TELEVISION
Miranda Cosgrove and the rest of the iCarly gang will keep on Webcasting and airing on Nickelodeon in 2010. Watch out for more hijinks—you never know what might be smashed, eaten, or set on fire during the show.

2010: What's Ahead

2010 is the **International Year of Biodiversity.**

JANUARY

11th

75th anniversary of Amelia Earhart becoming the first woman to fly solo across the Pacific Ocean. (See p. 265 for more on Amelia.)

FEBRUARY

12th-28th

The 2010 Winter Olympics. Athletes from more than 80 nations will take part in these games in Vancouver, Canada.

MARCH

12th-21st

The 2010 Winter Paralympics. Physically challenged athletes from more than 40 nations will take part in these winter games in Vancouver, Canada.

APRIL

National Kite Month Go fly a kite! Celebrate with your family and friends. Learn how to make a kite.

MAY

18th

30th anniversary of the eruption of Mount St. Helens in Washington State.

JUNE

11th

FIFA World Cup begins. For the first time, this world-class soccer tournament is being held in Africa.

JULY

26th

National Scout Jamboree begins. Boy Scouts from around the country will join together to celebrate this tradition.

AUGUST

Don't forget to vote for

The New 7 Wonders of Nature

Vote online. www.new7wonders.com

SEPTEMBER

1st

25th anniversary of the discovery of the sunken ship R.M.S. *Titanic* by National Geographic Explorer-in-Residence Robert Ballard.

OCTOBER

8th

National CHILDREN'S Day

NOVEMBER

3rd-7th

American Sandsculpting Championship Festival, held in Fort Myers, Florida.

DECEMBER

21st

Look up—is the moon gone? Nope, it's just a full lunar eclipse. That's when the sun, Earth, and moon align, causing the moon to fall in the Earth's shadow.

THE SECRETS OF STONEHENGE

How a new discovery may help solve an ancient mystery

No one really knows how or why Stonehenge—an ancient circle of giant stone slabs in southern England—was built in a grassy field about 4,500 years ago. But a new discovery reveals that Stonehenge had a neighboring village that may have housed its builders. Other remains found at the site include bones of barbecued pigs and cows—evidence that Stone Age neighbors probably gathered here for feasts. Today, these signs of village life are providing archaeologists with more clues about this mysterious place called Stonehenge.

Frozen Mammoth Mystery!

Lyuba with children
ir Siberia, Russia

The discovery of a baby mammoth reveals 40,000-year-old secrets.

When two brothers came upon what they thought was a funny-looking sleeping animal, the last thing they expected to find was a perfectly preserved body of a baby woolly mammoth. The female mammoth, named Lyuba, is one of only five well-preserved baby mammoths discovered in the past 200 years. Experts hope that by studying Lyuba, they can uncover secrets about the woolly mammoth species that have been frozen in time until now.
To find out more, go online.
www.kids.nationalgeographic.com

15

ROBOT SPY

It's a robot. It's a gecko. No, it's a gecko robot!

THIS ADORABLE ROBOT, named **Stickybot,** is the amazing creation of scientists who are studying the biology of animals and using that knowledge to create robots. Part of a new generation of small robots, Stickybot is similar to a real gecko. Stickybot moves swiftly, walks on vertical surfaces, and, of course, has sticky feet. Because of its amazing abilities, Stickybot has even raised the interest of military officials who see spy service in its future! (For more about robots see p. 314.)

The Great Turtle Race

WANT TO FOLLOW A GROUP OF leatherback turtles on a two-week swimming journey from Halifax, Nova Scotia, in Canada, to the Caribbean Sea? The Great Turtle Race happens every year. A group of leatherback turtles travel from their nesting sites as they "race" through the open ocean waters.

Leatherbacks are the largest turtles on Earth, growing up to 8.5 feet (2.6 m) in length and exceeding 2,000 pounds (907 kg). They may live 50 years or more, but human threats, such as fishing lines and nets, illegal egg harvesting, and loss of nesting habitat means tough times for leatherbacks. The species is critically endangered.

The Great Turtle Race was designed to help raise awareness about the plight of the leatherback turtles.

To track the race, go online. www.greatturtlerace.com

TOP 10 Extreme Sports

(by participation*)

1. Inline Skating: 10,814,000
2. Skateboarding: 8,429,000
3. Mountain Biking: 6,892,000
4. Snowboarding: 6,841,000
5. Paintball: 5,476,000
6. Cardio Kickboxing: 4,812,000
7. Rock-Climbing: 4,514,000
8. Trail Running: 4,216,000
9. Ultimate Frisbee: 4,038,000
10. Wakeboarding: 3,521,000

* 2008 U.S. data, from the Sporting Goods Manufacturers Association

Awesome Adventure

An ice climber scales a Fox Glacier crevasse in Westland National Park, South Island, New Zealand.

CHINA CONNECTION

DUDE: Marco Polo

EXPEDITION: One of the first Europeans to explore China

WHEN: Starting in 1271

Marco Polo's father and uncle ask him to travel with them from Italy to China—on horseback! The adventurous 17-year-old says yes! On his journey, Marco claims to hear "spirit voices" in the desert. But it's worth it when he reaches the huge, glittering palace of Kublai Khan, China's ruler. There he marvels at paper money, tattoos, and rhinoceroses. Marco turns his travels into a book, which later inspires another Italian with adventurous ambitions: Christopher Columbus.

WHAT'S IN IT FOR YOU: The discovery of America

These stories make *Survivor* look like episodes of the *Teletubbies*. Braving everything from raging seas to blazing deserts, these five awesome adventurers explored Earth's uncharted, unforgiving unknown. If you think *that's* extreme, along the way one of them wrestled a lion. Another chowed down on rats. And a third wore an American flag—as underwear. Explore on—if you dare!

WELCOME TO THE SUNSHINE STATE

DUDE: Ponce de León

EXPEDITION: Discovered Florida

WHEN: 1513

Wealth. Fame. The chance to be young again. That, according to legend, is what awaits the first person who dips his toes into the Fountain of Youth. But the problem is no one knows where the fabled fountain is located. Spanish explorer Ponce de León sails the Caribbean to Grand Turk Island. No fountain there. San Salvador Island, too, is fountain-free. Although Ponce never finds the fountain, he scores wealth and fame by being the first European to set foot in a land he calls Pascua Florida (Flowery Easter), or Florida to you and me.

WHAT'S IN IT FOR YOU: The discovery of the future home of Disney World

AFRICA

COOL DUDES WHO CHANGED THE WORLD

INTO AFRICA

DUDE: David Livingstone

EXPEDITION: First European to explore Central Africa extensively

WHEN: 1841 to 1873

For Scottish doctor-missionary David Livingstone, trudging through the deserts, rain forests, and mountains of unexplored Africa (and taking lots of notes) is a dream come true. He wrestles a lion and nearly loses an arm. He sees one of the world's largest waterfalls and names it Victoria, for England's queen. He searches for the source of the Nile River and drops from sight. Five years later newspaper reporter Henry Stanley tracks down Livingstone outside a grass hut and utters the famous line, "Dr. Livingstone, I presume?"

WHAT'S IN IT FOR YOU: The knowledge that you really *should* keep distance between yourself and a lion

IT'S LONELY AT THE TOP. COLD, TOO.

DUDE: Robert Peary

EXPEDITION: Led the expedition that was first to reach the geographic North Pole

WHEN: 1909

Robert Peary, his trusted partner Matthew Henson—a talented African-American explorer—and four other men are heading north. *Way* north. They scale 50-foot cliffs of ice and endure subzero temperatures and dark fog. When they finally reach the North Pole, Peary unfurls an American flag sewn by his wife—which he's worn as a warm undergarment—and rightfully feels he's on top of the world.

WHAT'S IN IT FOR YOU: The knowledge that when exploring new territory, you should always pack a flag—it could come in handy!

AROUND THE WORLD IN ... THREE YEARS

DUDE: Ferdinand Magellan

EXPEDITION: Led the first expedition to sail around the world

WHEN: Starting in 1519

Back then, people thought the world was round, but no one had actually *proven* it by sailing all the way around the world—until Magellan. Terrible storms nearly sink his ships. Food runs so low that they eat rats. Three years later, just one of five ships returns home. But it carries the first men to sail around the world.

WHAT'S IN IT FOR YOU: The knowledge that you won't ever fall off the edge of the Earth

NORTH POLE

21

1 START YOUR OWN BUSINESS.

2 MAKE A FRIEND WHO IS A DIFFERENT RACE OR RELIGION THAN YOU ARE.

3 WRITE A ROCK SONG.

4 BECOME AN EXPLORER. GET A MAP AND PUT PINS IN EVERY PLACE YOU VISIT. TRY TO VISIT A NEW LOCATION—SUCH AS A CITY OR A NATIONAL PARK—EACH YEAR.

5 ORGANIZE A "YEAR IN THE LIFE" PHOTO ALBUM ABOUT YOUR FAMILY.

6 CONVINCE YOUR PARENTS TO MAKE ONE BIG CHANGE FOR THE ENVIRONMENT.
- DRINK TAP WATER INSTEAD OF BOTTLED WATER.
- CHANGE TO COMPACT FLUORESCENT BULBS.
- WALK INSTEAD OF DRIVE IN YOUR NEIGHBORHOOD.

7 APOLOGIZE FOR SOMETHING YOU DID A LONG TIME AGO. (C'MON, YOU *KNOW* THERE'S SOMETHING!)

15 THINGS TO DO BEFORE YOU GROW UP

8 BE A MUST-HAVE GUEST. LEARN TO JUGGLE, TELL JOKES, OR WHISTLE.

9 TAKE THE BASIC FIRST-AID TRAINING COURSE FROM THE AMERICAN RED CROSS.

10 STAY UP ALL NIGHT (WITH YOUR PARENTS' PERMISSION).

11 MASTER ONE DISH FROM ANOTHER COUNTRY EVERY MONTH AND SERVE IT TO YOUR FAMILY.

12 LEARN A FOREIGN LANGUAGE.

13 MAKE A VIDEO ABOUT SOMETHING MEANINGFUL TO YOU: YOUR SPORTS TEAM, A VOLUNTEER CAUSE, A FESTIVAL, OR YOUR TOWN.

14 EAT AN EXOTIC FRUIT, SUCH AS NASHI (ASIAN PEAR) OR YANG TAO (KIWI).

15 RECORD YOUR RELATIVES TELLING YOU THEIR FAVORITE MEMORIES. THEN WRITE THEIR STORIES IN A MEMORY BOOK.

CLIFF Hanger

A FIRST-PERSON ACCOUNT OF A TOWERING CONQUEST

Yosemite Valley, California

I t's 1 a.m. I'm 2,500 feet above the ground, sleeping on a portable cot I've attached to the near-vertical face of the rocky valley wall, when— BOOM—my cot suddenly collapses, plunging me through darkness.

Suddenly my waist belt—tied to a bolt in the rock where my cot used to be—snatches me under the armpits and stops my fall. Dangling in midair, I realize how lucky I am that I didn't fall headfirst and slam into the rock. With frustration, I grunt it back up my rope to my gear and close my eyes.

That was at Yosemite National Park, in California. I was climbing 3,000 feet up a valley wall known as El Capitan for the fourth time. But even a fall from one of America's tallest and sheerest rock faces didn't stop me—I kept going, hand over hand, toe over toe, until I reached the top. You just can't admit failure in rock climbing.

To climb El Cap alone is kind of like climbing it twice. See, as I climb up the rock face, I pound tools into cracks in the rock to support my hands and feet. When I run out, I tie my rope to one of them. Then I rappel down to pull out my tools.

After I retrieve my 110 pounds of gear, I use my ascenders to slide back up the rope. Up, down, up, about every 160 feet.

The first time I made it to the top by myself was when I was 15. That makes me one of the youngest solo climbers to scale El Capitan's slick granite face.

Climbing El Cap is like putting together a big puzzle: figuring out which way to go, which crack to cram your toe in. I do everything while dangling from the rock— eat food, try to nap, even use a plastic "poop" tube. When I finally scramble to El Cap's summit, I always have this big smile on my face. Sure, El Capitan is tough, but I love it. Every time I get on, it teaches me who's boss.

—Scott Thelan

Adventurer Scott Thelan hangs from ropes as he scales the mountain.

To the Top

Want to climb a mountain? First get in shape with these tips.

Walk. Lots. Push yourself a little farther every day.

Keep your heart strong by biking, swimming, or running.

Build up your endurance: Always take the stairs.

Strong arms are essential. Strengthen them by carrying groceries in from the car.

Mental conditioning counts, so pay attention to the weather, wind, and geography around you.

GOING TO
EXTREMES

Researchers hunt for life that seems out of this world.

Diving into a maze of underwater caves is all in a day's work for scientists and researchers on a quest to find extremophiles. Extremophiles are microscopic life-forms that live in extreme environments that are too dry, too hot, too cold, too dark, or too toxic for the likes of us.

Microbiologist Hazel Barton eyes a small fish as she explores an underwater cave.

Scientists know that human beings are nature's wimps. We need a cushy environment to survive—lots of water, abundant sunshine, oxygen, and moderate temperatures. Most places on Earth—and in the rest of the solar system—just aren't like that.

SEARCHING THE DEEP

Finding extremophiles can be dangerous because of the remote places in which they live and grow. But some daring scientists are willing to take the risks because the rewards could be great.

The next important antibiotic could come from one of these organisms. Some have already helped scientists make new tests to identify people who are more likely to get certain diseases.

Heat-loving extremophiles were probably among the earliest forms of life on Earth. Scientists are even working with samples from caves to support the idea that microbes once lived under the surface of planets like Mars.

With so much to gain, scientists will keep chipping rock from cliffs, scraping scum from hot springs, and sampling the walls of deep ice caves to find extremophiles. Scientists are really going to extremes in the search for life.

Bet you didn't know

The average **person** walks about **80,000 miles** in a lifetime. That's more than **three times** around the world!

Rising to an elevation of almost 11,000 feet (3,353 m), Fitzroy Massif in southern Argentina's Patagonia region presents major challenges to adventurous climbers who must contend with strong winds and bitter cold.

DINOSAUR FOOTPRINTS

TRACKS TELL PREHISTORIC SECRETS

Footprints impressed on the Earth millions of years ago are changing the field of dinosaur paleontology.

"There is much to be learned from a corpse, even one that has been dead for millions of years," says Rich McCrea, a curator at the Peace Region Paleontology Research Centre. He is a member of a small but growing field of scientists who have dedicated themselves to the study of fossilized dinosaur tracks. "Tracks, even those millions of years old, represent the activity of animals that were living," he said.

LEARNING FROM TRACKS

Tracks are the closest a human can get to understanding dinosaurs as breathing, functioning animals. They show where and how dinosaurs walked, their posture, and gait. They show which dinosaurs roamed solo and which traveled in groups.

Coal mining sites have revealed thousands of footprints of dinosaurs. For example, McCrea spends much of his time studying tracks near the mining town of Grande Cache, Alberta, Canada. "There are only a couple of sites where there is a real diversity of tracks," says McCrea. In the few places with multiple tracks, he found traces of small, medium, and large meat-eating, two-footed theropod dinosaurs, and also those of birds.

TRACK HUNTING

When scientists hunt for dinosaur tracks they look for areas where ancient layers of sedimentary rock are exposed, such as cliffs, sea coasts, quarries, open-pit mines, and along the banks of rivers and streams.

Usually, tracks are not found in the same location as bones. This is mostly because the conditions that are ideal for preserving tracks are not very good for the fossilization of bone.

"It doesn't mean the bones weren't there, but after 70 million years the bones would dissolve whereas the tracks wouldn't," says Anthony Martin, an ichnologist (one who studies tracks). "We can look forward to the discovery of tracks of more groups of extinct animals."

Paleontologist Paul Sereno

MEET THE NAT GEO EXPLORERS

DERECK AND BEVERLY JOUBERT

Award-winning filmmakers from Botswana, the Jouberts have been filming, researching, and exploring Africa for over 25 years.

How did you become explorers?
We were both born to be explorers! You know how sometimes when you just know—we knew. School was just like going to the gym—a way to get mentally and physically fit to go exploring.

What was your closest call in the field?
We have been hit by elephants; bitten by snakes, scorpions, and mosquitoes; knocked down by buffalo; crashed two planes; and generally had a hard life—every day is potentially a close call.

What is one place or thing you'd still like to explore?
Exploration is as much of the mind as it is of a place. There are still things to be done, things to be discovered, and greater understanding to bring to humankind.

TREASURES OF THE TOMB

Discovering King Tut's incredible riches

It's pitch-black. His hands trembling, British archaeologist Howard Carter makes a small hole in the tomb's second door. He inserts a candle. Next to him, British millionaire Lord Carnarvon blurts out, "Can you see anything?" After a moment of stunned silence, Carter replies, "Yes, wonderful things."

What Carter sees looks like the inside of a giant treasure chest. Gold gleams everywhere! There are glittering statues, a throne, and fabulous golden beds with posts shaped like the heads of wild animals. Precious items are heaped all over the room.

It's 1922. It has taken years of digging in the Valley of the Kings—a graveyard for ancient Egypt's richest kings—and $500,000 (in today's money) of Lord Carnarvon's cash, but Carter hit the jackpot. He discovered the tomb of Tutankhamun (Tut, for short), who became pharaoh at age nine and died ten years later around 1323 B.C.

KEEPING ON YOUR TOES

Carter, Lord Carnarvon, and two others enter the cluttered first room, which they call the antechamber. Under a bed with posts in the shape of hippopotamus heads, Lord Carnarvon finds the entrance to another room. Soon known as the annex, this tiny chamber holds more than 2,000 everyday objects. They include boomerangs, shields, a box containing eye makeup, and 116 baskets of food. When Carter clears the annex out later, his workers need to be suspended by ropes to keep from stepping on things.

Curse of the Pharaohs

Many people believe in the curse of the pharaohs. They think that the souls of the ancient Egyptian dead will haunt those who uncover their bodies and disturb their rest. These ancient ghosts often get blamed when things go wrong, including accidents, illnesses, and even deaths.

Does Egyptologist and National Geographic Explorer-in-Residence Zahi Hawass believe in the curse? Nope. "Even if it does exist, I do not fear it, although many strange things have happened to me during my years excavating, or digging, at sites around Egypt," says Hawass.

Buckle showing King Tut and his queen

Collar on Tut's mummy

Ceremonial instruments of royal authority

Fan

26

Mummy's gold sandals

Hippo's head bedpost

Tut's mummy
The mummy wore a mask of solid gold.

Innermost coffin
Made of solid gold, this weighs nearly 250 pounds (113 kg). It held Tut's mummy.

Middle coffin
Real gold, colored glass, and semi-precious stones cover this wooden coffin.

Outermost coffin
This is made of gilded and inlaid wood.

The disorder in the annex indicates ancient grave robbers had looted the tomb. They left behind footprints and gold rings wrapped in cloth. Luckily, they'd been caught and the tomb resealed. That was more than 3,000 years ago.

ANCIENT GUARD

The explorers are fascinated by two tall statues in the antechamber showing Tut dressed in gold. The figures seem to be guarding another room. Sweltering in the heat, the group crawls through a hole created by the ancient robbers.

Before them stands a huge wooden box, or shrine, that glitters with a layer of gold. This room must be Tut's burial chamber! At the very center of the shrine is a carved sarcophagus, or coffin. Inside it are three nested coffins, each one more richly decorated than the one before. Inside the last, made of solid gold, lies the mummy of Tutankhamun. A 22-pound (10-kg) gold mask (far left) covers its head and shoulders. A collar made from 171 separate gold pieces rests on the mummy's chest, and gold sandals are on its feet.

On one side of the burial chamber is an open doorway revealing the fourth room of the tomb—the treasury. Towering over the other objects is a gold-covered shrine guarded by goddesses. It holds Tut's liver, lungs, stomach, and intestines. Each vital organ is preserved, wrapped in linen, and placed in its very own small coffin.

Today millions of people visit Cairo's Egyptian Museum each year to see Tut's treasures. The ancient Egyptians believed that "to speak the name of the dead is to make them live again." If that is true, Tutankhamun certainly lives on.

MUMMIES EVERYWHERE!

A city of the dead sat undisturbed for centuries. Then, in 1996, a donkey passing through the Egyptian oasis town of Bahariya stumbled into a hole. As the donkey's owner worked to free its hoof, he saw a flash of gold in the sand. The donkey had punched a hole in the roof of a long-buried tomb. Archaeologists found mummies—more than have ever been found in one place before. The mummies of Bahariya were entombed during Egypt's Greco-Roman period, which lasted from 332 B.C. until the fourth century A.D.

DARE TO EX

Do you have what it takes to be a great explorer? Read the stories of thre

THE EASTERN U.S.
AS SEEN FROM THE
SPACE SHUTTLE

SANDRA MAGNUS
SEES IT ALL.

THE EXTREME PHOTO-GRAPHER

Carsten Peter, on his face-to-face experience with an erupting volcano:

"When I was 17, a friend and I climbed the Stromboli volcano in Italy to capture its eruptions on film. We set up our cameras on the rim, but we didn't realize that we were too close. Suddenly, an explosion erupted from the volcano. Giant volcanic bombs—flaming rocks up to two feet wide—began spitting into the air. We started running and dodging them, and we were so scared we forgot to turn on the cameras! It frightened me to death, but that was when I realized I had magma in my blood. And that this was what I wanted to do with my life."

THE ASTRONAUT

Sandra Magnus, astronaut aboard the space shuttle *Atlantis*, on seeing Earth from space for the first time:

"Looking down on the Earth, everything just looks so peaceful and calm. Down there, billions of people are going to work, going to school, playing soccer. It makes you realize it's just one world, and we're all together on this ball of life. The oceans are so blue, the deserts so flowing. It's a beautiful, fragile planet, and you can see these treasures all at once from space."

Want to be an astronaut?

STUDY:
Math, science, engineering

WATCH: *Space Station*

READ: *To Space and Back*, by Sally Ride with Susan Okie

DO: Make star-watching your hobby.

ADVICE: "Have a plan. It may not happen exactly how you want it to happen. But be flexible, and you'll succeed."

Want to be a photographer?

STUDY: Anything—then take pictures!

WATCH: *Winged Migration*

READ: NATIONAL GEOGRAPHIC

DO: Learn physical skills—climbing, paragliding, skateboarding—to get you to great places to take photos.

ADVICE: "With digital cameras, it's easier than ever to become a photographer."

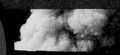

XPLORE

amous adventurers, and see how you can get started on the same path.

MIREYA MAYOR HANGS
OUT WITH WILD ANIMALS.

A SILVERBACK
GORILLA

THE PRIMATOLOGIST

Mireya Mayor, on making a connection with a family of gorillas:

"When I started observing western lowland gorillas in the Central African Republic, I was an outsider among the apes. But one day, a baby gorilla was irritating his father, a giant silverback, and the two started bickering. As the mother took the baby away for a time-out, she looked over at me as if to say, 'You understand why I have to do this.' These gorillas have been hunted for centuries, and yet when you look into a gorilla's eyes and see that she accepts you, you realize that you've gone from being an enemy to being a friend."

Want to be a primatologist?

STUDY: Ecology, English, science—even math will help for all the statistics

WATCH: *Madagascar, Gorillas in the Mist*

READ: *The Aye-Aye and I,* by Gerald Durrell

DO: Go camping, hiking, and bird-watching.

ADVICE: "Become involved and hands-on. Try things like volunteering at animal shelters or your local zoo."

CARSTEN PETER'S
JOB IS A BLAST.

29

Kids Did It!

Inches from the HUGE OPEN JAWS of a great white shark,

Wiley Dotzenroth's eyes bug out of their sockets. "Woo-hoo! Awesome!" he yells as he surfaces. He's standing safely in a protective steel shark cage lowered over the side of the boat.

Wiley, of Wayzata, Minnesota, was one of 15 explorers on the 2007 NATIONAL GEOGRAPHIC KIDS Expedition team who traveled to the country of South Africa. The 10- to 14-year-olds were winners of the annual NG KIDS photo and essay competition—the Hands-On Explorer Challenge (HOEC).

In just the first few hours of the expedition, the team saw great white sharks, Cape fur seals, and southern right whales. They also were granted special permission to go ashore on Dyer Island, a protected nesting ground for African penguins where injured penguins are cared for and released back to the wild once well.

The NG KIDS team traveled to Bush Lodge at Sabi Sabi Private Game Reserve, where mischievous vervet monkeys greeted them. Every morning and evening the team explored the reserve. They spotted many wild animals, including South Africa's "big five": elephants, rhinos, African buffalo, lions, and leopards.

Before the expedition began, team members raised more than $10,000. They used that money to buy a computer and Internet access for the Sam Nzima Primary School, in the village of Lilydale. Most exciting for the team: the knowledge that they can email new friends made during their visit to the school.

AFRICA

SOUTH AFRICA

Members of the 2007 NATIONAL GEOGRAPHIC KIDS expedition team

Caged team members got this view of a great white shark.

Burchell's zebras live in small herds.

For more about the NG KIDS Hands-On Explorer Challenge, go online. www.kids.nationalgeographic.com

WILL MY TOY CAR SURVIVE A CROC ATTACK?

My name is Brady Barr, and part of my job as a scientist is catching crocodiles. Crocs are big, fast, good at hiding, and always alert. They're not easy to catch, but I need to get hold of them to attach tracking tags and to gather data.

I talked with some creative kids who gave me a few great ideas to help me catch crocs. So on my next trip to Africa, I set off with my scientific equipment and toys (the kids' suggestion).

I'm helping wildlife biologists put tracking tags on a threatened population of Nile crocodiles. From our boat we spot a cluster of crocs. I set a remote-control car on the beach and steer it toward the basking crocs. I speed the car right up to one—chomp! The croc's teeth just miss the car, and it's not giving up! It chases the car and I work the joystick as if my life depends on it.

My little car is no match for a Nile crocodile—the croc's jaws close over my toy—and, temporarily, over my plans. The size and quick movements of the toy car must trigger a crocodile's predatory instinct. Conclusion: Use a faster car and improve my driving skills!

The kids' second idea: to disguise myself as a croc. I get into the water wearing a big rubber croc mask. My goal: Get close enough to wrestle a croc into our boat. When one giant male approaches, I raise the snout of my mask, which in "croc talk" lets him know I'm not looking for trouble. But he's angry—he arches his back and slaps the water with his chin. He thinks I'm a rival! At first I stand my ground, but as he comes closer, it gets too dangerous. I get out of the water ... fast! Conclusion: The disguise works.

Idea number three—I steer the remote-control boat, fitted with a small rubber croc head and a snare, toward the real crocs. Success! They act as if the boat's one of them and ignore it. Then, just as the boat's in position to snare one, the batteries die! Conclusion: The boat works, but next time I've got to remember more batteries!

A field test involves a lot of trial and error. What I learned this time will mean success the next time. Meanwhile, I reached my goal to be the first person to catch all 23 species of crocodilians!
— Brady Barr

FEAR FACTOR

EXTREME FEARS....	A FEAR OF
Lachanophobia	vegetables
Blennophobia	slime
Ephebiphobia	teenagers
Lutraphobia	otters
Octophobia	the number eight
Nephophobia	clouds
Metrophobia	poetry
Geliophobia	laughter
Genuphobia	knees
Anthophobia	flowers
Apeirophobia	infinity
Cometophobia	comets
Chrematophobia	money
Peladophobia	bald people
Didaskaleinophobia	going to school
Phobophobia	phobias

10 Thrilling World Adventures

Track mountain gorillas in Rwanda

Take an African safari in Zambia

Trek remote valleys of Bhutan

Explore the New Zealand backcountry

Cycle the Okanagan Valley of British Columbia, Canada

Track gray whales in Mexico

Climb the Grand Teton in Wyoming

Trek in Patagonia

Cruise the Inside Passage of Alaska

Discover a penguin colony in Antarctica

HOW TO SURVIVE...

ADRIFT AT SEA

1 GO UNDERCOVER
Slap on some sunscreen, a baseball cap, your best sunglasses, and a jacket. That will help you avoid sunburn, sunstroke, and dehydration—which could *so* ruin your day.

2 MADE IN THE SHADES
No sunglasses? No problem! Cut two narrow eye slits in your socks, and tie them around your head with string. Now you've got a smelly pair of shades!

3 OFF THE HOOK
Getting hungry? Fashion a fishing line from a rope, string, or scrap of cloth. Make a hook with the pop-top from a soda can. Soon you'll have sushi!

4 HERE'S FISH IN YOUR EYE
The ocean may look like one huge salt-flavored Big Gulp. But too much seawater can cause vomiting and hallucinations. Instead, catch rainwater. Or you can suck liquid out of a fish eye. Slurp!

5 CATCH SOME RAYS
Use a mirror to reflect sunlight and signal your search team. Then fix your hair. You'll want to be ready for your close-up when you're rescued!

QUICKSAND

BEWARE! QUICKSAND

1 NO MORE "SOUP-ERSTITIONS"
Quicksand isn't some bottomless pit waiting to suck you in. It's a soupy mixture of sand and water found near riverbanks, shorelines, and marshes. It's rarely more than a few feet deep, though it can be deeper.

2 GO WITH THE FLOAT
Not that you'd want to, but quicksand is actually easier to float on than water. So lean backward, place your arms straight out from your sides, and let the sopping sand support your weight.

3 YOU FLAIL, YOU FAIL
Don't kick or struggle. That creates a vacuum, which only pulls you down. Ignore the gritty goop squishing into your underpants and remain calm.

4 LEG LIFTS
Conquer the quicksand with a slow stand. As you're lying back with your arms out, carefully inch one leg, then the other, to the surface.

5 ROLL OVER!
When both legs are afloat, pretend you're performing a dog trick. Keeping your face out of the muck, gently roll over the quicksand until you're on solid ground.

"I Survived a SHARK ATTACK!"

Bethany Hamilton, then 14, lay on her surfboard waiting for a wave. Suddenly a tiger shark grabbed Bethany's left arm, tugging her back and forth as she clung to the board. Finally the shark disappeared, but it had torn off most of Bethany's arm.

Before that day, Bethany, of Hawai'i, wanted to be a pro surfer. Now all she wanted to do was make it back to shore.

GETTING HER FEET WET

Most people would give up surfing forever. Not Bethany. Just four weeks after the attack, she was back in the water. "I was a little scared but really excited," she said. Her supportive family and strong faith helped her focus on living her life—not on the loss of her arm.

Without two arms for balance, Bethany made some changes to her surfing style. She uses a lighter board that's easier to paddle, and she grabs a handle on her board to help her stand.

Today Bethany is back to surfing twice a day, training for future competitions. "If you have faith," she says, "it makes things a lot easier."

A tiger shark bit a huge chunk out of Bethany's board.

CONFESSIONS of a BUG EATER

TRUE STORY!

On the bottom shelf inside my refrigerator next to the apple-sauce is a bowl of grasshoppers in seasoned cooking oil. On the shelf above that is a tarantula, its eight hairy legs spread out on a dinner plate. OK, I know it sounds weird. But let me explain.

I started eating bugs many years ago, while studying the world's bug-eating cultures. In most countries worldwide, people merrily munch on bugs. Insects and their relatives are protein-rich and, in many cases, loaded with minerals and vitamins. So why not eat bugs?

Among the frozen packages in my freezer you'll see bags filled with crickets and mealworms. My real treasures hide behind the ice cream: a ten-inch-long centipede and some scorpions.

My favorite insect snack is the wax worm, a critter often sold as fishing bait or live food for pet lizards. In the wild, these sweet-tasting morsels feed on honey-combs from inside beehives.

When I'm cooking for an audience, I often invite kids to help make and sample my dishes. Sometimes the same kids who gulp down the grasshoppers will refuse to eat the mushrooms in a dish. See? It's all relative. When kids tease me about eating bugs, I tease them back. "I bet you eat chicken eggs," I say. "Now *that's* gross!"

David George Gordon is an expert and knows which bugs are safe to eat. Do not eat any bugs without expert advice and approval from your parents.

TIPS FROM A PRO
How to Take Great Photos

As far as the eye can see there are photographs waiting to be captured or to be created. Life swirls around us without stopping, but as a photographer, you can put a frame around moments in time. A lot more goes into taking a good photograph than just pushing a button, though.

Learn how to use a camera, but most of all, learn how to think like a photographer. Here are some valuable tips from expert photographer Neil Johnson to help you get started on your way.

LIGHT

- When lighting a subject, it is important to consider not only the direction of the light (front, side, back), but also the color of the background.
- Light does not always have to fall on the front of your subject.
- On-camera flash is most useful for subjects that are 10 to 15 feet away from you.

COMPOSITION

- Making your subject the focus of attention does not mean that you have to put it in the middle of the frame. Placing the subject slightly off center can help lead the viewer into the picture.

SUBJECTS

- When taking pictures of animals, getting down to their eye level and moving in close will improve your photographs.
- When taking pictures of people, try to get them to forget about the camera and just go about doing what they enjoy.

QUICK TIPS!

- Don't rush your pictures.
- Take your time and experiment.
- Snap. Snap. Snap. Take as many pictures as you can.
- Study them. Ask yourself why some work and others don't.
- Learn from your mistakes, but most important, keep shooting.

PHOTO TERMS

Composition: the arrangement of everything in your picture—the subject, foreground, background, and surrounding elements

Exposure: the amount of light coming into the camera and the length of time it strikes the film or digital medium

Lens: one or more pieces of glass or plastic designed to collect and focus light on a piece of film or digital medium

Shutter: the device in a camera that opens to allow light to strike the film or digital medium

Tripod: a three-legged stand for supporting a camera

CAUGHT ON CAMERA

up-close a...

Off the coast of Me...

I'm Annie Griffiths Belt, and as a National Geographic photographer, I am lucky enough to go to some pretty wild places. A big part of the fun is how I get there. I have ridden elephants and helicopters, fishing boats, hot air balloons, and camels.

One of the most exciting adventures I ever had was in Mexico, when I went to photograph gray whales. I was floating in a rubber raft and watching for whales. Suddenly, I felt a bump. The rubber raft actually began lifting out of the water!

A friendly whale had decided to play with us. She gently lifted our raft up out of the water, and slowly lowered us down again. She circled around us with her baby calf, so close that we could touch her nose and stroke her calf.

—*Annie Griffiths Belt*

For more, read Annie's book, *A Camera, Two Kids and a Camel: My Journey in Photographs.*

Cornered by a
King Cobra!

Photographers who shoot for the National Geographic Society often face scary situations and challenging conditions in pursuit of the perfect image. For example, an encounter with a king cobra in Thailand was an exciting challenge for photographer Mattias Klum.

"It was the angriest snake I'd ever seen. The king cobra, star of a village street show, was a fighter in the traditional 'sport' of king cobra boxing. King cobras are teased and provoked by their keepers until the snakes strike out at almost anything.

"The people who do this don't think they're being cruel. They believe they're in tune with their religion's spirits. And even though I wasn't teasing this snake—I was just standing there photographing the action—I was in quite a bit of danger.

"This ten-foot-long king cobra, whose bite contains a startling amount of deadly neurotoxin, was suddenly distracted by my movement. He reached out to strike me, but got my camera instead." Good thing. The venom in a single bite can kill an elephant!

WHAT IS IT?
A king cobra

PLACE
Ban Khok Sa-nga, Thailand

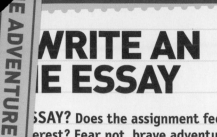

WRITE AN
E ESSAY

SSAY? Does the assignment feel as
erest? Fear not, brave adventurer.
You're up to the ch... ge! The following step-by-step tips
will help you with this monumental task.

1 **BRAINSTORM.** Sometimes the subject matter of your essay is assigned to you, sometimes it's not. Either way, you have to decide what you want to say. Start by brainstorming some ideas, writing down any thoughts you have about the subject on a piece of scratch paper. Then read over everything you've come up with and consider which idea you think is the strongest. Ask yourself what you want to write about the most. Keep in mind the goal of your essay. (The four main types of essays are described on the next page.) Can you achieve the goal of the assignment with this topic? If so, you're good to go.

2 **WRITE A TOPIC SENTENCE.** This is the main idea of your essay, a statement of your thoughts on the subject. Again, consider the goal of your essay. Think of the topic sentence as an introduction that tells your reader what the rest of your essay will be about.

3 **OUTLINE YOUR IDEAS.** Once you have a good topic sentence, you then need to support that main idea with more detailed information, facts, thoughts, and examples. These supporting points answer the question, "Why?" to your topic sentence. This is where research and perhaps more brainstorming comes in. Then organize these points in the way you think makes the most sense, probably in order of importance. Now you have an outline for your essay.

4 **ON YOUR MARK, GET SET, WRITE!** Follow your outline, using each of your supporting points as the topic sentence of its own paragraph. Use descriptive words to get your ideas across to the reader. Go into detail, using specific information to tell your story or make your point. Stay on track, making sure that everything you include is somehow related to the main idea of your essay. Use transitions (see p. 143) to make your writing flow.

5 **WRAP IT UP.** Finish your essay with a conclusion that summarizes your entire essay and restates your main idea.

6 **PROOFREAD AND REVISE.** Check for errors in spelling, capitalization, punctuation, and grammar. Look for ways to make your writing clear, understandable, and interesting. Use descriptive verbs, adjectives, or adverbs when possible. It also helps to have someone else read your work to point out things you might have missed. Then make the necessary corrections and changes in a second draft. Repeat this revision process once more to make your final draft as good as you can.

Types of Essays

NARRATIVE ESSAY

Purpose: A narrative essay tells a story about an event.

Example: "Caught on Camera" (p. 35)

Helpful Hints:
- Pick a topic that really interests you. Your excitement will come through in your writing.
- Tell your story with a clear beginning, middle, and end.
- Add fun or exciting details to highlight dramatic or unexpected moments.
- Use descriptive words to help give your reader a sense of what it was like to be there.

EXPOSITORY ESSAY

Purpose: An expository essay gives facts and information about a person, place, thing, or idea. Book reports, research papers, and biographies are types of expository writing.

Example: "Going to Extremes: Researchers Hunt for Life That Seems Out of This World" (p. 24)

Helpful Hints:
- Dig deep in your research to find interesting details.
- State your topic right away.
- Use transitional phrases to make your essay flow smoothly.

DESCRIPTIVE ESSAY

Purpose: A descriptive essay describes a person, place, or thing, using sensory details to give the reader a better idea of what the subject is really like.

Example: "Discovering King Tut's Incredible Riches" (p. 26)

Helpful Hints:
- Describe how the subject looks, sounds, tastes, smells, and feels.
- Use interesting comparisons.
- Be specific, find just the right adjectives and adverbs.

PERSUASIVE ESSAY

Purpose: A persuasive essay tries to convince the reader of your point of view using facts, statistics, details, and logic to make an argument.

Example: A newspaper editorial recommending new environmental protection laws

Helpful Hints:
- State your opinion in the topic sentence.
- Use evidence to support your point of view.
- Consider the opposing views.
- Present a strong conclusion.

NO COPYING!
All about plagiarism

Plagiarism is presenting an idea or piece of writing as your own original work when it was actually created by someone else. It's a serious offense and will get you into trouble. Obvious examples of plagiarism include buying an essay from the Internet and handing it in as your own, or copying from a friend. Plagiarism can also occur by not citing your sources, so be careful.

In writing, you must give credit whenever you use information taken from another source. This is called citing your sources. Follow these basic guidelines to avoid plagiarism.

- **Take good notes** when researching. Keep a list of all research material you use, including details (title, author, page numbers, websites, etc.) about where you got specific pieces of information.

- **Use your own words.** Copying sentence structure but changing a few words is still plagiarism. Don't use more than three words in a row taken directly from another source.

- **Plagiarism** is not restricted to textbooks—don't copy material from the Internet, either.

- **Place quotation marks** around any phrase or sentence you take directly from another source, and cite it.

- **Double check** your final text with your notes. Be sure that you've given credit where credit is due.

Beware! Plagiarism can result in suspension or expulsion from school.

Amazing Animals

An African lion and his cub on the Maasai Mara, in Kenya

WHAT IS
Taxonomy?

Since there are billions and billions of living things, called organisms, on the planet, people need a way of classifying them. Scientists created a system called **taxonomy**, which helps to classify all living things into ordered groups. By putting organisms into categories we are able to better understand how they are the same and how they are different. There are seven levels of taxonomic classification, beginning with the broadest group, called a domain, down to the most specific group, called a species.

Biologists divide life based on evolutionary history and place organisms in three domains depending on their genetic structure: Archaea, Bacteria, and Eukarya. (see p. 300 for "The Three Domains of Life").

SAMPLE CLASSIFICATION
GIRAFFE

Domain:	Eukarya
Phylum:	Chordata
Class:	Mammalia
Order:	Artiodactyla
Family:	Giraffidae
Genus:	*Giraffa*
Species:	*G. camelopardalis*

Where do animals come in?

Animals are a part of the Eukarya domain, which means they are organisms with cells. There are over one million species named, including humans. Like all living things, animals can be divided into smaller groups, called phyla. Generally, there are thought to be more than 30 phyla into which animals are grouped based on certain scientific criteria, such as body type or if the animal has a backbone or not. It can all be pretty confusing, so there is another, less complicated system of grouping animals into two categories: vertebrates and invertebrates. About 95 percent of all animals are invertebrates.

Chinese stripe-necked turtle

TIP
Here's a sentence to help you remember the classification order: **D**ear **P**hilip **C**ame **O**ver **F**or **G**ood **S**oup.

Bet you didn't know

Cold-blooded ANIMALS such as LIZARDS don't sweat.

Nobody really knows exactly **HOW MANY SPECIES** there are on Earth. **SCIENTISTS ESTIMATE** there may be anywhere from **3 to 30 MILLION** species of animals on our planet! **Hundreds of NEW SPECIES** are found **EVERY DAY.**

Vertebrates Animals WITH Backbones

Fish are cold-blooded and live in water. They breathe with gills, lay eggs, and usually have scales.

Amphibians are cold-blooded. Their young live in water and breathe with gills. Adults live on land and breathe with lungs.

Reptiles are cold-blooded and breathe with lungs.

Birds are warm-blooded and have feathers and wings. They lay eggs, breathe with lungs, and usually are able to fly.

Mammals are warm-blooded and feed on their mothers' milk. They also have skin that is usually covered with hair.

Whitefaced owl

Gray reef shark

Invertebrates Animals WITHOUT Backbones

Sponges are a very basic form of animal life. They live in water and do not move on their own.

Echinoderms have external skeletons and live in seawater.

Mollusks have soft bodies and can live either in or out of shells.

Arthropods are the largest group of animals. They have an external skeleton, called an exoskeleton, and segmented bodies with appendages.

Worms are soft-bodied animals with no legs.

Cnidaria live in water and have mouths surrounded by tentacles.

Brown tube sponges

Earthworms

Mexican red knee tarantula

Cold-blooded versus Warm-blooded

Cold-blooded animals, also called ectotherms, get their heat from outside their bodies.

Warm-blooded animals, also called endotherms, keep their bodies at a relatively level temperature regardless of the temperature of their environment.

Wolf Speak

Understanding the secret language of a wolf pack

If you want to understand wolf speak, you need to use your ears, eyes, and even your nose. Wolves talk to each other using their voices, body language, and, yes, body odor.

Wolves live in packs. Their survival depends on working as a team to find food, protect pack members, and raise pups. Being able to clearly read and express each wolf's rank is a matter of great importance.

Read My Lips and Ears and Shoulders

From head to tail, wolves express information through subtle and obvious body language. Facial expressions and how high a tail is held tell a wolf's confidence level or where it fits within the pack. The higher a wolf ranks, the higher it stands and holds its head, ears, and tail. The lower it ranks, the lower it drops everything, even flopping to the ground belly side up. Wolves puff up their fur or flatten it to express themselves.

From Growl to Howl

Yips, yaps, barks, and squeaks are all wolf sounds. Wolves usually use vocals when interacting with each other. Scientists have trouble eavesdropping on these shy animals, so little is known about wolves' private conversations. But they're sure vocalizations are important. Even a three-week-old puppy can mimic almost all the adult sounds.

The howl is a wolf's long-distance call. In a forest, a howl might be heard six miles away.

Calling all pack members! Meet us over here **to go hunt!**

To all who can hear: If you're not in our pack, **stay off our turf.**

It's all good. **C'mon, let's go.**

On the tundra it can be heard up to ten miles away. A wolf may howl to locate its pack. Or it may be announcing its availability to join or form a new pack. Packs howl together in a chorus to strengthen the team, warn other wolves away from their territory, or coordinate movements of pack members.

Talk to the Paw

With a sense of smell a hundred times better than humans', it's no wonder scent is an important part of wolf communication. Wolves intentionally leave their scent by marking trees and bushes with urine. They also secrete messages with scent glands in their feet and other body parts.

These odors aren't generally obvious to humans, but for wolves, sniffing tells all: the identity of an animal, its social status, whether it's an adult or a youth, how healthy it is, what it's been eating, if it's ready to breed, and much more.

As scientists keep learning how to understand wolf speak, they use their best tools—sniffing, spying, and eavesdropping.

42

GRAY WOLVES

You Are Here

CONTINENTS: EUROPE AND ASIA

COUNTRY: RUSSIA

SIZE: WORLD'S LARGEST COUNTRY, FOLLOWED BY CANADA, THE UNITED STATES, AND CHINA

LOCATION: NORTHWESTERN COUNTRYSIDE

Your plane lands in northern Russia. As you approach wolf territory, you hear them first. *Ow-oooo! Grrrr!* Then you spot the pack of wolves. Wrestling and playing, they look like they're celebrating. They're actually psyching themselves up for a hunt. Wolves' preferred prey includes moose. One moose can weigh twice as much as the entire pack. Confidence and teamwork mean survival. Only about one in ten attacks on a moose is successful.

Packs are led by the dominant male and female,

sometimes called the alpha wolves. Your heart pounds when you see the alpha female lunge toward a younger wolf in the pack. It falls down, exposing its neck to show submission. Growling, the alpha holds it down by its throat. Even from a distance, you understand the conversation. She's reminding the juvenile that she's in charge. The pup's submissive response means, "Yes, ma'am!" Communication and leadership help the pack survive.

You notice that the alpha pair really seem to like each other. The power couple nuzzles and cuddles; they're likely to remain lifelong partners. The two leaders rally the pack, and all but one adult trot off to hunt. Left behind: the pups and an adult babysitter. You watch as the wolves, working as a team, successfully bring down a moose. They eat their fill in about half an hour. Then they return home, and the pups nip at their snouts, begging for dinner. The adults immediately regurgitate undigested meat for the pups and babysitter to eat. Happy that a more appetizing meal is waiting for you on the plane, you slip away to begin your next adventure.

BY THE NUMBERS

1 litter of pups is born each year in a typical pack.

3 times bigger than a coyote, the gray wolf is the largest wild member of the dog family.

13 years is the average life span of a gray wolf in the wild.

22 pounds of meat may be wolfed down at one wolf's meal.

40 miles per hour is a wolf's top running speed.

100 times stronger sense of smell than a human's. A gray wolf can sense the presence of an animal up to three days after it's gone and smell prey more than a mile away.

43

ARCTIC ANIMALS

Wind whips across the ice at 45 miles per hour (72 kph). Blizzards cut visibility to zero. Temperatures plunge to -50°F (-45°C). Not many creatures can survive the fierce Arctic winter.

One survivor is the cunning arctic fox. It doesn't even try to escape. Nor does it sleep through the coldest and darkest months of the year. Instead, the arctic fox depends on three special survival skills.

TRICK 1: When hunger strikes, the arctic fox often steals a meal. It creeps across the sea ice in search of the leftovers of another Arctic winter resident—a polar bear.

TRICK 2: The arctic fox stores food, which is less risky than stealing from bears. In the spring, foxes steal snow goose eggs from nests and bury them in secret spots. Months later, the foxes come back, dig up the eggs, and have a feast.

Arctic foxes have been known to steal and store as many as 3,000 eggs during the nesting season. Burying the eggs in the cool ground keeps them fresh for months.

TRICK 3: The arctic fox dresses for success. Nature designed its whole body for heat conservation (see box below). The fox even changes coats with the seasons. In the summer, the arctic fox's back, sides, and tail are a dusky brown. But by mid-November the fox sheds the last traces of its summer look for pure white winter fur that helps it blend with the snowy background. This coat is super-thick and mostly made of fleece. The long, coiled hairs are especially good for holding in body heat.

During the worst winter weather the arctic fox curls up into a ball to save heat and stay cozy, even as the brutally cold Arctic winds blow.

THE ANATOMY OF A
SURVIVOR

Small ears, a short muzzle, rounded body, and squat legs are all less likely to lose body heat than larger, lankier body parts. Extensive, complicated networks of veins and capillaries within each pad on a fox's foot keep warm blood flowing through, supplying feet with extra heat.

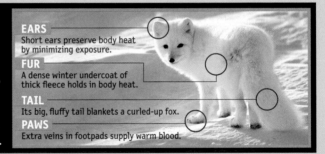

EARS
Short ears preserve body heat by minimizing exposure.

FUR
A dense winter undercoat of thick fleece holds in body heat.

TAIL
Its big, fluffy tail blankets a curled-up fox.

PAWS
Extra veins in footpads supply warm blood.

Wild Hare
Fur and speed: These are the keys to an arctic hare's survival.

Winter weather is often bitterly cold in the tundra of North America and Greenland where arctic hares live. But a coat of thick, luxurious fur, along with pads of thick hair on the soles of its feet, keep a hare toasty warm. By curling into a tight ball with only its hind feet touching the ground, a hare stays snug. The tighter the curl, the warmer it remains.

An arctic hare's fur helps conceal it from predators. White fur camouflages it as snow in winter. In the southern part of their range, hares grow darker coats that help them blend into the terrain.

Standing on its hind legs and using its excellent eyesight and sense of smell, a hare stays alert for enemies. If one gets too close, the hare hops to get away, leaping six to nine feet in one hop. At speeds of up to 30 miles per hour, an arctic hare could keep up with a car on a city street—though off-road cruising is more its style.

BEAR NECESSITIES

How Polar Bears Survive the Deep Freeze

In a polar bear's Arctic home, winter temperatures get unbelievably cold. But imagine running around outside in a heavy down jacket. Even if it's cold out, you might start to feel too warm. Much like you in that jacket, a polar bear is so well insulated that it can easily become overheated. Sometimes it cools off with a mouthful of snow or by lying flat to expose its belly directly to the snow. To keep from overheating, a polar bear usually moves slowly and doesn't run much.

So what keeps the polar bear so toasty? The most visible protection is its thick fur coat. The coat has two layers: an outer layer of long, dense guard hairs and an undercoat of short woolly hairs. A polar bear may look white, but underneath its hair its skin is black, which absorbs heat.

Another way a polar bear copes with the cold is with built-in insulation: a layer of blubber under its skin that can be more than four inches thick.

Many polar bears spend the winter living on slippery sea ice. Luckily, their paws are perfect for getting around on a slick, cold surface. Rough pads give them a nonslip grip, and thick fur between the pads keeps their feet warm. Sharp, curved claws act like hooks to climb and dig in the ice.

So bring on the snow, wind, and icy water. Because when it comes to keeping warm, a polar bear's got it covered!

KEY: WHERE POLAR BEARS LIVE

The Bear Facts

ICY HOME Polar bears live in the far north, on sea ice and on land. Scientists estimate that some 20,000 to 25,000 polar bears roam the Arctic.

HANDY PAWS Partially webbed front paws help polar bears swim. The bears may use their back paws like rudders—to steer.

SEA BEAR Polar bears, seen swimming as far as 150 miles offshore, are the only bears considered to be marine mammals.

GETTING BIG Polar bears usually give birth to twins. A newborn weighs about a pound; an adult male, 1,400 pounds.

SNACKING When a polar bear hunts, it looks for baby seals resting in dens under the snow near the water's edge.

SNOW BABIES

Baby polar bear cubs are born in mid- to late December inside a snow den built by their mother. She usually has one or two cubs. The den is about the size of a refrigerator, and so is mom, so it's not roomy.

As newborns, cubs are about the same size as a loaf of bread and weigh about a pound. They have no teeth, their eyes are closed, and their fur is not thick. They need their mother's warmth and protection 24/7.

By early April, when cubs leave the den for the first time, they already weigh 20 to 30 pounds. By two years old the cubs have learned all the bear lessons they'll need for their 30-year life span. Then the young bears find their own territory and start preparing for having their own cubs.

45

PANDAMONIUM

Like a toddler at snack time, a giant panda sits with its legs stretched out in front of it and munches on bamboo. The tough bamboo is no match for the panda's powerful jaws and the crushing force of its huge molars. In one day, it'll polish off 20 to 40 pounds of bamboo!

Bamboo—a grass that grows tall like a tree— sprouts so fast you can actually watch it grow. Even so, nearly 138 giant pandas starved to death in the mid-1970s.

Today, there are fewer than 2,500 pandas left in the wild. Another loss would devastate the endangered population.

BLOOMING BAMBOO

For pandas, bamboo is the perfect food and shelter. Ninety-nine percent of a panda's diet is bamboo. Stems, shoots, leaves—pandas devour it all. That is, until the bamboo begins to flower. Even the hungriest panda isn't likely to eat it at that stage, because bamboo is not nutritious or appetizing as it flowers.

One blooming plant wouldn't be a big deal, but bamboo is peculiar. Unlike most plants, when one bamboo flowers, all of the bamboo plants of the same species do, too. After flowering, bamboo drops its seeds to the forest floor. Then the plant dies. If a majority of a forest is the same species of bamboo, then pandas are suddenly out of food.

FINDING FOOD

You would think that a panda would be able to hunker down and wait out the flowering by surviving on other plants and small animals. But many species of bamboo sprouts aren't big enough to be edible for at least five to seven years. That means a small area—or an entire forest—goes from a bamboo buffet to starvation central practically overnight—and stays that way.

Scientists know very little about the bamboo flowering process because it happens so infrequently. Some haven't flowered in 120 years—when your great-grandparents or maybe even great-great-grandparents were still in diapers.

In the past, pandas would just search for other sources of bamboo. Today there's a short supply of dining digs because roads, farms, cities, logging, and mining isolate forests. The pandas can't get to a suitable new forest because their homes are surrounded by human activities.

LOOKING AHEAD

To halt habitat destruction, China has stopped most logging. The government also created some 50 nature reserves for pandas. And scientists are working with zoos worldwide to create an extensive panda breeding program with a goal of rebuilding the wild population. All this support gives giant pandas—and their bamboo habitat—a green future.

Where Bears Live

0   3,000 miles
0   4,000 kilometers

Bear Ranges

☐ American Black Bear   ▨ Polar Bear
▨ Asiatic Black Bear   ▨ Sloth Bear
▨ Brown Bear   ▨ Spectacled Bear
■ Giant Panda   ☐ Sun Bear

Striped pattern indicates overlapping ranges.

BROWN BEARS

📷 CLOSE-UP

Look, Ma. No Hands!

Open wide! Fish—it's what's for dinner. This salmon did not look before it leaped, so it's about to end up as brown bear food. Salmon by the thousands leave the ocean and head upstream to mate and lay eggs every fall. Attracted by the fish feast, brown bears by the dozen gather along the banks of Brooks Falls in Katmai National Park in Alaska to fatten up before their long winter hibernation. Timing, luck, and patience are what helped photographer Joel Sartore catch this fish—just before the bear did.

THE Great Koala RESCUE

Frightened and helpless, a baby koala clings to a tree branch. Below, his mother screams. Searching for their dinner, she has gotten her head stuck in a fence.

For Australians, spotting a koala isn't unusual, but finding one in distress is. Desperate to save the mother koala, a family who happened upon the scene calls the Queensland Parks and Wildlife Services. Koala rescuer Vicki Pender is sent to help.

Pender knows she must act quickly to save the terrified animal that is frantically struggling to free herself. After giving the koala a tranquilizer to calm her down, Pender carefully cuts away the fence with bolt cutters.

CAUGHT IN HER TRACKS

Just as she is about to rush to the animal hospital, a yipping sound stops Pender in her tracks. High in a nearby tree, the baby calls for his mother. The rescuer tries to coax him from the tree, but he scampers away. Knowing the baby will not survive alone, Pender needs to act fast.

Quick action, experience, and a little luck help the rescuer nab the confused baby before he gets far. At the hospital, veterinarians check both koalas for injuries.

Every day, rescuers, scientists, and citizens work to help save koalas. Not too long ago, millions of koalas thrived in Australian forests. Then people moved in, cutting down trees to build roads, houses, factories, and malls.

A Koala-Friendly Development

New South Wales, Australia

Dogs and cats are not allowed in Koala Beach Estates, a housing development in New South Wales, but koalas are more than welcome. The number of koalas in Australia has declined dramatically because eucalyptus trees, which koalas depend on for food and shelter, have been cut down to make room for houses and shopping centers. The builders of Koala Beach Estates, however, worked with the Australian Koala Foundation to preserve the existing eucalyptus trees and also plant new ones. All fences are raised one foot off the ground so koalas can move around easily. And residents agree not to keep cats or dogs because the pets might harm the koalas. The result? There are probably 30 or more koalas living at Koala Beach Estates!

A DANGEROUS LIFE

Koalas stay in the trees as much as possible, preferring to spend little time on the ground. A koala's life consists mainly of sleeping during the day and devouring up to two pounds of eucalyptus leaves at night. Now there are fewer trees, and koalas face more dangers as they walk greater distances to go from tree to tree. They must walk through yards, across streets, and often into danger to reach eucalyptus. On the ground, koalas can be hit by cars or attacked by dogs.

Since koalas are also sensitive to stress and unable to adapt to the changing environment, koalas' numbers have dropped drastically.

What are people doing to help save koalas? They're keeping pets in at night and planting trees for koalas to feed on. Warning signs remind drivers to watch out for koalas crossing roads. Most important, citizens continue to work hard to pass laws that protect koalas' remaining forests.

The rescued koala mother and joey had a short hospital stay. Then rescuers released the healthy animals back into the wild.

CONVERSATIONS WITH
APES

**SURPRISING WAYS
BONOBOS "TALK"
WITH HUMANS**

*HMM . . .
WHICH
RING TONE
DO I
WANT?*

RARING TO GO!

Panbanisha, a female bonobo (buh-NO-bo), often hitches a ride—but she'd probably rather drive. One day, while out in the woods of Georgia, Panbanisha suddenly leaped into a parked golf cart. By pushing the accelerator with her foot, she started the engine. Gripping the steering wheel with both hands, she looked over her shoulder and backed up. Next, she shifted gears and zoomed ahead. The only reason she stopped was because she rammed the cart into a tree! (She wasn't hurt.)

"We never taught her to drive," says Sue Savage-Rumbaugh, the primatologist who was in charge of the Georgia State University Language Research Center in Atlanta at the time. But that didn't prevent this smart ape from teaching herself.

JUST LIKE US

Of the great apes—bonobos, gorillas, orangutans, and chimpanzees—bonobos are the most like humans. Savage-Rumbaugh decided to study them to see whether they could pick up language on their own, as humans do. It turns out that they can. In fact, Savage-Rumbaugh discovered that bonobos can learn to do lots of things on their own.

Growing up in the language center lab, Panbanisha and her brother, Kanzi, had human caretakers, watched TV, and played with toys. Both drink from a glass, brush their teeth, and use the toilet. They also communicate.

At first, the apes simply listened—picking up the meanings of words by hearing people talk. Later they learned to say things by pressing symbols on a portable computer.

FIREFIGHTER?

Savage-Rumbaugh frequently took the apes hiking in the forest. Kanzi learned to make fires by watching her make them. Kanzi walks around picking up sticks, which he snaps with his foot and piles in a heap. Then he borrows a lighter to ignite the blaze. The apes use the fires for roasting marshmallows! When it's time to leave, Kanzi douses the flames with a bucket of water. (CAUTION: Never light a fire without adult supervision!)

Savage-Rumbaugh hopes that as people learn more about bonobos, they'll grow to respect them and feel as strongly as she does about protecting them in the wild.

Above and Beyond

NATIONAL ZOO, WASHINGTON, D.C.

Like a nervous tightrope walker, the orangutan stood poised on a platform tower 40 feet above the ground. At this zoo, towers and cables connect the Great Ape House with a primate language exhibition in another building. Called the O-line, it lets orangutans travel naturally and decide for themselves where to spend their days.

Bonnie was the first to use it. But before she did, she tested each cable. She shook it, stood on it, and bounced up and down. Finally, she ventured across, leaving her baby behind. But what happened next amazed everyone watching. At the halfway point Bonnie stopped ... and stared.

"I'll never forget the look on her face," says biologist Rob Shumaker. "It was thrilling for her to sit up there looking out over the zoo. She saw things she didn't know existed."

As employees cheered, Bonnie returned for her son. And together they retraced her steps—so she could expand his world, too.

49

5 COOL THINGS ABOUT ELEPHANTS

1 ELEPHANTS HAVE LONG MEMORIES
Elephants never forget. "They keep coming to places they like, no matter what," says photographer Frans Lanting, of Santa Cruz, California. One elephant herd has been visiting the same tree every November for at least 25 years!

2 ELEPHANTS CHAT WITH FRIENDS
Elephants are always "talking" in some way. This is fine in the wild. But it's a problem when elephants join sightseers on safari through the jungle. Noisy elephants spook wildlife away. "We depended on quiet," says John Roberts, who managed elephants at a lodge in the Royal Chitwan National Park in Nepal, in Asia.

When pachyderm pals Chan Chun Kali and Bhirikuti Kali worked together, they were too chatty, so Roberts moved the elephants to separate camps, six miles apart.

This worked during the day. But every night the chatterboxes started up again. They didn't rumble softly like most elephants do when "talking" long distance. "They shouted!" says Roberts. He wore earplugs to get some sleep.

3 ELEPHANTS THINK FOR THEMSELVES
In Thailand, the wild and wacky sport of elephant polo is popular. During one game, a player couldn't quite hit the ball—he just kept swinging and missing. Finally his quick-thinking elephant took matters into her own hands. She picked up the ball and handed it to the player!

4 ELEPHANTS ARE GENTLE
Tender touching is important among elephants. They hug, pet, and guide others with their trunks. Bob Norris, a cowboy from Colorado Springs, Colorado, adopted a baby African elephant named Amy. "We bonded immediately," he says.

5 ELEPHANTS HELP EACH OTHER
A retired circus elephant named Peggy might have drowned if another elephant hadn't come to her rescue! Peggy, an elephant with a partially paralyzed trunk, and her friend Betty Boop were bathing in the sanctuary pond, when Peggy laid down on her side. Swimming elephants use their trunks as snorkels, but Peggy's was completely underwater. The elephant couldn't breathe or stand! Luckily, Betty Boop rushed over and used her head to push Peggy back up on her feet and save her.

ELEPHANTS TO THE RESCUE

Trained elephants lent a helping "trunk" after a tsunami destroyed many of southern Asia's coastal towns in December 2004. In Thailand, the pachyderms used their trunks to lift motorcycles (right) and cars from the wreckage. Elephants also helped out in other countries hit by the tsunami. One elephant was walking with an eight-year-old girl on its back when the tsunami struck. In shoulder-high water, the elephant carried the girl to safety. Guess that makes these animals huge heroes!

SAFARI SEARCH

These young travelers have seen a lot of unusual African animals. The animal names in the box below are hidden in the safari jeep. They are horizontal, vertical, diagonal, even backwards. When you spot them, circle them. **BONUS:** Find the animals in the picture!

ANSWERS ON PAGE 339

aye-aye

flamingo

mamba

ibis

```
    J E R B O A L L I R O G
  N J E C H A M E L E O N X
  X O Z E B R A A A S A O O T
  K I M Q D H P M D I N K G O
A W D N A L E V V I E B D B E A N R
T N A I R A F A S Z N P A A I Y P I T
A B K H A I R Y F R O G B X E H I M O
E S K V N K R O T S U O B A R A M A I
T S E E B E D L I W O L Y R U N E L S
C H I C H I M P A N Z E E G R E T F E
P Q Y A S K        O G N O B F
  J P Q B          D V Z L
```

jerboa

bongo

wildebeest

Hidden Names

- aardvark
- addax
- ape
- baboon
- chameleon
- chimpanzee
- egret
- eland
- gorilla
- hairy frog
- hyena
- lion
- marabou stork
- okapi
- rhino
- safari ant
- skink
- tortoise
- zebra

51

The Weird World of FROGS

Frogs survived the cat-astrophic extinction of the dinosaurs. But strangely, the world's frogs and toads have suddenly begun to disappear. Some species that were common 25 years ago are now rare or extinct. And individual frogs are showing up with deformities such as too many legs. Scientists are not exactly sure what is going on.

But scientists do agree that because frogs drink and breathe through their thin skin, they are especially vulnerable to pesticides and pollution. A deformed frog often indicates that all is not well with the environment. And frogs live just about everywhere on Earth.

Frogs are amphibians, which means "double life." They generally hatch in water as tadpoles and end up living on land as fully formed frogs.

Frogs' skin must stay moist, so they're usually found in wet places.

Because frogs are so sensitive to environmental changes, they act as an early warning system. Their dwindling numbers may be a sign that our planet is not as clean and healthy as it once was. By studying how frogs are affected by the environment around them, scientists may be able to predict—and sound an alarm—that a neighborhood needs to cut back on lawn fertilizers or that a chemical-dumping factory should clean up its act. The hidden message in frogs' familiar peeps and croaks? "I'm jumpy for a reason!"

RANDOM *Question*

Q Has it ever rained frogs?

A Yes! Frogs fell from the sky in Kansas City, Missouri, in 1873, and again in De Witt, Arkansas, in 1942. Tornadoes and powerful storms sometimes vacuum up the surface of ponds, including the frogs living in the water. When the storm breaks up, frogs really *can* drop from the clouds!

CALLING ALL FROGS

Frogs bark, croak, cluck, click, grunt, snore, squawk, chirp, whistle, trill, and yap. Some are named for the noise they make. A chorus of barking tree frogs sounds like a pack of hounds on a hunt. The carpenter frog sounds like two carpenters hammering nails, and the pig frog grunts like—you guessed it—Porky's cousin! Here a male Australian red-eyed tree frog (above) inflates his throat pouch, which helps make his female-attracting calls louder.

TOADS and FROGS—WHICH IS WHICH?

Toads are actually a subgroup of the frog family. So scientifically speaking, all toads are frogs—but not all frogs are toads. Generally, the differences include the following:

versus

AMERICAN TOAD | **BRONZE FROG**

TOADS
- have bumpy, dry skin
- have short hind legs and move by short hops
- usually live in damp places, sometimes away from water

FROGS
- have smooth, moist skin
- have long, strong hind legs and move by long leaps
- often live in or near water, never found far from it

Superfrogs!

LARGEST
The Goliath frog, from West Africa, grows to about a foot long. As frogs grow, they shed their skins. After bending and twisting their bodies to loosen the skin, they pull it over their heads like a sweater—and eat it!

SMALLEST
One of the smallest frogs in the world, this leaf litter frog fits on a coin the size of a nickel. The tiny frog is found in Cuba. There are more than 4,500 species of frogs worldwide.

MOST POISONOUS
The bright colors of the golden poison-dart frog from Colombia, South America, warn predators to stay away. The skin of one golden poison-dart frog, the deadliest of all frog species, contains so much toxin it could kill 20,000 mice or 10 adult humans.

COOLEST
The North American wood frog spends two or three months frozen each winter. Its breathing and heartbeat stop, and most of the water in its body turns to ice. These frogs use a sugar called glucose in their blood as a kind of antifreeze to protect their organs from damage.

Frog Facts

Flashing open its big colorful eyes may help the red-eyed tree frog startle a predator just long enough for the frog to hop away.

The unusual gastric brooding frog of Australia is now probably extinct. But check this out: Mother frogs would swallow their eggs, and the young hatched in their stomachs. About six weeks later—*burp!*—up and out came fully formed froglets!

Some kinds of frogs lay as many as 30,000 eggs at a time.

Frogs can be different colors—green, brown, red, yellow, orange, and even blue!

Frogs have lived on Earth for so long—at least 190 million years—they were probably dodging dinosaurs!

Albino Animals

THESE ANIMALS FACE DANGER IN THE WILD

From mottled gray-and-white koalas to brilliantly hued reef fish, an animal's color serves a purpose. Color helps some species blend with their surroundings so they can hide from predators or sneak up on prey. The bright colors of some animals warn predators that they're poisonous, while others attract a mate with their color.

An animal's color comes from a pigment called melanin. Pigment cells color eyes, skin, fur, feathers, and scales. The specific colors the cells produce are determined by genes. Genes are a body's instructions on how to build the animal from head to toe, inside and out, down to the last detail.

But what happens if an animal's pigment cells cannot produce melanin? Animals without pigment have inherited a condition called albinism. In albinos, altered genes prevent pigment cells from making color. Albino animals are all white with pink or blue eyes. Many animal species can have the rare genes that cause albinism.

Albino animals face challenges in the wild. They stand out, which makes them targets for predators. Albino animals also may have trouble finding mates. Some birds, for example, reject albino partners. The reason may be that albinos lack the colors and patterns the birds rely on to choose a mate.

Below are a couple examples of rare albino animals. Many albino animals, like those shown below, live in captivity, where they are protected and live longer than they would in the wild.

ALLIGATOR

WALLABY

5 SUPER REASONS TO LOVE BATS

1 FLIP, FLAP, AND FLY
Bats are the only mammals that can truly fly. A bat's wings are basically folds of skin stretched between extra-long finger and hand bones.

2 VALUABLE DROPPINGS
Bat droppings, called guano, are super-rich in nitrogen, a main ingredient in plant food. The ancient Incas protected bats as a valuable source of fertilizer for their crops. Guano is still used in farming today.

3 MARVELOUS MOSQUITO MUNCHERS
Many bats are born bug eaters, filling their bellies with moths, mosquitoes, and other winged insects. The little brown bat gulps down as many as a thousand mosquito-size insects in an hour. Each night the bats from one Texas cave consume about 200 tons of bugs, many of them crop-eating pests. That's about the weight of six fully loaded cement trucks.

4 EXTREME FLIGHT
Hoary bats migrate up to 1,000 miles south from Canada each fall. Mexican free-tailed bats often fly up to 3 miles high, where tailwinds help speed them along at more than 60 miles an hour.

5 SUPERMOM STRENGTH
A newborn bat may weigh as much as one-third of its mother's weight, yet the mom can hold her baby while clinging by her toes to a crack in a cave's ceiling.

Different Bats

LITTLE BROWN BAT
"Little" is right—a brown bat weighs about as much as two nickels!

SHORT-TAILED FRUIT BAT
After just one night of dining, this bat can scatter up to 60,000 undigested seeds—crucial to rain forest plant growth.

COMMON VAMPIRE BAT
Vampires' main diet is the blood of cows and horses. Rarely do they take a bite out of humans.

WHITE TENT BATS
These fruit eaters often create "tents" to roost in. They make bites in a large leaf so it folds over itself. Then the bats snuggle under.

FLYING FOX
There are about 60 species of bats called flying foxes (above). This kind sometimes roosts in a "camp" of up to a million individuals.

VELVETY FREE-TAILED BAT
This bat fills its cheek pouches with insects in midair, then chews and swallows them later.

PALLID BAT
Using big ears to listen for rustlings, a pallid bat locates and grabs its prey from the ground.

DESERT LONG-EARED BAT
Sonar emitted by this kind of bat echoes off prey, signaling where its meal lies.

OLD WORLD LEAF-NOSED BAT
Complex nose structures for hunting gave this bat its name.

Bet you didn't know

Bat Spit May Save Lives
A substance in the saliva of vampire bats could help victims of strokes survive, according to researchers at the University of Monash in Melbourne, Australia. Strokes happen when a blood clot blocks blood flow to the brain. An anticlotting substance in bat spit makes blood flow freely, so a bat can continue to feed. The researchers think the same substance may be able to dissolve blood clots in stroke patients. Fortunately the substance would be contained in medicine, and bats would not be required to bite patients!

Whooo-o Are You?

5 Owls
you ought to know

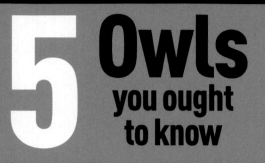

There are almost 200 species of owls. They range in size from 5 to 30 inches tall and live on every continent but Antarctica. Here are five owls and the surprising facts about whooo-o they are!

Yet another owl you should know—the pygmy owl.

1 SAW-WHET OWL

This tiny owl, just seven inches tall, gets its name from its call. The call sounds like a saw being whetted, or sharpened, on a stone. Owls make many different and distinct sounds, including hoots, screeches, trills, and chimes. Like most birds, owls sing to attract mates and call to keep other owls from intruding into their territory.

2 AFRICAN SPOTTED EAGLE-OWL

Owls' big eyes are ten times more sensitive to light than humans' eyes. That helps the birds see at night, which is when most owls, including the eagle-owl, hunt rabbits and other prey. Eyes that face forward give owls depth perception, or the ability to tell how far away things are—another useful ability for these hunters.

Sometimes even hunters have to hide—from pests such as crows and smaller birds. When startled, many owls flatten their feathers and lengthen their bodies to look like a tree branch. Some have "ear" tufts (which are just feathers, not really ears) that mimic broken twigs, helping the birds blend in even better.

3 BURROWING OWL

Most owls live in trees in nests abandoned by other birds. But a burrowing owl looks for an abandoned animal den in the ground. If it's in an area with very soft, loose soil, the owl digs its own burrow. To hunt, it stands on the dirt mound near its burrow, or on a higher perch if available, and watches the area for lizards, mice, or insects. Once the owl spots its prey, off it goes, sometimes on foot, to catch dinner. Most owls live alone, but burrowing owls often live in a group. A group of owls living together is called a parliament.

4 GREAT GRAY OWL

A tasty fresh mole caught by a parent means dinnertime for many great gray owl chicks. To feed the babies, an adult uses its sharp beak to tear the food into pieces. In owl families, both parents feed the young. A female lays an average of four to six eggs. She lays each egg on a different day, so the chicks hatch at different times. That means some are smaller than others. If food is scarce, the smallest owl chick often starves. Owlets quickly learn to hunt, and most are on their own by the first winter. Sometimes parents bring live insects and small rodents to the nest so the young can practice hunting.

5 BARN OWL

Silent flight lets owls surprise their victims. Owls with long wings, like barn owls, usually hunt from the air. After catching its prey, an owl carries it back to a perch where it swallows its meal, usually whole. It can't digest bones, feathers, or fur. A few hours after it eats, the owl closes its eyes, makes a pained face, and regurgitates a big, tightly wrapped pellet of leftovers.

Wonder what kind of owl Harry Potter has? Learn about this "snow white" wonder online. kids.nationalgeographic. com/Animals/Creature Feature/Snowy-owl

COOL CLICK

HORSE? ZEBRA? BOTH!

The name Eclyse (ee-KLEEZ) is a combination of her parents' names: mom Eclipse and dad Ulysses.

Schloss Holte-Stukenbrock, Germany

When Eclyse was about to be born, people figured the animal would be a zebra. After all, that's what the mother was. But the newborn's mix of stripe patterns and solid hair told a different story: Her father was a horse! Eclyse is a zorse: half horse, half zebra. How did this happen? In the wild, horses and zebras would never mate. But Eclyse's parents lived close together at a horse farm. The result was a rare, unintentional zorse.

Eclyse looks like two animals melded into one, but she behaves more like a horse. She eats hay, whinnies, and hangs out with Pedro the horse. "But she's a little wild like a zebra," says Susanna Stubbe of Zoo Safaripark Stukenbrock, where Eclyse now lives. "She's a bit jumpy, even if a fly lands on her back." Eclyse is definitely a horse of a different stripe!

PIG ATHLETES?

Moscow, Russia

Now even pigs can have gold medal dreams! During the third annual Pig Games in 2006, Russian pigs faced a fierce team of international competitors in sports such as pigball (like soccer), pig swimming, and pig racing.

Russia's sporting swine live in a special complex where vets and coaches keep them in fabulous form. Nariner Bagmanyan, whose company organizes the games, says the well-trained Russian pigs were calm and focused before their events. Or maybe they just had their eyes on the prize: a tub of cooked carrots with cream!

The home team left their challengers in the dust, winning all three events. Russia's pigball players defeated the international team by a whopping 16 to 3. But Bagmanyan cuts the visiting athletes some slack: "To play soccer in a foreign country is probably difficult for everybody, even pigs."

57

WILD CAT
Family Reunion

There Are 37 Species of Wild Cats

Scientists divided them into eight groups called lineages after studying their DNA. Here are representatives from each lineage. The domestic house cat comes from the lineage that includes the sand cat.

CHEETAH

(46–143 pounds)

(21–65 kilograms)

- Often scans for prey from a high spot.
- Can sprint up to 70 miles an hour.
- From puma lineage, which includes three species.

1

CANADA LYNX

(11–38 pounds)

(5–15 kilograms)

- Its main prey is the snowshoe hare.
- Big paws act like snowshoes.
- From lynx lineage, which includes four species.

2

3

OCELOT

(15–34 pounds)

(6.8–15.4 kilograms)

- Most of an ocelot's prey is small.
- Found from Texas to Argentina.
- From ocelot lineage, which includes seven species.

TIGER

(165–716 pounds)

(74.8–324.8 kilograms)

- Tigers are the only striped wild cats.
- These big cats will hunt almost any mammal in their territory.
- From Panthera lineage, which includes seven species, such as lion and jaguar.

4

58

5

SAND CAT (3–7½ pounds) (1.4–3.4 kilograms)
- The sand cat lives in dry deserts of northern Africa and the Middle East.
- Rarely drinks; gets water from food.
- From domestic cat lineage, which includes six species of cat.

MARBLED CAT
(4–11 pounds)
(1.8–5 kilograms)
- Its long, bushy tail is sometimes longer than its body.
- Very little is known about this rare, nocturnal, and shy wild cat.
- From bay cat lineage, which includes three species.

6

SERVAL **7**
(15–30 pounds)
(6.8–13.6 kilograms)
- Longest legs, relative to its body, of any cat species.
- Big ears used to listen for prey.
- From caracal lineage, which includes three species.

8

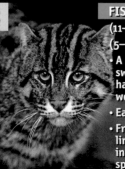

FISHING CAT
(11–35 pounds)
(5–15.8 kilograms)
- A strong swimmer, it has slightly webbed feet.
- Eats mainly fish.
- From leopard cat lineage, which includes five species.

How to tell a cat by its
SPOTS

JAGUAR: little dots in the middle of larger rings
Home: mainly Mexico, Central and South America
Average Size: 80 to 350 pounds
Cat Fact: Third-largest in the cat family after tigers and lions, the jaguar is the largest feline in the Western Hemisphere.

LEOPARD: rings without the jaguar's smaller dots inside
Home: much of Asia and Africa
Average Size: 62 to 200 pounds
Cat Fact: Some leopards are dark and look spotless. They're called black panthers.

CHEETAH: evenly spaced, solid black splotches the size of a human thumbprint
Home: parts of Africa
Average Size: 46 to 143 pounds
Cat Fact: Fastest land animal; dark lines mark a cheetah's face from the inner corner of each eye to the outer corners of its mouth.

SERVAL: usually a series of single black dots that can vary from the size of a freckle to that of a quarter
Home: many parts of Africa
Average Size: 15 to 30 pounds
Cat Fact: A serval uses its huge ears to hunt by sound, surprising prey with a pounce.

OCELOT: solid or open-centered dark spots that sometimes merge to look like links in a chain; fur in the center of open spots is often darker than background coat color
Home: South, Central, and North America
Average Size: 15 to 34 pounds
Cat Fact: An ocelot's main prey is rodents.

59

BENGAL TIGERS

You Are Here

CONTINENT: ASIA
COUNTRY: INDIA
LOCATION: KANHA NATIONAL PARK
INDIA'S POPULATION: OVER ONE BILLION; ONLY CHINA HAS MORE PEOPLE

Deep in a jungle in India, you're on an elephant's back searching for a tiger. Your elephant, controlled by a mahout, or driver and care-taker, provides the safest place from which to watch tigers in the wild. (Tigers usually don't attack adult elephants.) A tiny movement catches your eye: the flicker of a tiger's ear. The tiger's so well camouflaged that the rest of her 300-pound body melds with the background. To your great delight, you quickly realize she's not alone.

Two endangered bengal tiger cubs burst into sight, tumbling toward their mother. They leap and jump on each other. Their mother lies patiently as her cubs use her as an obstacle for playing hide, seek, and pounce.

As you watch, the playful cubs catch sight of a big grass-hopper. Practicing hunting skills they'll need when they're older, the cubs crouch, all eyes on the insect. They try hard to be patient, but they're so excited that they leap too soon and the grasshopper escapes easily.

The cubs are four months old. In a couple more months they'll be old enough to follow Mom when she hunts. They'll begin to learn her techniques and mimic her hunting behaviors. Cubs stay with their mother for as long as two years.

Rooaaarr! The roar came from a tiger in the distance. It may be a reminder to the mom and cubs to stay out of the other tiger's territory. You love watching the cubs, but decide it's time for you and your elephant to return to the lodge.

MEET THE LIGER

Sporting stripes and sometimes a shaggy mane, ligers roar like lions and chuff like tigers. That's because ligers are a rare mix of a male lion and a female tiger.

NOT A NATURAL MATCH

Giants among the big cats, ligers can weigh almost as much as a lion and tiger combined. They can devour up to 30 pounds of raw meat a day, and their heads are as big around as a kid's bicycle tire!

There may be fewer than 30 ligers living today. But they aren't endangered. Zoologists and other scientists don't even recognize ligers as a species. Ligers would not exist in the wild, because lions and tigers wouldn't mate. The solitary tiger and the group-minded lion wouldn't be good partners.

SO WHERE DO LIGERS COME FROM?

In captivity, some caretakers have allowed the two species to share space. But kept together, a lion and a tiger *can* mate, resulting in an "accidental" liger cub.

Most ligers are intentionally bred by humans—often for personal gain by being sold to private zoos. People like them because they are odd.

AN ACTIVE DEBATE

Is it wrong to allow this to happen, even if it's an accident? Almost all scientists say yes. "It's just not natural," says Ron Tilson, director of conservation at the Minnesota Zoo.

Besides that, ligers are often unhealthy because of their mismatched lion and tiger genes. They're prone to blindness, weak hearts, deafness, and short life spans. No matter how playful and happy some ligers may seem, this genetic mix isn't right.

HIDDEN HUNTER

How stripes help the tiger make a sneak attack

Crouching in the tall grass, a tiger waits patiently. Black stripes against a golden coat blend perfectly with brown and yellow stalks reflecting the sunlight. Perfectly still, the big cat is almost invisible as a large Indian bison approaches. The bison is unaware of the hidden danger. Suddenly the tiger springs from its hideout, pounces on its prey with a powerful leap, and pulls the bison to the ground. The bison didn't see its predator coming—until it was too late.

In their natural habitat, tigers live in a world of dappled sunlight and shadows. Patches of bright sunlight alternate with deep shadows in the dense, tangled forests and grasslands of Asia. A tiger's bold stripes break up the outline of its body and let it blend into the shadows.

SOLO STRIPES

Tigers are the only striped wild cat. Other wild cats are marked with spots or blotches, like cheetahs, or have coats with no pattern, like lions. Some scientists think that tigers' stripes may have evolved from a blotched coat pattern similar to that of the clouded leopard. Over time, the large spots may have disappeared, leaving the dark lines on the back edges of the blotches—the cloud patterns—to evolve into stripes.

No two tigers have exactly the same stripe pattern. Just as each human's fingerprints differ, so do each tiger's stripes.

Tigers' individual striping comes in very handy for scientists who study tigers in the wild—a difficult pursuit because the animals are hard to spot and most active at night.

TIGER PHOTOGRAPHERS

Biologists used to rely on finding tracks and signs of kills to get a tiger population count in an area under research. Now they just get tigers to take their own pictures! Choosing trails that the big cats are likely to use, researchers set out special motion-detecting cameras throughout a study area. As a tiger walks by, it trips the camera's shutter. Because each tiger's stripes are different, researchers can recognize individuals in the photographs by the unique markings on each animal's head and body.

Earn your stripes as a tiger researcher! Play the game to the right and see if you can tell the tigers apart.

Unlike most other cats, tigers actually enjoy water. On hot days, they spend hours playing in ponds or rivers, or just lounging in the water to beat the heat. Tigers are strong swimmers and are known to swim to islands as far as five miles offshore.

Yipes! Stripes!

Only one photograph below is exactly the same animal as tiger A above. Can you find the match? (Hint: Focus on eyebrow area.)
ANSWER ON PAGE 339

61

LIONS OF THE KALAHARI DESERT

How these specialized hunters adapted to their environment

E yes half-closed against the wind-blasted sand, a sleek, black-and-gold-maned lion (below) strides along a dry riverbed in the Kalahari Desert. He is one of the lions that roam the desolate sand dunes of southern Africa's Kalahari and Namib deserts. These lions thrive in an intensely hot landscape. They have learned to go without water for weeks.

Life for a desert lion is very different from life as a lion in the grassy plains of Africa, such as in the Serengeti of Kenya and Tanzania. There, large prides of up to 20 lions spend most of their time together. A pride is very much like a human family.

Fritz Eloff, a scientist who spent 40 years studying the desert lions of the Kalahari, found that desert lions live, on average, in smaller groups of fewer than six. Family ties are just as strong, but relationships are long-distance. They often break up into smaller groups.

BUSY NIGHTS

Life for Kalahari lions is a constant battle against thirst and high temperatures. In summer during the day, the surface temperature of the sand can be 150°F (66°C). That's hot enough to cook an egg. Not surprisingly, Kalahari lions hunt mostly after the sun has gone down. The big cats usually rest until the middle of the night, waiting for a cool desert wind. Then they spend the rest of the night walking—looking for food.

In the Serengeti, food is very plentiful. Lions rarely have to walk more than a couple of miles before they find a meal. But life in the desert is not so easy. With only a few scattered animals such as porcupines and gemsboks—horse-size antelopes—for prey, desert lions have to walk farther and work harder to catch dinner.

DANGEROUS DINNER

When Kalahari lions do find something to eat, it is usually spiky or dangerous. One out of every three animals they catch is a porcupine. The desert lion's main prey is the gemsbok, which can provide ten times as much meat as a porcupine. But gemsboks are difficult to bring down; they've been known to kill lions by skewering them on their three-foot-long, saberlike horns.

Water is scarce in the Kalahari, so the desert lions have to be as resourceful at finding a drink as they are at finding a meal. One hot day, just as a light rain began to fall, Eloff watched two lionesses. Side by side, they licked the raindrops off each other.

These lean, strong lions have amazingly learned to survive, and by cooperating they manage to thrive in an inhospitable, almost waterless world.

ROARRR!
On a still night the sound of lions roaring can carry for five miles. Roaring often is used to tell other lions, "This is my piece of land."

LION Around

Close encounter with an upside-down cat

Screams echo through the forest as alarmed animals, such as spotted deer, warn each other of a predator's approach. Lying on my stomach with my camera in front of me, I've been watching a nearby stream for hours, waiting. This may be it.

Yes! A 380-pound (172-kg) lioness steps from the trees and heads toward the stream. She crouches down to drink. She's close to me—no more than 50 yards away. She stands up and begins to walk toward me, not knowing I'm there.

When she is just about 20 yards away, I move my camera slightly so that she notices me. I don't want to shock or panic her. She freezes for a moment, then takes a crouching position and continues toward me—which was not really the reaction I wanted! I'm thinking, "Uh-oh, I'm about to become cat food!" I've approached lions before, but this is a first. The lion approaches me.

If I stand up and yell, will she leave? Maybe, maybe not. If I stand up and run, will she chase me? Probably. So I decide to stay put.

The lioness comes closer and closer until she's only about four yards from me—which is now only a couple of pounces away and the closest distance that still allows me to focus my camera lens.

Surprisingly, she lies down, posing like a sphinx in front of me. This makes me feel very small and humble. Then she rolls over and looks at me upside down! She seems a little puzzled and appears to be trying to figure me out—Hmm, are you edible? You don't look dangerous. I think you're OK.

Breathe slowly, I remind myself, even though my heart is pounding. I carefully back up my tripod just a bit to where I can focus and shoot this picture.

Suddenly—so fast that it startles me—she leaps up. In a flash, she bounds away. I'm left overwhelmed with emotion. Getting this shot took a long time.

I spent two years waiting for a permit to track the extremely rare Asiatic lions in the Gir Forest of India. Then I spent three months on foot searching for them. There are only about 300 of these endangered lions left.

Perhaps all the waiting in the forest gave the lioness time to get used to me. I tried not to intrude on her life. My reward? A moment I'll never forget.
—*Mattias Klum, National Geographic photographer*

BY THE NUMBERS

3 is the number of cubs in a typical litter of lions.

5 miles (8 km) is the distance the sound of a lion's roar can carry.

15 pounds (6.8 kg) of meat is a typical meal for an adult male lion.

36 miles per hour (58 kph) is a lion's top running speed.

2,200 pounds (998 kg) is the top weight of prey a pride can kill.

JAGUARS

CONTINENT: SOUTH AMERICA

COUNTRY: BRAZIL

LOCATION: AMAZON RIVER RAIN FOREST

LENGTH OF RIVER: 4,000 MILES; SECOND-LONGEST RIVER ON EARTH

As your plane lands, the sun rises in Brazil's rain forest along the Amazon River. You make your way into the lush growth of the hot, dense forest. You're eager to spot a jaguar hunting. You and your guide search for a cat that a scientist has been following using a tracking device. The jaguar's spots camouflage it so well that the cat is hard to find. Finally, it appears, leaping suddenly from the underbrush into a small clearing.

You notice the jaguar's short, compact body and big head. A jaguar easily drags prey two or three times its weight great distances. To match that strength, you'd have to be able to drag three of your friends at once— with your mouth!

You watch as the jaguar settles into a hidden spot, waiting to ambush a deer. As the unsuspecting animal wanders by, the cat pounces, killing the deer by piercing its skull with its powerful bite. The jaguar is the only big cat that uses this method to kill prey. It can even bite through a tortoise's shell.

Like the lion, this cat likes to swim—and fish. Your guide tells you about the time he watched a jaguar wait patiently at the edge of a stream until a fish swam by. Then *swoosh!* The cat scooped the fish out with its paw for a snack.

COOL CLICK

To learn more about lots of other amazing animals, go online. kids.nationalgeographic.com/Animals

Bet you **didn't know**

7 feline **facts** to **pounce on**

1 A **tiger's roar** can be heard **over** one mile away.

2 **Cats** were domesticated at least **3,000 years** ago in Egypt.

3 ALL CATS ARE BORN WITH **BLUE EYES.**

4 Unlike most cats, **lions** are **excellent** swimmers.

5 Today's domestic cats are **cousins** of **big** cats.

6 A **tiger's paw prints** are called pug marks.

7 **Cats communicate** using at least 16 known "**cat words.**"

5 Cool Things About Dolphins

1 Stunning SOUNDS

Like most bats, dolphins use sound to "see." They use echolocation—making a sound and listening to it bounce off objects—for finding food and navigating without bumping into things. While hunting for food underwater, some dolphins also make very loud clicking sounds that may knock out any small fish or squid within range. The dolphins then gobble up the sound-stunned prey.

2 Terrific TEAMWORK

Thousands of dolphins sometimes gather in huge pods, or groups. These superpods spread across several miles of open ocean. Dolphins often hunt together. That allows them to cover larger areas as they look for schools of fish. Dolphins also cooperate to round up their prey. Sometimes they work together to herd a big school of fish into a small, crowded clump. Then the dolphins take turns speeding through the trapped fish to eat.

3 Favorite AUNT

Cooperation among dolphins is crucial to a newborn. When a mother dolphin is ready to give birth, a second dolphin called an auntie will stay nearby to help. As soon as the baby is born, its mother gently nudges the newborn to the surface for its first breath of air. Often the auntie will help with this important chore.

4 Name-CALLERS

Dolphins communicate with whistles and use individual "names" to identify one another. Some research scientists who study dolphin communication think that wild dolphins have special high-pitched calls known as signature whistles that they use to tell pod pals apart. Each dolphin chooses its own signature whistle, usually by its first birthday. This name stays the same for at least ten more years.

5 Toothy JAWS

If dolphins had dentists, those docs would be busy. Some dolphins have even more teeth than crocodiles. Their extremely long jaws may contain as many as 250 pointy white teeth. Unlike predatory crocodiles, though, dolphins aren't interested in chomping on human swimmers. There are no reliable reports of wild dolphins attacking people.

Fin Kin
Dolphins are toothed whales. They come in many shapes and sizes. Take a closer look at the names, weights, home ranges, and surprising facts about a few of the 67 toothed whales that exist.

Art not to scale

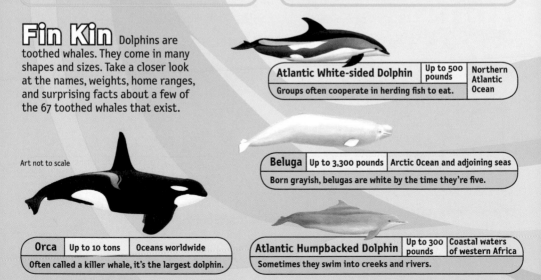

Atlantic White-sided Dolphin	Up to 500 pounds	Northern Atlantic Ocean
Groups often cooperate in herding fish to eat.		

Beluga	Up to 3,300 pounds	Arctic Ocean and adjoining seas
Born grayish, belugas are white by the time they're five.		

Orca	Up to 10 tons	Oceans worldwide
Often called a killer whale, it's the largest dolphin.		

Atlantic Humpbacked Dolphin	Up to 300 pounds	Coastal waters of western Africa
Sometimes they swim into creeks and rivers.		

CLOSE-UP

Splish. Splash!

DOLPHIN SPLASh FACTS

More than 30 species of dolphins swim in the world's oceans and rivers.

All dolphins are predators and are warm-blooded, air-breathing mammals.

Most dolphins' bodies are streamlined, making them fast, graceful swimmers.

The smallest species is the Maui's dolphin, found in the South Pacific. It's less than four feet long—about the same as the average height of a six-year-old boy.

The largest dolphin is the orca, or killer whale. An adult male orca can be about 32 feet long—8 times the size of the tiny Maui's.

Bottlenose dolphins, some of the best-known dolphins, live in groups called pods. These friendly dolphins use squeaks, whistles, and body language to communicate with each other. If we could only know what they're saying!

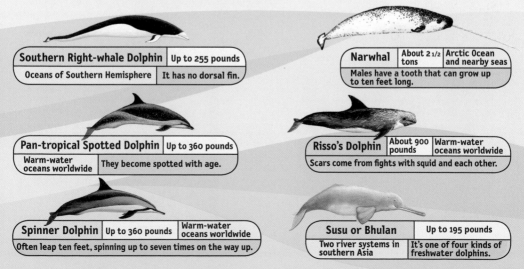

Southern Right-whale Dolphin	Up to 255 pounds
Oceans of Southern Hemisphere	It has no dorsal fin.

Narwhal	About 2 1/2 tons	Arctic Ocean and nearby seas
Males have a tooth that can grow up to ten feet long.		

Pan-tropical Spotted Dolphin	Up to 360 pounds
Warm-water oceans worldwide	They become spotted with age.

Risso's Dolphin	About 900 pounds	Warm-water oceans worldwide
Scars come from fights with squid and each other.		

Spinner Dolphin	Up to 360 pounds	Warm-water oceans worldwide
Often leap ten feet, spinning up to seven times on the way up.		

Susu or Bhulan	Up to 195 pounds
Two river systems in southern Asia	It's one of four kinds of freshwater dolphins.

MEET THE NAT GEO EXPLORER

SYLVIA EARLE

Sometimes termed "Her Deepness," Earle is an oceanographer, explorer, author, and lecturer, whose knowledge of the sea is immense. Earle has led more than 60 expeditions and logged more than 6,000 hours underwater, including leading the first team of women aquanauts during the Tektite Project in 1970 and setting a record for solo diving to a depth of 3,300 feet (1,000 meters).

How did you become an explorer?
It was really easy. I started out as a kid, asking questions—Who? How? What? Where? When? And especially, why? And I never stopped. Explorers and scientists never lose their sense of wonder, never stop asking questions, and always keep looking for answers.

What was your closest call in the field?
I have been surrounded by hundreds of sharks, dived in submersibles more than two miles under the sea, and had my air supply run out when I was more than a thousand feet away from my home base underwater.

How did you get involved with National Geographic?
I loved reading the NATIONAL GEOGRAPHIC magazine as a child, and I still do. Then, as a scientist, I lived underwater for two weeks in 1970, and I was asked to write about the experience for NATIONAL GEOGRAPHIC! Since then I have written more stories for the magazine and worked on a lot of films and books.

Would you suggest that kids follow in your footsteps?
I followed my heart—and it led into the sea. I hope every child will have a chance to realize his or her dreams. Every person has a special, unique pathway that unfolds as opportunities arise and choices are made. There is an urgent need for everyone who cares about exploring and protecting natural systems, above and below the sea, to get busy and go for it!

EMPEROR PENGUINS

1 Emperors are the largest of the 17 penguin species.

2 One colony can number as many as 60,000 penguins.

3 These penguins can live 20 years or more in the wild.

4 Emperors eat fish, squid, and shrimplike krill.

5 Parents feed chicks every three to four days.

IN SEARCH OF THE GIANT SQUID

Do huge sea monsters with eyes the size of human heads and multiple arms that could wrap around a large ship and drag it to the bottom of the sea exist? For centuries sailors have reported seeing such sea monsters. In fact, they sound a lot like a real deep-sea creature called the giant squid.

The giant squid may grow 60 feet long—about the length of six pool tables end to end—and can weigh, literally, a ton. It has a razor-sharp beak plus eight arms and two tentacles outfitted with hundreds of suckers. Its eyes are the largest of any animal. But scientists only know this from examining dead or dying squids that were trapped in fishing nets or washed up on beaches. The truth is no one has ever seen the giant squid alive in its natural habitat, thousands of feet beneath the ocean's surface.

BIG AND SCARY

There may be something even bigger and scarier than the giant squid lurking in the ocean depths: the colossal squid. According to some marine biologists, the colossal squid has a heavier body than the more common giant squid. Scarier still, the suckers that line the colossal squid's arms and tentacle ends boast hooks that can bend while they grip. Ouch!

SQUID VERSUS SQUID

In a watery wrestling match between the two enormous squids, which would come out alive? "It probably comes down to weight," says Mark Norman, a senior curator of mollusks at Museum Victoria in Melbourne, Australia. "So I'd be putting my money on the colossal squid."

GREAT WHITE SHARKS

"We've located a great white shark," the captain tells you and the shark expert you've been talking with on the deck of the research vessel. You're off the coast of South Australia, near Spencer Gulf. The captain points to the shark cage tied to the boat's stern. "Hop in!" he tells you. "This is an opportunity you won't want to miss."

You check your snorkeling gear and then slip down feet-first into the cage. (A shark cage is built to keep great white sharks out. The cage's metal bars protect divers like you.) Slowly you're lowered, inside the cage, to just below the ocean surface. Soon you spot what you came to see. Your heart races as a six-foot great white shark glides past the cage, turns, and swims by again. You are safe.

Great white sharks are the world's largest meat-eating fish. Their sharp teeth and powerful jaws are built to cut and tear their prey. The longest confirmed great white was longer than 20 feet—about the length of 4 bathtubs! Your six-footer is a young shark.

Suddenly you see the shark's impressive teeth. The predator you're watching speeds by again—this time following a school of large fish. The shark grabs one that lags a bit behind the rest. In two gulps, the fish is gone. The scientist on board told you that great white sharks also scavenge, or eat dead animals they come across. They particularly like whales. Whale blubber, or fat, gives these large sharks an excellent source of calories. Now the captain hoists you out of the water because the time has come to head for dry land.

Steering Clear of Shark Bites

Shark attacks on people are extremely rare. In the U.S., seven times as many people are bitten by squirrels as sharks every year. Here are tips to help you stay safe:

1 Stay out of the ocean at dawn, dusk, and night—when some sharks swim into shallow water to feed.

2 Don't swim in the ocean if you're bleeding.

3 Swim and surf at beaches with lifeguards on duty. They can warn you about shark sightings.

COOL CLICK

Want to color a picture of a great white shark? www.nationalgeographic.com/coloringbook/sharks.html

6 COOL THINGS YOU DIDN'T KNOW ABOUT SHARKS

TEETH TO SPARE

If great white sharks had tooth fairies, they'd be rich! A great white loses and replaces thousands of its teeth during its lifetime. Its upper jaw is lined with 26 front-row teeth; its lower jaw has 24. Behind these razor-sharp points are many rows of replacement teeth. The "spares" move to the front whenever the shark loses a tooth.

BOX OFFICE BULLY

Great white sharks are superstars. Before the *Star Wars* series, the 1975 movie *Jaws* was Hollywood's biggest moneymaker. *Jaws*, about a great white on the prowl, cost $12 million to film but made $260 million in the U.S. Not bad for a fish story!

SPEEDY SWIMMERS

Great white sharks can sprint through the water at speeds of 35 miles per hour—seven times faster than the best Olympic swimmer! Scientists on the California coast tracked one shark as it swam all the way to Hawaii—2,400 miles—in only 40 days.

CHOW DOWN, TUNA BREATH!

Picky eaters they're not. While great white sharks prefer to eat seals, sea lions, and the occasional dolphin, they've been known to swallow lots of other things. Bottles, tin cans, a straw hat, lobster traps, and a cuckoo clock are among the items found inside the bellies of great white sharks.

EAR THAT?

Great white sharks have ears. You can't see them, because they don't open to the outside. The sharks use two small sensors in the skull to hear and, perhaps, to zero in on the splashing sounds of a wounded fish or a struggling seal!

HOT ON THE TRAIL

Unlike most fish, great white sharks' bodies are warmer than their surroundings. The sharks' bodies can be as much as 27°F warmer than the water the fish swim in. A higher temperature helps the great white shark swim faster and digest its food more efficiently—very useful for an animal that's always on the go!

Sensitive Sharks

What's the secret weapon

a great white shark or a black-tip reef shark uses to track its prey? Gel in the snout! The clear gel acts like a highly sensitive thermometer, registering changes in water temperature as slight as a thousandth of a degree, according to a University of San Francisco physicist. Tiny changes in the ocean's temperature tend to occur in places where cold and warm water mix, feeding areas for smaller fish—a shark's next meal. Once the gel registers a change, it produces an electrical charge that causes nerves in the snout to send a message to the shark's brain that says, "Let's do lunch!"

BY THE NUMBERS

ABOUT **12** species of sharks are considered dangerous.

YOU ARE **250** times more likely to be killed by lightning than by a shark.

THERE ARE **375** different species of sharks found in the world's oceans.

THERE WERE **43,674** more injuries associated with toilets than with sharks.

71

UNDER the ICE

Jellyfish (right) with 30-foot-long tentacles ... sponges the size of bears ... these are just a few of the surprises beneath the surface of Antarctica's frozen seas.

One such surprise is **sea spiders.** Found in oceans worldwide, they are less than an inch long. But in Antarctica, they often reach the size of a human's hand. Luckily, people aren't their chosen snack food. They prefer to chow down on coral, anemones, and sponges.

SEABIRDS OF THE NORTH

Colorful Atlantic puffins perch on a grass-covered cliff in Iceland, Europe's westernmost country. These unusual birds are skilled fishers but have difficulty becoming airborne and often crash upon landing.

GO FISH!

Something's fishy at this aquarium. Find and circle the following items that are hidden in this scene.

surfboard
cowboy hat
sunflower
wrapped gift
bike wheel
teacup and saucer
plate of spaghetti
soft pretzel
guitar

ANSWERS ON PAGE 339

Human activity poses the greatest threat to Earth's biodiversity—its rich variety of species. Loss of habitat puts many species, including those in this section, at great risk. Experts estimate that species are becoming extinct at a rate 100 to 1,000 times higher than natural loss would cause.

Sea Turtle RESCUE

How people are saving these threatened creatures

Green sea turtles were important to the fishermen on Mafia Island off Tanzania's coast, in Africa—because they could sell the turtle meat!

That attitude began to change in 2002 when fishermen hauled in a 50-year-old green sea turtle with a shell as wide as a car tire. There was nothing special about the turtle. Mafia Island fishing boats had netted thousands just like her before. But what happened next was special: Instead of killing her, the fishermen spared the turtle's life.

Sea Life Needs Sea Turtles

Sea turtles play a key role in Mafia Island's chain of life. Green turtles act as natural undersea lawn mowers. Fish and other sea creatures use the huge sea grass beds near Mafia as a safe place with plenty of food for raising their young. Sea grass beds need sea turtles to graze on them in order to stay healthy.

Four of the world's seven sea turtle species swim in the waters off Mafia. Green turtles are the most common. Even though it's illegal to harm these threatened animals, Mafia Islanders had traditionally eaten turtle meat. They also ate turtle eggs found in nests. Other sea turtle species in the world include: hawksbill, leatherback, loggerhead, Kemp's ridley, flatback, and olive ridley turtles. Populations of all these sea turtles are in distress.

Success Saving Sea Turtles

Thanks to a program funded by the World Wildlife Fund, fishermen have learned about the value of sea turtles. Fishermen who guard a nest or turn over a live sea turtle to scientists—for data collection and release—can earn money. For fishermen, sea turtles have become the gift that keeps on giving.

The program seems to have worked. Killing turtles and taking their eggs almost completely stopped.

All this success started with that first green sea turtle saved in 2002. Unfortunately, sea turtles throughout the oceans still face many dangers, such as pollution and deep-sea fishing nets. But at least they're not being eaten anymore!

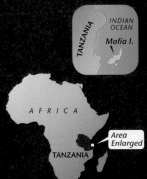

INDIAN OCEAN

TANZANIA

Mafia I.

AFRICA

Area Enlarged

TANZANIA

Will the RED PANDA survive?

A mask marks one of the cutest faces in the forest. The red panda looks a little like a raccoon, a bit like a fox, and somewhat like a puppy. Soft, cuddly reddish fur blankets its body, which is a tad larger than a big house cat's. These harmless creatures live in the high mountain forests of the Himalaya in southeastern Asia. But their numbers in the wild are dwindling.

As loggers and firewood collectors chop down trees, and ranchers allow overgrazing by domestic livestock, the fragile mountain habitat of the red panda erodes.

SPECIALIZED DIET

The diet of the red panda also makes it vulnerable because it is one of just a few mammal species in the world that eat mainly bamboo. It's not the most nutritious stuff. This giant grass has tough stems and leaves that make it difficult to chew and digest. A bamboo diet doesn't give red pandas much energy, so they have to conserve as much as possible.

SLOW-MOVING SLEEPYHEADS

Red pandas save energy simply by keeping activity to a minimum. They spend six to eight hours a day moving around and eating. The rest of their time is spent resting and sleeping. Their bodies are built to conserve energy. When the weather is cold, the pandas curl into a tight ball on a tree branch and go into a very deep sleep. This reduces their metabolism, or the amount of energy they use. When red pandas wake up, their metabolism returns to normal. But as soon as they go back to sleep their metabolism drops again, saving energy.

BALD EAGLES Are Home Free

The bald eagle is back! Once close to extinction, the national bird of the United States is officially out of danger. These raptors almost died off when a chemical used to control insects started polluting their fishing waters. As a result, the eagles' eggs became thin and cracked too early. "They couldn't raise any young," says Colin Rowan of the group Environmental Defense.

Decades later, the bald eagle population had dropped from thousands to only 400 nesting pairs in the entire U.S., not including Alaska. The government soon banned the dangerous chemical and passed a law to protect endangered species.

The changes worked! In 1995 the species was upgraded from endangered to threatened. Today the birds are thriving, with some 10,000 nesting pairs. In 2007, bald eagles soared off the national list of threatened and endangered species. Sounds like these birds are flying high!

By the Numbers

There are 8,462 vulnerable or endangered animal species in the world. The list includes:

- **1,141 mammals**, such as the snow leopard, the polar bear, and the fishing cat.
- **1,222 birds**, including the Steller's sea eagle and the Madagascar plover.
- **1,275 fish**, such as the Thailand giant catfish.
- **423 reptiles**, including the American crocodile.
- **626 insects**, including the Corsican swallowtail butterfly.
- **1,905 amphibians**, such as the Round Island day gecko.
- **and more**, including 18 arachnids, 606 crustaceans, 235 corals, 95 bivalves, and 883 snails and slugs.

COOL CLICK

To find endangered species by state, country, and other groupings, check out the U.S. Fish and Wildlife Service. ecos.fws.gov/tess_public

PANDA BABY BOOM!

If Su Lin the giant panda had thrown herself a one-year-old birthday party, she'd have had a lot of panda friends to play Pin the Tail on the Donkey. That's because she is one of 19 captive pandas who turned a year old that year.

Su Lin's home is the San Diego Zoo in California. She was born August 2, 2005, and weighed about the same as a stick of butter. By September 2008 she weighed about 165 pounds.

PANDAS AT RISK

The exact number of giant pandas in the wild is hard to estimate, but scientists think that fewer than 2,500 of these animals live in the mountains of central China. About another 300 giant pandas live in zoos and breeding stations, mostly in China. Giant pandas are among the rarest of the world's living mammals.

DAY 1
08-02-2005
22:37:35

Bai Yun gently holds her newborn in her mouth moments after giving birth.

DAY 3

A newborn panda doesn't have its parents' black-and-white markings.

WEEK 2

She's almost 10 inches long and weighs 13 ounces. Black markings begin to show.

WEEK 6

The cub grew fast. She already weighs more than four pounds!

WEEK 13

WEEK 11

The cub gets her first tooth. "Stay tuned," say zoo doctors. "More teeth to come!"

In keeping with Chinese tradition, the cub is named 100 days after her birth. Her name is Su Lin, which means "A Little Bit of Something Very Cute."

Polar Bears
Listed as Threatened

In 2008, polar bears were added to the list of threatened species and received special protection under U.S. law. In his statement, former U.S. secretary of the interior Dirk Kempthorne noted that the decline of Arctic sea ice is the greatest threat to the bears.

Polar bears live in the Arctic and hunt seals and other fatty marine mammals from sea ice. They also travel, mate, and sometimes give birth on the ice. But sea ice is melting as the planet warms, and it is predicted to continue to do so for several more decades. "Because polar bears are vulnerable to this loss of habitat, they are—in my judgment—likely to become endangered in the foreseeable future," Kempthorne said.

Although many scientists say that human activity is directly responsible for the melting sea ice, the polar bear protections will not by themselves change U.S. climate policy.

The listing of the bear adds protections for the animals, and provides means to limit the impacts from activities such as oil and gas production. Hunting of polar bears as a food source by certain native people and trade in native handicrafts made from polar bears will also continue. However, importing polar bear products from Canada (where trophy hunting is legal) will be banned.

A study in 2007 found that two-thirds of the world's polar bears could go extinct by 2050. Saving the polar bear will depend on international cooperation. Permanent sea-ice habitat is likely to remain in areas outside of the U.S., particularly in Canada and Greenland, until the end of the century,

Scientists view these areas as refuges that could allow some polar bear populations to survive over the long term and repopulate the Arctic if temperatures decrease and sea ice returns. Scientists believe that there is still time to save polar bears and their Arctic habitat if we take action on climate change soon.

When you're a Canada lynx's lunch, it's *always* a bad hare day.

An endangered Canada lynx perches on a stump. A snowshoe hare, ever alert, crouches on the snow. White on white, the hare is betrayed only by its black, marblelike eyes. Suddenly the lynx bounds, pounces ... and just misses as the hare flees. The cat sniffs briefly and then sits on its haunches in deep, melting snow. It's late spring in the far north.

Gorilla RESCUE

Orphaned and afraid, baby gorilla Dunia finally finds kindness in human arms.

When a terrified one-year-old baby gorilla was found in a sting operation against poachers (illegal hunters) in Rwanda, the authorities rushed the young gorilla to the nearby headquarters of the Mountain Gorilla Veterinary Project. The vets there realized that she had not been given enough food or water, but they were more worried about something else she hadn't been getting: touch.

Surprisingly, gorillas, animals well known for their great size and strength, are extremely fragile creatures—they need their mother's constant body contact to survive. The project's staff immediately began holding and cuddling the little female—a kind of touch first aid. They named her Dunia.

After six months of loving care that included around-the-clock attention, a good diet, and a comfortable home at the project's headquarters, Dunia was looking and acting like a healthy, happy young gorilla should. Eventually, the vets at the project hope to place Dunia and other orphaned gorillas in a sanctuary. No matter where she ends up, Dunia will never be alone again.

How you can help!

- Be careful with the products you buy. Don't buy or sell products from dead wildlife, such as ivory from elephants. Live cruelty-free.

- Reach out to animal rights groups to help make life better for wild animals and help protect their rights.

- Read all you can about animals and the issues surrounding them. Knowledge is power.

Cougar RESCUE

Chinook and another orphaned cougar cub snuggle at the Oregon Zoo.

When a scared and hungry orphaned cougar cub wandered into a neighborhood searching for food, the homeowners called the authorities for help. This cub was starving. She weighed only 20 pounds, half what she should have weighed. "She probably would have died in a matter of days," says state fish and wildlife officer Larry Baker. Cougars normally stay with their mothers until they're about two years old, nursing and then learning how to catch prey.

The cub needed medical attention right away. In addition to starvation, the cougar suffered from fleas and internal parasites. With the help of medicine and meaty meals, the cat quickly gained weight and strength. But she could not be released into the wild without the survival skills her mother would have taught her. After three months of recovery, Chinook, as she was named, was taken to a new, permanent home at the Oregon Zoo in Portland.

There, the zoo's staff keeps her busy and exercised. She "hunts" for meals and gets frozen meat treats. What does Chinook like to do the most? Sleep, like most cougars.

Saving Habitats

A habitat is a place where animals and plants live. Animals adapt to their specific habitats—forest, desert, ocean, prairie, wherever—to find food, hide from predators, and raise young. But if one thing changes, the habitat could be in trouble.

For instance, building houses and shopping malls can change or even destroy habitats. And constructing roads can divide habitats, creating barriers to food and shelter. Such changes make it hard for animals to survive.

Think of it this way: What if your refrigerator stopped working, or your faucets ran dry? One small change could make your house—your habitat—unlivable. And just like you, animals and plants need safe, livable habitats to survive.

Don Edwards San Francisco Bay National Wildlife Refuge (NWR*)
California
In this urban habitat, American avocets hunt on mudflats, which can contain 40,000 living things in a handful of mud.

Agassiz NWR
Minnesota
This refuge supports the largest population of gray wolves in the lower 48 states.

Horicon NWR
Wisconsin
Migrating birds such as redhead ducks nest at this freshwater refuge.

John Heinz NWR at Tinicum
Pennsylvania
Like many wildlife refuges, this NWR is within an hour's drive of a major U.S. city.

National Bison Range
Montana
American bison grow thick fur for the chilly winters here.

Rocky Mountain Arsenal NWR
Colorado
Bald eagles spread their wings over this prairie habitat, an inactive military site.

Canaan Valley NWR
West Virginia
Black bears roam in the swamps and forests of this refuge, the system's 500th.

Cabeza Prieta NWR
Arizona
Saguaro cactuses living here survive deserts by storing as much as seven tons of water.

Wichita Mountains NWR
Oklahoma
Prairie dogs dig burrows that become habitats for many grassland creatures.

Neal Smith NWR
Iowa
The regal fritillary butterfly is getting a helping hand from this refuge's 8,600-acre prairie restoration project.

Okefenokee NWR
Georgia
Although the American alligator is thriving, many of its unprotected wetland habitats are shrinking.

Pelican Island NWR
Florida
Protected at the first National Wildlife Refuge, brown pelicans live only near coasts.

Kenai NWR
Alaska
Salmon thrive in this watershed, a source of water for rivers and streams.

Kilauea Point NWR
Hawai'i
Laysan albatross chicks face little threat from predators on this coastal refuge.

***National Wildlife Refuges** (NWRs) are home to hundreds of species of birds, mammals, reptiles, fish, and plants, including endangered species. The U.S. Fish and Wildlife Service manages more than 540 refuges. Check out a few of them on this map, or go online to learn more—including how to visit one! www.fws.gov/refuges

AYE-AYES OF MADAGASCAR

The aye-aye's odd-looking fingers, pointy teeth, big eyes, and huge ears give some people the creeps.

Seeing an aye-aye is considered very bad luck to many superstitious residents of Madagascar, the African island country where these animals live in the wild. In parts of the country, people kill aye-ayes on sight, hoping to prevent anything "evil" from happening. The aye-aye's bad reputation isn't helped by the fact that it's active only at night, when things can seem a lot scarier to people.

The truth about this five-pound animal, a type of lemur, is that it's harmless. In the wild, aye-ayes live mostly in trees. When they leave their nests, where they spend daylight hours sleeping, their forest home is dark. Big eyes help them see as they look for food. Aye-ayes' favorite food is insect larvae.

The main threat to aye-ayes is loss of habitat due to farming and logging in Madagascar. Added to that danger are the people who kill them because of lingering beliefs that aye-ayes bring bad luck. We can only hope that fears about the animals will disappear at the same time aye-ayes' numbers grow.

AFRICA

MADAGASCAR

MADAGASCAR

■ AREAS WHERE AYE-AYES MAY LIVE

ANIMAL KILLERS
BUSTED!

GUNNING FOR TROUBLE

The bald eagle bodies arrived at the lab by the dozens, shot, with their tails and wings missing. No gun had been heard, and no hunter was sighted where police had discovered the corpses.

But the killer left key evidence. The casings, or outer shells, of his bullets littered the ground beneath the telephone wires where he'd shot the protected national birds.

A gun leaves telltale nicks and scratches on the bullets it fires. "We can match both the bullets and the casings to a particular weapon by the marks left on them after they've been fired from the gun," says deputy lab director Ed Espinoza.

Back in the lab, the forensic scientists recovered the bullets that killed several eagles. Then they fired a test round of bullets from a gun seized from a suspect.

Using a high-powered microscope, investigators compared scratches from the test round to scratches on bullets found in the eagles. They matched perfectly. Thanks to the scientists' eagle eyes, the suspect was charged. Bald eagles are now safe from this bad guy.

CRIME SCENE EVIDENCE

BULLET

CRIME SCENE EVIDENCE

FEATHER SAMPLE

ULTIMATE Animal RESCUE

Molly can relax in her new home.

Molly, an African lioness, was found prowling in a Dallas, Texas, neighborhood. She was starving, and a chain around her neck was choking her. Rescuers cut it off with bolt cutters and hurried her to a veterinarian. Fortunately a good permanent home awaited the ten-month-old abandoned pet as she began her journey back to health.

Located in Austin, Texas, the 20-acre Austin Zoo is a private, nonprofit organization that takes in and rehabilitates all sorts of confiscated, stray, or unwanted animals. The zoo staff never tries to make them act like pets. Like most zoos, it's open to the public, but the Austin Zoo does not breed or sell any of its animals. It even becomes home for animals that other zoos no longer want to keep.

Now Nikki has room to climb.

In her new home, Molly eats a proper diet, and she has gained weight. She lives there with other abandoned pets like Nikki, a ring-tailed lemur, and Teri, a Brazilian porcupine. Both Nikki and Teri like to climb around branches and platforms.

Nearby, Binny the bearcat lounges on his little house

or slowly stretches out on the tree branches in his large, private enclosure. That's a whole lot better than napping on someone's doorstep after escaping from the barn where he was kept illegally. Although he is called a bearcat, Binny isn't related to either bears or cats. *Bearcat* is another name for binturong, an animal species from Asia.

Teri the porcupine

The Austin Zoo gets nearly 200 calls a month about animals in

need of homes, but unfortunately they don't have room for all of them. The solution for neglected exotic pets, zoos' unwanted animals, and animals rescued from bad conditions isn't building more animal sanctuaries. It's important to stop breeding these animals instead. But for the lucky animals the zoo has helped to save, now numbering more than 300 individuals of more than 100 different species, the Austin Zoo is one home sweet home.

A worker makes sure Binny is OK.

Who's SMARTER ...
Cats or Dogs?

CATS FLUSH

Russ and Sandy Asbury were alone in their Whitewater, Wisconsin, home when they suddenly heard the toilet flush. "My husband's eyes got huge," says Sandy. "Did we have ghosts?"

Nope. Their cats just like to play with toilets. Boots, a Maine coon cat, taught himself to push on the handle that flushes. Then his copycat brother, Bandit, followed. "It's kind of eerie," Sandy admits. "Bandit follows me into the bathroom and flushes for me—sometimes even before I'm finished!"

Now the cats use the stunt to get attention. They go into a flushing frenzy if supper's late!

These cats just play in the bathroom, but some cats can be trained to use the toilet instead of a litter box. For their lucky owners, cleanup is just a flush (instead of a scoop) away. Meanwhile, Fido's just *drinking* from the toilet.

DOGS "GO" ON CUE

To housebreak a pup, take him outside and watch closely. When he starts to urinate, say the same phrase, such as "right there," each time. Within weeks, he'll associate the phrase with the action.

Buffy, a keeshond belonging to Wade Newman of Turin, New York, has never had an "accident" in the house. In fact, the smart dog sometimes plans ahead. Once, called in for the night, she came running. "But suddenly she stopped, cocked her head, and took off in the other direction," Newman says. "I was kind of annoyed." But it turned out Buffy was simply getting ready for bed—by "going" first, after which she obediently ran back to Newman. Now, *that's* thinking ahead!

DOGS SNIFF

Sometimes dogs can drive you crazy! That reportedly happened to one woman whose sheepdog started to sniff at her back every time she sat down. Exasperated, she asked her husband to take a look. All he saw was a dark mole. Nothing to worry about, thought the woman. Then one day she was sunbathing when her dog tried to nip off the mole with its teeth.

That did it. The woman went to the doctor and found out the mole was a deadly form of skin cancer. Her dog probably saved her life.

Dogs' noses have about 4 times as many scent cells as cats' noses and 14 times more than humans'. It makes some breeds terrific at sniffing out mold, termites, illegal drugs, missing persons, and, apparently, even cancer. Now, if only those noses didn't feel so cold.

CATS PREDICT EARTHQUAKES

Early one evening in 1976, people in northeastern Italy were all asking the same question: What is wrong with my cat? Many pets were running around, scratching on doors, and yowling to go out. Once out, they didn't come back (except for mother cats, who returned to get their kittens). Then, later that day, a major earthquake hit!

Cats may feel very early vibrations or sense the increase in static electricity that occurs before a quake. Whatever they're sensing, it's one more reason to pay attention to your cat.

So, which *is* smarter ... a cat or a dog?

Actually, this is a trick question, and there's no simple answer.

Dogs and cats have different abilities. Each species knows what it needs to know in order to survive. "For that reason, we can't design a test that is equal for both animals," says Dr. Bonnie Beaver, a veterinarian at Texas A&M University. "When people ask me which is smarter, I say it's whichever one you own!"

DOGS PLAY THE PIANO

Forget "sit" and "shake." Chanda-Leah, a toy poodle who died in 2006 at the age of twelve, settled down at a computerized keyboard and plunked out "Twinkle, Twinkle, Little Star." Flashing red lights under the white keys told her which notes to hit.

"She loved to show off," says owner Sharon Robinson of Hamilton, Ontario, in Canada, who says the secret to training is practice and patience. That must be true, because Chanda knew a record-breaking number of tricks! She's the trickiest canine ever listed in *The Guinness Book of World Records*.

CATS WALK TIGHTROPES

Animal trainers of cats that appear in movies and TV commercials train the feline actors to walk on tightropes, wave at crowds, and open doors.

"Cats can do a lot, like jump through hoops, retrieve toys, and give high fives," says veterinarian Bonnie Beaver of Texas A&M University. But unlike dogs, they won't work for praise. "Cats are motivated by food," she says, "and it's got to be yummy."

TOP TEN MOST POPULAR DOG BREEDS	TOP TEN MOST POPULAR CAT BREEDS
1. LABRADOR RETRIEVER	1. PERSIAN
2. YORKSHIRE TERRIER	2. EXOTIC
3. GERMAN SHEPHERD	3. MAINE COON
4. GOLDEN RETRIEVER	4. SIAMESE
5. BEAGLE	5. ABYSSINIAN
6. BOXER	6. RAGDOLL
7. DACHSHUND	7. SPYHNX
8. BULLDOG	8. AMERICAN SHORTHAIR
9. POODLE	9. BIRMAN
10. SHIH TZU	10. ORIENTAL
(According to the American Kennel Club)	(According to the Cat Fanciers' Association)

Is there a "WOLF" in your house?

All dogs, from Chihuahuas to chowchows, are descended from wolves. So every dog is a little bit wolf. For thousands of years humans have bred dogs for the qualities that make them our best friends. Wolves are not dogs, however. They don't make good pets, and neither do wolf-dog crosses. Wolves are wild animals with predator instincts, and they can't be fully tamed.

83

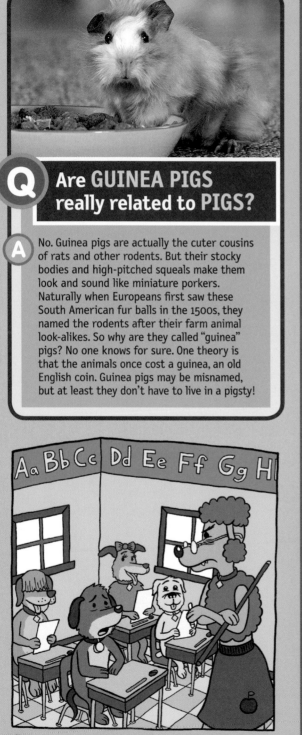

Q — Are GUINEA PIGS really related to PIGS?

A — No. Guinea pigs are actually the cuter cousins of rats and other rodents. But their stocky bodies and high-pitched squeals make them look and sound like miniature porkers. Naturally when Europeans first saw these South American fur balls in the 1500s, they named the rodents after their farm animal look-alikes. So why are they called "guinea" pigs? No one knows for sure. One theory is that the animals once cost a guinea, an old English coin. Guinea pigs may be misnamed, but at least they don't have to live in a pigsty!

"Um . . . my owner ate my homework."

OTHER ANIMAL FRIENDS

Why should cats and dogs get all the attention? Here's what makes other pets so special. See if one of them is right for you.

HORSE

If you have the time and money for a horse, pick one for its behavior, not its breed.

GOLDFISH

Too busy? Goldfish won't chew up your shoes if you come home late.

PARAKEET

Parakeets can be trained to talk and will perch on your finger.

Pampered PET

Today's celebrities may dress up their dogs in silly designer clothes and doggie jewelry, but that's nothing new. People have been spoiling their four-legged and feathered friends for thousands of years.

Pampering your pet could cost you an arm and a paw!

LUXURY SUITE AT PET SPA	$75 A NIGHT
PROFESSIONAL MASSAGE	$30
CUSTOM-BUILT DOGHOUSE	$6,000
CUSTOM-MADE PET SOFA	$400
HAND-KNITTED SWEATER	$250
GOURMET DOG TREATS	$5 FOR 13 OUNCES

In the 1800s, Hai Lung, a long-haired Pekingese, had his own servant and snoozed in a basket lined with red silk. The royal pup couldn't even chow down on his chopped liver until the food had been inspected by his owner—the ruler of China!

Dog Bed

Try This!

WHAT YOU'LL NEED

- FLEECE FABRIC IN TWO COLORS (AVAILABLE AT FABRIC STORES); THE AMOUNT OF FABRIC DEPENDS ON THE SIZE OF YOUR DOG.
- RULER
- FABRIC SCISSORS
- POLYESTER PILLOW STUFFING
- OPTIONAL: OTHER COLORS OF FLEECE TO DECORATE THE PILLOW

WHAT TO DO

Determine the dimensions your pillow needs to be to fit your dog; then add eight inches to the length and width. (This gives you extra fabric for fringe.) Measure two colors of fleece to this size and align both pieces. To create the fringe, cut strips four inches long by one inch wide along all four sides of both pieces of fleece. Cut out the squares of fabric at the corners. (If you like, cut extra fabric into fun shapes and sew them onto the fleece that will form the pillow's top.) Tightly knot the top strips to the bottom strips on three sides of the pillow. Stuff the pillow filling into the open side until the pillow is firm. Then tie the last side together.

85

Bugs, Bugs, and More Bugs!

Those creepy crawlers are the most diverse group of the animal kingdom. From the phylum Arthropoda, insects are considered to be the most successful life form on the planet! There are so many millions of insect species that scientists can't even agree on the number. They live everywhere—in every habitat—from the frozen tundra to the arid desert. They even live on you!

The most common thing among arthropods is that they have a hard outer shell, called an exoskeleton. They also have segmented bodies, which include three parts: **head**, **thorax**, and **abdomen**. There are two classes in the arthropod phylum: Hexapoda (insects) and Arachnida (spiders, ticks, mites, scorpions, and their relatives).

The study of insects is called entomology.

abdomen

head

thorax

INSECTS Helping Out

Insects aren't just about bugging you. There are lots of ways they are beneficial to humans. Here are some of the most common ways insects help us out.

FOOD: Bees make honey, and some insects are eaten by people.

PRODUCTS: Beeswax, dyes, and silk

POLLINATION: They pollinate plants so that humans can grow fruit and vegetable crops, making insects responsible for billions of dollars worth of the food we eat.

AND THEY'RE PRETTY TO LOOK AT, TOO!

Bet you didn't know

A **COCKROACH** can live for up to **nine days** without its head!

The world's termites *outweigh* the world's humans.

Dragonflies can fly at speeds up to 30 miles per hour.

LADY-BUGS SQUIRT SMELLY LIQUID FROM THEIR KNEES WHEN THEY GET SCARED.

CLOSE-UP

Stupid antennae.
I can't wait to get cable!

Some kinds of short-horned grasshoppers are called locusts. Locusts that migrate in swarms eat all the grasses, crops, and trees in their path.

Grasshoppers can't tune in to the Plant Channel with the antennae on top of their heads, but they *can* use them to find food. Antennae are like hands that can smell. Most grass-hoppers are plant eaters, so antennae come in, well, handy! Scientists separate the more than **11,000 kinds of grasshoppers** (which range from a quarter-inch to four inches long) into two groups. Based on the length of their anten-nae, grasshoppers are either short-horned or long-horned. This one's a "shortie." Maybe *that's* why it can't get good TV reception!

One giant swarm of locusts migrating through the U.S. Great Plains during the 1870s stretched 300 miles long and 100 miles wide.

Bee Mystery

Millions of honeybees are vanishing, and their disappearing act has experts stumped.

Honeybees are more important than many people realize. A lot of what we eat is directly or indirectly pollinated by the bees, including apples, oranges, and almonds. Ice cream manufacturers are even worried that they'll have to stop making fruit and nut flavors, such as strawberry, banana, raspberry, and rocky road.

So what is the cause of this bizarre *bee*-havior? No one knows for sure. In 2007–2008 beekeepers nationwide lost 36 percent of their colonies, with some beekeepers losing more than 70 percent. This is called colony collapse disorder.

According to bee expert Dennis vanEngelsdorp, he used to see up to 50,000 of the insects inside every hive. "Now many hives have no bees—dead or alive," he says. The insects just fly away and die.

Is the culprit a bee flu, or fungus, or poor nutrition? The experts know the bees' immune systems are having trouble fighting disease. "We don't know yet if this is a cause or a symptom," says vanEngelsdorp. But investigators are working hard to solve the puzzle and put these busy bees back in business.

WHAT'S ALL THE BUZZ ABOUT?

The ancient Egyptians were the first known beekeepers.

Honeybees dance to communicate with each other.

BY THE NUMBERS

- Honeybees fly **50,000** miles to collect enough nectar for one pound of honey.
- A honeybee's wings beat about **11,400** times a minute.

What in the World?

These photographs show close-up views of bugs. Unscramble the letters to identify what's in each picture.
ANSWERS ON PAGE 339

IRDPES

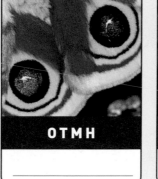

OTMH

YOLHSERF

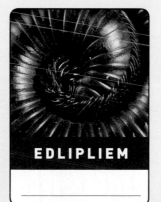

EDLIPLIEM

Bugging OUT!

RHRASGOPSEP

ETELEB

RACERAILPLT

RNADOYFLG

Voices from the Deep

What do your favorite rock bands have in common with male humpback whales? They sing amazing songs.

Hanging motionless at a depth of 60 feet, his head pointed downward and tail pointed upward, a humpback whale launches into his long, drawn-out song. Nearby, other male humpbacks sing the same tune—a 10- to 15-minute piece that is made up of as many as seven phrases, or themes, and may be repeated many times. The singers' voices overlap, blending to create a chorus of low moans, trumpetlike blasts, and high-pitched squeals.

Scientists used to think that only birds and people could sing. Then they discovered that humpbacks sing, too. In fact, other than those of humans, humpbacks' songs may be the longest and most complex of any creature on Earth—and they're filled with mystery.

"For starters, we don't really know how the whales make the singing sounds," says Louis Herman, president of the Dolphin Institute in Honolulu, Hawai'i. "They don't have vocal cords like people, and their mouths don't move when they sing."

Why humpbacks sing is also a mystery. "We once thought that individual male humpbacks sang for the same reason as birds—to attract mates," says Herman. "But when we played tape recordings of male humpbacks singing, the songs seemed to lure other males, not the females, to the recording."

Herman theorizes that singing whales are indeed trying to lure females, although probably not to one particular male. By sharing the same song, males may be helping each other broadcast their message more loudly—and farther—to females who are miles away. The whales change their tunes gradually over time, adding new notes and dropping others.

About 5,000 of these marine mammals migrate from Alaskan waters to Hawai'i for the breeding season—from November until May. The whales rarely sing in Alaska. Back in Hawai'i they pick up their songs where they left off six months before. Meanwhile, scientists continue to watch and listen, trying to solve the mysteries of the humpbacks' songs.

Acrobatic swimmers, humpbacks often leap out of the water belly-up, then somersault to dive back in headfirst.

Amazing Animal Friends

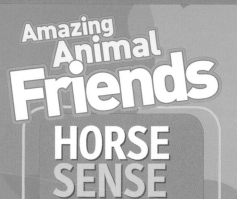

SAHARA AND ALEXA

HORSE SENSE

Victoria, Australia

Tigger the cat steers clear of people and animals—except for his best friend, Annie the pony. Jumping onto a fence, Tigger wraps his paws around Annie's face, then nuzzles her nose-to-nose. Annie then responds by rubbing *her* nose on Tigger's belly when he lies on his back! Tigger trusts Annie so much that he'll weave between her hooves and rub against her legs while she's trotting. "Most cats wouldn't go near an animal of Annie's size," owner Carolyn Bellman says. "But these two have a strong bond." How strong? Tigger even sleeps in Annie's food bin while she gently nibbles around him!

> About 50 million years ago, horses were nearly three times smaller than horses today and had padded feet similar to a dog's.

ANNIE AND TIGGER

CATS & DOGS

Cincinnati Zoo and Botanical Garden, Ohio

Sahara, a cheetah cub, hissed as she faced Alexa the Anatolian shepherd puppy for the first time. The Anatolian is a Turkish dog bred to protect goats and sheep from predators such as cheetahs.

In Namibia, in southern Africa, farmers don't want cheetahs around because they're concerned that the cats will kill their livestock. The Cheetah Conservation Fund (CCF) raises Anatolians and gives them to farmers to use as guard dogs.

Elissa Knights, manager of the Cat Ambassador Program for the CCF, was wondering what would happen between Sahara and Alexa when suddenly her pet dog, Bailey, intervened. Snatching up a long, braided rope, Bailey stuffed the toy into Alexa's open mouth. Then he picked up the other end and took it to Sahara. She grabbed hold. The animals played tug-of-war, and a lasting friendship began.

Today Sahara and Alexa live together. They sleep, play, and visit schools together. "They've worked out their differences," says Knights.

> Cheetahs purr, mew, hiss, and growl, but they can't roar.

91

Do Animals Have FEELINGS?

A scientist sat observing wild chimpanzees in Tanzania, in Africa. The chimp she called Flint had always been unusually attached to his mother. Even as an adolescent, he shared her nest at night. When his mother died, Flint withdrew from other chimps. He hardly ate. He climbed a tree to the nest he and his mother had shared. For a long time he stood there, staring into space. "It was as though he were remembering," says Jane Goodall, the world-famous National Geographic explorer-in-residence emeritus who witnessed the scene.

Stories like this suggest that animals have emotional feelings. Add up all such stories (there are many) and they suggest something more: evidence. It is evidence that researchers like Goodall hope will convince skeptics of something most people with pets already believe: that animals do have feelings.

Not everyone agrees that there is proof of animal emotions. Why the doubt? "You can't do an experiment to find out," says Joseph LeDoux, professor of neuroscience at New York University. "An animal can't tell you, 'Yes, that's how I feel.' So there's no way you can prove it."

Scientists used that same argument with Goodall nearly 50 years ago. But she didn't buy it. "Look into a chimp's eyes," she says, "and you know you're looking into the mind of a thinking, feeling being."

Sometimes that feeling is grief. Flint was so distraught after his mother's death that he starved to death—an unusual reaction to grief. But elephants also seem to mourn their dead. They stare at and touch their relatives' bodies and sometimes even carry their bones around.

But LeDoux says this doesn't prove feelings. Complex emotions—such as jealousy, grief, or embarrassment—may require a neocortex, the wrinkled outer part of the brain. Only primates and a few other animals have this brain structure.

Though most scientists believe that many animals do have some feelings, they also suspect that animal feelings are different from human feelings. How different? We may never know for sure.

Goodall believes that as researchers continue to observe animals and compare their findings, they will eventually gather enough data to draw some conclusions. "Until then, let's give all creatures the benefit of doubt," suggests Goodall.

Carefree young lions stretch out side by side. They played, pounced, and wrestled—and now snuggle in total contentment.

Animal SIBLINGS

TAKE MINE

Like early cavemen, Kanzi, a captive bonobo, and his sister Panbanisha smack rocks together to make stone tools. It's hard work, and Kanzi—being stronger—is better at it. "He can more quickly make a knife that cuts the first time," says William Fields, director of bonobo research at the Great Ape Trust of Iowa. Panbanisha might have to hammer out three to get one that's sharp.

One day Kanzi finished his knife, used it to cut the rope securing a food box, and ate the banana he found inside. Knowing her turn was next, Panbanisha reached for her brother's stone tool. "Nope," said the researcher. Panbanisha must make her own.

Instead the two creative apes plotted together. On his way out, when the scientist wasn't looking, Kanzi hid his knife where Panbanisha could find it. Minutes later she did and opened her box in a flash—thanks to her brother.

SEARCH AND RESCUE

Cashew and Macadamia, spotted hyena twins, were inseparable. One day, Cashew disappeared. Had a predator nabbed the little cub? Hyena cubs take care of each other when their mothers leave to find food. Without her twin and protector, Mac stood little chance of survival. Zoologist Sofia Wahaj, who was studying the hyenas in Kenya, in Africa, was concerned. Then she saw something puzzling. Macadamia and her mom were pawing frantically around a hole in the ground. "Mom's tail was bristly, and she was snarling and poking her head into the hole," says Wahaj. Finally a huge warthog burst out of the hole—followed by Cashew! The cub had been exploring the tunnel when the warthog entered and trapped her inside. Mac and Mom knew Cashew needed help because they had heard her muffled cries. Now Macadamia had her ally back, and the devoted duo have rarely been separated since.

93

ANIMALS THAT YOU MIGHT RUN INTO AT SCHOOL

HMMM — BOOKWORM

I SAW THAT! — BALD EAGLE

PSST! SHOW ME YOUR ANSWERS. — THE CHEETAH

I KNOW WHO DID IT. — A RAT

Try This!

CREATE YOUR OWN HYBRID ANIMAL.

DRAW A PICTURE THAT IS A COMBINATION OF TWO ANIMALS.

GROUPIES!

Fish swim in schools, and cattle hang out in herds, but check out these weird names for other animal groups:

- a cloud of grasshoppers
- a sloth of bears
- a business of ferrets
- a troop of monkeys
- a plague of locusts
- a bloat of hippos
- an army of caterpillars
- a crash of rhinos

- a stand of flamingos
- a murder of crows
- a gaggle of geese
- a string of ponies
- a skulk of foxes
- an ostentation of peacocks
- a knot of toads
- a trip of goats

- a rafter of turkeys
- a peep of chickens
- a husk of hares
- a paddling of ducks
- a bale of turtles
- a pod of whales
- a drift of hogs
- a smack of jellyfish

National Geographic photographer Darlene Murawski combines her background in art and biology to showcase the lives and ecology of lesser-known organisms. Here she lies on her back to photograph caterpillars.

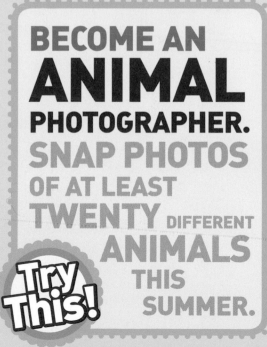

HOW TO GET GREAT ANIMAL PHOTOS

Tips from the pros at National Geographic

1. Learn as much as you can about the animal and observe it for a while before you take any pictures.

2. Get on the animal's schedule. This may mean getting out of bed early!

3. Get as close to the animal as possible without taking a risk. Crouch or lie down so that you're at the animal's eye level.

4. When photographing animals in zoos or aquariums, visit when the animals are most active—usually feeding time or early or late in the day.

5. Be patient. The best shots come when you photograph animals on their terms rather than your own.

BECOME AN **ANIMAL** PHOTOGRAPHER. SNAP PHOTOS OF AT LEAST TWENTY DIFFERENT ANIMALS THIS SUMMER.

Try This!

Prehistoric TIME LINE

HUMANS HAVE WALKED on Earth for some 200,000 years, a mere blip in Earth's 4.5-billion-year history. A lot has happened in that time. Earth formed, and oxygen levels rose in the millions of years of the Precambrian time. The productive Paleozoic era gave rise to hard-shelled organisms, vertebrates, amphibians, and reptiles. Dinosaurs ruled the earth in the mighty Mesozoic. And 64 million years after dinosaurs went extinct, modern humans emerged in the Cenozoic era. From the first tiny mollusks to the dinosaur giants of the Jurassic, Earth has seen a lot of transformation.

THE PRECAMBRIAN TIME

4.5 Billion to 542 Million Years Ago

- Earth forms from exploding stars when a new star gathered a swirling disk of dust and gases around it.
- Low levels of oxygen made Earth a suffocating place.

THE PALEOZOIC ERA

542 Million to 251 Million Years Ago

- The first plants, insects, and animals conquered the land.
- 450 million years ago (m.y.a.), the ancestors of sharks began to swim in the oceans.
- 430 m.y.a. plants began to take root on land.
- Over 360 m.y.a., amphibians emerged from the water.
- Slowly the major landmasses began to come together, creating Pangaea, a single supercontinent.
- By 300 m.y.a., reptiles had begun to dominate the land.

What Is a Dinosaur?

Strong, huge, fierce—these are some words people generally associate with dinosaurs. But not all dinosaurs were big or mean; in fact, they had lots of different characteristics. One quality stands out about dinosaurs, though—they endured. Dinosaurs were some of the most successful animals that have ever lived. After all, they managed to stay on Earth for more than 150 million years! They lived all over the world and dominated all other land creatures. Dinosaurs were reptiles, animals with many common features including a backbone, and scaly, waterproof skin. To date, there are at least 1,000 known species, and more are discovered every day.

DINO TIMES

THE MESOZOIC ERA

251 Million to 65 Million Years Ago
The Mesozoic era, or the age of the reptiles, consisted of three consecutive time periods (shown below). This is when the first dinosaurs began to appear. They would reign supreme for more than 150 million years.

TRIASSIC PERIOD

251 Million to 199 Million Years Ago
- Appearance of the first mammals. They were rodent-sized.
- Appearance of the first dinosaur.
- Ferns were the dominant plants on land.
- The giant supercontinent of Pangaea began breaking up toward the end of the Triassic.

JURASSIC PERIOD

199 Million to 145 Million Years Ago
- Giant dinosaurs dominated the land.
- Pangaea continued its breakup, and oceans formed in the spaces between the drifting land masses, allowing for sea life, including sharks and marine crocodiles, to thrive.
- Conifer trees spread across the land.

CRETACEOUS PERIOD

145 Million to 65 Million Years Ago
- The modern continents developed.
- The largest dinosaurs developed.
- Flowering plants spread across the landscape.
- Mammals flourished and giant pterosaurs ruled the skies over the small birds.
- Temperatures grew more extreme. Dinosaurs lived in deserts, swamps, and forests from the South Pole to the Arctic.

Early Dinosaurs

Appearing first in western South America, dinosaurs began to make their impact about 230 million years ago. One of the first dinosaurs was Eoraptor. It weighed about 20 pounds—the size of a small dog and a quick and skillful hunter. The first flying reptiles, the pterosaurs, took to the skies.

Who Ate What?

Herbivores
- Primarily eat plants
- Grew up to 100 tons—the largest animals ever to walk the Earth
- Up to 1,000 blunt or flat teeth to grind vegetation
- Many had cheek pouches to store food
- Examples: *Styracosaurus, Parasaurolophus*

Carnivores
- Meat-eaters
- Long, strong legs to run faster than plant-eaters; ran up to 30 miles per hour
- Most had good eyesight, strong jaws, and sharp teeth
- Both scavengers and hunters; often hunted in packs

- Grew to 45 feet long
- Examples: *Velociraptor, Tyrannosaurus rex, Gigantoraptor*

TYRANNOSAURUS REX

Dino Poo

You may wonder how we could possibly know what dinosaurs actually ate. Well, paleontologists search for coprolites, or fossilized waste. Yep, that's right, the poo of the prehistoric world has told us everything we know about what plants dinosaurs ate. Coprolites contain digested plant material, which can help us learn about a dinosaur's diet. Coprolites aren't the only things that can help scientists learn about the dinosaur diet—teeth, habitat, and plant fossils also provide insight.

GIGANTORAPTOR

DID YOU KNOW?
Different species of dinosaurs lived at different times. Some dinosaurs would have never met, being separated by as much as 164 million years!

VELOCIRAPTOR   **SINOSAUROPTERYX**

MAMENCHISAURUS

PARASAUROLOPHUS

ERKETU

Paleontologists learn about dinosaurs by studying fossils—animal remains that have often been preserved in rock.

Bet you **didn't know**

Many of the **dinosaurs** known as **SAUROPODS** had **TINY** heads and few **TEETH.** They did most of their digesting in their **HUGE STOMACHS!**

TUOJIANGOSAURUS

STYRACOSAURUS

MONONYKUS

Dino Classification

Classifying dinosaurs and all other living things can be a complicated matter, so scientists have devised a system to help with the process. Dinosaurs are put into groups based on a very large range of characteristics.

Scientists put dinosaurs into two major groups: the bird-hipped ornithischians and the reptile-hipped saurischians.

Ornithischian

"Bird-hipped"
(pubis bone in hips point backward)

Ornithischians have the same shaped pubis as birds of today, but today's birds are actually more closely related to the saurischians.

Example: *Styracosaurus*

Saurischian

"Reptile-hipped"
(pubis bone in hips point forward)

Saurischians are further divided into two groups, the meat-eating Theropoda and the plant-eating Sauropodomorpha.

Example: *Tyrannosaurus rex*

Within these two main divisions, dinosaurs are then separated into orders and then families, such as Stegosauria. Like other members of the Stegosauria, *Stegosaurus* had spines and plates along the back, neck, and tail.

COOL CLICK

Want to learn about the largest, most complete, best preserved *T. rex*? Learn about a fossil named Sue at the Field Museum.
www.fieldmuseum.org/sue

Dinosaur Superlatives

Smallest:
Early Cretaceous *Microraptor* was a tiny dinosaur, reaching about 22 inches (55.9 cm) in length.

Scariest looking:
Tyrannosaurus rex was a huge, flesh-eating dinosaur.

One of the heaviest:
Argentinosaurus is thought to have weighed up to 100 tons! Only the modern blue whale is larger.

Smartest:
If a large brain compared to body size indicates intelligence, then the *Troodon* may have been the smartest. This fast little meat-eater with excellent eyesight lived during the Cretaceous period.

Dumbest:
Stegosaurus was among the dumbest—it had a brain the size of a walnut!

Longest name:
Micropachycephalosaurus (23 letters)

First dinosaur to be named:
Megalosaurus, named in 1822 by the Reverend William Buckland.

21 DINOS YOU SHOULD KNOW

Dinosaur
What the name means
Example:
Length: XX ft (X m)
Time Range: When they lived
Where: Where they are found

Aucasaurus
Lizard from Auca
Length: 13 feet (4 m)
Time Range: Late Cretaceous
Where: Argentina

Brachiosaurus
Arm lizard
Length: 98 ft (29.9 m)
Time Range: Late Jurassic
Where: Colorado, U.S.; Tanzania

Camptosaurus
Bent lizard
Length: 23 ft (7 m)
Time Range: Late Jurassic
Where: Wyoming, South Dakota, Colorado, Utah, U.S.; England

Carcharodontosaurus
Shark-toothed lizard
Length: 40 ft (12.2 m)
Time Range: Late Cretaceous
Where: Algeria; Egypt; Morocco

Carnotaurus
Meat-eating bull
Length: 25 ft (7.6 m)
Time Range: Late Cretaceous
Where: Argentina; Patagonia

DINOSAUR GALLERY

Herrerasaurus
Herrera's lizard
Length: 16.5 ft (5 m)
Time Range: Late Triassic
Where: Argentina

Lambeosaurus
Lambe's lizard
Length: Up to 54 ft (16.5 m)
Time Range: Late Cretaceous
Where: Montana, U.S.; Alberta, Canada

Hypsilophodon
High-ridged tooth
Length: 7.5 ft (2.3 m)
Time Range: Early Cretaceous
Where: England; Spain; Portugal

Lesothosaurus
Lesotho lizard
Length: 3 ft (1 m)
Time Range: Early Jurassic
Where: Lesotho

Iguanodon
Iguana tooth
Length: 33 ft (10.1 m)
Time Range: Early Cretaceous
Where: Europe

Maiasaura
Good-mother lizard
Length: 30 ft (9.1 m)
Time Range: Late Cretaceous
Where: Montana

DINOSAUR GALLERY

Microraptor
Small thief
Length: 22 inches (55.9 cm)
Time Range: Early Cretaceous
Where: Liaoning Province, southern China

Stegosaurus
Roofed reptile
Length: 29.5 ft (9 m)
Time Range: Late Jurassic
Where: Wyoming, Utah, Colorado, U.S.

Oviraptor
Egg thief
Length: 8 ft (2.4 m)
Time Range: Late Cretaceous
Where: Mongolia

Protoceratops
First horned face
Length: 8 ft (2.1 m)
Time Range: Late Cretaceous
Where: Mongolia; China

Bet you didn't know

SOME DINOSAURS HAD 1,000 TEETH.

DINOSAUR GALLERY

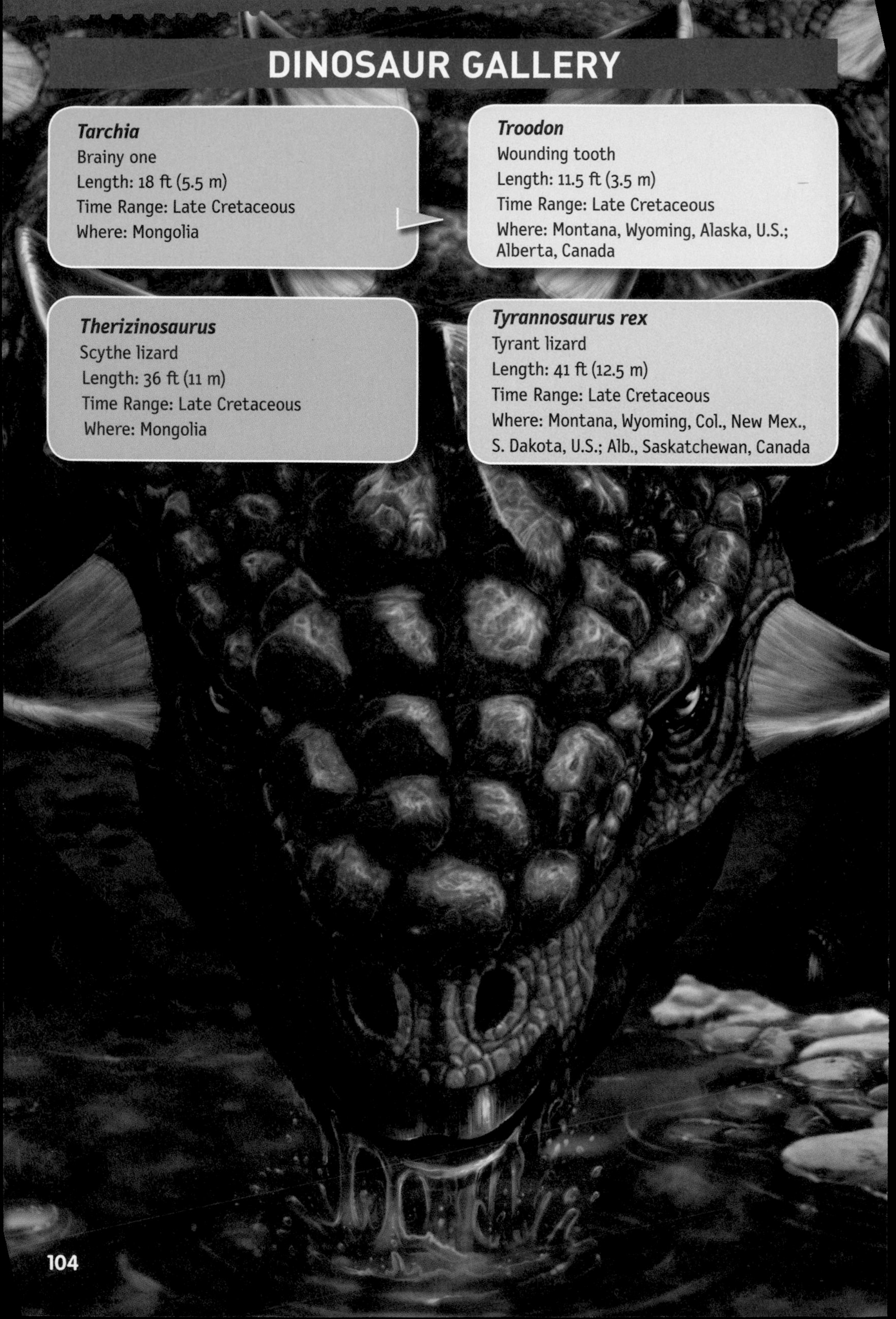

Tarchia
Brainy one
Length: 18 ft (5.5 m)
Time Range: Late Cretaceous
Where: Mongolia

Troodon
Wounding tooth
Length: 11.5 ft (3.5 m)
Time Range: Late Cretaceous
Where: Montana, Wyoming, Alaska, U.S.;
Alberta, Canada

Therizinosaurus
Scythe lizard
Length: 36 ft (11 m)
Time Range: Late Cretaceous
Where: Mongolia

Tyrannosaurus rex
Tyrant lizard
Length: 41 ft (12.5 m)
Time Range: Late Cretaceous
Where: Montana, Wyoming, Col., New Mex.,
S. Dakota, U.S.; Alb., Saskatchewan, Canada

DINOSAUR GALLERY

Utahraptor
Utah plunderer
Length: 19.5 ft (5.9 m)
Time Range: Early Cretaceous
Where: Utah, U.S.

Velociraptor
Swift robber
Length: 6.5 ft (2 m)
Time Range: Late Cretaceous
Where: Mongolia; China

3 PREHISTORIC BIRDS

Baptornis
Diving bird
Length: 3.9 ft (1.2 m)
Time Range: Late Cretaceous
Where: Kansas, U.S.

Archaeopteryx
Ancient wing
Length: 12–20 in (30–50 cm)
Time Range: Late Jurassic
Where: Germany; Portugal

Iberomesornis
Intermediate Spanish bird
Length: 8-in (20-cm) wingspan
Time Range: Early Cretaceous
Where: Spain

Archaeopteryx is the first known bird—birds are descendants of dinosaurs.

DID DINOSAURS HAVE SOCIAL LIVES?

Not much is known about whether dinosaurs liked to hang out with their friends, but a "dance floor" found in Arizona may have shed some light on this social question.

At a remote site in northern Arizona, paleontologists believe they may have found more than a thousand footprints and marks made by Jurassic dinosaurs. Scientists say the site, 190 million years old, was a watering hole surrounded by a huge desert.

DINO PATHS

The footprints were made in soft sand, which was soon covered over. It hardened, preserving the footprints. Because we can see the dinosaur tracks, scientists can make conclusions about their habits. Tracks both large and small were found, suggesting they may have been made by mothers walking around with their babies, or a crowd of dinosaurs of varying sizes. At least four types of dinosaurs were identified through the footprints. Three-toed tracks, for instance, were made by a meat-eating dinosaur smaller than *Tyrannosaurus rex*, according to the scientists.

NOT CONVINCED

However, some paleontologists question whether dinosaurs made any of these marks. Some think that the footprints, which look like potholes in the rock, were made by modern erosion. Tail drag marks are rare and can be extremely difficult to verify. It may take a long time for scientists to decide whether these are actually dinosaur tracks or just holes in the ground, but then again, that is what science is all about.

Q Did PEOPLE and DINOSAURS ever live at the same time?

A Absolutely not! Dinosaurs died out 65 million years ago, long before people were on Earth.

What Does a Paleontologist Do?

Ask a Scientific Question
Example: Did reptile-hipped dinosaurs hunt? If so, what did they eat?

Find a Fossil
Example: Map the area, search, and record finds

Get It Out of the Ground
Example: Dig up the remains

Conserve
Example: Clean it up, repair it as needed

Reconstruct
Example: Compare it with other fossils and living things to learn about what it was

Tell People
Example: Write about or exhibit the discovery

For more detailed information on the paleontology process, check out the Project Exploration website. projectexploration.org

What Killed the Dinosaurs?

Sixty-five million years ago the last of the nonbird dinosaurs went extinct. So did the giant mosasaurs and plesiosaurs in the seas and the pterosaurs in the skies. Many kinds of plants died, too. Perhaps half of the world's species died in this mass extinction that marks the end of the Cretaceous and the beginning of the Paleogene period.

Why did so many animals die out while most mammals, turtles, crocodiles, salamanders, and frogs survived? Birds escaped extinction. So did many plants and insects. Scientists are searching for answers.

Asteroid or Volcano?

Scientists have a couple of hypotheses: a huge impact, such as an asteroid or comet, or a massive bout of volcanic activity. Any of these might have choked the skies with debris that starved Earth of the sun's energy. Once the dust settled, greenhouse gases locked in the atmosphere may have caused the temperature to soar.

Regardless of what caused the extinction, it marked the end of *Tyrannosaurus rex*'s reign of terror and opened the door for mammals to take over.

Bet you didn't know Modern-day **BIRDS** are descendents of THEROPOD DINOSAURS; that means theropods **NEVER WENT EXTINCT!**

SEA MONSTERS
A PREHISTORIC ADVENTURE

Prehistoric animals didn't just live on the land—they swam through the sea, too. These wondrous sea monsters ruled the deep with supersize eyes, fearsome teeth, and extremely long necks.

The National Geographic giant-screen film *Sea Monsters: A Prehistoric Adventure* features many of these prehistoric marine creatures.

TYLOSAUR
Tylosaurus proriger

The 29-foot-long tylosaur is the unchallenged ruler of the cretaceous ocean. It ambushed its prey, crushing victims with its sharp, cone-shaped teeth.

OTHER COOL STUFF Tylosaur had a nose for nastiness. Some scientists think its long, bony snout had dozens of nerve endings that sensed prey in murky waters. As soon as the meal was detected, the nerves triggered a bite response to quickly seize the prey.

Filmed in the Bahamas, *Sea Monsters: A Prehistoric Adventure* features computer-generated sea monsters and real water backgrounds. The digital sea monsters were added later.

To find out even more, check out the film and its website. www.nationalgeographic.com/seamonsters/index.html

WHEN MARINE REPTILES AND DINOSAURS LIVED

About 250 million years ago

The first marine reptiles appeared.

About 230 million years ago

Dinosaurs first walked on Earth.

About 65 million years ago

Most marine reptiles and dinosaurs became extinct.

XIPHACTINUS

Xiphactinus audax

This 17-foot-long fish had fangs that seized prey so it could swallow its victims whole. But this fierce predator sometimes got choked up. Many *Xiphactinus* fossils have been found with undigested fish in their rib cages—a sign that the prey may have choked the killer fish.

OTHER COOL STUFF
Shaped like a torpedo, *xiphactinus* was a fast swimmer.

DOLLY

Dolichorhynchops osborni

Living 82 million years ago, these dolphin-size air breathers hunted fish and squid in shallow waters. But they had to brave dangerous, unknown seas when their prey migrated into deeper water.

OTHER COOL STUFF Dollies used large, wing-like flat paddles to "fly" through the water. But they had to be careful. Dollies that dived too deep and surfaced too quickly could suffer a deadly condition called "the bends," according to Kenneth Carpenter of the Denver Museum of Nature and Science in Colorado.

CRETOXYRHINA

Cretoxyrhina mantelli

Like today's great white shark, the 20-foot-long *Cretoxyrhina* had razor-sharp teeth that cut victims into chunks.

OTHER COOL STUFF
Cretoxyrhina never ran out of teeth! Worn-out teeth were replaced by new ones. Good thing, because *Cretoxyrhina* would even eat bones. Anything it couldn't digest, it would just throw up.

WILDLY GOOD ANIMAL REPORTS

Your teacher wants a written report on the velvety free-tailed bat. By Monday! Not to worry. Use the tools of good writing to organize your thoughts and research, and you'll create an animal report a bat would flap about.

Velvety free-tailed bats in flight

STEPS TO SUCCESS Your report will follow the format of a descriptive or expository essay (see p. 36 for "How To Write an Awesome Essay") and should consist of a main idea followed by supporting details and finished off with a conclusion. Use this basic structure for each paragraph as well as the whole report and you'll be on the right track.

1. Introduction

State your main idea about your subject.

The velvety free-tailed bat is a common and important species of bat.

2. Body

Provide **details (supporting points)** for your main idea.

The velvety free-tailed bat eats insects and can have a large impact on insect populations.

It ranges from Mexico to South America, even parts of Florida.

Like other bats, its wings are built for fast, efficient flight.

Then **expand (elaborate)** on those points with further description, explanation, or discussion.

The velvety free-tailed bat eats insects and can have a large impact on insect populations.

> *Their diet consists primarily of mosquitoes and other airborne insects.*

It ranges from Mexico to South America, even parts of Florida.

> *They are often encountered in attics.*

Like other bats, its wings are built for fast, efficient flight.

> *They have trouble, however, taking off from low or flat surfaces and must drop from a place high enough to gain speed to start flying.*

3. Conclusion

Wrap it all up with a summary of your whole paper.

Because of its large numbers, the velvety free-tailed bat holds an important position in the food chain.

KEY INFORMATION

Here are some things you should consider including in your report:

> What does your animal look like?
> To what other species is it related?
> How does it move?
> Where does it live?
> What does it eat?
> What eats it?
> How long does it live?
> Is it endangered?
> Why do you find it interesting?

FACT FROM FICTION: Your animal may have been featured in a movie or in myths and legends. Compare and contrast how the animal has been portrayed with how it behaves in reality. For example, sharks don't ordinarily feed on people, snakes just want to be left alone, and penguins can't fly airplanes.

PROOFREAD AND REVISE: As with any awesome essay, when you're finished, check for misspellings, grammatical mistakes, and punctuation errors. It often helps to have someone else proofread your work, too, as they may catch things you have missed. Also look for ways to make your sentences and paragraphs even better. Add more descriptive language, choosing just the right verbs, adverbs, and adjectives to make your writing come alive.

BE CREATIVE: Use visual aids to make your report come to life. Include an animal photo file with interesting images found in magazines or printed from websites. Or draw your own! You can also build a miniature animal habitat diorama. Use your creativity to help communicate your passion for your subject.

THE FINAL RESULT: Put it all together in one final, polished draft. Make it neat and clean, and remember to cite your references (see p. 269 for "Reveal Your Sources").

WATCH OUT!
How to conduct an animal observation

BOOKS, ARTICLES, and other secondhand sources are great for learning about animals, but there's another way to find out even more. Direct observation means watching, listening to, and smelling an animal yourself. To truly understand animals you need to observe them.

VISIT

YOU CAN FIND ANIMALS in their natural habitats almost anywhere, even your own backyard. Or take a drive to a nearby mountain area, river, forest, wetland, or other ecosystem. There are animals to be seen in every natural setting you can visit. To observe more exotic varieties, plan a trip to a national park, aquarium, zoo, wildlife park, or aviary.

OBSERVE

GET NEAR ENOUGH to an animal to watch and study it, but do not disturb it. be patient, as it may take a while to spot something interesting. And be safe. Don't take any risks; wild animals can be dangerous. Take notes and write down every detail. Use all of your senses. How does it look? How does it act? What more can you learn?

RESEARCH

COMPARE YOUR own observations with those found in textbooks, encyclopedias, nonfiction books, Internet sources, and nature documentaries. Even classic stories from literature can provide great information and context as you do your research. National Geographic's series **Face to Face with Animals** has a lot of great in-the-field encounters.

TIP:
Binoculars are a good way to get up-close and personal with wild animals while still keeping a safe distance.

COOL CLICK

To learn about Crittercam, a really inventive way that animal behavior is being observed, go to its website. There's a bunch of great footage, information, games, and more. Have fun!
www.nationalgeographic.com/crittercam

111

Culture
Connection

Young boys play soccer in a park
in Dubai, United Arab Emirates.

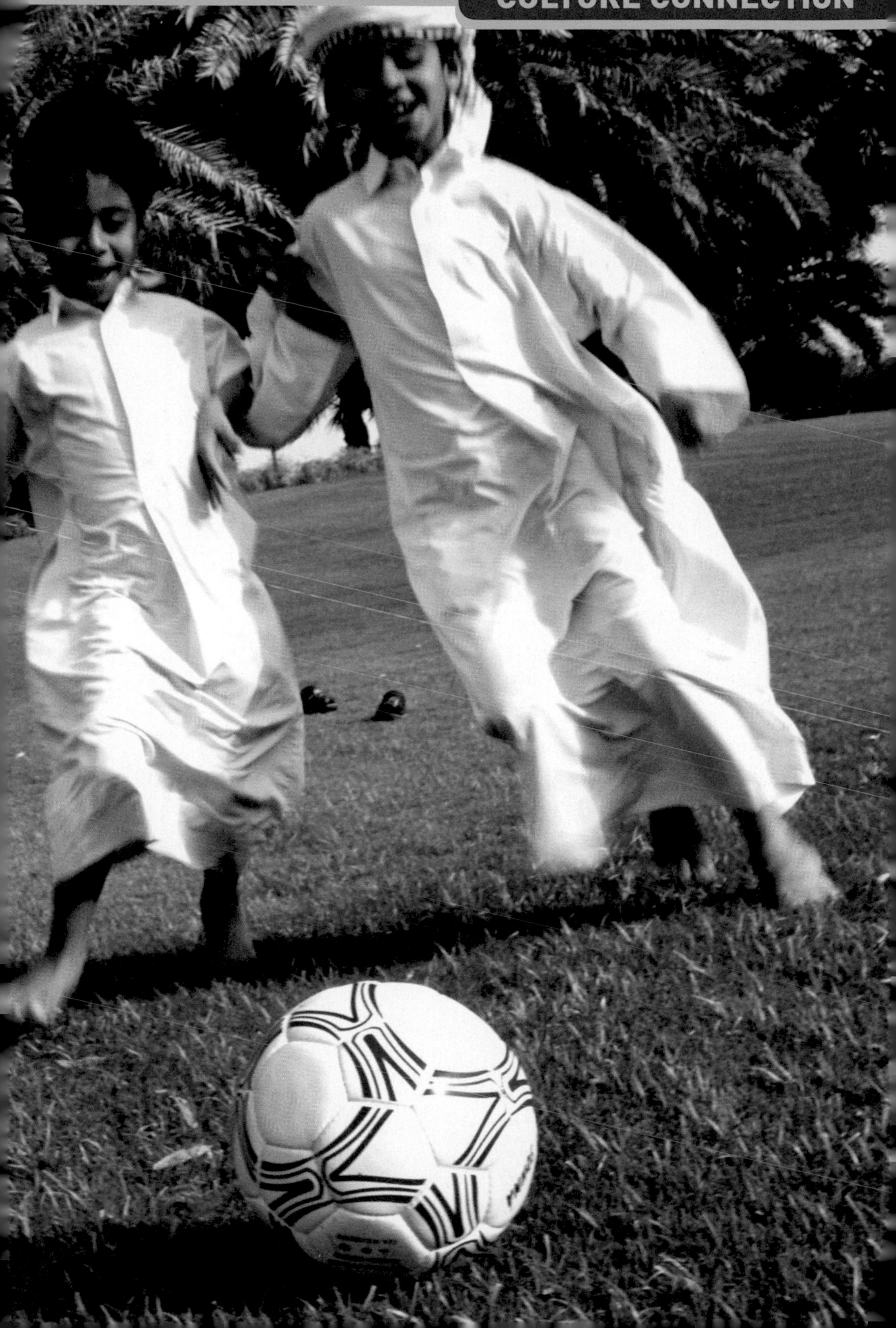

STRAIGHT TALK

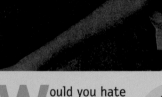

DIFFERENT IS GOOD!

Accepting differences is like eating a burrito—without all the different meats, veggies, and cheeses, all you get is a boring tortilla. "And when I chew all the ingredients together, it's good!" says Deborah Crockett, a school psychologist in Atlanta, Georgia. Sometimes it's hard to keep an open mind about things—or people—you don't understand. So to really enjoy your next "cultural burrito," use Crockett's tips below.

COMMON GROUND. Everyone's different. But everyone also has things in common. Do you wear a baseball cap, a Jewish yarmulke, or a Muslim hijab? Yeah, they're from different cultures. But the point is, they're all head coverings.

CULTURE CLUB. Learning about other groups of people helps you understand them. Try eating foods from another culture. Or teach yourself words in another language.

BLAME GAME. Has your entire class ever had to stay in from recess because one kid couldn't keep his mouth shut? That's not fair! It's also not fair to blame an entire group of people for the actions of a few individuals.

TIME-OUT

friends?

TYPECAST. It's normal to make assumptions, we all do it. But the key is to be aware that you've done it—then try to be more open-minded the next time around.

Would you hate someone just because they looked different? Unfortunately, after the terrorist attacks of September 11, 2001, many people did. Muslim and Arab-American kids were bullied on playgrounds. Some were even too afraid to go to school. All because they looked similar to the small number of men who participated in the attacks. But it doesn't matter where you are from, what your culture is, or what religion you practice. We're all people and everyone should be accepted as an individual.

11 WAYS TO BE POLITE IN DIFFERENT COUNTRIES

SLURP your SOUP in **China** and **Japan**.

KEEP your **napkin** on the table at **MEALS** in **Hungary**.

ARRIVE 15 minutes late to parties in **India**.

AVOID mopping your dinner plate with **bread** in **Italy**.

AVOID snapping your **fingers** in **Belgium**.

STICK the **TIP** of your **index finger** in your **ear** and then **kiss it** to show that you **ENJOYED** your **dinner** in **Portugal.**

WHISTLE in **Russia ONLY** outdoors— or you might bring **bad luck.**

TALK to people with your **hands** out of your pockets in some parts of **Canada.**

APOLOGIZE if you accidentally **TOUCH** someone's head in **Thailand.**

Leave FOOD on your **PLATE** in **Egypt**

AVOID facing someone while **crossing** your arms in **TURKEY.**

INDIGENOUS PEOPLE OF SOUTH AMERICA

Country	Percentage
Bolivia	55%
Peru	45%
Ecuador	25%
Guyana	9.1%
Chile	5%
Paraguay	5%
Argentina	4.1%
Uruguay	4%
Colombia	3.4%
Suriname	2%
Venezuela	2%
Brazil	.4%

The indigenous people of South America are concentrated largely in the countries of the Andes mountains, as shown in this chart.

INDIGENOUS PEOPLE

are an ethnic group of people who live in a place to which they have the earliest known historical connection.

115

Celebration Nation

① NEW YEAR'S DAY*
January 1
Marking the beginning of a new year, celebrations for this holiday usually begin the night before. Parties, wishes for a good new year, and resolutions are among the usual festivities.

② BIRTHDAY OF MARTIN LUTHER KING, JR.*
3rd Monday in January
A remembrance day for Martin Luther King, Jr., an African-American minister who strove in a nonviolent way to secure civil rights in the United States.

③ VALENTINE'S DAY
February 14
Named for Saint Valentine, this day is celebrated with gifts of candy and flowers.

④ PRESIDENTS' DAY*
3rd Monday in February
Honors all the past U.S. Presidents, especially George Washington and Abraham Lincoln.

⑤ EASTER SUNDAY
varies
A Christian holiday that celebrates the resurrection of Jesus Christ. Easter is often celebrated by giving baskets filled with gifts or candy to children.

⑥ PASSOVER
varies
A Jewish holiday that commemorates the ancient exodus of the Jews from Egypt and their liberation from slavery. Passover is an eight-day holiday (seven days in Israel) during which observers have seders, or ritual feasts, and abstain from eating leavened bread.

* Denotes a U.S. federal holiday.

⑦ MEMORIAL DAY*
Last Monday in May
First created to honor soldiers in the U.S. Civil War, today this holiday honors all members of the armed services who have died in war.

⑧ INDEPENDENCE DAY*
July 4
Celebrating the signing of the Declaration of Independence in 1776, better known as "the fourth of July," this holiday often features parades, flags, and fireworks.

⑨ LABOR DAY*
1st Monday in September
Honors America's workers, generally with parades and picnics.

⑩ COLUMBUS DAY*
2nd Monday in October
Commemorates explorer Christopher Columbus's landing in the New World on October 12, 1492.

⑪ ROSH HASHANAH & YOM KIPPUR
varies
Rosh Hashanah is a Jewish holiday marking the beginning of a new year on the Hebrew calendar. The two-day holiday is celebrated with prayer, ritual foods, and a day of rest. Yom Kippur, known as the Day of Atonement, is the most solemn of all Jewish holidays. It is observed with fasting and prayer, and is marked by a feast at sundown. Together, these two celebrations are known as the High Holidays.

⑫ HALLOWEEN
October 31
A day for costumes, candy, scary stories, and trick-or-treating, Halloween has its roots in a Celtic festival celebrating the end of the harvest season.

13 **DIWALI**
varies
Also known as the Festival of Lights, this Hindu holiday celebrates the triumph of good over evil and the lifting of spiritual darkness.

14 **VETERANS DAY***
November 11
Originally created to honor Americans who served in World War I, this holiday now honors all American veterans.

15 **THANKSGIVING***
4th Thursday in November
This holiday remembers the 1621 feast of the Pilgrims and the Native Americans. An American tradition, Thanksgiving is celebrated with feasts shared with family and friends.

16 **CHRISTMAS DAY***
December 25
A Christian holiday marking the birth of Jesus Christ. Christmas is usually celebrated by decorating trees, exchanging presents, and having festive gatherings.

17 **HANUKKAH**
varies
Also known as the Festival of Lights, this Jewish holiday is eight days long. It commemorates the re-dedication of the Temple in Jerusalem. It is generally observed with celebrations, the lighting of candles in a menorah, and the exchange of gifts.

18 **KWANZAA**
December 26 – January 1
A weeklong celebration honoring African heritage, which includes lighting candles in a kinara and gift giving. It ends with a feast.

19 **RAMADAN AND EID AL-FITR**
varies
A Muslim holiday, Ramadan is one month long, and culminates in the Eid Al-Fitr celebration. Observers fast during this month, eating only after sunset, and do good deeds for others. Muslims pray for forgiveness and hope to purify themselves with observance.

2010 CALENDAR

JANUARY

S	M	T	W	T	F	S
					1	2
3	4	5	6	7	8	9
10	11	12	13	14	15	16
17	18	19	20	21	22	23
24	25	26	27	28	29	30
31						

FEBRUARY

S	M	T	W	T	F	S
	1	2	3	4	5	6
7	8	9	10	11	12	13
14	15	16	17	18	19	20
21	22	23	24	25	26	27
28						

MARCH

S	M	T	W	T	F	S
	1	2	3	4	5	6
7	8	9	10	11	12	13
14	15	16	17	18	19	20
21	22	23	24	25	26	27
28	29	30	31			

APRIL

S	M	T	W	T	F	S
				1	2	3
4	5	6	7	8	9	10
11	12	13	14	15	16	17
18	19	20	21	22	23	24
25	26	27	28	29	30	

MAY

S	M	T	W	T	F	S
						1
2	3	4	5	6	7	8
9	10	11	12	13	14	15
16	17	18	19	20	21	22
23	24	25	26	27	28	29
30	31					

JUNE

S	M	T	W	T	F	S
		1	2	3	4	5
6	7	8	9	10	11	12
13	14	15	16	17	18	19
20	21	22	23	24	25	26
27	28	29	30			

JULY

S	M	T	W	T	F	S
				1	2	3
4	5	6	7	8	9	10
11	12	13	14	15	16	17
18	19	20	21	22	23	24
25	26	27	28	29	30	31

AUGUST

S	M	T	W	T	F	S
1	2	3	4	5	6	7
8	9	10	11	12	13	14
15	16	17	18	19	20	21
22	23	24	25	26	27	28
29	30	31				

SEPTEMBER

S	M	T	W	T	F	S
			1	2	3	4
5	6	7	8	9	10	11
12	13	14	15	16	17	18
19	20	21	22	23	24	25
26	27	28	29	30		

OCTOBER

S	M	T	W	T	F	S
					1	2
3	4	5	6	7	8	9
10	11	12	13	14	15	16
17	18	19	20	21	22	23
24	25	26	27	28	29	30
31						

NOVEMBER

S	M	T	W	T	F	S
	1	2	3	4	5	6
7	8	9	10	11	12	13
14	15	16	17	18	19	20
21	22	23	24	25	26	27
28	29	30				

DECEMBER

S	M	T	W	T	F	S
			1	2	3	4
5	6	7	8	9	10	11
12	13	14	15	16	17	18
19	20	21	22	23	24	25
26	27	28	29	30	31	

What's Your Chinese Horoscope?
Locate your birth year to find out.

In Chinese astrology, the zodiac runs on a 12-year cycle, based on the lunar calendar. Each year corresponds to one of twelve animals, each representing one of twelve personality types. Read on to find out which animal year you were born in and what that might say about you.

RAT
1972, '84, '96, '08
Say cheese! You're attractive, charming, and creative. When you get mad, you can really have sharp teeth!

RABBIT
1975, '87, '99, '11
Your ambition and talent make you jump at opportunity. You also keep your ears open for gossip.

HORSE
1966, '78, '90, '02
Being happy is your "mane" goal. And while you're a smart, hard worker, your teacher may ride you for talking too much.

ROOSTER
1969, '81, '93, '05
You crow about your adventures, but inside you're really shy. You're thoughtful, capable, brave, and talented.

OX
1973, '85, '97, '09
You're smart, patient, and as strong as an—well, you know what. Though you're a leader, you'd never brag.

DRAGON
1976, '88, '00, '12
You're on fire! Health, energy, honesty, and bravery make you a living legend.

SHEEP
1967, '79, '91, '03
Gentle as a lamb, you're also artistic, compassionate, and wise. You're often shy.

DOG
1970, '82, '94, '06
Often the leader of the pack, you're loyal and honest. You can also keep a secret.

TIGER
1974, '86, '98, '10
You may be a nice person, but no one should ever enter your room without asking—you might attack!

SNAKE
1977, '89, '01, '13
You may not speak often, but you're very smart. You always seem to have a stash of cash.

MONKEY
1968, '80, '92, '04
No "monkey see, monkey do" for you. You're a clever problem solver with an excellent memory.

PIG
1971, '83, '95, '07
Even though you're courageous, honest, and kind, you never hog all the attention.

DAY OF THE DEAD

YOU'LL HAVE TOO MUCH FUN TO BE FRIGHTENED DURING THIS **MEXICAN** HOLIDAY.

Skeletons are scary, right?

Not if you're celebrating *Dia de los Muertos*, or Day of the Dead. The holiday, which is celebrated mostly in Mexico on November 1 and 2, is like a family reunion—except dead ancestors are the guests of honor. Day of the Dead is a joyful time that helps people remember the deceased and celebrate their memory.

First, people set up a candlelit altar in their homes so spirits can find their way back to their relatives. Then it's off to the graveyard for a big party. Families bring a huge feast to eat while they clean tombstones, sing songs, and talk to their ancestors.

And don't forget the skeletons. Life-size papier-mâché skeletons and miniature skeletons are everywhere. Why? Mexicans honor their ancestors, but they're also reminding themselves that death is just a part of life. Hanging out with skeletons reminds people that one day they will be skeletons, too!

Holi

A wild festival throws color on spring—and everything else!

Incoming! Colored water flies through the air, drenching people on the street. Everyone's sticky in pink, red, yellow, and green as if someone dumped a thousand melted crayons over them.

But no one's trying to escape this colorful monsoon. Getting messy is the point during Holi, a festival in India that celebrates spring.

With a mix of water and colored powder called *gulal*, people in India get ready to rumble. Long tubes called *pichkaris* squirt bright liquid. Buckets of colored water are tossed as if to douse a campfire. Water balloons used to come out of nowhere—till launching a balloon attack was outlawed for Holi!

People laugh so hard they can barely say the standard chant: *Bura na mano, Holi hai*—don't feel offended, it's Holi! And what more can you say when you're being drenched in colored water?

119

Try This!

CINCO DE MAYO
FIESTA

Cinco de Mayo celebrates Mexico's victory over the French at the Battle of Puebla on May 5, 1862. *Cinco de Mayo* means "fifth of May."

YOUR FAMILY CAN CELEBRATE THIS MEXICAN HOLIDAY WITH FLAVORS FROM SOUTH OF THE BORDER.

MEXICAN SUNDAE

YOU WILL NEED

- 3 ounces semisweet chocolate
- 2/3 cup heavy cream
- 1/2 teaspoon cinnamon
- 1 pint vanilla ice cream
- 1/2 cup chopped salted peanuts

WHAT TO DO

Place the chocolate, heavy cream, and cinnamon in a medium saucepan. Warm over low heat, stirring occasionally until the chocolate melts and the sauce is smooth. Remove from the heat and let cool for ten minutes. Drizzle over ice cream and top with peanuts. Makes four servings.

MOLLETES (mo-YEH-tehs)

YOU WILL NEED

- French bread baguette
- 2 cups refried beans
- 12 ounces shredded cheddar cheese
- pico de gallo

WHAT TO DO

Preheat oven to 400°F. Slice the baguette in half lengthwise, then cut it into thick pieces. Spread with the beans and top with cheese. Place on a baking sheet, and bake for about five minutes, or until the cheese melts and the beans are hot. Top with store-bought pico de gallo, or make your own (see recipe at right).

Ask an adult for help when you try these activities.

PICO DE GALLO (pee-koh deh GUY-yo)

YOU WILL NEED

- 1/4 cup chopped fresh cilantro
- 2 1/2 cups chopped ripe tomatoes
- 1 chopped jalapeño, without seeds (optional)
- 1 medium diced onion
- juice of 1 lime
- salt to taste

WHAT TO DO

Mix all ingredients in a bowl and stir well.

CUBAN Carnival

Stilt walkers in brightly colored costumes tower above this street in Old Havana, Cuba, during the annual celebration of Carnival. The festival includes dancing, music, and parades. Introduced by Catholic colonizers from Spain, Carnival occurs prior to the beginning of the religious season of Lent.

Fun Winter Gift Idea

Snow Globes

Make this easy and inexpensive present for the holidays!

YOU WILL NEED
- small jar (a baby food jar works well)
- plastic animal or figurine that fits in the jar
- sandpaper
- instant-bonding glue (follow directions on the tube and use with adult supervision)
- nail polish remover
- baby oil
- 1/2 teaspoon white glitter

WHAT TO DO
Turn the jar's lid upside down. Use sandpaper to scuff the inside of the lid. Glue the bottom of the figurine to the center of the lid. (Nail polish remover cleans glue off skin and surfaces.) Dry for four hours. Fill the jar with baby oil. Add glitter. To seal, put glue around the rim of the jar. Close the lid tightly and dry for four hours. Turn the jar over and let it snow!

Bet you didn't know

NEW YEAR'S CELEBRATIONS ACROSS THE GLOBE

IN THAILAND, giant water fights ring in the New Year in early spring.

IN IRAN, festivities kick off with the arrival of spring and last 13 days.

IN BELGIUM, kids write letters to their parents and godparents, and read them aloud on New Year's Day.

IN SCOTLAND, residents open their front doors before midnight on New Year's Eve to let the old year out and the new year in.

IN ETHIOPIA, New Year's comes in September, which is the end of the rainy season.

IN OKLAHOMA, the Muscogee Indians' new year starts in midsummer, after the corn ripens.

121

OFF THE DEEP END

UNDERWATER PUMPKIN CARVING

The grossest thing about carving pumpkins is pulling out the slimy guts with your bare hands, right? Well, try dodging those slimy guts as they float by your face while fish attack!

The "sport" is underwater pumpkin carving. Each Halloween, scuba divers flipper their way to the bottom of oceans, lakes, and swimming pools to participate in these wacky contests.

And talk about fun: "Where else can you see someone carving a pumpkin while they're upside down?" says Trish Lee, who participated in a contest in Monterey Bay, California.

SMASHING PUMPKINS

Armed with their carving knives and pumpkins, divers make their way to the bottom. Easy, right?

Like a 15-pound balloon, a pumpkin is filled with air—so it floats. Puncturing the pumpkin and filling the air pockets with water helps weigh it down, but uncooperative pumpkins tend to pop back to the surface like big orange bubbles.

Once divers get to the bottom (usually only about 20 feet down), they can start carving. When they pull the pumpkin's top off, fish swarm to the scene to devour a free meal.

Some divers draw their pumpkin faces before carving; others sculpt freestyle. Either way, it's challenging when you're under the sea.

Trish Lee steadies the gourd as her partner takes a turn carving.

Halloween Hometowns

Bloody Springs, Mississippi	Mummy Island, Alaska
Cape Fear, North Carolina	Panic, Pennsylvania
Coffins Corner, New Jersey	Scary, West Virginia
Dark Hollow, Indiana	Screamer, Alabama
Deadman Crossing, Ohio	Shady, New York
Deadwood, South Dakota	Shivers, Mississippi
Death Valley, California	Skull Valley, Arizona
Eek, Alaska	Spook City, Colorado
Frankenstein, Missouri	Tombstone, Arizona
Graves Mill, Virginia	Trickum, Georgia
Midnight, Mississippi	Warlock, Texas
Moon, Virginia	Witch Lake, Michigan

A GREAT COSTUME FOR UNDER $10

Jelly beans

Make holes for your arms and legs in the bottom and sides of a large, clear plastic bag. (A lawn bag or a dry-cleaner bag will work great.) Put the bag on over your clothes, then fill it with different colored balloons that are not completely blown up. Gather the bag opening at your neck and loosely tie on a ribbon with a tag.

We Spent
$3

122

A Picture-Perfect
Turkey Day

Ask a friend or parent to give you words to fill in the blanks in this Thanksgiving tale, without showing it to him or her. Then read it out loud for a laugh.

Thanksgiving started out just like it does every year, but _____,
exclamation

it sure ended differently. As usual, I woke up to the _____ sound of
adjective

my dad singing _____ as he stuffed our _____ into
song you hate _plural noun_

the car. Meanwhile, Mom made _____ sandwiches for the
food

_____—hour drive to grandma's _____. The whole way
large number _type of shelter_

there, _____ and I fought over who would have to sit next to Uncle
relative's name

Larry at dinner. Last year, he _____ so bad that I could barely eat my
past-tense verb

_____! But this year Uncle Larry sat next to his new girlfriend,
favorite Thanksgiving dish

_____. I couldn't believe it! She was just as _____
female pop star _adjective_

in person as she looks on TV! Unfortunately, _____
male relative's name

wouldn't stop _____ at her. She got so mad that she took
verb ending in -ing

a scoop of mashed _____ and _____ it at him across
vegetable, plural _past-tense motion verb_

the table. It landed on Grandma's _____! Then he picked up
body part

a(n) _____ leg and _____ it at her! The next thing
animal _past-tense motion_

I knew, my uncle yelled " _____ fight!" Soon we were all covered in
noun

_____ sauce, _____ casserole, and slices of roasted
fruit _vegetable_

_____. For once, Mom's family photos turned out really _____.
type of bird _adjective_

And I'm making a fortune selling the shots of _____ on eBay.
same female pop star

Who knew she had such a great arm?

World Religions

Rooted in people's attempts to explain the unknown, religion takes many forms. Some belief systems, such as Christianity, Islam, and Judaism, are monotheistic, meaning that followers believe in just one supreme being. Others, like Hinduism, Shintoism, and most native belief systems, are polytheistic, meaning that many of their adherents believe in multiple gods.

All of the major religions have their origins in Asia, but they have spread around the world. Christianity, with the largest number of followers, has three divisions—Roman Catholic, Eastern Orthodox, and Protestant. Islam, with about one-fifth of all believers, has two main divisions—Sunni and Shiite. Hinduism and Buddhism account for almost another one-fifth of believers. Judaism, dating back some 4,000 years, is the oldest of all the major monotheistic religions.

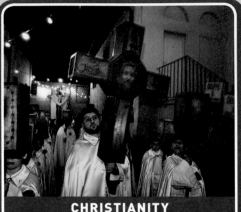

CHRISTIANITY

Based on the teachings of Jesus Christ, a Jew born some 2,000 years ago in the area of modern-day Israel, Christianity has spread worldwide and actively seeks converts. Followers in Switzerland (above) participate in a procession with lanterns and crosses.

BUDDHISM

Founded about 2,500 years ago in northern India by a Hindu prince, Gautama Buddha, Buddhism spread throughout East and Southeast Asia. Buddhist temples have statues, such as the Mihintale Buddha (above) in Sri Lanka.

HINDUISM

Dating back more than 4,000 years, Hinduism is practiced mainly in India. Hindus follow sacred texts known as the Vedas and believe in reincarnation. During the festival of Diwali, Hindus light candles (above) to symbolize the victory of good over evil.

CLOSE-UP

Now that's a BIG crowd!

It has been 1,200 years since the bishop of Rome became known as the pope. Today, the pope is still the head of the Roman Catholic Church. Every Easter Sunday, about 100,000 people gather in St. Peter's Square in Rome to receive his blessing.

To learn more about ancient and medieval religions, go online.
www.historyforkids.org/learn/religion

COOL CLICK

ISLAM

Muslims believe that the Koran, Islam's sacred book, records the words of Allah (God) as revealed to the Prophet Muhammad around A.D. 610. Believers (above) circle the Kabah in the Haram Mosque in Mecca, Saudi Arabia, the spiritual center of the faith.

JUDAISM

The traditions, laws, and beliefs of Judaism date back to Abraham (the Patriarch), and the Torah (the first five books of the Old Testament). Followers pray before the Western Wall (above), which stands below Islam's Dome of the Rock in Jerusalem.

Languages & Literacy

Earth's nearly 7 billion people live in 194 independent countries, but they speak more than 7,000 languages. Some countries, such as Japan, have one official language. Others have many languages. India has 22 official languages. Experts believe that humans may once have spoken as many as 10,000 languages, but that number has dropped by one-third and is still declining.

Language defines a culture, through the people who speak it and what it allows speakers to say. Throughout human history, the languages of powerful groups have spread while the languages of smaller cultures have become extinct.

Literacy is the ability to read and write in one's native language. Almost 84 percent of the people in the world (age 15 and over) are literate.

Literacy rates vary greatly from country to country and region to region. Many factors play a role in whether people are literate; some of those factors are wealth, gender, educational availability, and locale.

There are 774 million illiterate adults (those who cannot read and write) in the world. Two-thirds of those are women, generally because women in less-developed countries often lack access to education.

COOL CLICK

To read more about preserving languages, go online.
www.nationalgeographic.com/mission/enduringvoices

> Every 14 days a language dies. By 2100, more than half of the more than 7,000 languages spoken on Earth—many of them not yet recorded—may disappear, taking with them a wealth of knowledge about history, culture, the environment, and the brain.

LEADING LANGUAGES

Some languages have only a few hundred speakers, but 23 languages stand out with more than 50 million speakers each. Earth's population giant, China, has 874 million speakers of Mandarin, more than double the next-largest group of language speakers. Colonial expansion, trade, and migration account for the spread of the other most widely spoken languages. With growing use of the Internet, English is becoming the language of the technology age.

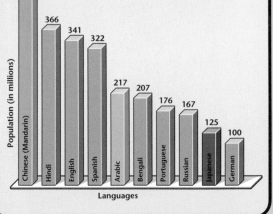

Population (in millions) vs. Languages

Language	Population (in millions)
Chinese (Mandarin)	874
Hindi	366
English	341
Spanish	322
Arabic	217
Bengali	207
Portuguese	176
Russian	167
Japanese	125
German	100

The widespread use of technology—for example, the electronic games that hold the attention of these children in France—has crossed over the language barrier. Computers, the Internet, and electronic communication devices use a universal language that knows no national borders.

MEET THE NAT GEO EXPLORER

WADE DAVIS

An ethnographer, writer, filmmaker, and photographer, Wade Davis is dedicated to the cause of protecting the world's vanishing cultures.

How did you become an explorer?

I was with my roommate in the Harvard Square cafeteria, and there was a National Geographic map in front of us. He looked at me, and I looked at him. He pointed to the Arctic, and I pointed to the Amazon. Two weeks later we were each there.

How would you suggest kids follow in your footsteps?

Just do it. It's as simple as that. But there are two lessons I like to share with kids. First, people often suggest to kids that life is linear and the only way to get through the alphabet is A to B to C. I think it's the critical crossroads that determine life's path. Cultivate your inner compass so when you come to a crossroads, you know which way to go. Second, be patient. Learn to put yourself in the way of opportunities. Do the work, and give your destiny time to find you.

What is one place or thing you'd still like to explore?

There are so many. But here's the top of my list:
— Walk Asia's Silk Road.
— Traverse the Sahara in Africa from west to east.
— Walk the network of ancient Incan highways in South America.

BRAILLE

Braille is an alphabet system used by blind people to read and write using touch. It consists of groups of dots arranged in various ways to designate certain letters, numbers, words, and punctuation marks. Each character is made up of six dots, which can be raised or not raised, creating the codes. People can read Braille by running their fingers over the text and feeling the dot arrangements.

a b c d e f g h i j k l m

n o p q r s t u v w x y z

To learn more about Braille, go online. www.brailler.com/braille.htm

ASL AMERICAN SIGN LANGUAGE

ASL is the main language used by the deaf in the United States and other areas of North America. Manipulation of the fingers and hands to form letters (shown below) and words (signs), combined with facial expressions and postures, is how ASL is spoken.

It is interesting to know that sign language is not the same around the world—there are other sign languages used in different countries.

Aa Bb Cc Dd Ee Ff Gg Hh Ii Jj Kk Ll Mm

Nn Oo Pp Qq Rr Ss Tt Uu Vv Ww Xx Yy Zz

See more information on ASL online. www.nidcd.nih.gov/health/hearing/asl.asp

15 Ways to Say Hello

Armenian *Barev*	**Mandarin** *Ni hao*	**Dutch** *Goedendag*
Finnish *Hei*	**French** *Bonjour*	**Greek** *Yia sou*
Hebrew *Shalom*	**Hindi** *Namaste*	**Icelandic** *Halló*
Italian *Ciào*	**Russian** *Privyet*	**Spanish** *Hola*
Swahili *Jambo*	**Turkish** *Merhaba*	**Welsh** *Dweud*

Bet you didn't know

The word **NERD** was first used in a **Dr. Seuss book.**

There are more than **250,000 different words** in the English language.

VALENTINE'S DAY BREAKFAST

DO SOMETHING *SWEET* FOR YOUR FAMILY ON VALENTINE'S DAY. Whip up this quick recipe for heart-shaped pancakes with strawberry sauce, then serve them with a Valentine's Day note. Work with your parents when using the kitchen.

MAYBE THIS WILL MAKE UP FOR MY MESSY ROOM.

Happy Valentine's Day to the BEST mom in the world!

HEART-SHAPED STRAWBERRY PANCAKES

YOU WILL NEED

LARGE CONTAINER OF FRESH STRAWBERRIES, WASHED

RASPBERRIES AND BLUEBERRIES, WASHED

1 1/4 CUPS STRAWBERRY PRESERVES

1/4 CUP APPLE JUICE

1 TEASPOON LEMON JUICE

PANCAKE MIX

ALL INGREDIENTS LISTED ON THE BOX OF PANCAKE MIX

LARGE HEART-SHAPED COOKIE CUTTER

WHAT TO DO

1. First, prepare the strawberry sauce. Ask an adult to help you cut 1 1/2 cups of sliced fresh strawberries. Set aside. Stir together the strawberry preserves and the apple and lemon juices in a saucepan on low heat. When it gently bubbles, add the sliced strawberries. Cook for one minute. Puree the sauce in a blender until it's smooth. Cover and set aside. Serves four.
2. To prepare the pancakes, follow the directions on the box of pancake mix. Press the cookie cutter into each finished pancake. Ask for an adult's help, and be careful not to burn yourself.
3. If necessary, reheat the strawberry sauce. Dress up the plate with strawberries, raspberries, and blueberries.

THE SECRET SCROLL

YOU WILL NEED

SCISSORS

DECORATIVE PAPER

RULER

COLORFUL STRAWS

TAPE

PEN

RIBBON

WHAT TO DO

1. Cut the paper so it's longer than it is wide.
2. Fold in both ends of the scroll about a half-inch.
3. Cut two straws to the same length, a little longer than the width of the scroll.
4. Tape one straw in the crease of each fold, then tape down the folds.
5. Turn the scroll over and write your Valentine's Day message.
6. Roll the folds toward each other until they meet in the middle. Tie with a ribbon.

Popsicles
WERE INVENTED BY AN
11-year-old.

Most Americans eat about
1,500
peanut butter-and-jelly sandwiches before
graduating from high school.

KETCHUP was originally **SOLD AS MEDICINE.**

Try This!

TRY AN ETHNIC FOOD
that you've never eaten before,
such as Japanese sushi (shown at left),
Indian *naan* (a type of bread), or
Ethiopian *wats* (stews).

Caviar, a distinctly Russian luxury food item, is the **eggs** (called roe) of **sturgeon fish** caught in the Caspian Sea. The eggs are aged in a salty brine before being packaged in cans (right). Unfortunately, most sturgeon are endangered.

Chocolate

CHOCOLATE COMES FROM THE BEAN of the cacao tree, and people have been delighting in it since the time of the Aztecs. In fact, they often used it in a spicy drink for royal and religious celebrations. Here are some cool things you probably never knew about the yummy stuff:

- *Theobroma cacao*, the name of the tree that produces chocolate, means "food of the gods" in Greek.

- In the 19th century, people began adding condensed milk to cocoa to produce milk chocolate. (*Cacao* refers to the bean or tree; *cocoa* is a product derived from cacao.)

- The Aztecs used cacao seeds as money.

- The Aztecs sometimes fed their sacrificial victims chocolate beverages to calm them before the sacrifice.

- During World War I, chocolate began to be shaped in the form of bars for eating.

- Mexicans today use chocolate in molé, a spicy sauce made with chilies and chocolate.

Pop History

BUBBLE GUM IS MADE FROM SWEETENERS like sugar, a variety of different flavorings, and a chewy gum base. The gum base originally was made from a product called *chicle*, which actually comes from *Manilkara chicle* trees! Today, the gum base is sometimes made from a latex product or a type of rubber. But these products also come from trees. Think it's weird to chew gum from a tree? People have been doing it for thousands of years, ever since the Ancient Mayans.

Interested in learning about other food history and fun facts?
www.foodfunandfacts.com/foodfun.htm

COOL CLICK

SMASHING FUN!

It's OK to play with your food in Buñol, Spain. That's where the largest annual food fight is held. Every August, about 120 tons of tomatoes are tossed off of trucks to more than 38,000 people. The food fighters crush the tomatoes and then send them flying. Just don't try this in your school cafeteria!

Try This!

Rabbi Shira's Honey Cake*

This delicious honey cake, a traditional Jewish dessert, is light and airy because of the egg whites.

Ingredients
5 eggs
3/4 cup brown sugar
1/4 cup oil
3/4 cup honey

2 teaspoons cinnamon
1/2 teaspoon nutmeg
1/2 teaspoon vanilla
1 3/4 cups self-rising flour

You will need
An electric mixer to beat the egg whites
A whisk and a wooden spoon
A 10-inch cake pan sprayed with vegetable oil and then lightly dusted with flour
Confectioner's sugar
Slivered almonds, lightly toasted (optional).

What to do

1. Preheat oven to 350°F.

2. Separate egg whites and egg yolks.

3. Beat egg whites with a mixer until they look stiff.

4. Slowly add sugar to egg whites with mixer at lowest speed.

5. Add egg yolks and oil to egg-white mixture with a whisk. Be gentle. Keep stirring.

6. Add honey, cinnamon, nutmeg, vanilla, and flour using a wooden spoon. Remember to be gentle. Stir until all the flour is absorbed.

7. Pour batter into prepared pan.

8. Bake at 350°F for 45 minutes.

9. Check for doneness by inserting a toothpick into the center of the cake. If it comes out gooey, the cake's not done yet.

10. Cool in pan for 15 minutes. Loosen the edges and bottom of the cake with a long knife. Turn the cake onto a rack.

11. Once the cake is completely cool, place it on a plate. To make it look pretty, shake confectioner's sugar on top. Sprinkle with the almonds if you like.

*This recipe is from Deborah Heiligman's *Celebrate Rosh Hashanah and Yom Kippur.*

World Economies

What is an economy? In terms of countries, it's the way a country manages its resources (money, land, etc.) to produce, distribute, and consume goods (cars, foods, etc.) and services (transportation, etc.).

The United States has a free-market economy, which means that people are free to buy and trade goods and services. In addition, prices are determined by consumer demand.

A country's economy can be divided into three parts, or sectors—agriculture, industry, and services. The economies of the United States, Western Europe, and Japan are dominated by the service sector. These economies enjoy a high GDP (gross domestic product) per capita—the value of goods and services produced each year, averaged per person in each country. In contrast, some economies in Africa and Asia still depend mostly on agriculture. Many farmers produce only enough crops to support their own families, and therefore have a low standard of living. Other economies, such as those of oil-producing countries of the Middle East, have a very high GDP per capita, but wealth is very unevenly divided among the population.

No country produces everything its people need or want. Therefore, trade is a critical part of the world economy.

HIGHEST GDP PER CAPITA*

1.	Liechtenstein	$118,000
2.	Qatar	$101,000
3.	Luxembourg	$85.100
4.	Bermuda	$69,900
5.	Kuwait	$60,800
6.	Norway	$57,500
7.	Brunei	$54,100
8.	Singapore	$52,000
9.	United States	$48,000
10.	Ireland	$47,800

LOWEST GDP PER CAPITA**

1.	Zimbabwe	$200
2.	Democratic Republic of the Congo	$300
3.	Burundi	$400
4.	Liberia	$500
5.	Somalia	$600
6.	Guinea-Bissau	$600
7.	Eritrea	$700
8.	Sierra Leone	$700
9.	Niger	$700
10.	Central African Republic	$700

* Data from 2004–2008
**All data as of 2008

MIDEAST OIL RESERVES

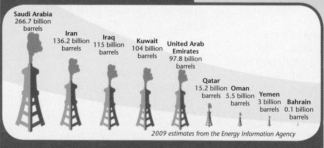

Saudi Arabia 266.7 billion barrels
Iran 136.2 billion barrels
Iraq 115 billion barrels
Kuwait 104 billion barrels
United Arab Emirates 97.8 billion barrels
Qatar 15.2 billion barrels
Oman 5.5 billion barrels
Yemen 3 billion barrels
Bahrain 0.1 billion barrels

2009 estimates from the Energy Information Agency

Saudi Arabia leads the region and the world in oil reserves and production, but four other countries in the Middle East also rank near the top.

AUTO GIANTS

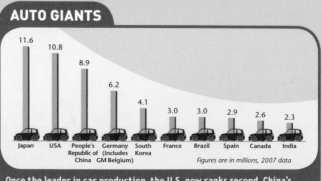

Japan	USA	People's Republic of China	Germany (includes GM Belgium)	South Korea	France	Brazil	Spain	Canada	India
11.6	10.8	8.9	6.2	4.1	3.0	3.0	2.9	2.6	2.3

Figures are in millions, 2007 data

Once the leader in car production, the U.S. now ranks second. China's expanding production makes it a contender for a top place in the future.

FISHING AND AQUACULTURE

The world's yearly catch of ocean fish is more than four times what it was in 1950. The most heavily harvested areas are in the North Atlantic and western Pacific Oceans. Overfishing is becoming a serious problem. At least seven of the most-fished species are considered to be at their limit.

Aquaculture—raising fish and seaweed in controlled ponds—accounts for some 40 percent of the fish people eat. This practice began some 4,000 years ago in China, where it continues today. Fish are among the most widely traded food products, with 75 percent of the total catch sold on the international market each year.

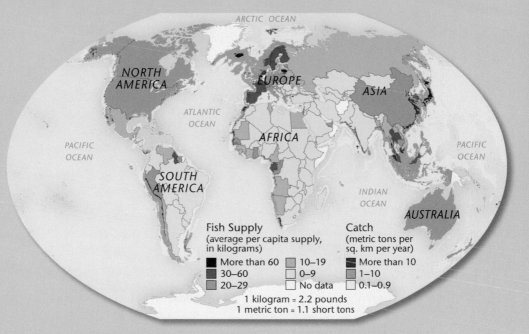

ARCTIC OCEAN

NORTH AMERICA

EUROPE

ASIA

ATLANTIC OCEAN

AFRICA

PACIFIC OCEAN

PACIFIC OCEAN

SOUTH AMERICA

INDIAN OCEAN

AUSTRALIA

Fish Supply
(average per capita supply, in kilograms)

- More than 60
- 30–60
- 20–29
- 10–19
- 0–9
- No data

Catch
(metric tons per sq. km per year)

- More than 10
- 1–10
- 0.1–0.9

1 kilogram = 2.2 pounds
1 metric ton = 1.1 short tons

STAPLE GRAINS

CORN

A staple in prehistoric Mexico and Peru, corn (or maize) is native to the New World. By the time Columbus's crew first tasted it, corn was already a hardy crop in much of North and South America.

WHEAT

Among the two oldest grains, wheat (barley is the other) was important in ancient Mediterranean civilizations. Today, it is the most widely cultivated grain. Wheat grows best in temperate climates.

RICE

Originating in Asia many millennia ago, rice is the staple grain for about half the world's people. It is a labor-intensive plant that grows primarily in paddies (flooded fields) and thrives in the hot, humid tropics.

Currency Around the World

Currency is different from country to country, but most use bills and coins of varying shapes, sizes, and values. There is such a huge variety of money out there (some are really colorful) that you might even think it is play money! Here are the names of some types of currency used around the world.

U.S.	Dollar
Japan	Yen
Venezuela	Bolivar
Israel	Shekel
United Kingdom	Pound
Sweden	Krona
Gambia	Dalasi
Turkey	Lira
Russia	Ruble
Argentina	Peso
Iraq	Dinar
Thailand	Baht
Italy	Euro
Ethiopia	Birr

COOL CLICK

For more on currency, go online. www.xe.com

Weird but true

DON'T SPEND IT ALL IN ONE PLACE!
3¢

THE UNITED STATES ONCE ISSUED A THREE-CENT BILL.

There are **293** ways to make change for a dollar.

THE AVERAGE **$100** BILL CIRCULATES FOR **9** YEARS.

If you spent a dollar every second, **it would take about 32 YEARS to spend a billion dollars.**

MORE THAN 10,000,000 **MILLIONAIRES** ARE ALIVE TODAY.

Try This! MONEY FUN

Transform a dollar bill into a butterfly with this cool design by John Montroll, author of the book *Dollar Bill Animals in Origami*.

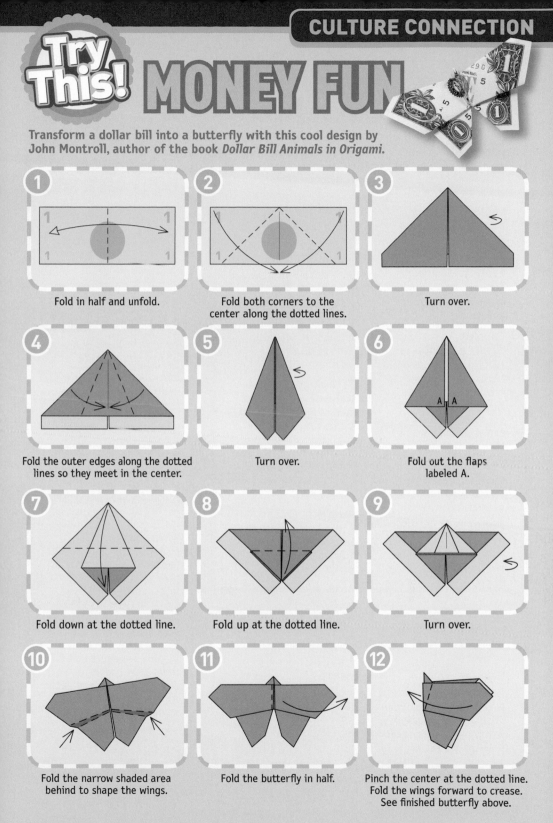

1 Fold in half and unfold.

2 Fold both corners to the center along the dotted lines.

3 Turn over.

4 Fold the outer edges along the dotted lines so they meet in the center.

5 Turn over.

6 Fold out the flaps labeled A.

7 Fold down at the dotted line.

8 Fold up at the dotted line.

9 Turn over.

10 Fold the narrow shaded area behind to shape the wings.

11 Fold the butterfly in half.

12 Pinch the center at the dotted line. Fold the wings forward to crease. See finished butterfly above.

Types of Literature

FICTION A category that refers to narratives, or stories, that are made up from the imagination, as opposed to based on fact. Within fiction, there are many genres:

Fable
A story, generally with animals as the main characters, which has a moral.

Fairy Tale
A story that has magical or imaginary creatures and people.

Fantasy/Science Fiction
Fantasy involves suspending reality, and generally involves other worlds. Science fiction is similar but more scientific, and is generally set in the future.

Folklore
Stories, songs, and myths passed down orally through generations of people.

Historical
Fictional characters and events used within actual historical settings.

Horror
Writing that evokes fear, shock, or aversion.

Humor
Funny stories with the main goal of entertainment of the reader.

Mystery
Writing that deals with crime or suspicious activities.

Mythology/Legend
Mythology and legend are often based on historical events, but also include imaginative material and symbolism. Myths are often about gods, while legends generally deal with heroes.

Poetry
Writing that is rhythmic and often rhymes. The intent is to create an emotional response.

NONFICTION An overarching category that refers to informational narratives or collective of information, which are true. There are several genres within nonfiction, as well:

Biography/Autobiography
Writing about a person's life history. A biography is written by someone other than the subject, while an autobiography is written by the subject.

Essay
A short piece of writing that uses facts to support an author's analysis.

Almanac
Annual publication listing information across a wide breadth of general-interest topics.

MILLION-DOLLAR BOOK

THE TREASURE: AN ORIGINAL MARK TWAIN MANUSCRIPT

FOUND: IN A TRUNK IN AN ATTIC

NOW WORTH: 1.5 MILLION DOLLARS

An attic trunk turned out to be a treasure chest. Inside, a woman found half of the original handwritten manuscript of Mark Twain's *Adventures of Huckleberry Finn*. A century before, Twain had sent the manuscript in parts to the woman's grandfather at the Buffalo and Erie County Library in New York. He took part of Twain's work home to bind, but it was packed in the trunk—and forgotten—when he died. In 1992, the papers were reunited with the rest of the manuscript, now valued at 1.5 million dollars.

COOL CLICK

Take a look at a great online literature library.
www.literature.org

Movie Munchies

FAVORITE SNACKS FROM AROUND THE GLOBE

AUSTRALIA Meat pies

CHINA Pickled dried fruit

COLOMBIA Fried ants

CROATIA Roasted pumpkin seeds

ENGLAND Sugar-coated popcorn

FRANCE Roasted chestnuts

GREECE Yogurt with honey

HONG KONG Shredded, dried cuttlefish

INDIA Caramel popcorn

JAPAN Fried octopus pancakes

MALAYSIA Spicy green peas

PHILIPPINES Fried banana chips

SINGAPORE Shrimp-flavored crackers

TONGA Guavas, mangoes, and oranges

TURKEY Frozen chocolate pudding

10⁺ must-see MOVIES

Feel like watching some good movies? Check out some of these, which are among the most popular movies for kids of all time:

The Wizard of Oz – 1939

Fantasia – 1940

It's a Wonderful Life – 1946

The *Star Wars* films

Raiders of the Lost Ark – 1981

E.T.: The Extra-Terrestrial – 1982

Back to the Future – 1985

The Princess Bride – 1987

The *Harry Potter* films

Pirates of the Caribbean films

VISUAL Arts

Beginning with drawings on the walls of caves and rocks, visual art has helped to connect people and to tell the story of human cultures. Styles vary with time, location, artist, and other factors, but the presence of art in a culture always remains throughout time and around the world. A sampling of visual art genres—each with a unifying set of conventions—is given here to demonstrate the wide range of styles.

Abstract
Objects and people do not need to appear as they do in the real world; instead, color and shape are used to evoke emotions. What emotions do you see when you look at a Jackson Pollock abstract painting?

Cubism
Modern art gone geometric. Check out some Georges Braque and see if you think it's cool or just plain square.

Expressionism
Expressionist artists wanted feelings to shine through their paintings, like in Edvard Munch's *The Scream*.

Impressionism
Originating in France in the late 19th century, impressionist paintings are bold and lack details. They are often landscapes, such as many in the work of Claude Monet.

Pointillism
Tons of small dots or strokes come together in pointillist paintings to form beautiful pictures. Artists like Paul Seurat really put the point on this genre.

Pop Art
Beginning in the 1950s, pop art hit the scene with bold, tradition-challenging pieces using themes from mass culture, including comic books and advertisements. Artists like Andy Warhol made themselves legends by depicting everyday objects, such as soup cans.

Realism
Originating in the 18th century, realist paintings strive to represent life as it actually appears. Most Realists were French, but American painters like Thomas Eakins were also prominent in the genre.

Surrealism
Surrealist paintings invoke feelings based on odd representations. Salvador Dali was a master surrealist who shouldn't be missed.

Bet you didn't know

The *Mona Lisa* has no eye-brows.

MUSIC Genres

A genre is a type or style of something—in this case, music. There are many kinds of music in the world. Each genre has its own unique history and sound. The various styles can make you feel different things. To discover a music genre you've never heard before, download some new tunes and see how it makes you feel. Here's a list of some common music genres and musicians who are associated with them.

Blues

Arising out of the oral tradition of African-American poetry set to music that uses "blue" notes (a note sung or played at a slightly lower pitch than that of the major scale), blues is a genre that influenced the development of jazz, rock-and-roll, and R&B. Hum a tune with B. B. King.

Classical

A style of music originating in Europe, classical music includes a lot of operas and symphonies. Relax to some soothing Mozart.

Country

Country music came from the blending of music found in the South and the Appalachian Mountains. Kick up your boots with a little Carrie Underwood.

Folk

A traditional music, folk reflects the beliefs of the community and times from which it comes. Take a listen to Woody Guthrie.

Hip-Hop/Rap

A relatively new genre, started in the 1970s, hip-hop or rap music has a rhythmic style with a strong beat. Listen to an original hip-hop group, like the Sugarhill Gang.

Jazz

One of the only truly American art forms (the other is quilting), jazz originated in the early 1900s in the South. Jazz is based on European and African music traditions, combined with contemporary American popular music. Chill out with a little Louis Armstrong.

Reggae

From the islands of the West Indies, reggae features repetitive sounds, generally played on the off beat. Get jammin' with Bob Marley.

Rhythm & Blues

A combination of two other genres, jazz and blues, R&B was developed in the United States by African-American musicians. It had a strong influence on rock-and-roll. Stay smooth with Alicia Keys.

Rock-and-Roll

Originating in the late 1940s and 50s, rock-and-roll was a combination of R&B and country music. Today, it is a large, all-encompassing genre, generally called rock, which includes other types of music, such as punk rock, heavy metal, and alternative. Dance to the early rock-and-roll of Bill Haley & The Comets.

...COUNTRY!
...e a
...y report

YOU'RE A STUDENT, but you're also a citizen of the world. Writing a report on a foreign country is a great way to better understand and appreciate how people in other parts of the world live. Pick the country of your ancestors, one that's been in the news, or one that you'd like to visit someday.

Passport to Success

A country report follows the format of an expository essay (see p. 36 for "How to Write an Awesome Essay") because you're "exposing" information about the country you choose.

Simple Steps

1 RESEARCH. Gathering information is the most important step in writing a good country report. Look to Internet sources, encyclopedias, books, magazine and newspaper articles, and other sources to find important and interesting details about your subject.

2 ORGANIZE YOUR NOTES. Put the information you gathered into a rough outline. For example, sort everything you found about the country's system of government, climate, etc. Remember to take note of your sources for each piece of information. (See p. 269 for "Reveal Your Sources.")

3 WRITE IT UP. Follow the basic structure of good writing: introduction, body, and conclusion. Remember that each paragraph should have a topic sentence that is supported by facts and details. Incorporate the information from your notes, but make sure it's in your own words. And make your writing flow with good transitions and descriptive language.

4 JAZZ IT UP. Include maps, diagrams, photos, and other visual aides.

5 PROOFREAD AND REVISE. Correct any mistakes and put a polish on your language. Do your best!

6 CITE YOUR SOURCES. Be sure to keep a record of your sources for each piece (See p. 269 for "Reveal Your Sources.")

TIP: Choose a country that's in the news. For example, Canadians are excited to host the 2010 Winter Olympics in Vancouver. This exciting world event makes Canada an ideal topic for your next country report.

Key Information

You may be assigned to write a report on a specific aspect of a country, such as its political system, or your report may be more general. In writing a broad survey, be sure to touch on the following areas:

GEOGRAPHY—the country's location, size, capital and major cities, topography, and other physical details

NATURE—the country's various climates, ecosystems (rain forest, desert, etc.), and unique wildlife

HISTORY—major events, wars, and other moments that affected the country and its people

GOVERNMENT—the country's political system (democracy, dictatorship, etc.) and the role of the individual citizen in the country's governance

ECONOMY / INDUSTRY—the country's economic system (capitalism, socialism, etc.), major industries and exports, and the country's place in the world economy

PEOPLE AND CULTURE—the country's major religions, spoken languages, unique foods, holidays, rituals, and traditions

GO BEYOND THE BASICS.

Explain the history of the country's flag and the meaning of its colors and symbols. www.crwflags.com/fotw/flags

Play the country's national anthem. Download the anthems, words, and sheet music. www.nationalanthems.info

Figure out how much a dollar is worth in the country. www.xe.com/ucc

Check the local weather. Click on "World" at the top of the page, then search for the country. Click on a city to know if it's sunny and clear or subzero. www.weather.com

Figure out the time difference between the country you're studying and where you live. www.worldtimeserver.com

Still want more information? Go to National Geographic's One-Stop Research site for maps, photos, art, games, and other information to make your report stand out. www.nationalgeographic.com/onestop

COOL CLICK

Write With Power

Using good transitions makes any kind of writing read more smoothly. It gives organization and helps the reader to understand and improve connections between thoughts. Here are a few examples of good transitions you might want to use:

Addition
also, again, as well as, besides, coupled with, furthermore, in addition, likewise, moreover, similarly

Generalizing
as a rule, as usual, for the most part, generally, generally speaking, ordinarily, usually

Emphasis
above all, chiefly, with attention to, especially, particularly, singularly

Similarity
comparatively, coupled with, correspondingly, identically, likewise, similar, moreover, together with

Restatement
in essence, in other words, namely, that is, that is to say, in short, in brief, to put it differently

Contrast and Comparison
contrast, by the same token, conversely, instead, likewise, on one hand, on the other hand, on the contrary, rather, similarly, yet, but, however, still, nevertheless, in contrast

143

Geography
Rocks

GEOGRAPHY ROCKS

Iguazú Falls of Brazil and Argentina,
as seen from the Brazilian side

THE POLITICAL WORLD

Earth's land area is made up of seven continents, but people have divided much of the land into smaller political units called countries. Australia is a continent with a single country, and Antarctica is set aside for scientific research. But the other five continents include almost 200 independent countries. The political map shown here depicts boundaries—imaginary lines created by treaties—that separate countries. Some boundaries, such as the one between the United States and Canada, are very stable and have been recognized for many years.

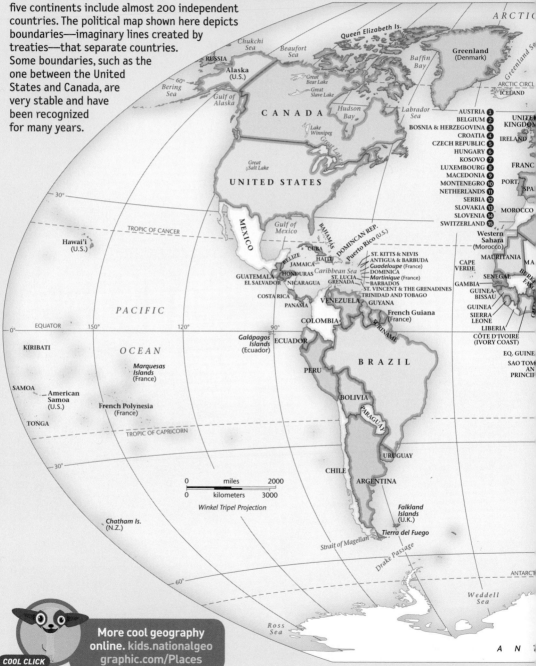

ARCTIC

Chukchi Sea
Beaufort Sea
Queen Elizabeth Is.
Baffin Bay
Greenland (Denmark)
Greenland Sea
RUSSIA
Alaska (U.S.)
60°
Bering Sea
Gulf of Alaska
Great Bear Lake
Great Slave Lake
Hudson Bay
Labrador Sea
ARCTIC CIRCLE
ICELAND

CANADA
Lake Winnipeg
Great Lakes

AUSTRIA ①
BELGIUM ②
BOSNIA & HERZEGOVINA ③
CROATIA ④
CZECH REPUBLIC ⑤
HUNGARY ⑥
KOSOVO ⑦
LUXEMBOURG ⑧
MACEDONIA ⑨
MONTENEGRO ⑩
NETHERLANDS ⑪
SERBIA ⑫
SLOVAKIA ⑬
SLOVENIA ⑭
SWITZERLAND ⑮

UNITE KINGDO
IRELAND
FRANC
PORT.
SPA
MOROCCO

Great Salt Lake

UNITED STATES

30°
TROPIC OF CANCER

Hawai'i (U.S.)

MEXICO
Gulf of Mexico
BAHAMAS
CUBA
HAITI
DOMINCAN REP.
Puerto Rico (U.S.)
Western Sahara (Morocco)

BELIZE
JAMAICA
GUATEMALA
HONDURAS
EL SALVADOR NICARAGUA
COSTA RICA
PANAMA

ST. KITTS & NEVIS
ANTIGUA & BARBUDA
Guadeloupe (France)
DOMINICA
Martinique (France)
ST. LUCIA
GRENADA
BARBADOS
ST. VINCENT & THE GRENADINES
TRINIDAD AND TOBAGO

Caribbean Sea

MAURITANIA
MA
CAPE VERDE
SENEGAL
GAMBIA
GUINEA-BISSAU
GUINEA
SIERRA LEONE
LIBERIA
CÔTE D'IVOIRE (IVORY COAST)
EQ. GUINE
SAO TOM
AN
PRINCIP

VENEZUELA GUYANA
COLOMBIA
SURINAME
French Guiana (France)

PACIFIC

EQUATOR
150°
120°
90°

KIRIBATI

OCEAN

Galápagos Islands (Ecuador) ECUADOR
PERU
BRAZIL

Marquesas Islands (France)

SAMOA
American Samoa (U.S.)
French Polynesia (France)

TONGA

BOLIVIA
PARAGUAY

TROPIC OF CAPRICORN

30°

0 miles 2000
0 kilometers 3000
Winkel Tripel Projection

CHILE
URUGUAY
ARGENTINA

Chatham Is. (N.Z.)

Falkland Islands (U.K.)
Tierra del Fuego
Strait of Magellan
Drake Passage

60°
ANTARC

Weddell Sea

Ross Sea

A N

More cool geography online. kids.nationalgeographic.com/Places

COOL CLICK

Other boundaries, like the one between Ethiopia and Eritrea in northeast Africa, are relatively new and still disputed. Countries come in all shapes and sizes. Russia and Canada are giants; others, like Luxembourg, are small. Some countries are long and skinny—look at Chile in South America! Still other countries—like Indonesia and Japan in Asia—are made up of groups of islands. The political map is a clue to the diversity that makes Earth so fascinating.

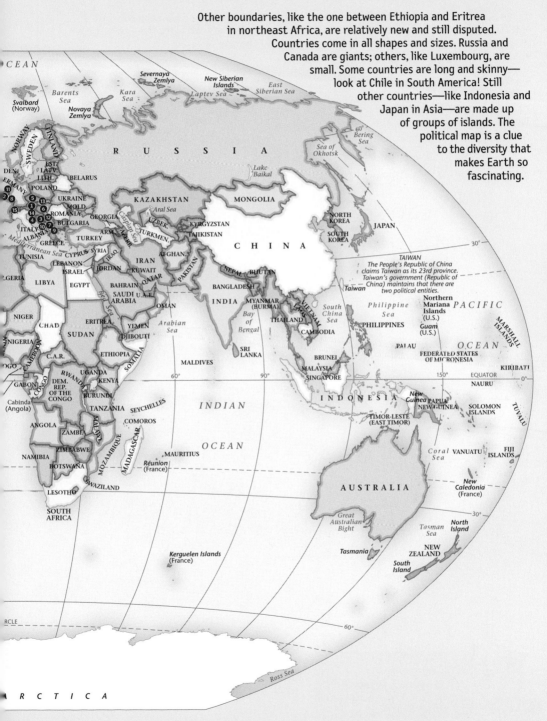

TAIWAN
The People's Republic of China claims Taiwan as its 23rd province. Taiwan's government (Republic of China) maintains that there are two political entities.

THE PHYSICAL WORLD

Earth is dominated by large landmasses called continents—seven in all—and by an interconnected global ocean that is divided into four parts by the continents. More than 70 percent of Earth's surface is covered by oceans, and the remaining 30 percent is made up of land areas.

Different landforms give variety to the surface of the continents. The Rockies and Andes mark the western edge of the Americas, and the Himalaya tower above southern Asia. The Plateau of Tibet forms the rugged core of Asia, while the

ARCTIC

Queen Elizabeth Islands

GREENLAND

Chukchi Sea
Beaufort Sea
Brooks Ra.
Victoria Island
Baffin Bay
ARCTIC CIRCLE
Iceland

SIERRA
+ Mt. McKinley
20,320 ft
(6,194 m)
Bering Sea
Great Slave Lake
Great Bear Lake
Hudson Bay
Labrador Sea
British Isles
Ireland
Great Britain

60°

Aleutian Islands

NORTH
AMERICA

Vancouver Island

Canadian Shield

Nova Scotia
Island of Newfoundland

Missouri
Lake Winnipeg
Great Lakes
Appalachian Mountains

Azores
Madeira Islands

Great Salt Lake
Death Valley
-282 ft
(-86 m)
Colorado
Rio Grande
Central Lowland
Mississippi

30°

Hawaiian Islands

TROPIC OF CANCER

Baja California

Gulf of Mexico

West Indies

Canary Islands

Greater Antilles

Cape Verde Islands

CENTRAL
AMERICA
Caribbean Sea
Lesser Antilles

ATLANTIC

PACIFIC

Llanos
Orinoco

0°

Line Islands
150°
120°
EQUATOR
90°

Galápagos Islands

Amazon
Amazon

OCEAN

OCEAN

POLYNESIA

Marquesas Islands

Basin

SOUTH
AMERICA

Samoa
Cook Islands
Tuamotu Archipelago
Society Is.
Tahiti
Austral Is.
Fiji Is.
Tonga Is.

Andes

Lake Titicaca

Brazilian Highlands

TROPIC OF CAPRICORN

Easter Island

Atacama Desert

Gran Chaco
Paraná

30°

Cerro Aconcagua +
22,834 ft
(6,960 m)

Pampas
ANDES

Isla Grande de Chiloé

Patagonia

Laguna del Carbón
-344 ft
(-105 m)
Falkland Is.
Tierra del Fuego

Strait of Magellan

South Sandwich Islands

South Shetland Islands

ANTARCTIC

60°

Bellingshausen Sea
Ellsworth Land
Antarctic Peninsula
Weddell Sea

Q

Marie Byrd Land
Vinson Massif +
16,067 ft
(4,897 m)
MOUNTAINS

TRANSANTARCTIC

COOL CLICK

Northern European Plain extends from the North Sea to the Ural Mountains. Much of Africa is a plateau, and dry plains cover large areas of Australia. Beneath massive ice sheets, mountains rise over 16,000 ft (4,877 m) in Antarctica.

Mountains and trenches make the ocean floors as varied as any continent.

A mountain chain called the Mid-Atlantic Ridge runs the length of the Atlantic Ocean.

In the western Pacific, trenches drop deep into the ocean floor.

CEAN
Svalbard
Norwegian Sea
Barents Sea
Kara Sea
Novaya Zemlya
Severnaya Zemlya
New Siberian Islands
Laptev Sea
East Siberian Sea
Yenisey
Central Siberian Plateau
Lena
Bering Sea
Kamchatka Peninsula
Aleutian Is.
Kuril Islands
Sea of Okhotsk
Scandinavia
West Siberian Plain
Ob
Irtysh
Angara
Lena
Sea of Japan (East Sea)
Hokkaido
JAPAN
Honshu
Northern European Plain
Ural Mountains
Volga
Lake Baikal
Amur
EUROPE
Alps
Danube
El'brus 18,510 ft (5,642 m)
The Steppes
Aral Sea
Altay Mountains
Tian Shan
ASIA
GOBI
North China Plain
Yellow (Huang)
Korea
Nampo Shoto
Caucasus Mts.
Black Sea
Caspian Sea
Kunlun Mountains
Sea of Japan (East Sea)
East China Sea
Ryukyu
Zagros Mts.
Dead Sea -1,380 ft (-421 m)
HIMALAYA
Plateau of Tibet
Brahmaputra
Yangtze (Chang)
Taiwan
PACIFIC
mediterranean Sea
Nile
ARABIAN PENINSULA
Indus
Ganges
Mt. Everest 29,035 ft (8,850 m)
Salween
Mekong
East China Sea
OCEAN
HARA
Libyan Desert
Arabian Sea
INDIA
Bay of Bengal
Indochina Peninsula
Hainan
Luzon
Philippine Sea
Mariana Islands
AHEL
Gulf of Aden
Somali Peninsula
Andaman Islands
Andaman Sea
South China Sea
Philippine Islands
MICRONESIA
Lake Chad
Ethiopian Highlands
Sri Lanka
Nicobar Is.
Malay Peninsula
Marshall Islands
AFRICA
Maldive Islands
Borneo
Gilbert Islands
Congo
Lake Victoria
Kilimanjaro +19,340 ft (5,895 m)
INDONESIA
Greater Sunda
Celebes
New Guinea
Bismarck Archipelago
Solomon Islands
MELANESIA
Congo Basin
Great Rift Valley
Lake Tanganyika
Seychelles
Sumatra
Java
Islands
INDIAN
EQUATOR
Zambezi
Comoros Is.
Madagascar
OCEAN
Timor
Arafura Sea
Coral Sea
Vanuatu
Fiji Islands
Kalahari Desert
Mascarene Is.
Great Sandy Desert
AUSTRALIA
Lake Eyre -52 ft (-16 m)
Great Victoria Desert
Central Lowlands
Darling
Great Dividing Range
New Caledonia
Kerguelen Islands
miles 2000
kilometers 3000
Winkel Tripel Projection
Mt. Kosciuszko 7,310 ft (2,228 m)
Tasman Sea
Tasmania
North Island
NEW ZEALAND
South Island
Auckland Islands
RCLE
en Maud Land
Transantarctic Mountains
Victoria Land
ANTARCTICA

30°
60°
90°
150°
0°
30°
60°

149

KINDS OF MAPS

Maps are special tools that geographers use to tell a story about Earth. Maps can be used to show just about anything related to places. Some maps show physical features, such as mountains or vegetation. Maps can also show climates or natural hazards and other things we cannot easily see. Other maps illustrate different features on Earth—political boundaries, urban centers, and economic systems.

AN IMPERFECT TOOL

Maps are not perfect. A globe is a scale model of Earth with accurate relative sizes and locations. Because maps are flat, they involve distortions of size, shape, and direction. Also, cartographers—people who create maps—make choices about what information to include. Because of this, it is important to study many different types of maps to learn the complete story of Earth. Three commonly found kinds of maps are shown on this page.

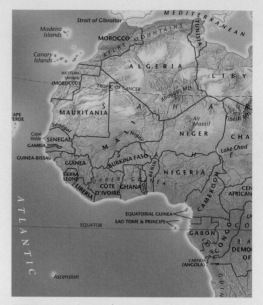

PHYSICAL MAPS. Earth's natural features—landforms, water bodies, and vegetation—are shown on physical maps. The map above uses color and shading to illustrate mountains, lakes, rivers, and deserts of western Africa. Country names and borders are added for reference, but they are not natural features.

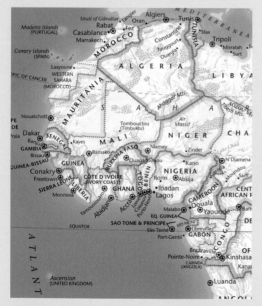

POLITICAL MAPS. These maps represent characteristics of the landscape created by humans, such as boundaries, cities, and place names. Natural features are added only for reference. On the map above, capital cities are represented with a star inside a circle, while other cities are shown with black dots.

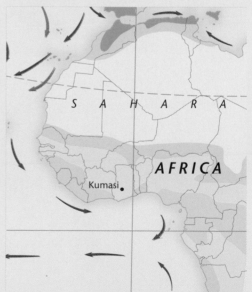

THEMATIC MAPS. Patterns related to a particular topic, or theme, such as population distribution, appear on these maps. The map above displays the region's climate zones, which range from tropical wet (bright green) to tropical wet and dry (light green) to semiarid (dark yellow) to arid or desert (light yellow).

KINDS OF ENVIRONMENTS

The world is full of a wondrous selection of natural geographic features. If you take a look around, you'll be amazed by the beauty of our world. From roaring rivers to parched deserts, from underwater canyons to jagged mountains, Earth is covered with beautiful and diverse environments.

Here are some examples of the most common types of geographic features found around the world.

RIVER

As a river moves through flatlands, it twists and turns. Above, the Rio Los Amigos winds through a rain forest in Peru.

CANYON

Steep-sided valleys called canyons are created mainly by running water. Buckskin Gulch (above) is the deepest slot canyon in the American Southwest.

DESERT

Deserts are land features created by climate, specifically by a lack of water. Above, a camel caravan crosses the Sahara, in North Africa.

OASIS

Occasionally, water rises from deep below a desert, creating a refuge that supports trees and sometimes crops, as in this oasis in Africa.

MOUNTAIN

Mountains are Earth's tallest landforms, and Mount Everest (above) rises highest of all, at 29,035 feet (8,850 m) above sea level.

GLACIER

Glaciers—"rivers" of ice—such as Alaska's Hubbard Glacier (above) move slowly from mountains to the sea. Global warming is shrinking them.

VALLEY

Valleys, cut by running water or moving ice, may be broad and flat or narrow and steep, such as the Indus River Valley in Ladakh, India (above).

WATERFALL

Waterfalls form when a river reaches an abrupt change in elevation. Above, Kaitur Falls, in Guyana, descends 800 feet (244 m).

A GREEN MAP

Check out green action around the globe.

Maps can show all sorts of information. This thematic map shows how protecting the planet isn't just a concern in the United States—it's a global issue. Everyone needs to pitch in, no matter where they live. Take a look at what's happening around the world in the mission to save Earth.

UNITED STATES

Recycling in Seattle, Washington, and Madison, Wisconsin, isn't optional. It's backed by aggressively enforced laws.

UNITED STATES

As of 2009, 200 miles of bicycle lanes were available in New York City.

BRAZIL & ARGENTINA

Many cars and trucks in Brazil and Argentina run on biodiesel fuel—an eco-friendly blend of diesel fuel and alcohols made from plants, such as algae or sugarcane (below).

ALASKA
(U.S.)

NORTH
AMERICA

Seattle

Madison

UNITED STATES

New
York
City

HAWAI'I
(U.S.)

SOUTH
AMERICA

BRAZIL

ARGENTINA

ANTARCTICA

IRELAND

In Ireland, shoppers must pay an extra 33 cents for each plastic shopping bag they take home.

GERMANY

Germany produces more electricity from wind power than any other European country. Unlike coal or oil, wind power is clean and renewable.

CHINA

One day a week, residents of Beijing, China, are encouraged not to drive, and everyone walks, bicycles, or rides public transportation.

ASIA

IRELAND
GERMANY
EUROPE

Beijing

CHINA

JAPAN

PAKISTAN

AFRICA

KENYA

JAPAN

Many office buildings in Japan are no cooler than 82.4°F (28°C) in the summer. To keep comfy, employees are encouraged to trade in their suits for short sleeves.

PHILIPPINES

MALAYSIA

PAKISTAN

Pakistan is beginning to provide some citizens with energy produced by wind.

PHILIPPINES

More than a fourth of the electricity in the Philippines is from clean, renewable geothermal energy, which comes from heat beneath Earth's surface.

AUSTRALIA

MALAYSIA

Many Malaysians will be required to use rainwater for things such as watering plants and flushing toilets. Treated water is saved for drinking and cooking.

KENYA

In Kenya, a woman started a project that has planted more than 40 million trees so far.

AUSTRALIA

Incandescent lightbulbs have been banned in Australia as of 2010. Residents are replacing them with energy-efficient compact fluorescent bulbs (right).

AFRICA

PHYSICAL

Land area
11,608,000 sq mi
(30,065,000 sq km)

Highest point
Kilimanjaro,
Tanzania
19,340 ft
(5,895 m)

Lowest point
Lake Assal,
Djibouti
-512 ft (-156 m)

Longest river
Nile
4,241 mi (6,825 km)

Largest lake
Victoria
26,800 sq mi
(69,500 sq km)

POLITICAL

Population
967,049,000

Largest country
Sudan
967,500 sq mi
(2,505,813 sq km)

**Largest
metropolitan area**
Cairo, Egypt
Pop. 11,893,000

**Most densely
populated country**
Mauritius
1,609 people per sq mi
(622 per sq km)

Economy
Farming: fruit, grains
Industry: chemicals,
    mining, cement
Services

Africa spans nearly as far from west to east as it does from north to south. The Sahara—the world's largest desert— covers Africa's northern third, while to the south lie bands of grassland, tropical rain forest, and more desert. The rain forests of Africa are home to half of the continent's animal species. Wild creatures, such as lions (right), roam sub-Saharan Africa, and water-loving hippos live near the great lakes of this large continent.

Africa, where humankind is believed to have begun millions of years ago, is second only to Asia in size. The 53 independent countries of Africa are home to a wide variety of cultures and traditions. In many areas, traditional tribal life is still very common, such as with the Maasai people (shown above).

Africa also has a wealth of languages—some 1,600—more than any other continent. The first great civilization in Africa arose 6,000 years ago on the banks of the lower Nile. Today, though still largely rural, Africans increasingly migrate to booming cities like Cairo, Egypt; Lagos, Nigeria; and Johannesburg, South Africa.

While rich in natural resources, from oil to coal to gemstones and precious metals, Africa is the poorest continent, long plagued by outside interference, corruption, and disease.

MORE THAN 12,000 SQUARE MILES — SURFACE AREA OF THE CENTRAL AFRICAN FRESHWATER LAKE, LAKE TANGANYIKA

3,475,000 SQUARE MILES — AREA OF THE SAHARA, LARGEST HOT DESERT ON EARTH

14.2 — PERCENT OF THE WORLD'S POPULATION THAT LIVES IN AFRICA

A LION'S BIG, DARK MANE INTIMIDATES OTHER MALES ● FEMALES HUNT

7 COOL THINGS ABOUT AFRICA

1. Africa could hold the land occupied by China, Europe, and the United States—with room to spare!

2. The Great Pyramid of Khufu in Egypt stood as the world's tallest man-made structure for more than 4,400 years.

3. South Africa is the largest gold-producing country in the world.

4. The venomous gaboon viper of Central Africa can have fangs that are more than two inches long, the longest of any snake.

5. Africa has more countries than any other continent.

6. All humans today are descended from people who lived in Africa tens of thousands of years ago.

7. Africa is almost an island. Its only connection to other land is the tiny Sinai Peninsula in Egypt.

GLITTERING WEALTH

Botswana	Democratic Republic of the Congo	South Africa	Angola	Namibia	Zimbabwe	Ghana
34.3	29.0	15.2	9.2	2.4	1.0	0.97

Millions of carats, 2006 data

Diamonds are prized both for jewelry and for industrial uses. More than half of the world's diamond production comes from mines in Africa.

MORE THAN MALES. CUBS DEPEND ON ADULTS FOR FOOD FOR 6 MONTHS

155

ANTARC

PHYSICAL

Land area
5,100,000 sq mi
(13,209,000 sq km)

Highest point
Vinson Massif
16,067 ft (4,897 m)

Lowest point
Bentley Subglacial
Trench
-8,383 ft (-2,555 m)

Coldest place
Plateau Station, annual
average temperature
−70°F (-56.7°C)

**Average precipitation
on the polar plateau**
Less than 2 in (5 cm)
per year

POLITICAL

Population
There are no indig-
enous inhabitants,
but there are both
permanent and
summer-only staffed
research stations.

**Number of
independent countries**
0

**Number of countries
claiming land**
7

**Number of countries
operating year-round
research stations**
19

**Number of year-round
research stations**
45

I t may be an interesting place to see, but unless you're a penguin, you probably wouldn't want to hang out in Antarctica for long. The fact that it's the coldest, windiest, and driest continent helps explain why humans never colonized this ice-covered land surrounding the South Pole.

No country actually owns Antarctica. Dozens of countries work together to study and care for its barren landscape. Photographers and tourists visit. Scientists live there temporarily to study such things as weather, environment, and wildlife.

Visitors can observe several species of penguins that breed in Antarctica, including the Adélie penguin (right). Antarctica's shores also serve as breeding grounds for six kinds of seals. And the surrounding waters provide food for whales.

People and animals share Antarctica. But there are still places on this vast, icy continent where you could be the first person to set foot.

2 PERCENT — AMOUNT OF ANTARCTICA THAT IS ICE-FREE

3 MILES — DEPTH OF THICKEST ICE COVERING THE CONTINENT

OVER 25,000 — AVERAGE NUMBER OF TOURISTS WHO VISIT ANTARCTICA ANNUALLY

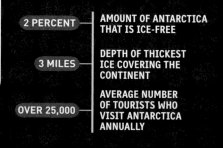

ADÉLIE PENGUINS MAY WALK 30 MILES TO THE SEA • ADÉLIES BUILD

TICA

7 COOL THINGS ABOUT ANTARCTICA

1. Summer in Antarctica is essentially one long day, and winter is one long night.

2. For nine months of the year intense cold makes it too dangerous for planes to fly.

3. All water at the South Pole is melted ice, some of the purest and coldest water on Earth.

4. The largest land animal in Antarctica is a wingless insect (penguins are marine animals).

5. Roald Amundsen and his team were the first people to reach the South Pole, in 1911.

6. Antarctica is often called the "white continent" because it's ice covered.

7. The continent was discovered in 1820 by a Russian expedition, but it took nearly 100 years before scientific exploration took off.

ESTS OF PEBBLES ● THE RECORD DIVE FOR AN ADÉLIE IS 574 FEET

ASIA

The Taj Mahal,
a domed mausoleum
in Agra, India

PHYSICAL

Land area
17,208,000 sq mi
(44,570,000 sq km)

Highest point
Mount Everest,
China-Nepal
29,035 ft (8,850 m)

Lowest point
Dead Sea, Israel-
Jordan
-1,380 ft (-421 m)

Longest river
Yangtze (Chang), China
3,964 mi (6,380 km)

**Largest lake entirely
in Asia**
Lake Baikal
12,200 sq mi
(31,500 sq km)

POLITICAL

Population
4,052,332,000

**Largest metropolitan
area**
Tokyo, Japan
Pop. 35,676,000

**Largest country
entirely in Asia**
China 3,705,405 sq mi
(9,596,960 sq km)

**Most densely
populated country**
Singapore
18,784 people
per sq mi
(7,258 per sq km)

Economy
Farming: rice, wheat
Industry: petroleum,
   electronics
Services

ABOUT 4,000 TO 7,000 SNOW LEOPARDS LIVE IN THE WILD • THEIR

7 COOL THINGS ABOUT ASIA

1. Asia is home to many endangered species, including the giant panda, the Sumatran rhino, and the orangutan.

2. Dragons are considered good luck in China.

3. The Hanging Gardens of Babylon, one of the Seven Wonders of the Ancient World (see p. 212), were thought to have originated around 600 B.C. in what is now Iraq.

4. Popular pizza toppings in Japan include seaweed and octopus.

5. Nepal's flag is the only national flag in the world that is not rectangular in shape.

6. Jerusalem, in Israel, has holy sites related to Islam, Christianity, and Judaism.

7. Tae kwon do originated about 2,000 years ago in Korea, which is now North and South Korea.

From Turkey to the eastern tip of Russia, Asia sprawls across nearly 180 degrees of longitude—almost half the globe! It boasts the highest (Mount Everest) and the lowest (the Dead Sea) places on Earth's surface.

Then there are Asia's people—over four billion of them. Three out of five people on the planet are found here—that's more than live on all the other continents put together. Asia has both the most farmers and the most million-plus cities.

The world's first civilization arose in Sumer, in what is now Iraq. Rich cultures also emerged along rivers in present-day India and China, strongly influencing the world ever since.

Asia is also home to a large number of different religions. And while religion plays a role in almost every culture, it is especially true of Buddhism in Tibet. Surrounded by the Himalaya mountains, Tibetan Buddhists practice peace, patience, and respect for all life. They even respect the mysterious snow leopards (above) who often attack their cattle.

Technology meets tradition as this woman takes a cell phone picture.

ONE-THIRD	PORTION OF THE WORLD'S POPULATION THAT LIVES IN CHINA AND INDIA
1,500	NUMBER OF SPECIES OF PLANTS AND ANIMALS WHO LIVE IN LAKE BAIKAL IN RUSSIA
8.6	PERCENT OF EARTH'S TOTAL SURFACE AREA THAT ASIA COVERS

OATS ARE SO THICK IN WINTER THAT THEIR EARS ARE BARELY VISIBLE

AUSTRA
NEW ZEALAND, AND

PHYSICAL

Land area
3,278,000 sq mi
(8,490,000 sq km)

Highest point
Mount Wilhelm,
Papua New Guinea
14,793 ft (4,509 m)

Lowest point
Lake Eyre, Australia
-52 ft (-16 m)

Longest river
Murray-Darling,
Australia 2,310 mi
(3,718 km)

Largest lake
Lake Eyre, Australia
3,430 sq mi
(8,884 sq km)

POLITICAL

Population
35,157,000

Largest metropolitan area
Sydney, Australia
Pop. 4,327,000

Largest country
Australia
2,969,907 sq mi
(7,692,024 sq km)

Most densely populated country
Nauru
1,250 people per sq mi
(476 per sq km)

Economy
Farming: livestock,
   wheat, fruit
Industry: mining, wool,
   oil
Services

This vast region includes Australia—the world's smallest and flattest continent—New Zealand, and a fleet of mostly tiny islands scattered across the Pacific Ocean. Apart from Australia, New Zealand, and Papua New Guinea, Oceania's other 11 independent countries cover about 25,000 square miles (65,000 sq km), an area only slightly larger than half of new Zealand's North Island. Twenty-one other island groups are dependencies of the United States, France, Australia, New Zealand, or the United Kingdom. Long isolation has allowed the growth of diverse marine communities such as Australia's Great Barrier Reef and the evolution of platypuses, kangaroos, and other land animals that live nowhere else on the planet.

"Aussies," as Australians like to call themselves, nicknamed their continent "the land down under." That's because the entire continent lies south of, or "under" the Equator. Most Australians live in cities along the coast. But Australia also has huge cattle and sheep ranches. Many ranch children live far from school. They get their lessons by mail or from the Internet or the radio. Their doctors even visit by airplane!

Aerial view, Bay of Islands, North Island, New Zealand

RED KANGAROOS ARE THE LARGEST POUCHED MAMMALS ★ THEIR JOEYS AR

LIA,
OCEANIA,

7 COOL THINGS ABOUT AUSTRALIA, NEW ZEALAND, & OCEANIA

1. The entire continent of Australia is approximately the same size as the United States (excluding Alaska and Hawai'i).

2. A kiwi is not just a fruit, it's a bird native to New Zealand and a slang term for a New Zealander.

3. Tonga, a country in the South Pacific, has 170 islands, but only 36 are inhabited.

4. Sheep outnumber people in Australia and New Zealand.

5. The vast interior of Australia, called the outback, consists mainly of desert plains.

6. The Great Barrier Reef, off the coast of Australia, is the longest reef system in the world.

7. The ceilings of grottoes in New Zealand's Waitomo Caves look like starry night skies due to the light given off by thousands of glowworms.

50,000 TO 60,000 YEARS OLD	AGE OF THE FIRST ABORIGINAL CULTURES IN AUSTRALIA
54	SPECIES OF KANGAROOS
MORE THAN 20,000 MILES	LENGTH OF AUSTRALIAN COASTLINE

ORN AN INCH LONG • A RED KANGAROO CAN LEAP 30 FEET IN ONE HOP

EUROPE

PHYSICAL

Land area
3,841,000 sq mi
(9,947,000 sq km)

Highest point
El'brus, Russia
18,510 ft (5,642 m)

Lowest point
Caspian Sea
-92 ft (-28 m)

Longest river
Volga, Russia
2,290 mi
(3,685 km)

Largest lake entirely in Europe
Ladoga, Russia
6,835 sq mi
(17,703 sq km)

POLITICAL

Population
735,427,000

Largest metropolitan area
Moscow, Russia
Pop. 10,452,000

Largest country entirely in Europe
Ukraine
233,090 sq mi
(603,700 sq km)

Most densely populated country
Monaco
42,500 people per sq mi (17,000 per sq km)

Economy
Farming: vegetables, fruit, grains
Industry: chemicals, machinery
Services

Eiffel Tower in Paris, France

A cluster of islands and peninsulas jutting west from Asia, Europe is bordered by the Atlantic and Arctic Oceans and more than a dozen seas, which are linked to inland areas by canals and navigable rivers such as the Rhine and the Danube. The continent boasts a bounty of landscapes. Sweeping west from the Ural Mountains in Russia and Kazakhstan is the fertile Northern European Plain. Rugged uplands form part of the western coast. The Alps shield Mediterranean lands from frigid northern winds.

Geographically small, Europe is home to more than 700 million people representing a shifting mosaic of cultures, languages, and borders. There is great ethnic diversity, which includes many groups of people indigenous to the land. One such native group is the Sami (shown below), who have lived for centuries in Norway, Sweden, Finland, and a small corner of Russia as roaming reindeer herders.

It is in Europe that first Greek and then Roman civilizations laid the world's cultural foundation. Europe's colonial powers built vast empires, while its inventors and thinkers revolutionized world industry, economy, and politics.

The challenge facing Europe in the 21st century is to create peace and prosperity—built on freedom and diversity—that embraces all its countries.

EUROPE'S GREAT RIVERS

Volga	3,685 km (2,290 mi)
Danube	2,888 km (1,795 mi)
Dnieper	2,290 km (1,423 mi)
Rhine	1,320 km (820 mi)
Elbe	1,091 km (678 mi)
Vistula	1,047 km (651 mi)
Tagus	1,038 km (645 mi)
Loire	1,012 km (629 mi)
Rhône	800 km (497 mi)
Po	652 km (405 mi)

Europe's rivers, many linked by canals, form a transportation network that connects its people and places to each other and the world beyond.

7 COOL THINGS ABOUT EUROPE

1. Made up of 46 countries, Europe is the second-smallest continent.

2. The first circus was held in Rome, Italy.

3. More chocolate is consumed in Switzerland than anywhere else in the world—22 pounds of chocolate per person per year.

4. The first subway in the world opened in 1863 in London, England, in the United Kingdom.

5. France produces more than 360 kinds of cheese.

6. The first jet plane was flown in Germany.

7. About 85 percent of homes in Iceland are warmed using underground heat from geothermal hot springs.

143,200 SQUARE MILES — AREA OF THE CASPIAN SEA, LARGEST LAKE ON EARTH

5,354 FEET — DEPTH OF THE DEEPEST CAVE IN EUROPE, AUSTRIA'S LAMPRECHTSOFEN-VOGELSCHACHT

798 — PEOPLE LIVING IN VATICAN CITY, SMALLEST COUNTRY IN THE WORLD

Neuschwanstein castle in Bavaria, Germany

,000 MILES A YEAR • REPORTS OF "FLYING REINDEER" DATE TO A.D. 1052

NORTH AMERICA

PHYSICAL

Land area
9,449,000 sq mi
(24,474,000 sq km)

Highest point
Mount McKinley
(Denali), Alaska
20,320 ft (6,194 m)

Lowest point
Death Valley,
California
-282 ft (-86 m)

Longest river
Mississippi-Missouri,
United States
3,710 mi (5,971 km)

Largest lake
Lake Superior, U.S.-
Canada; 31,700 sq mi
(82,100 sq km)

POLITICAL

Population
528,547,000

**Largest metropolitan
area**
New York, United
States
Pop. 19,040,000

Largest country
Canada
3,855,101 sq mi
(9,984,670 sq km)

**Most densely
populated country**
Barbados
1,687 people per sq
mi (651 per sq km)

Economy
Farming: cattle,
grains, cotton,
sugar
Industry: machinery,
metals, mining
Services

From the Great Plains of the United States and Canada to the rain forest of Panama, the third-largest continent stretches 5,500 miles (8,850 km), spanning natural environments that support wildlife from polar bears to jaguars.

North America can be chiefly divided into four large regions: the Great Plains, the mountainous west, the Canadian Shield of the northeast, and the eastern region.

Before Columbus even "discovered" the New World, it was a land of abundance for its inhabitants. Cooler, less seasonal, and more thickly forested than today, it contained a wide variety of species. Living off the land, Native American groups spread across these varied landscapes. Although the rich mosaic of native cultures largely disappeared before the onslaught of European fortune hunters and land seekers, some native groups remain. One such group is the Inuit, like the girl shown below, who live in the far north of Canada, Greenland, and Alaska. The majority of North Americans are actually descendants of immigrants.

While abundant resources and fast-changing technology have brought prosperity to Canada and the United States, other North American countries wrestle with the most basic needs. Promise and problems abound across this contrasting realm of 23 countries and more than 528 million people.

2 BILLION YEARS	AGE OF THE GRAND CANYON'S OLDEST ROCKS
9 MILLION	APPROXIMATE NUMBER OF CANADIANS WHO SPEAK FRENCH
-87°F (-66°C)	COLDEST TEMPERATURE RECORDED IN NORTH AMERICA (IN GREENLAND)

MOST BABY BISON ARE BORN IN MAY • BISON STAND 5 TO 6.5 FEE

7 COOL THINGS ABOUT NORTH AMERICA

1. Mexico is the most populous Spanish-speaking country in the world.

2. Greenland is the largest island in the world (excluding Australia).

3. The beaver is a national symbol of Canada.

4. The United States grows nearly all of the world's popcorn.

5. About 35 species of sharks live off the coast of Cuba.

6. The movie *Pirates of the Caribbean: The Curse of the Black Pearl* was actually filmed in the Caribbean.

7. An Aztec emperor in what is now Mexico introduced hot chocolate to Europeans.

Bison on the American Prairie

Mexico City, Mexico

LL AT THE SHOULDER • THEY ARE THE SYMBOL OF THE GREAT PLAINS

SOUTH AMERICA

PHYSICAL

Land area
6,880,000 sq mi
(17,819,000 sq km)

Highest point
Cerro Aconcagua,
Argentina
22,834 ft (6,960 m)

Lowest point
Laguna del Carbón,
Argentina
-344 ft (-105 m)

Longest river
Amazon
4,000 mi (6,437 km)

Largest lake
Lake Titicaca, Bolivia-
Peru; 3,200 sq mi
(8,290 sq km)

POLITICAL

Population
386,815,000

**Largest metropolitan
area**
São Paulo, Brazil
Pop. 18,845,000

Largest country
Brazil
3,300,171 sq mi
(8,547,403 sq km)

**Most densely
populated country**
Ecuador
126 people per sq mi
(49 per sq km)

Economy
Farming: cattle,
    coffee, fruit
Industry: mining, oil,
    manufacturing
Services

A jaguar in
a South American
rain forest

3	SOUTH AMERICAN COUNTRIES THE EQUATOR RUNS THROUGH (ECUADOR, COLOMBIA, AND BRAZIL)
3,212 FEET	DROP OF VENEZUELA'S ANGEL FALLS, THE WORLD'S TALLEST WATERFALL
2 MILLION SQUARE MILES	SIZE OF THE AMAZON RAIN FOREST

MOST JAGUARS LIVE IN THE AMAZON RAIN FOREST • A FEW HAVE BEE

South America stretches from the warm waters of the Caribbean to the frigid ocean around Antarctica. Draining a third of the continent, the mighty Amazon carries more water than the world's next ten biggest rivers combined. Its basin contains the planet's largest rain forest. The Andes tower along the continent's western edge from Colombia to southern Chile.

The Amerindian peoples who lived in the Andes were no match for the gold-seeking Spanish who arrived in 1532. They, along with the Portuguese, ruled most of the continent for almost 300 years. As in North America, the conquest of South America by Europeans took a heavy toll on its indigenous peoples.

Luckily, many remnants of early South American cultures remain. One such artifact of the old world is Machu Picchu (below), Peru, a mountaintop royal city built by an Incan ruler between 1460 and 1470. Centuries of ethnic blending have woven Amerindian, European, African, and Asian heritage into South America's rich cultural fabric.

Despite its relatively small population and wealth of natural resources, South America today is burdened by economic, social, and environmental problems. But with the majestic Andean mountain chain, the mighty Amazon River, and the most extensive rain forest on Earth, South America has nearly unlimited potential.

Soccer is one of the most popular sports in South America.

Machu Picchu in Peru

7 COOL THINGS ABOUT SOUTH AMERICA

1. One-fifth of the world's birds come from the Amazon rain forest—over 1,200 different species.

2. Marine iguanas are found only in Ecuador's Galápagos Islands.

3. The world's largest soccer stadium, which seats 200,000 people, is in Rio de Janeiro, in Brazil.

4. Pink dolphins live in the Amazon River.

5. The Andes make up the world's longest mountain range above sea level.

6. The guinea pig was first domesticated in South America.

7. Many of the most important dinosaur fossils were found in South America.

COUNTRIES OF THE WORLD

The following pages present a general overview of all 194 independent countries recognized by the National Geographic Society, including the youngest nation, Kosovo, which gained independence in 2008.

Flags of each independent country symbolize diverse cultures and histories. The statistical data provide highlights of geography and demography. They are a brief overview of each country; they present general characteristics and are not intended to be comprehensive. For example, not every language spoken in a specific country can be listed. Thus, languages shown are the most representative of that area. This is also true of the religions mentioned.

A country is defined as a political body with its own independent government, geographical space, and, in most cases, laws, military, and taxes.

Disputed areas like Northern Cyprus and Taiwan, and dependencies like Bermuda, Greenland, and Puerto Rico, which belong to independent nations, are not included in this listing.

Note the color key at the bottom of the pages, which assigns a color to each country based on the continent in which it is located.

Afghanistan

Area: 251,773 sq mi (652,090 sq km)
Population: 32,738,000
Capital: Kabul, pop. 3,324,000
Currency: afghani
Religions: Sunni Muslim, Shiite Muslim
Languages: Afghan Persian (Dari), Pashtu, Turkic languages (primarily Uzbek and Turkmen), Baluchi, 30 minor languages (including Pashai)

Andorra

Area: 181 sq mi (468 sq km)
Population: 85,000
Capital: Andorra la Vella, pop. 24,000
Currency: euro
Religion: Roman Catholic
Languages: Catalan, French, Castilian, Portuguese

Albania

Area: 11,100 sq mi (28,748 sq km)
Population: 3,241,000
Capital: Tirana, pop. 406,000
Currency: lek; note: the plural of *lek* is *leke*
Religions: Muslim, Albanian Orthodox, Roman Catholic
Languages: Albanian, Greek, Vlach, Romani, Slavic dialects

Angola

Area: 481,354 sq mi (1,246,700 sq km)
Population: 16,752,000
Capital: Luanda, pop. 4,007,000
Currency: kwanza
Religions: indigenous beliefs, Roman Catholic, Protestant
Languages: Portuguese, Bantu, and other African languages

Algeria

Area: 919,595 sq mi (2,381,741 sq km)
Population: 34,694,000
Capital: Algiers, pop. 3,355,000
Currency: Algerian dinar
Religion: Sunni Muslim
Languages: Arabic, French, Berber dialects

Antigua and Barbuda

Area: 171 sq mi (442 sq km)
Population: 86,000
Capital: St. John's, pop. 26,000
Currency: East Caribbean dollar
Religions: Anglican, Seventh-day Adventist, Pentecostal, Moravian, Roman Catholic, Methodist, Baptist, Church of God, other Christian
Languages: English, local dialects

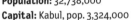

Argentina

Area: 1,073,518 sq mi
(2,780,400 sq km)
Population: 39,746,000
Capital: Buenos Aires, pop. 12,795,000
Currency: Argentine peso
Religion: Roman Catholic
Languages: Spanish, English, Italian, German, French

Armenia

Area: 11,484 sq mi
(29,743 sq km)
Population: 3,084,000
Capital: Yerevan, pop. 1,102,000
Currency: dram
Religions: Armenian Apostolic, other Christian
Language: Armenian

Australia

Area: 2,969,906 sq mi
(7,692,024 sq km)
Population: 21,347,000
Capital: Canberra, pop. 378,000
Currency: Australian dollar
Religions: Roman Catholic, Anglican
Language: English

Austria

Area: 32,378 sq mi (83,858 sq km)
Population: 8,352,000
Capital: Vienna, pop. 2,315,000
Currency: euro
Religions: Roman Catholic, Protestant, Muslim
Language: German

Azerbaijan

Area: 33,436 sq mi
(86,600 sq km)
Population: 8,679,000
Capital: Baku, pop. 1,892,000
Currency: Azerbaijani manat
Religion: Muslim
Language: Azerbaijani (Azeri)

Bahamas

Area: 5,382 sq mi (13,939 sq km)
Population: 337,000
Capital: Nassau, pop. 240,000
Currency: Bahamian dollar
Religions: Baptist, Anglican, Roman Catholic, Pentecostal, Church of God
Languages: English, Creole

Bahrain

Area: 277 sq mi (717 sq km)
Population: 780,000
Capital: Manama, pop. 157,000
Currency: Bahraini dinar
Religions: Shiite Muslim, Sunni Muslim, Christian
Languages: Arabic, English, Farsi, Urdu

Bangladesh

Area: 56,977 sq mi (147,570 sq km)
Population: 147,285,000
Capital: Dhaka, pop. 13,485,000
Currency: taka
Religions: Muslim, Hindu
Languages: Bangla (Bengali), English

Barbados

Area: 166 sq mi (430 sq km)
Population: 280,000
Capital: Bridgetown, pop. 116,000
Currency: Barbadian dollar
Religions: Anglican, Pentecostal, Methodist, other Protestant, Roman Catholic
Language: English

Belarus

Area: 80,153 sq mi
(207,595 sq km)
Population: 9,678,000
Capital: Minsk, pop. 1,806,000
Currency: Belarusian ruble
Religions: Eastern Orthodox, other (includes Roman Catholic, Protestant, Jewish, Muslim)
Languages: Belarusian, Russian

Belgium

Area: 11,787 sq mi (30,528 sq km)
Population: 10,695,000
Capital: Brussels, pop. 1,743,000
Currency: euro
Religions: Roman Catholic, other (includes Protestant)
Languages: Dutch, French

Bosnia and Herzegovina

Area: 19,741 sq mi (51,129 sq km)
Population: 3,843,000
Capital: Sarajevo, pop. 377,000
Currency: konvertibilna marka (convertible mark)
Religions: Muslim, Orthodox, Roman Catholic
Languages: Bosnian, Croatian, Serbian

Belize

Area: 8,867 sq mi (22,965 sq km)
Population: 318,000
Capital: Belmopan, pop. 16,000
Currency: Belizean dollar
Religions: Roman Catholic, Protestant (includes Pentecostal, Seventh-day Adventist, Mennonite, Methodist)
Languages: Spanish, Creole, Mayan dialects, English, Garifuna (Carib), German

Botswana

Area: 224,607 sq mi (581,730 sq km)
Population: 1,842,000
Capital: Gaborone, pop. 224,000
Currency: pula
Religions: Christian, Badimo
Languages: Setswana, Kalanga

Benin

Area: 43,484 sq mi (112,622 sq km)
Population: 9,309,000
Capitals: Porto-Novo, pop. 257,000; Cotonou, pop. 762,000
Currency: Communauté Financière Africaine franc
Religions: Christian, Muslim, Vodoun
Languages: French, Fon, Yoruba, tribal languages

Brazil

Area: 3,300,171 sq mi (8,547,403 sq km)
Population: 195,138,000
Capital: Brasília, pop. 3,594,000
Currency: real
Religions: Roman Catholic, Protestant
Language: Portuguese

Bhutan

Area: 17,954 sq mi (46,500 sq km)
Population: 671,000
Capital: Thimphu, pop. 83,000
Currencies: ngultrum; Indian rupee
Religions: Lamaistic Buddhist, Indian- and Nepalese-influenced Hindu
Languages: Dzongkha, Tibetan dialects, Nepalese dialects

Brunei

Area: 2,226 sq mi (5,765 sq km)
Population: 379,000
Capital: Bandar Seri Begawan, pop. 22,000
Currency: Bruneian dollar
Religions: Muslim, Buddhist, Christian, other (includes indigenous beliefs)
Languages: Malay, English, Chinese

Bolivia

Area: 424,164 sq mi (1,098,581 sq km)
Population: 10,028,000
Capitals: La Paz, pop. 1,590,000; Sucre, pop. 243,000
Currency: boliviano
Religions: Roman Catholic, Protestant (includes Evangelical Methodist)
Languages: Spanish, Quechua, Aymara

Bulgaria

Area: 42,855 sq mi (110,994 sq km)
Population: 7,621,000
Capital: Sofia, pop. 1,186,000
Currency: lev
Religions: Bulgarian Orthodox, Muslim
Languages: Bulgarian, Turkish, Roma

COLOR KEY ● Africa ● Australia, New Zealand, & Oceania

Burkina Faso

Area: 105,869 sq mi (274,200 sq km)
Population: 15,213,000
Capital: Ouagadougou, pop. 1,148,000
Currency: Communauté Financière Africaine franc
Religions: Muslim, indigenous beliefs, Christian
Languages: French, native African languages

Cameroon

Area: 183,569 sq mi (475,442 sq km)
Population: 18,468,000
Capital: Yaoundé, pop. 1,610,000
Currency: Communauté Financière Africaine franc
Religions: indigenous beliefs, Christian, Muslim
Languages: 24 major African language groups, English, French

Burundi

Area: 10,747 sq mi (27,834 sq km)
Population: 8,856,000
Capital: Bujumbura, pop. 430,000
Currency: Burundi franc
Religions: Roman Catholic, indigenous beliefs, Muslim, Protestant
Languages: Kirundi, French, Swahili

Canada

Area: 3,855,101 sq mi (9,984,670 sq km)
Population: 33,304,000
Capital: Ottawa, pop. 1,143,000
Currency: Canadian dollar
Religions: Roman Catholic, Protestant (includes United Church, Anglican), other Christian
Languages: English, French

Cambodia

Area: 69,898 sq mi (181,035 sq km)
Population: 14,656,000
Capital: Phnom Penh, pop. 1,465,000
Currency: riel
Religion: Theravada Buddhist
Language: Khmer

Cape Verde

Area: 1,558 sq mi (4,036 sq km)
Population: 503,000
Capital: Praia, pop. 125,000
Currency: Cape Verdean escudo
Religions: Roman Catholic (infused with indigenous beliefs), Protestant (mostly Church of the Nazarene)
Languages: Portuguese, Crioulo

MOST POPULOUS COUNTRIES
(mid-2008 data)

1. China 1,355,251,000
2. India 1,149,285,000
3. United States . . 304,486,000
4. Indonesia 239,945,000
5. Brazil 195,138,000
6. Pakistan 172,800,000
7. Nigeria 148,071,000
8. Bangladesh 147,285,000

MOST CROWDED COUNTRIES
Population Density
(people per sq mi/sq km; mid-2008 data)

1. Monaco 42,500/17,000
2. Singapore 18,784/7,258
3. Vatican City . . .3,990/1,995
4. Malta 3,377/1,304
5. Bahrain 2,816/1,088
6. Maldives 2,696/1,040
7. Bangladesh 2,585/998
8. Barbados 1,687/651

● Asia ● Europe ● North America ● South America

Central African Republic

Area: 240,535 sq mi (622,984 sq km)
Population: 4,435,000
Capital: Bangui, pop. 672,000
Currency: Communauté Financière Africaine franc
Religions: indigenous beliefs, Protestant, Roman Catholic, Muslim
Languages: French, Sangho, tribal languages

Comoros

Area: 719 sq mi (1,862 sq km)
Population: 732,000
Capital: Moroni, pop. 46,000
Currency: Comoran franc
Religion: Sunni Muslim
Languages: Arabic, French, Shikomoro

Chad

Area: 495,755 sq mi (1,284,000 sq km)
Population: 10,111,000
Capital: N'Djamena, pop. 987,000
Currency: Communauté Financière Africaine franc
Religions: Muslim, Catholic, Protestant, animist
Languages: French, Arabic, Sara, over 120 languages and dialects

Congo

Area: 132,047 sq mi (342,000 sq km)
Population: 3,847,000
Capital: Brazzaville, pop. 1,332,000
Currency: Communauté Financière Africaine franc
Religions: Christian, animist
Languages: French, Lingala, Monokutuba, local languages

Chile

Area: 291,930 sq mi (756,096 sq km)
Population: 16,770,000
Capital: Santiago, pop. 5,719,000
Currency: Chilean peso
Religions: Roman Catholic, Evangelical
Language: Spanish

Costa Rica

Area: 19,730 sq mi (51,100 sq km)
Population: 4,519,000
Capital: San José, pop. 1,284,000
Currency: Costa Rican colon
Religions: Roman Catholic, Evangelical
Languages: Spanish, English

China

Area: 3,705,405 sq mi (9,596,960 sq km)
Population: 1,355,251,000
Capital: Beijing, pop. 11,106,000
Currency: renminbi (yuan)
Religions: Taoist, Buddhist, Christian
Languages: Standard Chinese or Mandarin, Yue, Wu, Minbei, Minnan, Xiang, Gan, Hakka dialects

Côte d'Ivoire (Ivory Coast)

Area: 124,503 sq mi (322,462 sq km)
Population: 20,677,000
Capitals: Abidjan, pop. 3,801,000; Yamoussoukro, pop. 669,000
Currency: Communauté Financière Africaine franc
Religions: Muslim, indigenous beliefs, Christian
Languages: French, Dioula, other native dialects

Colombia

Area: 440,831 sq mi (1,141,748 sq km)
Population: 44,447,000
Capital: Bogotá, pop. 7,764,000
Currency: Colombian peso
Religion: Roman Catholic
Language: Spanish

Croatia

Area: 21,831 sq mi (56,542 sq km)
Population: 4,433,000
Capital: Zagreb, pop. 689,000
Currency: kuna
Religions: Roman Catholic, Orthodox
Language: Croatian

COLOR KEY   ● Africa   ● Australia, New Zealand, & Oceania

Cuba

Area: 42,803 sq mi
(110,860 sq km)
Population: 11,233,000
Capital: Havana, pop. 2,178,000
Currency: Cuban peso
Religions: Roman Catholic, Protestant, Jehovah's Witness, Jewish, Santeria
Language: Spanish

Cyprus

Area: 3,572 sq mi (9,251 sq km)
Population: 1,060,000
Capital: Nicosia, pop. 233,000
Currencies: euro; new Turkish lira in Northern Cyprus
Religions: Greek Orthodox, Muslim, Maronite, Armenian Apostolic
Languages: Greek, Turkish, English

Czech Republic (Czechia)

Area: 30,450 sq mi (78,866 sq km)
Population: 10,428,000
Capital: Prague, pop. 1,162,000
Currency: Czech koruna
Religion: Roman Catholic
Language: Czech

Democratic Republic of the Congo

Area: 905,365 sq mi
(2,344,885 sq km)
Population: 66,515,000
Capital: Kinshasa, pop. 7,851,000
Currency: Congolese franc
Religions: Roman Catholic, Protestant, Kimbanguist, Muslim, syncretic sects, indigenous beliefs
Languages: French, Lingala, Kingwana, Kikongo, Tshiluba

Denmark

Area: 16,640 sq mi (43,098 sq km)
Population: 5,490,000
Capital: Copenhagen, pop. 1,086,000
Currency: Danish krone
Religions: Evangelical Lutheran, other Protestant, Roman Catholic
Languages: Danish, Faroese, Greenlandic, German, English as second language

Djibouti

Area: 8,958 sq mi
(23,200 sq km)
Population: 848,000
Capital: Djibouti, pop. 583,000
Currency: Djiboutian franc
Religions: Muslim, Christian
Languages: French, Arabic, Somali, Afar

Dominica

Area: 290 sq mi (751 sq km)
Population: 73,000
Capital: Roseau, pop. 14,000
Currency: East Caribbean dollar
Religions: Roman Catholic, Seventh-day Adventist, Pentecostal, Baptist, Methodist, other Christian
Languages: English, French patois

Dominican Republic

Area: 18,704 sq mi
(48,442 sq km)
Population: 9,890,000
Capital: Santo Domingo, pop. 2,154,000
Currency: Dominican peso
Religion: Roman Catholic
Language: Spanish

Ecuador

Area: 109,483 sq mi
(283,560 sq km)
Population: 13,801,000
Capital: Quito, pop. 1,697,000
Currency: U.S. dollar
Religion: Roman Catholic
Languages: Spanish, Quechua, other Amerindian languages

COOL CLICK

For more country facts, visit the CIA World Factbook online.
https://www.cia.gov/library/publications/the-world-fact-book/index.html

Egypt

Area: 386,874 sq mi
(1,002,000 sq km)
Population: 74,946,000
Capital: Cairo, pop. 11,893,000
Currency: Egyptian pound
Religions: Muslim (mostly Sunni), Coptic Christian
Languages: Arabic, English, French

Ethiopia

Area: 437,600 sq mi
(1,133,380 sq km)
Population: 79,087,000
Capital: Addis Ababa,
pop. 3,102,000
Currency: birr
Religions: Christian, Muslim, traditional
Languages: Amharic, Oromigna, Tigrinya, Guaragigna

El Salvador

Area: 8,124 sq mi (21,041 sq km)
Population: 7,218,000
Capital: San Salvador,
pop. 1,433,000
Currency: U.S. dollar
Religions: Roman Catholic, Protestant
Languages: Spanish, Nahua

Fiji Islands

Area: 7,095 sq mi (18,376 sq km)
Population: 864,000
Capital: Suva, pop. 224,000
Currency: Fijian dollar
Religions: Christian (Methodist, Roman Catholic, Assembly of God), Hindu (Sanatan), Muslim (Sunni)
Languages: English, Fijian, Hindustani

Equatorial Guinea

Area: 10,831 sq mi (28,051 sq km)
Population: 617,000
Capital: Malabo, pop. 96,000
Currency: Communauté Financière Africaine franc
Religions: Christian (predominantly Roman Catholic), pagan practices
Languages: Spanish, French, Fang, Bubi

Finland

Area: 130,558 sq mi
(338,145 sq km)
Population: 5,312,000
Capital: Helsinki, pop. 1,115,000
Currency: euro
Religion: Lutheran Church of Finland
Languages: Finnish, Swedish

Eritrea

Area: 46,774 sq mi (121,144 sq km)
Population: 5,006,000
Capital: Asmara, pop. 600,000
Currency: nakfa
Religions: Muslim, Coptic Christian, Roman Catholic, Protestant
Languages: Afar, Arabic, Tigre, Kunama, Tigrinya, other Cushitic languages

France

Area: 210,026 sq mi
(543,965 sq km)
Population: 62,046,000
Capital: Paris, pop. 9,902,000
Currency: euro
Religions: Roman Catholic, Muslim
Language: French

Estonia

Area: 17,462 sq mi (45,227 sq km)
Population: 1,340,000
Capital: Tallinn, pop. 397,000
Currency: Estonian kroon
Religions: Evangelical Lutheran, Orthodox
Languages: Estonian, Russian

Gabon

Area: 103,347 sq mi (267,667 sq km)
Population: 1,350,000
Capital: Libreville, pop. 576,000
Currency: Communauté Financière Africaine franc
Religions: Christian, animist
Languages: French, Fang, Myene, Nzebi, Bapounou/Eschira, Bandjabi

Gambia

Area: 4,361 sq mi (11,295 sq km)
Population: 1,559,000
Capital: Banjul, pop. 407,000
Currency: dalasi
Religions: Muslim, Christian
Languages: English, Mandinka, Wolof, Fula, other indigenous vernaculars

Georgia

Area: 26,911 sq mi (69,700 sq km)
Population: 4,639,000
Capital: T'bilisi, pop. 1,099,000
Currency: lari
Religions: Orthodox Christian, Muslim, Armenian-Gregorian
Languages: Georgian, Russian, Armenian, Azeri, Abkhaz

Germany

Area: 137,847 sq mi (357,022 sq km)
Population: 82,170,000
Capital: Berlin, pop. 3,405,000
Currency: euro
Religions: Protestant, Roman Catholic, Muslim
Language: German

Ghana

Area: 92,100 sq mi (238,537 sq km)
Population: 23,947,000
Capital: Accra, pop. 2,120,000
Currency: Ghana cedi
Religions: Christian (Pentecostal/Charismatic, Protestant, Roman Catholic, other), Muslim, traditional beliefs
Languages: Asante, Ewe, Fante, Boron (Brong), Dagomba, Dangme, Dagarte (Dagaba), Akyem, Ga, English

Greece

Area: 50,949 sq mi (131,957 sq km)
Population: 11,242,000
Capital: Athens, pop. 3,242,000
Currency: euro
Religion: Greek Orthodox
Languages: Greek, English, French

Grenada

Area: 133 sq mi (344 sq km)
Population: 106,000
Capital: St. George's, pop. 32,000
Currency: East Caribbean dollar
Religions: Roman Catholic, Anglican, other Protestant
Languages: English, French patois

Guatemala

Area: 42,042 sq mi (108,889 sq km)
Population: 13,677,000
Capital: Guatemala City, pop. 1,025,000
Currency: quetzal
Religions: Roman Catholic, Protestant, indigenous Mayan beliefs
Languages: Spanish, 23 official Amerindian languages

5 cool things about GREECE

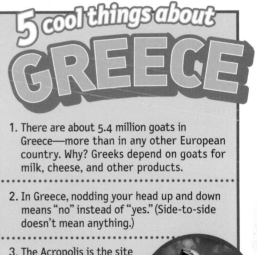

1. There are about 5.4 million goats in Greece—more than in any other European country. Why? Greeks depend on goats for milk, cheese, and other products.

2. In Greece, nodding your head up and down means "no" instead of "yes." (Side-to-side doesn't mean anything.)

3. The Acropolis is the site of several temples dedicated to the Greek goddess Athena, such as the nearly 2,500-year-old Parthenon (right).

4. If you were a Greek kid, your father's first name would be a part of your name—even if you are a girl!

5. Greece has over 2,000 islands. One of them, Mykonos, has a pelican named Petros as its official mascot.

Guinea

Area: 94,926 sq mi (245,857 sq km)
Population: 10,302,000
Capital: Conakry, pop. 1,494,000
Currency: Guinean franc
Religions: Muslim, Christian, indigenous beliefs
Languages: French, ethnic languages

Hungary

Area: 35,919 sq mi (93,030 sq km)
Population: 10,034,000
Capital: Budapest, pop. 1,675,000
Currency: forint
Religions: Roman Catholic, Calvinist, Lutheran
Language: Hungarian

Guinea-Bissau

Area: 13,948 sq mi (36,125 sq km)
Population: 1,746,000
Capital: Bissau, pop. 330,000
Currency: Communauté Financière Africaine franc
Religions: indigenous beliefs, Muslim, Christian
Languages: Portuguese, Crioulo, African languages

Iceland

Area: 39,769 sq mi (103,000 sq km)
Population: 319,000
Capital: Reykjavík, pop. 192,000
Currency: Icelandic krona
Religion: Lutheran Church of Iceland
Languages: Icelandic, English, Nordic languages, German

Guyana

Area: 83,000 sq mi (214,969 sq km)
Population: 773,000
Capital: Georgetown, pop. 133,000
Currency: Guyanese dollar
Religions: Christian, Hindu, Muslim
Languages: English, Amerindian dialects, Creole, Hindustani, Urdu

India

Area: 1,269,221 sq mi (3,287,270 sq km)
Population: 1,149,285,000
Capital: New Delhi, pop. 15,926,000 (part of Delhi metropolitan area)
Currency: Indian rupee
Religions: Hindu, Muslim
Languages: Hindi, 21 other official languages, Hindustani (popular Hindi/Urdu variant in the north)

Haiti

Area: 10,714 sq mi (27,750 sq km)
Population: 9,104,000
Capital: Port-au-Prince, pop. 2,002,000
Currency: gourde
Religions: Roman Catholic, Protestant (Baptist, Pentecostal, other)
Languages: French, Creole

Indonesia

Area: 742,308 sq mi (1,922,570 sq km)
Population: 239,945,000
Capital: Jakarta, pop. 9,143,000
Currency: Indonesian rupiah
Religions: Muslim, Protestant, Roman Catholic
Languages: Bahasa Indonesia (modified form of Malay), English, Dutch, Javanese, local dialects

Honduras

Area: 43,433 sq mi (112,492 sq km)
Population: 7,322,000
Capital: Tegucigalpa, pop. 947,000
Currency: lempira
Religions: Roman Catholic, Protestant
Languages: Spanish, Amerindian dialects

Iran

Area: 636,296 sq mi (1,648,000 sq km)
Population: 72,212,000
Capital: Tehran, pop. 7,875,000
Currency: Iranian rial
Religions: Shiite Muslim, Sunni Muslim
Languages: Persian, Turkic, Kurdish, Luri, Baluchi, Arabic

COLOR KEY   ● Africa ● Australia, New Zealand, & Oceania

Iraq

Area: 168,754 sq mi
(437,072 sq km)
Population: 29,492,000
Capital: Baghdad, pop. 5,500,000
Currency: Iraqi dinar
Religions: Shiite Muslim, Sunni Muslim
Languages: Arabic, Kurdish, Assyrian, Armenian

Italy

Area: 116,345 sq mi
(301,333 sq km)
Population: 59,865,000
Capital: Rome, pop. 3,340,000
Currency: euro
Religions: Roman Catholic, Protestant, Jewish, Muslim
Languages: Italian, German, French, Slovene

Ireland

Area: 27,133 sq mi
(70,273 sq km)
Population: 4,475,000
Capital: Dublin, pop. 1,060,000
Currency: euro
Religions: Roman Catholic, Church of Ireland
Languages: Irish (Gaelic), English

Jamaica

Area: 4,244 sq mi
(10,991 sq km)
Population: 2,692,000
Capital: Kingston, pop. 581,000
Currency: Jamaican dollar
Religions: Protestant (Church of God, Seventh-day Adventist, Pentecostal, Baptist, Anglican, other)
Languages: English, English patois

KISS ME, I'M IRISH!

The shamrock (a three-leaf clover) is the national plant of Ireland. • Ireland's nickname is the Emerald Isle because of its green landscape. • Ireland is slightly smaller than South Carolina. • Muckanaghederdauhaulia is the longest place-name in Ireland. • Green is Ireland's national color. • Legend has it that all leprechauns (fictional Irish elves) possess a hidden pot of gold. • Thousands of people kiss Ireland's famous Blarney Stone every year. It's said to bring the gift of eloquence. • About 34 million Irish Americans live in the United States.

Japan

Area: 145,902 sq mi (377,887 sq km)
Population: 127,720,000
Capital: Tokyo, pop. 35,676,000
Currency: yen
Religions: Shinto, Buddhist
Language: Japanese

5 cool things about JAPAN

1. The Japanese call their country *Nippon* or *Nihan,* which means "source of the sun."

2. Japan is made up of four large islands and thousands of smaller ones.

3. Streets in Japan are identified mostly by numbers instead of names.

4. Every year about 1,500 earthquakes occur in Japan.

5. Sumo is the national sport of Japan.

Israel

Area: 8,550 sq mi (22,145 sq km)
Population: 7,482,000
Capital: Jerusalem, pop. 736,000
Currency: new Israeli sheqel
Religions: Jewish, Muslim
Languages: Hebrew, Arabic, English

● Asia ● Europe ● North America ● South America

Jordan

Area: 34,495 sq mi (89,342 sq km)
Population: 5,849,000
Capital: Amman, pop. 1,064,000
Currency: Jordanian dinar
Religions: Sunni Muslim, Christian
Languages: Arabic, English

Kuwait

Area: 6,880 sq mi (17,818 sq km)
Population: 2,669,000
Capital: Kuwait City, pop. 2,061,000
Currency: Kuwaiti dinar
Religions: Sunni Muslim, Shiite Muslim
Languages: Arabic, English

Kazakhstan

Area: 1,049,155 sq mi (2,717,300 sq km)
Population: 15,651,000
Capital: Astana, pop. 594,000
Currency: tenge
Religions: Muslim, Russian Orthodox
Languages: Kazakh (Qazaq), Russian

Kyrgyzstan

Area: 77,182 sq mi (199,900 sq km)
Population: 5,242,000
Capital: Bishkek, pop. 837,000
Currency: som
Religions: Muslim, Russian Orthodox
Languages: Kyrgyz, Uzbek, Russian

Kenya

Area: 224,081 sq mi (580,367 sq km)
Population: 37,954,000
Capital: Nairobi, pop. 3,011,000
Currency: Kenyan shilling
Religions: Protestant, Roman Catholic, Muslim, indigenous beliefs
Languages: English, Kiswahili, many indigenous languages

Laos

Area: 91,429 sq mi (236,800 sq km)
Population: 5,850,000
Capital: Vientiane, pop. 746,000
Currency: kip
Religions: Buddhist, animist
Languages: Lao, French, English, various ethnic languages

Kiribati

Area: 313 sq mi (811 sq km)
Population: 98,000
Capital: Tarawa, pop. 42,000
Currency: Australian dollar
Religions: Roman Catholic, Protestant (Congregational)
Languages: I-Kiribati, English

Latvia

Area: 24,938 sq mi (64,589 sq km)
Population: 2,266,000
Capital: Riga, pop. 722,000
Currency: Latvian lat
Religions: Lutheran, Roman Catholic, Russian Orthodox
Languages: Latvian, Russian, Lithuanian

Kosovo

Area: 4,203 sq mi (10,887 sq km)
Population: 2,191,000
Capital: Pristina, pop. 600,000
Currencies: euro
Religions: Muslim, Serbian Orthodox, Roman Catholic
Languages: Albanian, Serbian, Bosnian, Turkish, Roma

Lebanon

Area: 4,036 sq mi (10,452 sq km)
Population: 3,981,000
Capital: Beirut, pop. 1,857,000
Currency: Lebanese pound
Religions: Muslim, Christian
Languages: Arabic, French, English, Armenian

COLOR KEY ● Africa ● Australia, New Zealand, & Oceania

Lesotho

Area: 11,720 sq mi (30,355 sq km)
Population: 1,801,000
Capital: Maseru, pop. 212,000
Currencies: loti; South African rand
Religions: Christian, indigenous beliefs
Languages: Sesotho, English, Zulu, Xhosa

Liberia

Area: 43,000 sq mi (111,370 sq km)
Population: 3,942,000
Capital: Monrovia, pop. 1,165,000
Currency: Liberian dollar
Religions: Christian, indigenous beliefs, Muslim
Languages: English, some 20 ethnic languages

Libya

Area: 679,362 sq mi (1,759,540 sq km)
Population: 6,283,000
Capital: Tripoli, pop. 2,189,000
Currency: Libyan dinar
Religion: Sunni Muslim
Languages: Arabic, Italian, English

Liechtenstein

Area: 62 sq mi (160 sq km)
Population: 36,000
Capital: Vaduz, pop. 5,000
Currency: Swiss franc
Religions: Roman Catholic, Protestant
Languages: German, Alemannic dialect

COOL CLICK

Want to see interactive maps and videos of the countries? Go online to National Geographic.
travel.nationalgeographic.com/places/countries/index.html

Lithuania

Area: 25,212 sq mi (65,300 sq km)
Population: 3,357,000
Capital: Vilnius, pop. 553,000
Currency: litas
Religions: Roman Catholic, Russian Orthodox
Languages: Lithuanian, Russian, Polish

Luxembourg

Area: 998 sq mi (2,586 sq km)
Population: 488,000
Capital: Luxembourg, pop. 84,000
Currency: euro
Religions: Roman Catholic, Protestant, Jewish, Muslim
Languages: Luxembourgish, German, French

Macedonia

Area: 9,928 sq mi (25,713 sq km)
Population: 2,049,000
Capital: Skopje, pop. 480,000
Currency: Macedonian denar
Religions: Macedonian Orthodox, Muslim
Languages: Macedonian, Albanian, Turkish

Madagascar

Area: 226,658 sq mi (587,041 sq km)
Population: 18,912,000
Capital: Antananarivo, pop. 1,697,000
Currency: Madagascar ariary
Religions: indigenous beliefs, Christian, Muslim
Languages: English, French, Malagasy

Malawi

Area: 45,747 sq mi (118,484 sq km)
Population: 13,630,000
Capital: Lilongwe, pop. 732,000
Currency: Malawian kwacha
Religions: Christian, Muslim
Languages: Chichewa, Chinyanja, Chiyao, Chitumbuka

Malaysia

Area: 127,355 sq mi (329,847 sq km)
Population: 27,711,000
Capital: Kuala Lumpur, pop. 1,448,000
Currency: ringgit
Religions: Muslim, Buddhist, Christian, Hindu
Languages: Bahasa Malaysia, English, Chinese, Tamil, Telugu, Malayalam, Panjabi, Thai, indigenous languages

Mali

Area: 478,841 sq mi (1,240,192 sq km)
Population: 12,716,000
Capital: Bamako, pop. 1,494,000
Currency: Communauté Financière Africaine franc
Religions: Muslim, indigenous beliefs
Languages: Bambara, French, numerous African languages

Maldives

Area: 115 sq mi (298 sq km)
Population: 310,000
Capital: Male, pop. 111,000
Currency: rufiyaa
Religion: Sunni Muslim
Languages: Maldivian Dhivehi, English

Malta

Area: 122 sq mi (316 sq km)
Population: 412,000
Capital: Valletta, pop. 199,000
Currency: euro
Religion: Roman Catholic
Languages: Maltese, English

Mali

How would your world be different if animals had magical powers? Just ask the Dogon (DOH-gahn) people of Mali, a country in West Africa. While many Dogon are Muslim or Christian, others follow a belief system called animism. These people believe that everything in nature has a spirit, including rocks, plants, animals, and even thunder. The Dogon go to great lengths to live in harmony with their animal neighbors.

Hanging Out

The Dogon still follow many of their ancestors' traditions. A few kids go to school, but more often girls learn to cook, boys tend livestock, and everyone helps farm the land. Many of their villages are built into the bases and on plateaus of rocky cliffs that tower more than 500 feet high.

Animal Dancers

In the Dama ritual ceremony (right), animals are said to help free the spirits of dead people. Men disguise themselves with masks and imitate the movements of the animals. For some Dogon people, showing respect for animals keeps the natural and spiritual worlds at peace.

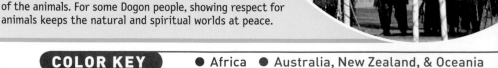

COLOR KEY ● Africa ● Australia, New Zealand, & Oceania

Marshall Islands

Area: 70 sq mi (181 sq km)
Population: 53,000
Capital: Majuro, pop. 28,000
Currency: U.S. dollar
Religions: Protestant, Assembly of God, Roman Catholic
Language: Marshallese

Mauritania

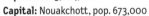

Area: 397,955 sq mi (1,030,700 sq km)
Population: 3,204,000
Capital: Nouakchott, pop. 673,000
Currency: ouguiya
Religion: Muslim
Languages: Arabic, Pulaar, Soninke, French, Hassaniya, Wolof

Mauritius

Area: 788 sq mi (2,040 sq km)
Population: 1,268,000
Capital: Port Louis, pop. 150,000
Currency: Mauritian rupee
Religions: Hindu, Roman Catholic, Muslim, other Christian
Languages: Creole, Bhojpuri, French

Mexico

Area: 758,449 sq mi (1,964,375 sq km)
Population: 107,677,000
Capital: Mexico City, pop. 19,028,000
Currency: Mexican peso
Religions: Roman Catholic, Protestant
Languages: Spanish, Mayan, Nahuatl, other indigenous

Micronesia

Area: 271 sq mi (702 sq km)
Population: 108,000
Capital: Palikir, pop. 7,000
Currency: U.S. dollar
Religions: Roman Catholic, Protestant
Languages: English, Trukese, Pohnpeian, Yapese, other indigenous languages

Moldova

Area: 13,050 sq mi (33,800 sq km)
Population: 4,136,000
Capital: Chisinau, pop. 592,000
Currency: Moldovan leu
Religion: Eastern Orthodox
Languages: Moldovan, Russian, Gagauz

Monaco

Area: 0.8 sq mi (2.0 sq km)
Population: 34,000
Capital: Monaco, pop. 34,000
Currency: euro
Religion: Roman Catholic
Languages: French, English, Italian, Monegasque

Mongolia

Area: 603,909 sq mi (1,564,116 sq km)
Population: 2,655,000
Capital: Ulaanbaatar, pop. 884,000
Currency: togrog/tugrik
Religions: Buddhist Lamaist, Shamanist, Christian
Languages: Khalkha Mongol, Turkic, Russian

Montenegro

Area: 5,415 sq mi (14,026 sq km)
Population: 627,000
Capital: Podgorica, pop. 142,000
Currency: euro
Religions: Orthodox, Muslim, Roman Catholic
Languages: Serbian (Ijekavian dialect), Bosnian, Albanian, Croatian

Morocco

Area: 274,461 sq mi (710,850 sq km)
Population: 31,177,000
Capital: Rabat, pop. 1,705,000
Currency: Moroccan dirham
Religion: Muslim
Languages: Arabic, Berber dialects, French

Mozambique

Area: 308,642 sq mi
(799,380 sq km)
Population: 20,387,000
Capital: Maputo, pop. 1,445,000
Currency: metical
Religions: Roman Catholic, Muslim, Zionist Christian
Languages: Emakhuwa, Xichangana, Portuguese,
Elomwe, Cisena, Echuwabo, other local languages

Myanmar (Burma)

Area: 261,218 sq mi (676,552 sq km)
Population: 49,221,000
Capitals: Nay Pyi Taw, pop. 200,000;
Yangon (Rangoon), pop. 4,088,000
Currency: kyat
Religions: Buddhist, Christian, Muslim
Languages: Burmese, minority ethnic languages

Namibia

Area: 318,261 sq mi
(824,292 sq km)
Population: 2,089,000
Capital: Windhoek, pop. 313,000
Currencies: Namibian dollar;
South African rand
Religions: Lutheran, other Christian, indigenous beliefs
Languages: Afrikaans, German, English

Nauru

Area: 8 sq mi (21 sq km)
Population: 10,000
Capital: Yaren NA
Currency: Australian dollar
Religions: Protestant, Roman Catholic
Languages: Nauruan, English

Nepal

Area: 56,827 sq mi
(147,181 sq km)
Population: 276,997,000
Capital: Kathmandu, pop. 895,000
Currency: Nepalese rupee
Religions: Hindu, Buddhist, Muslim, Kirant
Languages: Nepali, Maithali, Bhojpuri, Tharu, Tamang,
Newar, Magar

Netherlands

Area: 16,034 sq mi
(41,528 sq km)
Population: 16,433,000
Capital: Amsterdam, pop. 1,031,000
Currency: euro
Religions: Roman Catholic, Dutch Reformed,
Calvinist, Muslim
Languages: Dutch, Frisian

New Zealand

Area: 104,454 sq mi
(270,534 sq km)
Population: 4,272,000
Capital: Wellington, pop. 366,000
Currency: New Zealand dollar
Religions: Anglican, Roman Catholic, Presbyterian,
other Christian
Languages: English, Maori

Nicaragua

Area: 50,193 sq mi
(130,000 sq km)
Population: 5,669,000
Capital: Managua, pop. 920,000
Currency: gold cordoba
Religions: Roman Catholic, Evangelical
Language: Spanish

Niger

Area: 489,191 sq mi (1,267,000 sq km)
Population: 14,731,000
Capital: Niamey, pop. 915,000
Currency: Communauté
Financière Africaine franc
Religions: Muslim, other (includes indigenous beliefs
and Christian)
Languages: French, Hausa, Djerma

Nigeria

Area: 356,669 sq mi
(923,768 sq km)
Population: 148,071,000
Capital: Abuja, pop. 1,579,000
Currency: naira
Religions: Muslim, Christian, indigenous beliefs
Languages: English, Hausa, Yoruba, Igbo (Ibo), Fulani

North Korea

Area: 46,540 sq mi
(120,538 sq km)
Population: 23,479,000
Capital: Pyongyang, pop. 3,301,000
Currency: North Korean won
Religions: Buddhist, Confucianist, some Christian and syncretic Chondogyo
Language: Korean

Norway

Area: 125,004 sq mi
(323,758 sq km)
Population: 4,765,000
Capital: Oslo, pop. 834,000
Currency: Norwegian krone
Religion: Church of Norway (Lutheran)
Languages: Bokmal Norwegian, Nynorsk Norwegian, Sami

Oman

Area: 119,500 sq mi
(309,500 sq km)
Population: 2,719,000
Capital: Muscat, pop. 621,000
Currency: Omani rial
Religions: Ibadhi Muslim, Sunni Muslim, Shiite Muslim, Hindu
Languages: Arabic, English, Baluchi, Urdu, Indian dialects

Pakistan

Area: 307,374 sq mi
(796,095 sq km)
Population: 172,800,000
Capital: Islamabad, pop. 780,000
Currency: Pakistani rupee
Religions: Sunni Muslim, Shiite Muslim
Languages: Punjabi, Sindhi, Siraiki, Pashtu, Urdu, Baluchi, Hindko, English

Palau

Area: 189 sq mi (489 sq km)
Population: 20,000
Capital: Melekeok NA
Currency: U.S. dollar
Religions: Roman Catholic, Protestant, Modekngei, Seventh-day Adventist
Languages: Palauan, Filipino, English, Chinese

Panama

Area: 29,157 sq mi (75,517 sq km)
Population: 3,391,000
Capital: Panama City, pop. 1,280,000
Currencies: balboa; U.S. dollar
Religions: Roman Catholic, Protestant
Languages: Spanish, English

MEET THE NAT GEO EXPLORER

SPENCER WELLS

A leading population geneticist and director of the Genographic Project (https://genographic.nationalgeographic.com), Wells is studying humankind's family tree.

What was your closest call in the field?
I've had a few, but the most difficult physically was when I lived with Chukchi reindeer herders in the Russian Far East, inside the Arctic Circle. The temperatures fell as low as -70°C, which freezes unprotected skin and can kill you in a matter of minutes!

How would you suggest kids follow in your footsteps?
Find something in school you are passionate about, focus on it, and study hard. Don't let people tell you that it's not a practical subject to study—if you are excited enough about it, you will find a way to do it for a living. Take risks. Challenging yourself will give you confidence, and you'll learn something that may be useful in your future work.

● Asia ● Europe ● North America ● South America

PAPUA NEW GUINEA

FOR HULI WIG MEN, IT'S ALL ABOUT THE HAIR.

Imagine if your future depended on having perfect hair. For teenage boys in the Huli culture, it does. Members of this remote tribe believe that hair is a symbol of health and strength for men. Men who wear elaborate wigs (right) made from their own locks earn the respect of their tribe.

A Hidden Tribe

The Huli live deep in the rain forest of Papua New Guinea—an island nation 100 miles north of Australia. They remained unknown to the outside world until the 1930s, when a gold rush brought Western explorers to their home. Today about 70,000 people make up the Huli tribe, most following their traditional way of life.

The Secrets of Wig School

Some Huli kids go to grade school to study reading and math. But as teenagers, girls garden and babysit their younger siblings, while many boys go to wig school. Learning to grow their hair for wigs is serious business. The rules? 1) No running—you'll make your hair bounce; 2) Stay away from campfires; they could burn your hair; 3) Water your hair 12 times a day to make it grow faster. Breaking the rules could lead to suspension or even worse—bad hair!

Becoming a Wig Man

When ready, the boys' hair is cut off and woven into wigs. A Huli teen wears his first wig as a sign that he is strong enough for adult duties, such as warfare and marriage.

Papua New Guinea

Area: 178,703 sq mi (462,840 sq km)
Population: 6,458,000
Capital: Port Moresby, pop. 299,000
Currency: kina
Religions: indigenous beliefs, Roman Catholic, Lutheran, other Protestant
Languages: Melanesian Pidgin, 820 indigenous languages

Peru

Area: 496,224 sq mi (1,285,216 sq km)
Population: 27,903,000
Capital: Lima, pop. 8,007,000
Currency: nuevo sol
Religion: Roman Catholic
Languages: Spanish, Quechua, Aymara, minor Amazonian languages

Paraguay

Area: 157,048 sq mi (406,752 sq km)
Population: 6,230,000
Capital: Asunción, pop. 1,870,000
Currency: guarani
Religions: Roman Catholic, Protestant
Languages: Spanish, Guarani

Philippines

Area: 115,831 sq mi (300,000 sq km)
Population: 90,457,000
Capital: Manila, pop. 11,100,000
Currency: Philippine peso
Religions: Roman Catholic, Muslim, other Christian
Languages: Filipino (based on Tagalog), English

COLOR KEY ● Africa ● Australia, New Zealand, & Oceania

Poland

Area: 120,728 sq mi
(312,685 sq km)
Population: 38,110,000
Capital: Warsaw, pop. 1,707,000
Currency: zloty
Religion: Roman Catholic
Language: Polish

Portugal

Area: 35,655 sq mi
(92,345 sq km)
Population: 10,621,000
Capital: Lisbon, pop. 2,811,000
Currency: euro
Religion: Roman Catholic
Languages: Portuguese, Mirandese

Qatar

Area: 4,448 sq mi
(11,521 sq km)
Population: 928,000
Capital: Doha, pop. 386,000
Currency: Qatari rial
Religions: Muslim, Christian
Languages: Arabic, English commonly a second language

Romania

Area: 92,043 sq mi
(238,391 sq km)
Population: 21,498,000
Capital: Bucharest, pop. 1,940,000
Currency: new leu
Religions: Eastern Orthodox, Protestant, Roman Catholic
Languages: Romanian, Hungarian

Russia

Area: 6,592,850 sq mi
(17,075,400 sq km)
Population: 141,875,000
Capital: Moscow, pop. 10,452,000
Currency: ruble
Religions: Russian Orthodox, Muslim
Languages: Russian, many minority languages

Rwanda

Area: 10,169 sq mi
(26,338 sq km)
Population: 9,609,000
Capital: Kigali, pop. 852,000
Currency: Rwandan franc
Religions: Roman Catholic, Protestant, Adventist, Muslim
Languages: Kinyarwanda, French, English, Kiswahili

Samoa

Area: 1,093 sq mi (2,831 sq km)
Population: 188,000
Capital: Apia, pop. 43,000
Currency: tala
Religions: Congregationalist, Roman Catholic, Methodist, Church of Latter-day Saints, Assembly of God, Seventh-day Adventist
Languages: Samoan (Polynesian), English

San Marino

Area: 24 sq mi (61 sq km)
Population: 31,000
Capital: San Marino, pop. 4,000
Currency: euro
Religion: Roman Catholic
Language: Italian

Sao Tome and Principe

Area: 386 sq mi (1,001 sq km)
Population: 158,000
Capital: São Tomé, pop. 58,000
Currency: dobra
Religions: Roman Catholic, Evangelical
Language: Portuguese

It gets so cold in **SIBERIA**
(in northern Russia) that your
BREATH can TURN TO ICE in midair.

RUSSIA IS ONLY 2½ MILES FROM ALASKA.

Saudi Arabia

Area: 756,985 sq mi
(1,960,582 sq km)
Population: 28,147,000
Capital: Riyadh, pop. 4,462,000
Currency: Saudi riyal
Religion: Muslim
Language: Arabic

Senegal

Area: 75,955 sq mi
(196,722 sq km)
Population: 12,688,000
Capital: Dakar, pop. 2,603,000
Currency: Communauté
Financière Africaine franc
Religions: Muslim, Christian (mostly Roman Catholic)
Languages: French, Wolof, Pulaar, Jola, Mandinka

Serbia

Area: 29,913 sq mi (77,474 sq km)
Population: 7,354,000
Capital: Belgrade, pop. 1,100,000
Currency: Serbian dinar
Religions: Serbian Orthodox, Roman Catholic, Muslim
Languages: Serbian, Hungarian,

Seychelles

Area: 176 sq mi (455 sq km)
Population: 87,000
Capital: Victoria, pop. 26,000
Currency: Seychelles rupee
Religions: Roman Catholic, Anglican, other Christian
Languages: Creole, English

Sierra Leone

Area: 27,699 sq mi (71,740 sq km)
Population: 5,450,000
Capital: Freetown, pop. 826,000
Currency: leone
Religions: Muslim, indigenous beliefs, Christian
Languages: English, Mende, Temne, Krio

Singapore

Area: 255 sq mi (660 sq km)
Population: 4,790,000
Capital: Singapore, pop. 4,790,000
Currency: Singapore dollar
Religions: Buddhist, Muslim, Taoist, Roman Catholic, Hindu, other Christian
Languages: Mandarin, English, Malay, Hokkien, Cantonese, Teochew, Tamil

Slovakia

Area: 18,932 sq mi
(49,035 sq km)
Population: 5,405,000
Capital: Bratislava, pop. 424,000
Currency: Slovak koruna
Religions: Roman Catholic, Protestant, Greek Catholic
Languages: Slovak, Hungarian

Slovenia

Area: 7,827 sq mi
(20,273 sq km)
Population: 2,034,000
Capital: Ljubljana, pop. 244,000
Currency: euro
Religion: Roman Catholic, Muslim, Orthodox
Languages: Slovene, Serbo-Croatian

Solomon Islands

Area: 10,954 sq mi
(28,370 sq km)
Population: 507,000
Capital: Honiara, pop. 66,000
Currency: Solomon Islands dollar
Religions: Church of Melanesia, Roman Catholic, South Seas Evangelical, other Christian
Languages: Melanesian pidgin, 120 indigenous languages

Somalia

Area: 246,201 sq mi
(637,657 sq km)
Population: 8,956,000
Capital: Mogadishu, pop. 1,450,000
Currency: Somali shilling
Religion: Sunni Muslim
Languages: Somali, Arabic, Italian, English

186

COLOR KEY ● Africa ● Australia, New Zealand, & Oceania

South Africa

Area: 470,693 sq mi (1,219,090 sq km)
Population: 48,315,000
Capitals: Pretoria, pop. 1,336,000;
Bloemfontein, pop. 417,000;
Cape Town, pop. 3,211,000
Currency: rand
Religions: Zion Christian, Pentecostal, Catholic,
Methodist, Dutch Reformed, Anglican, other Christian
Languages: IsiZulu, IsiXhosa, Afrikaans, Sepedi, English

South Korea

Area: 38,321 sq mi
(99,250 sq km)
Population: 48,607,000
Capital: Seoul, pop. 9,799,000
Currency: South Korean won
Religions: Christian, Buddhist
Languages: Korean, English

Spain

Area: 195,363 sq mi (505,988 sq km)
Population: 46,501,000
Capital: Madrid, pop. 5,567,000
Currency: euro
Religion: Roman Catholic
Languages: Castilian Spanish, Catalan, Galician, Basque

Sri Lanka

Area: 25,299 sq mi
(65,525 sq km)
Population: 20,296,000
Capital: Colombo, pop. 656,000
Currency: Sri Lankan rupee
Religions: Buddhist, Muslim, Hindu, Christian
Languages: Sinhala, Tamil

St. Kitts and Nevis

Area: 104 sq mi (269 sq km)
Population: 48,000
Capital: Basseterre, pop. 13,000
Currency: East Caribbean dollar
Religions: Anglican, other Protestant, Roman Catholic
Language: English

St. Lucia

Area: 238 sq mi (616 sq km)
Population: 171,000
Capital: Castries, pop. 14,000
Currency: East Caribbean
dollar
Religions: Roman Catholic, Seventh-day Adventist,
Pentecostal
Languages: English, French patois

St. Vincent and the Grenadines

Area: 150 sq mi (389 sq km)
Population: 111,000
Capital: Kingstown, pop. 26,000
Currency: East Caribbean dollar
Religions: Anglican, Methodist, Roman Catholic
Languages: English, French patois

Sudan

Area: 967,500 sq mi
(2,505,813 sq km)
Population: 39,445,000
Capital: Khartoum, pop. 4,762,000
Currency: Sudanese pound
Religions: Sunni Muslim, indigenous beliefs, Christian
Languages: Arabic, Nubian, Ta Bedawie, many diverse
dialects of Nilotic, Nilo-Hamitic, Sudanic languages

Suriname

Area: 63,037 sq mi (163,265 sq km)
Population: 500,000
Capital: Paramaribo, pop. 252,000
Currency: Surinam dollar
Religions: Hindu, Protestant (predominantly Moravian),
Roman Catholic, Muslim, indigenous beliefs
Languages: Dutch, English, Sranang Tongo, Hindustani,
Javanese

COOL CLICK

The United Nations
has a great website with
information, games, and more.
Check it out online.
cyberschoolbus.un.org

● Asia ● Europe ● North America ● South America

Swaziland

Area: 6,704 sq mi (17,363 sq km)
Population: 1,129,000
Capitals: Mbabane, pop. 78,000; Lobamba NA
Currency: lilangeni
Religions: Zionist, Roman Catholic, Muslim
Languages: English, siSwati

Sweden

Area: 173,732 sq mi (449,964 sq km)
Population: 9,214,000
Capital: Stockholm, pop. 1,264,000
Currency: Swedish krona
Religion: Lutheran
Languages: Swedish, Sami, Finnish

Switzerland

Area: 15,940 sq mi (41,284 sq km)
Population: 7,633,000
Capital: Bern, pop. 337,000
Currency: Swiss franc
Religions: Roman Catholic, Protestant, Muslim
Languages: German, French, Italian, Romansh

Syria

Area: 71,498 sq mi (185,180 sq km)
Population: 19,933,000
Capital: Damascus, pop. 2,467,000
Currency: Syrian pound
Religions: Sunni, other Muslim (includes Alawite, Druze), Christian
Languages: Arabic, Kurdish, Armenian, Aramaic, Circassian

Tajikistan

Area: 55,251 sq mi (143,100 sq km)
Population: 7,285,000
Capital: Dushanbe, pop. 553,000
Currency: somoni
Religions: Sunni Muslim, Shiite Muslim
Languages: Tajik, Russian

Tanzania

Area: 364,900 sq mi (945,087 sq km)
Population: 40,213,000
Capitals: Dar es Salaam, pop. 2,930,000; Dodoma, pop. 183,000
Currency: Tanzanian shilling
Religions: Muslim, indigenous beliefs, Christian
Languages: Kiswahili, Kiunguja (Kiswahili in Zanzibar), English, Arabic, local languages

Thailand

Area: 198,115 sq mi (513,115 sq km)
Population: 66,148,000
Capital: Bangkok, pop. 6,706,000
Currency: baht
Religions: Buddhist, Muslim
Languages: Thai, English, ethnic dialects

Timor-Leste (East Timor)

Area: 5,640 sq mi (14,609 sq km)
Population: 1,081,000
Capital: Dili, pop. 159,000
Currency: U.S. dollar
Religion: Roman Catholic
Languages: Tetum, Portuguese, Indonesian, English, indigenous languages

Togo

Area: 21,925 sq mi (56,785 sq km)
Population: 6,761,000
Capital: Lomé, pop. 1,451,000
Currency: Communauté Financière Africaine franc
Religions: indigenous beliefs, Christian, Muslim
Languages: French, Ewe, Mina, Kabye, Dagomba

Tonga

Area: 289 sq mi (748 sq km)
Population: 102,000
Capital: Nukuʻalofa, pop. 25,000
Currency: paʻanga
Religion: Christian
Languages: Tongan, English

COLOR KEY   ● Africa ● Australia, New Zealand, & Oceania

Trinidad and Tobago

Area: 1,980 sq mi (5,128 sq km)
Population: 1,338,000
Capital: Port-of-Spain, pop. 54,000
Currency: Trinidad and Tobago dollar
Religions: Roman Catholic, Hindu, Anglican, Baptist
Languages: English, Caribbean Hindustani, French, Spanish, Chinese

Tunisia

Area: 63,170 sq mi (163,610 sq km)
Population: 10,337,000
Capital: Tunis, pop. 746,000
Currency: Tunisian dinar
Religion: Muslim
Languages: Arabic, French

Turkey

Area: 300,948 sq mi (779,452 sq km)
Population: 74,766,000
Capital: Ankara, pop. 3,715,000
Currency: new Turkish lira
Religion: Muslim (mostly Sunni)
Languages: Turkish, Kurdish, Dimli (Zaza), Azeri, Kabardian, Gagauz

Turkmenistan

Area: 188,456 sq mi (488,100 sq km)
Population: 5,180,000
Capital: Ashgabat, pop. 744,000
Currency: Turkmen manat
Religions: Muslim, Eastern Orthodox
Languages: Turkmen, Russian, Uzbek

Tuvalu

Area: 10 sq mi (26 sq km)
Population: 10,000
Capital: Funafuti, pop. 5,000
Currencies: Australian dollar; Tuvaluan dollar
Religion: Church of Tuvalu (Congregationalist)
Languages: Tuvaluan, English, Samoan, Kiribati

Uganda

Area: 93,104 sq mi (241,139 sq km)
Population: 29,194,000
Capital: Kampala, pop. 1,420,000
Currency: Ugandan shilling
Religions: Protestant, Roman Catholic, Muslim
Languages: English, Ganda, other local languages, Kiswahili, Arabic

Ukraine

Area: 233,090 sq mi (603,700 sq km)
Population: 46,237,000
Capital: Kiev, pop. 2,705,000
Currency: hryvnia
Religions: Ukrainian Orthodox, Orthodox, Ukrainian Greek Catholic
Languages: Ukrainian, Russian

United Arab Emirates

Area: 30,000 sq mi (77,700 sq km)
Population: 4,486,000
Capital: Abu Dhabi, pop. 604,000
Currency: Emirati dirham
Religion: Muslim
Languages: Arabic, Persian, English, Hindi, Urdu

United Kingdom

Area: 93,788 sq mi (242,910 sq km)
Population: 61,291,000
Capital: London, pop. 8,566,000
Currency: British pound
Religions: Anglican, Roman Catholic, Presbyterian, Methodist
Languages: English, Welsh, Scottish form of Gaelic

United States

Area: 3,794,083 sq mi (9,826,630 sq km)
Population: 304,486,000
Capital: Washington, DC, pop. 591,833
Currency: U.S. dollar
Religions: Protestant, Roman Catholic
Languages: English, Spanish

Uruguay

Area: 68,037 sq mi
(176,215 sq km)
Population: 3,334,000
Capital: Montevideo, pop. 1,514,000
Currency: Uruguayan peso
Religion: Roman Catholic
Language: Spanish

Venezuela

Area: 352,144 sq mi
(912,050 sq km)
Population: 27,935,000
Capital: Caracas, pop. 2,986,000
Currency: bolivar
Religion: Roman Catholic
Languages: Spanish, numerous indigenous dialects

Uzbekistan

Area: 172,742 sq mi
(447,400 sq km)
Population: 27,199,000
Capital: Tashkent,
pop. 2,184,000
Currency: Uzbekistani sum
Religions: Muslim (mostly Sunni), Eastern Orthodox
Languages: Uzbek, Russian, Tajik

Vietnam

Area: 127,844 sq mi
(331,114 sq km)
Population: 86,185,000
Capital: Hanoi, pop. 4,377,000
Currency: dong
Religions: Buddhist, Roman Catholic
Languages: Vietnamese, English, French, Chinese, Khmer

Vanuatu

Area: 4,707 sq mi (12,190 sq km)
Population: 240,000
Capital: Port-Vila, pop. 40,000
Currency: vatu
Religions: Presbyterian, Anglican, Roman Catholic, other Christian, indigenous beliefs
Languages: over 100 local languages, pidgin (known as Bislama or Bichelama)

Yemen

Area: 207,286 sq mi
(536,869 sq km)
Population: 22,198,000
Capital: Sanaa, pop. 2,008,000
Currency: Yemeni rial
Religions: Muslim including Shaf'i (Sunni) and Zaydi (Shiite)
Language: Arabic

Vatican City

Area: 0.2 sq mi (0.4 sq km)
Population: 798
Capital: Vatican City, pop. 798
Currency: euro
Religion: Roman Catholic
Languages: Italian, Latin, French

Zambia

Area: 290,586 sq mi
(752,614 sq km)
Population: 12,197,000
Capital: Lusaka, pop. 1,328,000
Currency: Zambian kwacha
Religion: Christian, Muslim, Hindu
Languages: English, Bemba, Kaonda, Lozi, Lunda, Luvale, Nyanja, Tonga, about 70 other indigenous languages

HOW SMALL CAN A COUNTRY BE?

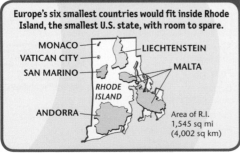

Europe's six smallest countries would fit inside Rhode Island, the smallest U.S. state, with room to spare.

MONACO
VATICAN CITY
SAN MARINO
LIECHTENSTEIN
MALTA
RHODE ISLAND
ANDORRA
Area of R.I.
1,545 sq mi
(4,002 sq km)

Zimbabwe

Area: 150,872 sq mi
(390,757 sq km)
Population: 13,481,000
Capital: Harare, pop. 1,572,000
Currency: Zimbabwean dollar
Religions: Syncretic (part Christian, part indigenous beliefs), Christian, indigenous beliefs
Languages: English, Shona, Sindebele, tribal dialects

COLOR KEY ● Africa ● Australia, New Zealand, & Oceania

Bet you didn't know

8 ways people try to get good luck around the globe

1 CARRYING **bat bones** IN YOUR POCKET in **Greece**

2 watching a ladybug fly into your bedroom in **Italy**

3 wearing yellow **under-wear** on New Year's Day in **Peru**

4 HOLDING A **rabbit's foot** IN PARTS OF **West Africa**

5 riding a **camel** in **Turkey**

6 touching A CHIMNEY SWEEP'S BRUSH in **Germany**

7 SEEING A WHITE **HORSE** FACING YOU IN WALES, IN THE **UNITED** KINGDOM

8 breaking **GLASS** in **Bulgaria**

● Asia ● Europe ● North America ● South America

THE POLITICAL
UNITED STATES

9:00 AM PACIFIC TIME

10:00 AM MOUNTAIN TIME

Cape Flattery

Seattle
Olympia ⊛ Tacoma
WASHINGTON
Spokane
Yakima
Portland
Columbia
Salem ⊛
Eugene
OREGON
Lewiston
IDAHO
Great Falls
Missouri
Butte ⊛ Helena
MONTANA
Billings
Minot
Grand Forks
NORTH DAKOTA
⊛ Bismarck
Farg
Aberdeen
SOUTH DAKOTA
⊛ Pierre
Sioux Fall

Medford
Klamath Falls
⊛ Boise
Idaho Falls
Snake
Pocatello
Cody
Yellowstone L.
WYOMING
Casper
Rapid City
Missouri

Eureka
Redding
Reno
Carson City ⊛
Lake Tahoe
Great
Salt
Lake
NEVADA
Ogden
Salt Lake City ⊛
Provo
UTAH
Cheyenne
Laramie
Fort Collins
N. Platte
Grand Island
Linco
NEBRASKA
Platte
S. Platte

Sacramento ⊛
San Francisco
Oakland San Jose
Salinas
Fresno
Sierra Nevada
CALIFORNIA
Basin
Grand Junction
Lake Powell
Colorado
COLORADO
Denver ⊛ Boulder
Colorado Springs
Pueblo
KANSAS
Dodge City
Arkansas
Wichi

Bakersfield
Point Conception
Mojave
Desert
Las Vegas
St. George
Lake Mead
Grand Canyon
Flagstaff
Santa Fe
Albuquerque
Amarillo
OKLAH
Oklahom Cit
Lawton
Red

Los Angeles
Long Beach
Riverside
Salton Sea
San Diego ⊛
Yuma
Phoenix ⊛ Mesa
ARIZONA
Tucson
NEW MEXICO
Roswell
Las Cruces
El Paso
Lubbock
Wichita Falls
Fort Worth
Midland
Odessa
Abilene
Waco
TEXAS

7:00 AM
HAWAI'I-ALEUTIAN TIME
North Slope
Brooks Range
Yukon
Alaska Range
Juneau
Anchorage
ALASKA
0   400 miles
0   400 kilometers
ALEUTIAN ISLANDS
Alaska Peninsula

8:00 AM
ALASKA TIME

Kaua'i
Ni'ihau
O'ahu
Moloka'i
Honolulu
Lana'i
Maui
Kaho'olawe
Hilo
Hawai'i
HAWAI'I
0   150 mi
0   150 km

7:00 AM
HAWAI'I-ALEUTIAN TIME

San Antonio ⊛ Aust
Corp Chris
Laredo
Rio Grande
Brownsvi

192

Like a giant quilt, the United States is made up of 50 states. Each is unique, but together they make a national fabric held together by a constitution and a federal government. State boundaries, outlined in various colors on the map, set apart internal political units within the country. The national capital—Washington, D.C.—is marked by a star in a double circle. The capital of each state is marked by a star in a single circle.

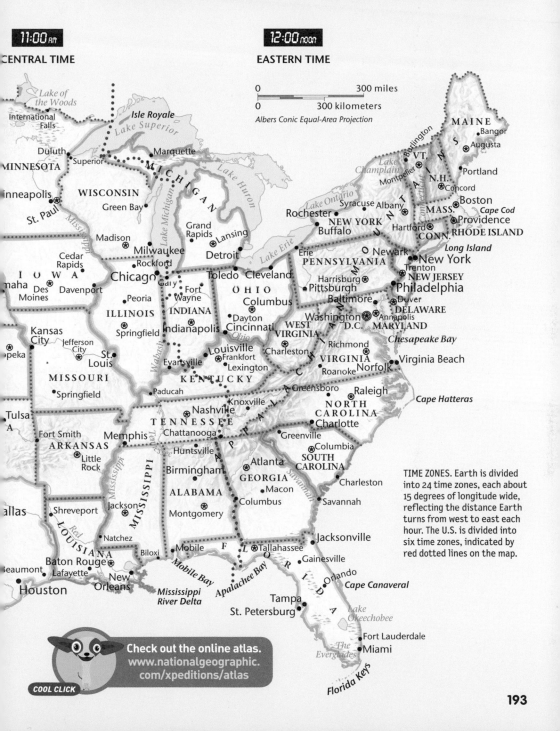

11:00 AM

CENTRAL TIME

12:00 noon

EASTERN TIME

0 ——————— 300 miles
0 ——————— 300 kilometers
Albers Conic Equal-Area Projection

TIME ZONES. Earth is divided into 24 time zones, each about 15 degrees of longitude wide, reflecting the distance Earth turns from west to east each hour. The U.S. is divided into six time zones, indicated by red dotted lines on the map.

Check out the online atlas.
www.nationalgeographic.com/xpeditions/atlas

COOL CLICK

THE PHYSICAL UNITED STATES

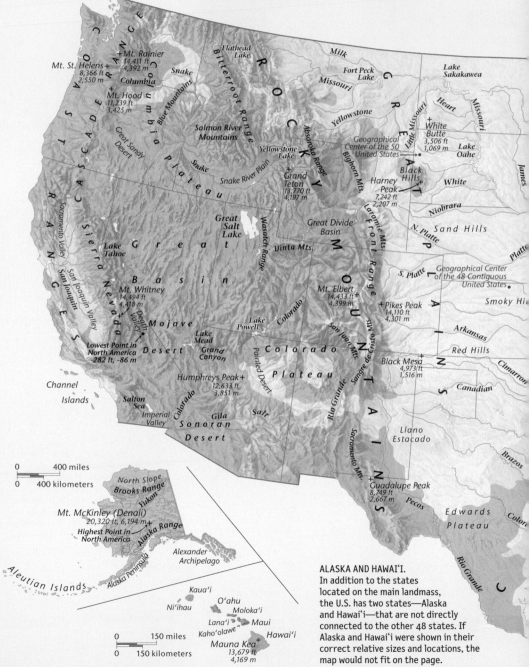

Mt. St. Helens +
8,366 ft
2,550 m

CASCADE RANGE

Mt. Rainier
14,411 ft
4,392 m

Columbia

Mt. Hood
11,239 ft
3,425 m

Snake

Columbia Plateau

Blue Mountains

Great Sandy
Desert

Flathead
Lake

Bitterroot Range

Salmon River
Mountains

Snake

Snake River Plain

Milk

Fort Peck
Lake

Missouri

Yellowstone

Yellowstone
Lake

Absaroka Range

Bighorn Mts.

ROCKY

Grand
Teton
13,770 ft
4,197 m

Little Missouri

Geographical
Center of the 50
United States.

Laramie Mts.

Harney
Peak +
7,242 ft
2,207 m

Black Hills

GREAT

Lake
Sakakawea

Heart

White
Butte
3,506 ft
1,069 m

Lake
Oahe

White

Missouri

Niobrara

James

Missouri

Sacramento Valley

Sierra Nevada

Lake
Tahoe

Great

Basin

Great
Salt
Lake

Wasatch Range

Uinta Mts.

Great Divide
Basin

MOUNTAINS

Front Range

Sand Hills

N. Platte

S. Platte

Geographical Center
of the 48 Contiguous
United States.

Platte

San Joaquin Valley

San Joaquin

Mt. Whitney
14,494 ft
4,418 m

Death
Valley

Mojave

Lake
Mead

Lake
Powell

Colorado

Grand
Canyon

Painted Desert

Mt. Elbert
14,433 ft+
4,399 m

San Juan Mts.

Sangre de Cristo Mts.

+ Pikes Peak
14,110 ft
4,301 m

Arkansas

Red Hills

Smoky Hi

Lowest Point in
North America
-282 ft, -86 m

Desert

Colorado
Plateau

Black Mesa
4,973 ft +
1,516 m

Canadian

Cimarron

Channel
Islands

Salton
Sea

Imperial
Valley

Colorado

Humphreys Peak +
12,633 ft
3,851 m

Gila

Sonoran

Desert

Salt

Rio Grande

Sacramento Mts.

Llano
Estacado

Guadalupe Peak +
8,749 ft
2,667 m

Pecos

Brazos

Edwards
Plateau

Colo

Rio Grande

Scale

0   400 miles
0   400 kilometers

North Slope

Brooks Range

Yukon

Mt. McKinley (Denali)
20,320 ft, 6,194 m +
Highest Point in
North America

Alaska Range

Alexander
Archipelago

Aleutian Islands

Alaska Peninsula

Kaua'i

Ni'ihau

O'ahu

Moloka'i

Lana'i

Kaho'olawe

Maui

Hawai'i

Mauna Kea +
13,679 ft
4,169 m

0   150 miles
0   150 kilometers

ALASKA AND HAWAI'I.
In addition to the states
located on the main landmass,
the U.S. has two states—Alaska
and Hawai'i—that are not directly
connected to the other 48 states. If
Alaska and Hawai'i were shown in their
correct relative sizes and locations, the
map would not fit on the page.

Stretching from the Atlantic Ocean in the east to the Pacific Ocean in the west, the United States is the third-largest country (by area) in the world. Its physical diversity ranges from mountains to fertile plains and dry deserts. Shading on the map indicates changes in elevation, while colors show different vegetation patterns.

0 | | 400 miles
0 | | 400 kilometers
Albers Conic Equal-Area Projection

NATURAL VEGETATION

- NEEDLELEAF FOREST
- BROADLEAF FOREST
- MIXED FOREST
- GRASSLAND
- TROPICAL VEGETATION
- DESERT
- TUNDRA

Lake of the Woods
Isle Royale
Eagle Mt. 2,301 ft 701 m
Lake Superior
Source of the Mississippi (Lake Itasca)
Upper Peninsula
Minnesota
Mississippi
Wisconsin
Lake Winnebago
North
Cedar
C E N T R A L
Des Moines
Illinois
L O W L A N D
Missouri
Lake of the Ozarks
Harry S. Truman Res.
Ozark Plateau
Kentucky
Lake Barkley
Magazine Mt. 2,753 ft 839 m
Arkansas
Ouachita Mts.
Red
Ouachita
Trinity
Sabine
Red
A S
Lake Pontchartrain
Mississippi River Delta

Lake Michigan
Lower Peninsula
Lake Huron
Lake St. Clair
Lake Erie
Ohio
Ohio
Lake
Tennessee
Cumberland
Cumberland Plateau
Appalachian Plateau
Black Belt
Alabama
Chattahoochee
Okefenokee Swamp

Lake Ontario
Niagara Falls
Allegheny Plateau
Allegheny Mts.
Susquehanna
Potomac
James
Roanoke
A P P A L A C H I A N
Mt. Mitchell 6,684 ft, 2,037 m
Cape Fear
Great Pee Dee
Savannah
Altamaha
C O A S T A L   P L A I N
Cape Canaveral
Lake Okeechobee
The Everglades
Florida Keys

Lake Champlain
Adirondack Mts.
Green Mts.
Connecticut
Mt. Washington 6,288 ft 1,917 m
Catskill Mts.
Hudson
Delaware
Long Island
Cape Cod
Delaware Bay
Chesapeake Bay
Cape Hatteras
Cape Fear

To see more great maps, go online. maps.nationalgeographic.com/maps

COOL CLICK

THE STATES

From sea to shining sea, the United States of America is a nation of diversity. In the more than 230 years since its creation, the nation has grown to become home to a wide range of geography, people, and cultures. The following pages present a general overview of all 50 states in the U.S.

The country is generally divided into five large regions: the Northeast, the Southeast, the Midwest, the Southwest, and the West. Though loosely defined, these zones tend to share important similarities, including climate, history, and geography. The color key below provides a guide to which states are in each region.

Flags of each state and highlights of geography and demography, are also included. These details offer a brief overview of each state; there are a lot more facts online to learn about the states that are not included here. You can check out important state stuff, such as state trees, mottos, and songs.

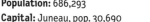

COOL CLICK

Interested in more about the states? Go online. travel.nationalgeographic.com/places/countries/country_unitedstates.html

Alabama

Area: 52,419 sq mi (135,765 sq km)
Population: 4,661,900
Capital: Montgomery, pop. 204,086
Largest city: Birmingham, pop. 229,800
Industry: Retail and wholesale trade, services, government, finance, insurance, real estate, transportation, construction, communication
State flower/bird: Camellia/northern flicker

Alaska

Area: 663,267 sq mi (1,717,862 sq km)
Population: 686,293
Capital: Juneau, pop. 30,690
Largest city: Anchorage, pop. 279,671
Industry: Petroleum products, government, services, trade
State flower/bird: Forget-me-not/willow ptarmigan

Arizona

Area: 113,998 sq mi (295,256 sq km)
Population: 6,500,180
Capital: Phoenix, pop. 1,552,259
Largest city: Phoenix, pop. 1,552,259
Industry: Real estate, manufactured goods, retail, state and local government, transportation and public utilities, wholesale trade, health services, tourism
State flower/bird: Saguaro cactus/wren

Arkansas

Area: 53,179 sq mi (137,732 sq km)
Population: 2,855,390
Capital: Little Rock, pop. 187,452
Largest city: Little Rock, pop. 187,452
Industry: Services, food processing, paper products, transportation, metal products, machinery, electronics
State flower/bird: Apple blossom/mockingbird

California

Area: 163,696 sq mi (423,972 sq km)
Population: 36,756,666
Capital: Sacramento, pop. 460,242
Largest city: Los Angeles, pop. 3,834,340
Industry: Electronic components and equipment, computers and computer software, tourism, food processing, entertainment, clothing
State flower/bird: Golden poppy/California quail

Colorado

Area: 104,094 sq mi (269,602 sq km)
Population: 4,939,456
Capital: Denver, pop. 588,349
Largest city: Denver, pop. 588,349
Industry: Real estate, government, durable goods, communications, health and other services, non-durable goods, transportation
State flower/bird: Columbine/lark bunting

Alaska is the biggest U.S. state in area but ranks 47th in population.

Sled dog racing is the official state sport of Alaska.

Careful! *Mukluks* are winter boots; *Muktuk* is a whale blubber snack.

No roads lead to Juneau, the state capital. The only way in is by boat or plane.

COLOR KEY ● Northeast ● Southeast

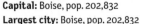

Connecticut

Area: 5,543 sq mi (14,357 sq km)
Population: 3,501,252
Capital: Hartford, pop. 124,563
Largest city: Bridgeport, pop. 136,695
Industry: Transportation equipment, metal products, machinery, electrical equipment, printing and publishing, scientific instruments, insurance
State flower/bird: Mountain laurel/robin

Delaware

Area: 2,489 sq mi (6,447 sq km)
Population: 873,092
Capital: Dover, pop. 35,811
Largest city: Wilmington, pop. 72,868
Industry: Food processing, chemicals, rubber and plastic products, scientific instruments, printing and publishing, financial services
State flower/bird: Peach blossom/blue hen chicken

Florida

Area: 65,755 sq mi (170,304 sq km)
Population: 18,328,340
Capital: Tallahassee, pop. 168,979
Largest city: Jacksonville, pop. 805,605
Industry: Tourism, health services, business services, communications, banking, electronic equipment, insurance
State flower/bird: Orange blossom/mockingbird

Georgia

Area: 59,425 sq mi (153,910 sq km)
Population: 9,685,744
Capital: Atlanta, pop. 519,145
Largest city: Atlanta, pop. 519,145
Industry: Textiles and clothing, transportation equipment, food processing, paper products, chemicals, electrical equipment, tourism
State flower/bird: Cherokee rose/brown thrasher

Hawai'i

Area: 10,931 sq mi (28,311 sq km)
Population: 1,288,198
Capital: Honolulu, pop. 375,571
Largest city: Honolulu, pop. 375,571
Industry: Tourism, trade, finance, food processing, petroleum refining, stone, clay, glass products
State flower/bird: Hibiscus/Hawaiian goose (nene)

Idaho

Area: 83,570 sq mi (216,447 sq km)
Population: 1,523,816
Capital: Boise, pop. 202,832
Largest city: Boise, pop. 202,832
Industry: Electronics and computer equipment, tourism, food processing, forest products, mining
State flower/bird: Syringa (Lewis' Mock orange)/mountain bluebird

Illinois

Area: 57,914 sq mi (149,998 sq km)
Population: 12,901,563
Capital: Springfield, pop. 117,090
Largest city: Chicago, pop. 2,836,658
Industry: Industrial machinery, electronic equipment, food processing, chemicals, metals, printing and publishing, rubber and plastics, motor vehicles
State flower/bird: Violet/cardinal

Indiana

Area: 36,418 sq mi (94,322 sq km)
Population: 6,376,792
Capital: Indianapolis, pop. 795,458
Largest city: Indianapolis, pop. 795,458
Industry: Transportation equipment, steel, pharmaceutical and chemical products, machinery, petroleum, coal
State flower/bird: Peony/cardinal

5 cool things about HAWAI'I

1. The endangered Hawaiian green sea turtle and the endangered Hawaiian monk seal live around the Hawaiian Islands.

2. The volcano Kilauea, on Hawai'i's Big Island, is one of the most active in the world. Legend says that the goddess Pele lives in it.

3. The Hawaiian language has only 12 letters: A, E, I, O, U, H, K, L, M, N, P, and W.

4. The only royal palace in the United States, the Iolani Palace, is in Hawai'i. The state's last queen was overthrown in 1893.

5. Surfers in Hawai'i prefer winter, when storms in the Pacific Ocean create huge 25- to 30-foot-tall waves.

● Midwest   ● Southwest   ● West

COOL CLICK

Check out great
state facts online.
www.state.me.us
This is for Maine. For each
state insert the two-letter state
abbreviation where "me" is now.

Maine

Area: 35,385 sq mi (91,646 sq km)
Population: 1,316,456
Capital: Augusta, pop. 18,367
Largest city: Portland, pop. 62,825
Industry: Health services, tourism, forest products, leather products, electrical equipment, food processing
State flower/bird: White pine cone and tassel/chickadee

Iowa

Area: 56,272 sq mi (145,743 sq km)
Population: 3,002,555
Capital: Des Moines, pop. 196,998
Largest city: Des Moines, pop. 196,998
Industry: Real estate, health services, industrial machinery, food processing, construction
State flower/bird: Wild rose/American goldfinch

Maryland

Area: 12,407 sq mi (32,133 sq km)
Population: 5,633,597
Capital: Annapolis, pop. 36,603
Largest city: Baltimore, pop. 637,455
Industry: Real estate, federal government, health services, business services, engineering services
State flower/bird: Black-eyed Susan/northern (Baltimore) oriole

Kansas

Area: 82,277 sq mi (213,097 sq km)
Population: 2,802,134
Capital: Topeka, pop. 122,642
Largest city: Wichita, pop. 361,420
Industry: Aircraft manufacturing, transportation equipment, construction, food processing, printing and publishing, health care
State flower/bird: Sunflower/western meadowlark

Massachusetts

Area: 10,555 sq mi (27,336 sq km)
Population: 6,497,967
Capital: Boston, pop. 599,351
Largest city: Boston, pop. 599,351
Industry: Electrical equipment, machinery, metal products, scientific instruments, printing and publishing, tourism
State flower/bird: Mayflower/chickadee

Kentucky

Area: 40,409 sq mi (104,659 sq km)
Population: 4,269,245
Capital: Frankfort, pop. 27,098
Largest city: Louisville, pop. 557,789
Industry: Manufacturing, services, government, finance, insurance, real estate, retail trade, transportation, wholesale trade, construction, mining
State flower/bird: Goldenrod/cardinal

Michigan

Area: 96,716 sq mi (250,495 sq km)
Population: 10,003,422
Capital: Lansing, pop. 114,947
Largest city: Detroit, pop. 916,952
Industry: Motor vehicles and parts, machinery, metal products, office furniture, tourism, chemicals
State flower/bird: Apple blossom/robin

Louisiana

Area: 51,840 sq mi (134,265 sq km)
Population: 4,410,796
Capital: Baton Rouge, pop. 227,071
Largest city: New Orleans, pop. 239,124
Industry: Chemicals, petroleum products, food processing, health services, tourism, oil and natural gas extraction, paper products
State flower/bird: Magnolia/brown pelican

Minnesota

Area: 86,939 sq mi (225,172 sq km)
Population: 5,220,393
Capital: St. Paul, pop. 277,251
Largest city: Minneapolis, pop. 377,392
Industry: Health services, tourism, real estate, banking and insurance, industrial machinery, printing and publishing, food processing, scientific equipment
State flower/bird: Showy lady's slipper/common loon

COLOR KEY   ● Northeast   ● Southeast

Mississippi

Area: 48,430 sq mi (125,434 sq km)
Population: 2,938,618
Capital: Jackson, pop. 175,710
Largest city: Jackson, pop. 175,710
Industry: Petroleum products, health services, electronic equipment, transportation, banking, forest products, communications
State flower/bird: Magnolia/mockingbird

Missouri

Area: 69,704 sq mi (180,534 sq km)
Population: 5,911,605
Capital: Jefferson City, pop. 40,564
Largest city: Kansas City, pop. 450,375
Industry: Transportation equipment, food processing, chemicals, electrical equipment, metal products
State flower/bird: Hawthorn/eastern bluebird

Montana

Area: 147,042 sq mi (380,840 sq km)
Population: 967,440
Capital: Helena, pop. 28,726
Largest city: Billings, pop. 101,876
Industry: Forest products, food processing, mining, construction, tourism
State flower/bird: Bitterroot/western meadowlark

Nebraska

Area: 77,354 sq mi (200,346 sq km)
Population: 1,783,432
Capital: Lincoln, pop. 248,744
Largest city: Omaha, pop. 424,482
Industry: Food processing, machinery, electrical equipment, printing and publishing
State flower/bird: Goldenrod/western meadowlark

Nevada

Area: 110,561 sq mi (286,352 sq km)
Population: 2,600,167
Capital: Carson City, pop. 54,939
Largest city: Las Vegas, pop. 558,880
Industry: Tourism and gaming, mining, printing and publishing, food processing, electrical equipment
State flower/bird: Sagebrush/mountain bluebird

New Hampshire

Area: 9,350 sq mi (24,216 sq km)
Population: 1,315,809
Capital: Concord, pop. 42,392
Largest city: Manchester, pop. 108,874
Industry: Machinery, electronics, metal products
State flower/bird: Purple lilac/purple finch

New Jersey

Area: 8,721 sq mi (22,588 sq km)
Population: 8,682,661
Capital: Trenton, pop. 82,804
Largest city: Newark, pop. 280,135
Industry: Machinery, electronics, metal products, chemicals
State flower/bird: Violet/American goldfinch

New Mexico

Area: 121,590 sq mi (314,917 sq km)
Population: 1,984,356
Capital: Santa Fe, pop. 73,199
Largest city: Albuquerque, pop. 518,271
Industry: Electronic equipment, state and local government, real estate, business services, federal government, oil and gas extraction, health services
State flower/bird: Yucca/roadrunner

New York

Area: 54,556 sq mi (141,300 sq km)
Population: 19,490,297
Capital: Albany, pop. 94,172
Largest city: New York City, pop. 8,274,527
Industry: Printing and publishing, machinery, computer products, finance, tourism
State flower/bird: Rose/eastern bluebird

THE TOWN OF **MONOWI, NEBRASKA,** HAS A POPULATION **OF ONE.**

● Midwest   ● Southwest   ● West

North Carolina

Area: 53,819 sq mi (139,390 sq km)
Population: 9,222,414
Capital: Raleigh, pop. 375,806
Largest city: Charlotte, pop. 671,588
Industry: Real estate, health services, chemicals, tobacco products, finance, textiles
State flower/bird: Flowering dogwood/cardinal

North Dakota

Area: 70,700 sq mi (183,113 sq km)
Population: 641,481
Capital: Bismarck, pop. 59,503
Largest city: Fargo, pop. 92,660
Industry: Services, government, finance, construction, transportation, oil and gas
State flower/bird: Wild prairie rose/western meadowlark

Ohio

Area: 44,825 sq mi (116,097 sq km)
Population: 11,485,910
Capital: Columbus, pop. 747,755
Largest city: Columbus, pop. 747,755
Industry: Transportation equipment, metal products, machinery, food processing, electrical equipment
State flower/bird: Scarlet carnation/cardinal

Oklahoma

Area: 69,898 sq mi (181,036 sq km)
Population: 3,642,361
Capital: Oklahoma City, pop. 547,274
Largest city: Oklahoma City, pop. 547,274
Industry: Manufacturing, services, government, finance, insurance, real estate
State flower/bird: Mistletoe/scissor-tailed flycatcher

Oregon

Area: 98,381 sq mi (254,806 sq km)
Population: 3,790,060
Capital: Salem, pop. 151,913
Largest city: Portland, pop. 550,396
Industry: Real estate, retail and wholesale trade, electronic equipment, health services, construction, forest products, business services
State flower/bird: Oregon grape/western meadowlark

Pennsylvania

Area: 46,055 sq mi (119,283 sq km)
Population: 12,448,279
Capital: Harrisburg, pop. 47,196
Largest city: Philadelphia, pop. 1,449,634
Industry: Machinery, printing and publishing, forest products, metal products
State flower/bird: Mountain laurel/ruffed grouse

Rhode Island

Area: 1,545 sq mi (4,002 sq km)
Population: 1,050,788
Capital: Providence, pop. 172,459
Largest city: Providence, pop. 172,459
Industry: Health services, business services, silver and jewelry products, metal products
State flower/bird: Violet/Rhode Island red

South Carolina

Area: 32,020 sq mi (82,932 sq km)
Population: 4,479,800
Capital: Columbia, pop. 124,818
Largest city: Columbia, pop. 124,818
Industry: Service industries, tourism, chemicals, textiles, machinery, forest products
State flower/bird: Yellow jessamine/Carolina wren

South Dakota

Area: 77,117 sq mi (199,732 sq km)
Population: 804,194
Capital: Pierre, pop. 14,032
Largest city: Sioux Falls, pop. 151,505
Industry: Finance, services, manufacturing, government, retail trade, transportation and utilities, wholesale trade, construction, mining
State flower/bird: Pasqueflower/ring-necked pheasant

TOWER OF HISTORY

The 125-foot (38-m) Astoria Column, built in 1926 near the mouth of the Columbia River in Oregon, is decorated with historic scenes of exploration and settlement along the Pacific Northwest coast.

COLOR KEY ● Northeast ● Southeast

Tennessee

Area: 42,143 sq mi (109,151 sq km)
Population: 6,214,888
Capital: Nashville, pop. 590,807
Largest city: Memphis, pop. 674,082
Industry: Service industries, chemicals, transportation equipment, processed foods, machinery
State flower/bird: Iris/mockingbird

Texas

Area: 268,581 sq mi (695,624 sq km)
Population: 24,326,974
Capital: Austin, pop. 743,074
Largest city: Houston, pop. 2,208,180
Industry: Chemicals, machinery, electronics and computers, food products, petroleum and natural gas, transportation equipment
State flower/bird: Bluebonnet/mockingbird

Utah

Area: 84,899 sq mi (219,888 sq km)
Population: 2,736,424
Capital: Salt Lake City, pop. 180,651
Largest city: Salt Lake City, pop. 180,651
Industry: Government, manufacturing, real estate, construction, health services, business services, banking
State flower/bird: Sego lily/California gull

Vermont

Area: 9,614 sq mi (24,901 sq km)
Population: 621,270
Capital: Montpelier, pop. 7,806
Largest city: Burlington, pop. 38,531
Industry: Health services, tourism, finance, real estate, computer components, electrical parts, printing and publishing, machine tools
State flower/bird: Red clover/hermit thrush

Virginia

Area: 42,774 sq mi (110,785 sq km)
Population: 7,769,089
Capital: Richmond, pop. 200,123
Largest city: Virginia Beach, pop. 434,743
Industry: Food processing, communication and electronic equipment, transportation equipment, printing, shipbuilding, textiles
State flower/bird: Flowering dogwood/cardinal

Washington

Area: 71,300 sq mi (184,666 sq km)
Population: 6,549,224
Capital: Olympia, pop. 44,925
Largest city: Seattle, pop. 594,210
Industry: Aerospace, tourism, food processing, forest products, paper products, industrial machinery, printing and publishing, metals, computer software
State flower/bird: Coast rhododendron/Amer. goldfinch

West Virginia

Area: 24,230 sq mi (62,755 sq km)
Population: 1,814,468
Capital: Charleston, pop. 50,478
Largest city: Charleston, pop. 50,478
Industry: Tourism, coal mining, chemicals, metal manufacturing, forest products, stone, clay, oil, glass products
State flower/bird: Rhododendron/cardinal

Wisconsin

Area: 65,498 sq mi (169,639 sq km)
Population: 5,627,967
Capital: Madison, pop. 228,775
Largest city: Milwaukee, pop. 602,191
Industry: Industrial machinery, paper products, food processing, metal products, electronic equipment, transportation
State flower/bird: Wood violet/robin

Wyoming

Area: 97,814 sq mi (253,337 sq km)
Population: 532,668
Capital: Cheyenne, pop. 55,641
Largest city: Cheyenne, pop. 55,641
Industry: Oil and natural gas, mining, generation of electricity, chemicals, tourism
State flower/bird: Indian paintbrush/western meadowlark

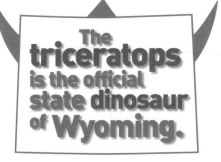

The **triceratops** is the official **state dinosaur** of **Wyoming.**

THE TERRITORIES

The United States has 14 territories, political divisions that are not states. Three of these are in the Caribbean Sea, and the other eleven are in the Pacific Ocean.

The brown tree snake probably arrived in Guam on cargo ships in the 1950s. The snake has greatly reduced the island's bird and small mammal populations and causes power outages when it climbs electrical poles.

U.S. CARIBBEAN TERRITORIES

Puerto Rico

Area: 3,508 sq mi (9,086 sq km)
Population: 3,958,000
Capital: San Juan (proper), pop. 424,951
Languages: Spanish, English

U.S. Virgin Islands

Area: 149 sq mi (386 sq km)
Population: 108,000
Capital: Charlotte Amalie, pop. 52,000
Languages: English, Spanish or Spanish Creole, French or French Creole

U.S. PACIFIC TERRITORIES

American Samoa

Area: 77 sq mi (199 sq km)
Population: 70,000
Capital: Pago Pago, pop. 58,000
Language: Samoan

Guam

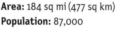

Area: 217 sq mi (561 sq km)
Population: 177,000
Capital: Hagåtña (Agana), pop. 149,000
Languages: English, Chamorro, Philippine languages

Northern Mariana Islands

Area: 184 sq mi (477 sq km)
Population: 87,000
Capital: Saipan, pop. 75,000
Languages: Philippine languages, Chinese, Chamorro, English

Other U.S. Territories

Baker Island, Howland Island, Jarvis Island, Johnston Atoll, Kingman Reef, Midway Islands, Palmyra Atoll, Wake Island, Navassa Island (in the Caribbean)

THE NATION'S CAPITAL

District of Columbia

Area: 68 sq mi (177 sq km)
Population: 591,833

Abraham Lincoln, who was President during the Civil War and a strong opponent of slavery, is remembered in a monument that houses this seated statue at the west end of the National Mall.

The Smithsonian Institution, the world's largest museum, is actually made up of 19 museums. Established in 1846, the Smithsonian is sometimes referred to as the nation's attic because of its large collections.

COLOR KEY ● Territories ● Northeast

Bet you didn't know

All state flags are rectangular **except Ohio's.** It's pennant-shaped.

Louisiana's state flag features a **mother pelican** feeding three chicks.

A 13-year-old designed **Alaska's flag.**

Georgia has the **newest flag** of any state, **adopted in 2003.**

George Washington **is the only real person** to be represented on a state flag—**Washington State's, of course.**

The United States' national bird, the **bald eagle,** appears on **ten state flags.**

Arkansas, one of the only states in the U.S. where **diamonds have been found,** features **two diamonds on its flag.**

Two-Letter Postal Abbreviations

AK	Alaska
AL	Alabama
AR	Arkansas
AS	American Samoa
AZ	Arizona
CA	California
CO	Colorado
CT	Connecticut
DC	District of Columbia
DE	Delaware
FL	Florida
GA	Georgia
GU	Guam
HI	Hawai'i
IA	Iowa
ID	Idaho
IL	Illinois
IN	Indiana
KS	Kansas
KY	Kentucky
LA	Louisiana
MA	Massachusetts
MD	Maryland
ME	Maine
MI	Michigan
MN	Minnesota
MO	Missouri
MP	Northern Mariana Islands
MS	Mississippi
MT	Montana
NC	North Carolina
ND	North Dakota
NE	Nebraska
NH	New Hampshire
NJ	New Jersey
NM	New Mexico
NV	Nevada
NY	New York
OH	Ohio
OK	Oklahoma
OR	Oregon
PA	Pennsylvania
PR	Puerto Rico
RI	Rhode Island
SC	South Carolina
SD	South Dakota
TN	Tennessee
TX	Texas
UT	Utah
VA	Virginia
VI	US Virgin Islands
VT	Vermont
WA	Washington
WI	Wisconsin
WV	West Virginia
WY	Wyoming

URBAN GIANT

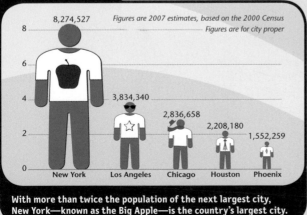

Figures are 2007 estimates, based on the 2000 Census
Figures are for city proper

- New York: 8,274,527
- Los Angeles: 3,834,340
- Chicago: 2,836,658
- Houston: 2,208,180
- Phoenix: 1,552,259

With more than twice the population of the next largest city, New York—known as the Big Apple—is the country's largest city.

Moving Along

Migration is when people move from one locality to another, often over long distances. Immigration is when this occurs between countries. Sounds simple, right? It's actually a lot more complicated than it sounds.

Migration, and, in turn, immigration, is an evolutionary force—a powerful pattern that can have a tremendous impact—on people, land, economy, history, and more. For example, imagine if you had a whole city of people who just got up and left. What would happen? The city would collapse because there would be no one to support it. That may be an extreme example of migration, but it does help to show just how influential it can be—and it's not so far off from the truth! After World War II, white Americans began leaving the major cities in droves to head for the newly created suburbs. This "suburbanization" occurred because people started to believe that the cities were dangerous and that the suburbs were safer places to raise families. As a result, the demographics of American cities changed greatly. Although most migrations are elective, they are generally out of a desire to change something about the circumstances in which the people currently live. People migrate to other places for economic reasons, environmental reasons, societal reasons, and even religious freedom. After all, what do you think the Puritans were doing when they first came to the New World?

Some migrations are forced, as a result of environmental or natural disasters, or authoritarian regimes trying to drive away groups of people. This international problem, known as human displacement, can be accompanied by a great deal of violence, particularly when it is conflict-induced. This can also cause large numbers of refugees, or people who flee to a foreign country to escape danger.

Migration of all types is a hot-button issue in our ever-changing world. It generates a tremendous amount of international economic, political, and ethical debate over policies toward immigrants and refugees.

POPULATION SHIFT

Since its creation, the United States has seen a number of migration shifts. In the latter half of the 20th century, people moved from the historical, industrial, and agricultural regions of the Northeast and Midwest toward the South and West. This move was motivated by the promise of jobs, generally lower living costs, and a more relaxed way of life. States such as Nevada, Arizona, and Idaho saw more than a 25 percent change in their total population.

Percent Change in Total Population from 1990 to 2000 (by State)

More than 25 | 13–25 | Less than 13

NATION OF IMMIGRANTS

Mexico
3,310,000

Figures represent the total number of legal permanent residents, 2006

Philippines
540,000

India
510,000

People's Republic of China
460,000

Dominican Republic
430,000

Since its founding, the United States has attracted people from other lands. Today, most immigrants to the U.S. come from Latin America and Asia.

Ellis Island, New York

United States/Mexico border fence

COOL CLICK

Learn about the American immigrant experience online. www.ellisisland.org

205

Wacky America

Check out these **5** strange-but-true roadside attractions.

Enchanted Highway **1**

REGENT, NORTH DAKOTA

Don't freak out when you spy a 40-foot-tall pheasant standing next to a highway— there's a 45-foot-tall farmer and a 60-foot-long grasshopper just down the road. The Enchanted Highway is a stretch of metal sculptures displayed for 32 miles along the road. You won't get bored on this drive!

2 Fremont Troll
SEATTLE, WASHINGTON

Even though this 18-foot-tall troll under a bridge is—*yikes!*—clutching a real car in his left hand, a person climbing up his arm won't bother him a bit. Made of concrete over steel rods and wire, the troll took about seven weeks to build. City officials hoped that the art would prevent people from dumping trash under the bridge. Or maybe they wanted to scare away the litterbugs.

3 The Topiary Garden
COLUMBUS, OHIO

You're supposed to think you're in a work of art when strolling through this park. The Topiary Garden is based on a 19th-century painting by Georges Seurat and includes hedges trimmed to look like 54 people, three dogs, a monkey, and more. Talk about life imitating art!

4 Noah Purifoy Outdoor Desert Art Museum
JOSHUA TREE, CALIFORNIA

Got junk? Maybe it'll end up here. This outdoor museum is two and a half acres of sculptures made from discarded materials such as toilets, vacuum cleaners, mannequin legs, bowling balls, and VCRs. That's one way to recycle!

5 Muskie the Fiberglass Fish
HAYWARD, WISCONSIN

If you're wondering what life looks like from the mouth of a giant fish, this sculpture is for you. A ramp takes you into the four-and-a-half story fish and up to a lookout deck in its mouth. From there, gaze down on other giant fiberglass fish in front of the National Freshwater Fishing Hall of Fame. Don't worry—there aren't any giant hooks!

ADULT HUMAN!

WORLD'S WILDEST THEME PARKS

T hink theme park thrills are just an American thing? Think again! Kids all over the world flock to parks in their own countries, with good reason. Check out these awesome attractions with their own national flair.

OCEAN PARK

HONG KONG, CHINA

WHY IT'S COOL Almost completely surrounded by the South China Sea, Ocean Park mixes wildlife with wild rides. For instance, visitors can watch the exciting *Sea Dreams* live show at Ocean Theatre, or they can wade in a pool to pet dolphins.

SIGNATURE RIDE High-rise cable cars carry people 673 feet to the top of the hilly park.

PLUS Animals at Ocean Park aren't all wet: Bamboo-munching giant pandas share the Lowland Gardens with birds and butterflies.

DREAMWORLD

GOLD COAST, QUEENSLAND, AUSTRALIA

WHY IT'S COOL Tired of roller coasters? Dreamworld has more than just rides. Get up close and personal with Aussie animals such as kangaroos, crocodiles, and koalas.

SIGNATURE RIDE Thrill seekers plummet 39 stories in 5 seconds on Giant Drop, the world's tallest free-fall ride.

PLUS Guests love the endangered Bengal tigers that romp around on Dreamworld's Tiger Island.

> A hotel in Las Vegas, Nevada, has a two-story-tall chocolate fountain.

I n the summer, there's no cooler place to be than a water park! And the coolest parks in the world for splishing, splashing, slipping, sliding, and getting soaked are located in the United States. See below for what riders have to say about two of the slides and rides that make these water parks such a big splash!

WILDWATER KINGDOM

ALLENTOWN, PENNSYLVANIA

"The blue slide is dark inside the whole time, which I like. But the red slide is my favorite. It has lots of bumps and hills on the way down. When I went over the bumps, I screamed—but because it was fun! I rode it seven times!"

Lindsay Cochran, Oak Harbor, Ohio

SCHLITTERBAHN

NEW BRAUNFELS, TEXAS

"At the top, you're so high up you can see everything. When you push off, you drop fast and the wind pulls back your hair. It feels like you're flying. It's over so fast that you want to do it again right away!"

Sarah Adams, New Braunfels, Texas

Funny FILL-IN
On the Road

Ask someone to give you words to fill in the blanks in this story without showing it to him or her. Then read it out loud for a laugh.

MOTEL

EAT

U.S. 301

OPEN

GAS

DINE

ALL-NIGHT DINER

CATTLE CROSSING

I'm so happy because my parents are taking me to _____ (your favorite vacation place).

I'll be able to swim in the _____ (adjective) _____ (a liquid) and play _____ (your favorite game) as much as I want. I just hope it's not like last year's _____ (adjective) trip. My parents, _____ (a relative), and I took the scenic route to _____ (a famous place). When we got on the road, my mother popped in a CD of _____ (famous person) and started _____ (verb ending in -ing) along to _____ (a song you hate). I was just about to get my _____ (adjective ending in -est) score ever on my favorite video game, when I heard a huge _____ (loud noise).

The car _____ (past-tense action verb) to a stop in front of a(n) _____ (something deep) in the road. I yelled, "_____ (exclamation)!" as my game _____ (past-tense action verb) out of the _____ (car part) and was _____ (past-tense action verb) over by a(n) _____ (adjective) _____ (large object) speeding by. Then I must have fallen asleep, because the next thing I knew, I heard _____ (animal sound, plural) and smelled _____ (something stinky). _____ (animal, plural) were crossing the road right in front of us!

By the time we finally arrived at _____ (same famous place), the hotel had given our _____ (noun) away and we had to sleep in a(n) _____ (type of shelter). Luckily, this year we're taking a cruise!

209

EARTH-FRIENDLY VACATIONS
How to have fun and protect the planet, too!

Going green can be a blast—especially if you do it while you're on vacation. Nothing's more fun than traveling to new places, but tourism can also hurt the environment. Cars and airplanes pollute the air. And tourists sometimes litter or damage the sites they come to see. So why be a regular tourist, when you can be an ecotourist? Earth-friendly travelers live by a golden rule: **Take only photographs, leave only footprints.** That means traveling to natural areas to observe—but not disturb—wild animals and plants. Ecotourists also explore local cultures, conserve resources such as water and fuel, and give back to the environment. Check out these cool vacations to find out how you can see the world and still be kind to the Earth.

GUIDE TO YOUR VACATION PERSONALITY

Find the symbols below that sound like you. Look for them on the right to pick a vacation that could be right for you.

- My favorite vacations are near the water.
- I love wildlife.
- I'm really active.
- I like learning about other cultures.

GIVE BACK TO THE EARTH

DESTINATION BELIZE

THE ADVENTURE Keep your eyes peeled for manatees and bottlenose dolphins as your boat floats around tropical islands. Then plunge into the crystal blue ocean for "swim breaks"—like recess in the water!

WHY IT'S ECO-FRIENDLY Counting manatees and dolphins helps scientists find out if the animals' habitat is thriving.

LEARN ABOUT ANIMALS

DESTINATION INDIA

THE ADVENTURE *Shh!* You're trying to spot tigers in Ranthambore National Park without disturbing the secretive cats. Spy on leopards and crocodiles, too. You also visit the Taj Mahal and other amazing sites.

WHY IT'S ECO-FRIENDLY The entrance fee to the park helps promote tiger conservation.

ECO-FRIENDLY LOCATIONS

DESTINATION PERU

THE ADVENTURE At the ExplorNapo eco-lodge in the Amazon River Rain Forest, you won't find electricity in your palm-thatched bedroom. But you will catch your own piranha fish for dinner, search for pink dolphins in the Amazon River, and climb up to a 115-foot-high walkway through the rain forest canopy.

WHY IT'S ECO-FRIENDLY The lodge conserves natural resources and donates profits toward saving the rain forest.

ECO-LINGO

eco-friendly Anything that's helpful, rather than harmful, to the environment.

green It's easy to be green. Just use less, and think renewable, sustainable, and eco-friendly.

Galápagos Islands
VACATION

Dozens of Pacific green sea turtles slowly glide by as you snorkel along a rugged reef. Suddenly a snorkeler cuts you off. Then another. Then you realize: These aren't snorkelers. They're sea lions! That's what might happen if you visit the Galápagos Islands, a group of islands straddling the equator near Ecuador, in South America.

Humans aren't allowed to live on most of the Galápagos Islands, which makes the animals very friendly. You can walk along hardened lava to see even more wildlife— a fur seal, bright red crabs, blue-footed booby's (right), shiny orcas, marine iguanas, flightless birds called cormorants, and penguins.

"The Galápagos Islands seem to break all the rules of nature," says a 14-year-old named Hannah who visited them.

A trip to the Galápagos Islands may change the way you think about the world.

TOP HISTORIC
Places to Visit

1	Wachau/Melk Abbey, Austria
2	Niagara-on-the-Lake, Ontario, Canada
3	Historic Center of Ghent, Belgium
4	Nikko historic areas, Japan
5	Graz, Austria
6	Stockholm's Gamla Stan, Sweden
7	Aix-en-Provence, France
8	Potsdam historic areas, Germany
9	Dijon and Bourgogne region, France
10	Mendoza wine estancias, Argentina

For more on these and other historic destinations, go online.
www.traveler.national
geographic.com

Just Joki

Q What travels a world but ne its corner?

A

SHOPPER'S PARADISE

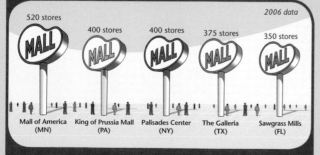

2006 data

520 stores — Mall of America (MN)
400 stores — King of Prussia Mall (PA)
400 stores — Palisades Center (NY)
375 stores — The Galleria (TX)
350 stores — Sawgrass Mills (FL)

Americans love to shop, and Bloomington, Minnesota's Mall of America has more retail stores than any other mall in the country.

The ORIGINAL 7 of the WONDERS of the WORLD

More than 2,000 years ago, many travelers wrote about sights they had seen on their journeys. Over time, seven of those places made history as the "wonders of the ancient world." There are seven because the Greeks, who made the list, believed the number seven to be magical.

THE PYRAMIDS OF GIZA, EGYPT
BUILT: ABOUT 2600 B.C.
MASSIVE TOMBS OF EGYPTIAN PHARAOHS, THE PYRAMIDS ARE THE ONLY ANCIENT WONDERS STILL STANDING TODAY.

HANGING GARDENS OF BABYLON, IRAQ
BUILT: DATE UNKNOWN
LEGEND HAS IT THAT THIS GARDEN PARADISE WAS PLANTED ON AN ARTIFICIAL MOUNTAIN, BUT MANY EXPERTS SAY IT NEVER REALLY EXISTED.

TEMPLE OF ARTEMIS AT EPHESUS, TURKEY
BUILT: SIXTH CENTURY B.C.
THIS TOWERING TEMPLE WAS BUILT TO HONOR ARTEMIS, THE GREEK GODDESS OF THE HUNT.

...ATUE OF ZEUS, GREECE
...ETH CENTURY B.C.
...STATUE ...KING ...DS.

MAUSOLEUM AT ...HALICARNASSUS, TURKEY
...UILT: FOURTH CENTURY B.C.
...S ELABORATE TOMB WAS ...T FOR KING MAUSOLUS.

...G...

...YPT
...RY B.C.
...HT-

212

The NEW 7 of the WONDERS of the WORLD

Why name new wonders of the world?
Most of the original ancient wonders no longer exist. To be eligible for the new list, the wonders had to be man-made before 2000 and in preservation. They were selected through a poll of over 100 million voters!

TAJ MAHAL, INDIA
COMPLETED: 1648
THIS LAVISH TOMB WAS BUILT AS A FINAL RESTING PLACE FOR THE BELOVED WIFE OF EMPEROR SHAH JAHAN.

PETRA, SOUTHWEST JORDAN
COMPLETED: ABOUT 200 B.C.
SOME 30,000 PEOPLE ONCE LIVED IN THIS ROCK CITY CARVED INTO CLIFF WALLS.

MACHU PICCHU, PERU
COMPLETED: ABOUT 1450
OFTEN CALLED "THE LOST CITY IN THE CLOUDS," MACHU PICCHU IS PERCHED 7,972 FEET HIGH IN THE ANDES MOUNTAINS.

THE COLOSSEUM, ITALY
COMPLETED: A.D. 80
WILD ANIMALS—AND HUMANS— FOUGHT EACH OTHER TO THE DEATH BEFORE 50,000 BLOOD- THIRSTY SPECTATORS.

CHRIST THE REDEEMER STATUE, BRAZIL
COMPLETED: 1931
TOWERING ATOP 2,310-FOOT- HIGH CORCOVADO MOUNTAIN, THIS STATUE IS TALLER THAN A 12-STORY BUILDING AND WEIGHS ABOUT 2.5 MILLION POUNDS.

CHICHÉN ITZÁ, MEXICO
COMPLETED: TENTH CENTURY
ONCE THE CAPITAL CITY OF THE ANCIENT MAYA EMPIRE, CHICHÉN ITZÁ IS HOME TO THE FAMOUS PYRAMID OF KUKULCÁN.

GREAT WALL OF CHINA, CHINA
COMPLETED: 1644
THE LONGEST MAN-MADE STRUCTURE EVER BUILT, THE GREAT WALL WINDS OVER AN ESTIMATED 4,500 MILES.

Cathedral
on the Square

AGELESS TIME
The famous astronomical clock, built in 1410 in Prague, Czech Republic, has an astronomical dial on top of a calendar dial. Together they keep track of time, as well as the movement of the sun, moon, and stars.

The onion-dome-topped towers of St. Basil's are a key landmark on Moscow's Red Square in Russia. Built between 1554 and 1560 to commemorate military campaigns by Ivan the Terrible, the building is rich in Christian symbolism.

THE UPRIGHT STUFF

The Tower of Pisa in Italy started tilting soon after its construction began more than 800 years ago. It was built on an ancient riverbed, which proved to be a foundation too soft to support a structure weighing 21 million pounds! By 1990 Italy's famously tilted landmark leaned so much that officials closed it to visitors, fearing it might fall over. But after years of repair work, the marble monument is again open to the public. And although you can't see the difference, it now leans 19 inches less. To straighten it, some 80 tons of soil was dug from below the side opposite the lean. When the ground underneath settled, the tower corrected itself slightly. Officials say it should be safe for tourists to walk up for another 200 years. That gives you plenty of time to plan a visit!

10 Cool Things About the WHITE HOUSE

Only a few families know what it's like to live in the White House, but we've got inside access. Here are ten reasons why it rocks when the White House is your home.

1 The President doesn't have to wait in an airport. Whenever he flies, a **helicopter** called *Marine One* lands right on the South Lawn of the White House to pick him up. The helicopter takes him to an air force base, where he walks right onto his plane, known as *Air Force One*.

2 Like sports? You'd love living in the White House. It has a basketball court, tennis court, swimming pool, **pool table**, putting green, and horseshoe pit.

3 If you're a guest at the White House, you might sleep in the **Lincoln Bedroom.** But Abe never slept there—it was his office. The Queens' Bedroom, next door, is named for the many queens who have stayed there.

4 There's no helping Dad paint the house at the White House. Workers use **570 gallons of paint** to cover the outside. A tower of 570 gallon-size cans is taller than the Statue of Liberty!

5 You probably won't wait for a **bathroom** at the White House. It has 35 of them, 15 of which contain bathtubs or showers.

6 Holidays at the White House are always fun for kids. On the Monday after every Easter, an Easter Egg Roll is held on the South Lawn. During Christmas the First Family holds a special party just for kids. The White House **Christmas tree** is usually almost 20 feet tall!

7 How'd you like to ride to school in this? The President is picked up in Cadillac One, a **special limousine** that's driven only by Secret Service agents. It's so safe that no one will even hint at what kind of security devices are installed in the car. All we can tell you is that only Secret Service agents can open and close the doors. The limo is even flown overseas when the President travels!

8

If you want a midnight snack, somewhere in the White House there's one waiting 24/7. The White House has five kitchens—a main one on the ground floor, an upstairs kitchen for the family, an underground one for the staff, one for guests, and a **pastry kitchen** just for desserts. With five chefs on duty, the food staff can prepare dinner for 140 people and snacks for more than 1,000.

9

Some claim the White House is haunted. Legend has it that President **John Adams's ghostly wife, Abigail,** hangs laundry. Other people say they've glimpsed Lincoln's ghost pacing the floor. One tale even tells of the ghost of Dolley Madison shouting at workers about to tear up her rose garden.

10

The First Family never has to go out to the movies—the White House has a **59-seat theater.** The President sees movies with family and friends, sometimes before the flicks open at the box office.

Ever wonder what's hanging on the walls of the White House? Well, it has quite the fine art collection, and it is featured throughout the building. Go online to find out more about this beautiful national collection. www.whitehouse.gov/history/art

COOL CLICK

FINDING YOUR WAY AROUND

EVERY MAP HAS A STORY TO TELL, but first you have to know how to read one. Maps represent information by using a language of symbols. Knowing how to read these symbols provides access to a wide range of information. Look at the scale and compass rose or arrow to understand distance and direction (see box below).

To find out what each symbol on a map means, you must use the key. It's your secret decoder—identifying information by each symbol on the map.

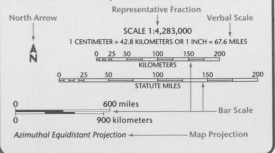

Latitude

Longitude

SYMBOLS

There are three main types of map symbols: points, lines, and areas. Points, which can be either dots or small icons, represent locations of things, such as schools, cities, or landmarks. Lines are used to show boundaries, roads, or rivers and can vary in color or thickness. Area symbols use patterns or color to show regions, such as a sandy area or a neighborhood.

POINT
A point symbol, a black dot, indicates a city, such as 'Omdurman.

LINE
Sudan's country boundary appears as a line symbol: a dotted line with a colored edge.

AREA
Sandy places, such as parts of the Sahara Desert, are shown by a tan, speckled area.

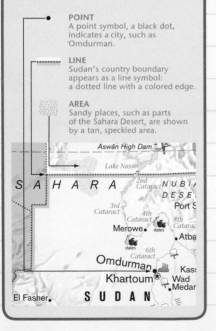

LATITUDE AND LONGITUDE LINES (above) help us determine locations on Earth. Every place on Earth has a special address called absolute location. Imaginary lines, called lines of latitude, run west to east, parallel to the equator. These lines measure distance in degrees north or south from the equator (0° latitude) to the North Pole (90°N) or to the South Pole (90°S). One degree of latitude is approximately 70 miles (113 km).

Lines of longitude run north to south, meeting at the poles. These lines measure distance in degrees east or west from 0° longitude (prime meridian) to 180° longitude. The prime meridian runs through Greenwich, England.

SCALE & DIRECTION

The scale on a map is shown as a fraction, as words, or as a line or bar. It relates distance on the map to distance in the real world. Sometimes the scale identifies the type of map projection. Maps may include an arrow or compass rose to indicate north on the map.

North Arrow

Representative Fraction

Verbal Scale

SCALE 1:4,283,000

1 CENTIMETER = 42.8 KILOMETERS OR 1 INCH = 67.6 MILES

N

| 0 | 25 | 50 | 100 | 150 | 200 |
KILOMETERS

| 0 | 25 | 50 | 100 | 150 | 200 |
STATUTE MILES

| 0 | 600 miles |
| 0 | 900 kilometers |

Bar Scale

Azimuthal Equidistant Projection ◄———— Map Projection

WHAT'S AN ATLAS?

An atlas, or collection of maps, is usually chock-full of information, charts, and illustrations. For example, the *National Geographic World Atlas For Young Explorers* is full of photographs, statistics, quick facts, and—most of all—lots of detailed maps and charts. Plus, there is a companion website, which adds even more. The website expands upon specific subjects in the atlas and also helps you explore on your own, taking you deep into the resources of National Geographic and beyond.

Fun stuff you can do on the atlas website:
- watch animal videos
- listen to animal sounds
- listen to music from different cultures
- find country information
- download pictures and maps for your reports
- play games that allow you to explore
- send e-postcards to your friends

COOL CLICK

www.nationalgeographic.com/kids-world-atlas

HOW TO USE THE ATLAS WEBSITE

START HERE: www.nationalgeographic.com/kids-world-atlas
Here are three ways to find what you are looking for from the home page: If you have the book, you can search (1) BY ATLAS PAGE NUMBER or (2) BY ICON. If you don't have the book, search (3) BY TOPIC.

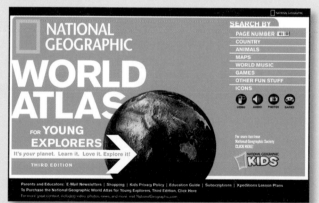

2. SEARCH BY ICON

If you want to find all the videos referenced in the atlas, or all of the audio, photos, or games, click on one of the icons. A list will drop down, and you choose. Clicking on King Tut takes you to several King Tut videos.

3. SEARCH BY TOPIC

If you want to explore a specific topic, click on the entry in the topic list. You'll find vast quantities of information, photos, videos, games, and more, all arranged by subject. Say you're interested in animals. One click takes you to the animals choice page.

1. SEARCH BY ATLAS PAGE NUMBER

If you find an icon in the atlas and want to go directly to that link, use the page number pull-down menu. Just drag and click.

Going Green

A kid in Cedarburg, Wisconsin, climbs an old maple tree.

6 ways YOU affect Earth

IN YOUR LIFETIME, YOU WILL...

1 eat an amount of **hamburger meat** (if you eat meat) equal to the weight of a family car.

2 own **8** microwave ovens, **10 TV sets,** and **13** cars.

3 use more than **1.2 million** gallons of water— enough to overflow two Olympic-size swimming pools.

5 gobble down **9,917** pounds of potatoes. That's the weight of about eight average-size racehorses.

4 throw away enough **trash** to fill up about five garbage trucks.

6 drive approximately **627,000 miles—** or 25 times around the world—using enough gasoline to fill 3 fuel tankers.

All statistics are based on estimated overall U.S. consumption.
Based on the average life span in the U.S. of 77 years and 9 months.

Try This!

REDUCE, REUSE, and RECYCLE are three important things you can do to be eco-friendly. Can you think of a way you might be able to reuse and recycle old clothes?

Don't throw out old clothes that don't fit you. Someone else may be able to use them. You and your siblings may have outgrown many of the clothes taking up space in your closets and drawers. Your parents also may have clothing they don't wear anymore. Challenge your family to sort through their closets. Donate clean clothes in good shape to a charity that will distribute them to people in need— survivors of a flood, tornado, or fire, for example, or people who are going through hard times and can't afford new clothes.

ECO-LINGO

climate change

A long-term and worldwide change in temperature, rainfall, snowfall, fog, frost, hail, wind, and storms. Gradual warming and cooling of Earth's climate has been a natural process throughout its history.

fossil fuel

Coal, petroleum, and natural gas that is burned to generate heat or power. The less we use, the better.

carbon dioxide (CO_2)

Every time you breathe out, you release CO_2 gas. Burning forests to clear land and using fossil fuels for energy emit carbon into the atmosphere, where it combines with oxygen to form CO_2. A little CO_2 in the atmosphere is a good thing; a lot is bad. Trees and other plants filter out CO_2, but their destruction reduces this natural filtering process.

global warming

An increase in Earth's average surface temperature. The increase in CO_2 and other gases—such as methane—is the major cause of this warming. By 2100, Earth's temperature may rise by several degrees, melting glaciers, drying up wetlands, and raising sea levels.

Environmental Hot Spots

Around the world people are putting more and more pressure on the environment. They are dumping pollutants into the air and water, and removing natural vegetation to extract mineral resources or turn the land into cropland for farming. In more developed countries, industries create waste and pollution; farmers use fertilizers and pesticides that run off into water supplies; and motor vehicles release exhaust fumes into the air. In less developed countries, forests are cut down for fuel or to clear land for farming; grasslands are turned into deserts as farmers and herders overuse the land; and expanding urban areas face problems of water quality and sanitation.

Old Phones Get New Homes

Boulder, Colorado

There are more than 200 million cell phone users in the United States alone. When old cell phones end up in landfills, they can leak dangerous chemicals into the water supply. Collective Good International, based in Colorado, has come up with a clever solution. The company partners with charitable groups to collect old cell phones. It then repairs and distributes them to developing countries where many people have never owned a telephone at all.

221

Pollution

Cleaning Up Our Act

So what's the big deal about a little dirt on the planet? Just ask this sea otter (below). Pollution can affect animals, plants, and people. In fact, some studies show that more people die every year from diseases linked to air pollution than from car accidents. And right now, about 17 percent of the world's people don't have access to clean drinking water.

A LITTLE POLLUTION= BIG PROBLEMS

You can probably clean your room in a couple of hours. (At least we hope you can!) But you can't shove air and water pollution under your bed or cram them into the closet. Once released into the environment, pollution—whether it's oil leaking from a boat or chemicals spewing from a factory's smokestack—can have a lasting environmental impact.

KEEP IT CLEAN

It's easy to blame things like big factories for pollution problems. But some of the mess comes from everyday activities. Exhaust fumes from cars and garbage in landfills can seriously trash Earth's health. We all need to pitch in and do some house-cleaning on Earth. It may mean bicycling more and riding in cars less. Or not dumping water-polluting oil or household cleaners down the drain. Look at it this way: Just like your room, it's always better not to let Earth get messed up in the first place.

A sea otter at the Monterey Bay National Marine Sanctuary, Monterey, California.

Light Pollution

Seattle, Washington, at night

Bright lights threaten more than stargazing.
For some wildlife, it's a matter of "light" and death.
Light pollution, which is excessive or obtrusive artificial light, can affect ecosystems in many ways.
For example, it blocks bugs from navigating their way, disorients birds, and misdirects turtles and frogs.

Declining Biodiversity
Saving All Creatures Great and Small

Earth is home to such a huge mix of plants and animals—perhaps 100 million—that scientists have officially identified and named only about 1.75 million! Scientists call this healthy mix biodiversity.

THE BALANCING ACT
The bad news is that half of the planet's plant and animal species may be on the path to extinction, mainly because of human activity. People cut down trees, build roads and houses, pollute rivers, and overfish and overhunt. The good news is that people care. Many scientific groups and volunteers race against the clock every day, working to save wildlife before time runs out. By building birdhouses, planting trees, and following the rules for hunting and fishing, you can be a positive force for preserving biodiversity, too. Every time you do something to help a species survive, you help keep Earth rich.

A white tip reef shark atop a coral reef location

BIODIVERSITY OF EARTH'S WILDLIFE

Insects, Centipedes, and Millipedes

Other Animals

Mammals

Habitat Destruction
Living on the Edge

Even though tropical rain forests cover only about seven percent of the planet's total land surface, they are home to half of all known species of plants and animals. Because people cut down so many trees for lumber and firewood and clear so much land for farms, hundreds of thousands of acres disappear every year.

SHARING THE LAND
Wetlands are also important feeding and breeding grounds. People have drained many wetlands, turning them into farm fields or sites for industries. Over half the world's wetlands have disappeared within the past century, squeezing wildlife out. Finding a balance between the needs humans and animals have for land is the key to lessening habitat destruction.

A captive jaguar lives in his natural rain forest habitat.

223

Overpopulation

It's Getting Crowded in Here

Every 60 seconds, more than 250 people are born. Based on expected birth and death rates, experts predict that our planet could be home to more than 9 billion people by the early 2040s. That's a big increase from the nearly 7 billion who populate Earth now. The world's two most populous countries are China and India. They have more than a billion people each.

TOO LITTLE FOR TOO MANY

The United States and other wealthy countries have fewer people but use up much more of the world's resources. Countries that use a lot of resources and countries that have a lot of people put pressure on the planet. To feed everyone, we must either grow more food on existing farms or carve new farmland out of wilderness areas, which is not as simple as it seems. Disposing of massive amounts of waste, producing enough heat and electricity, and curbing rising pollution are some of the other challenges that must be met before everyone on Earth can live comfortably. In an effort to slow population growth in China, most couples there must ask permission from the government to have more than one child. Some countries have found that providing citizens with more education and better job opportunities has helped slow population growth. But still the world population continues to increase.

Farmers working in a rice paddy field

World Food

Earth produces enough food for all its inhabitants—the nearly 7 billion and growing—but not everyone gets enough to eat. It's a matter of distribution. Food-producing regions are unevenly spread around the world, and it is sometimes difficult to move food supplies from areas of surplus to areas of great need.

STILL NOT ENOUGH

In recent decades, food production has increased, especially production of meat and cereals, such as corn, wheat, and rice. But increased yields of grain require intensive use of fertilizers and irrigation, which are not only expensive but also possibly a threat to the environment.

MORE PEOPLE, FEWER RESOURCES

"Developing countries, with so many people, can't afford to waste food, water, and energy," says Karen Kasmauski, who photographed a story on population growth for NATIONAL GEOGRAPHIC. "In the U.S. we think we can afford to waste resources, but we can't. We're stealing from future generations. Rich societies like ours often think that overpopulation is only a problem in countries where the birth rate is very high. But a family with a gas-gulping SUV and a huge house they must heat and cool is a bigger environmental threat."

Do your part to help conserve resources.

1. Learn to recognize the difference between *wanting* things and *needing* them. Advertising aimed at kids often targets "wants."
2. Don't waste food. Think about what went into growing, packaging, and transporting the things you eat.
3. Recycle glass, paper, and plastic.

CHANGING THE LAND

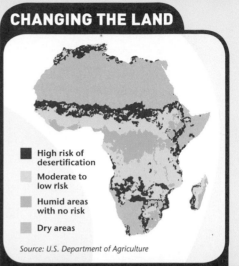

- High risk of desertification
- Moderate to low risk
- Humid areas with no risk
- Dry areas

Source: U.S. Department of Agriculture

Overgrazing, removal of vegetation by farmers, and unreliable rainfall are turning some land in Africa into deserts—a process called desertification.

ENVIRONMENTAL TRAGEDY
These giants of the rain forest dwarf two children in the Amazon village of Paragominas in Brazil. Harvesting such trees provides income for villagers but poses a serious long-term threat to the environment.

📷 **CLOSE-UP**

Phew! That STINKS!

The biggest flower in the world is this very stinky Sumatran Corpse Flower. This rare, ancient lily, from the tropical rain forests of Sumatra, is best known for its sickening smell (much like rotting dead animals!). Luckily, it doesn't bloom very often!

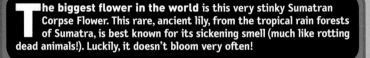

MEET THE NAT GEO EXPLORERS

CID SIMÕES AND PAOLA SEGURA

As sustainable agriculturists and development experts, this husband-wife team are protecting the planet—and Brazil's small farmers—one fruit tree at a time.

What was your closest call in the field?
Fortunately we have not had any close calls—only fun troubles, like fighting angry ants and bees, getting stuck in mud, getting covered with dust, and having to walk a lot when the car is broken or without gas.

How would you suggest kids follow in your footsteps?
Many people believe that agriculture is boring and hard work, but you can have a lot of fun. Like genetics, agriculture is one of a few sciences in the world where you can create a new "creature," like when we breed two flowers together to make a new one. A new creature can help hungry people, cure diseases, or even help bring peace and harmony. You just need to play with soil, plants, and water!

What is one place or thing you'd still like to explore?
We would love to keep exploring the world of microorganisms. There are millions and billions of them working for and against us. To learn how to control them and use their power in our favor is very important for the balance of the planet.

9 Tips to Save Earth

1 **Recycle** newsprint, cardboard, plastic, and other household waste. This can reduce carbon dioxide (CO_2) emissions, a greenhouse gas that many scientists believe contribute to global warming.

2 **Walk, ride your bike, or carpool.** Driving 15 minutes less a week can save 900 pounds (408 kg) of CO_2 a year.

3 **Buy snacks in bulk.** By doing away with individual wrappers, you'll throw away less of the 4.6 pounds (2 kg) of trash each person pitches every day.

4 **Put on a sweater.** Don't turn up the heat in the house when you're chilly. Wear more clothes! That can keep 300 pounds (136 kg) of CO_2 out of the air each year.

5 **Always turn off the lights** when you leave a room.

6 **Plant a tree** to put more oxygen into the atmosphere.

7 **Change lightbulbs** to compact fluorescent lights. Just one could save 500 pounds (227 kg) of coal a year.

8 **Drive better.** Ask your parents to drive a more fuel-efficient car. An electric or hybrid car can save 5,600 pounds (2,540 kg) of CO_2 a year.

9 **Stop water waste.** In many homes, toilets use more water than anything else. An older toilet may use more than five gallons of water each time it's flushed! Try this only with an older toilet and with a parent's permission. Clean out a one-gallon plastic jug (a milk or juice container will work), and make sure you take off any labels. Fill the jug with stones to make it heavy. Place the jug into the toilet tank, being very careful that it doesn't touch any of the toilet's inner workings. Now every time that toilet is flushed, it's using a gallon less water than it used to!

Try This! MAKE AN herb garden

YOU WILL NEED
• SMALL HERB PLANTS SUCH AS THYME, BASIL, AND ROSEMARY • SANDWICH BAG FULL OF SMALL STONES • POTTING SOIL • TROWEL OR LARGE SPOON • HOMEMADE LABELS FOR HERBS (WE MADE THEM BY GLUEING CRAFT FOAM ONTO WOODEN SKEWERS) • GARDENING GLOVES • LARGE FLOWERPOT TO PLANT ALL THE ITEMS

WHAT TO DO
Cover the bottom of the large flowerpot with stones for drainage. Fill the pot partway with soil. Carefully remove the plants from their containers and position them in the larger pot, leaving some space between each plant. Fill in soil around the plants. Water until the soil is damp, then place the flowerpot in a sunny spot. Water the herbs when the soil dries out—about once a week. Then watch your garden grow.

Global Warming

Bet you didn't know

It's getting hot in here.

In the past century, average temperatures rose one degree Fahrenheit. That may not seem like a lot, but evidence shows that it is enough to change weather patterns and shift the directions of ocean currents. This is an effect of global warming. The heat is melting glaciers and polar ice sheets, causing sea levels to rise and habitats to shrink. This makes survival for many animals a big challenge. Warming also means flooding along the coasts and drought for inland areas.

The world's climate changes naturally, but now people are speeding up the process. Everyday activities, such as driving cars that use gasoline and burning fossil fuels, contribute to global warming. These kinds of activities produce "greenhouse gases," which seep into the atmosphere and trap heat. Scientists predict that temperatures may continue to rise by as much as 10°F over the next hundred years.

Windmills on a wind farm **capture** the breeze and turn it into **energy.**

Wind is the world's **fastest-** growing **energy** source.

The **U.S.** is the world's **biggest producer** of **WIND POWER.**

A World at RISK

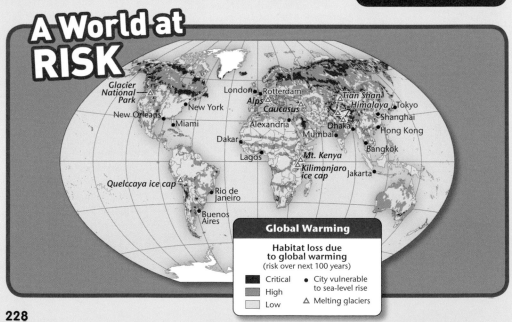

Glacier National Park
London
Rotterdam
Alps
Caucasus
Tian Shan
Himalaya
Tokyo
New York
Shanghai
New Orleans
Miami
Alexandria
Dhaka
Hong Kong
Dakar
Mumbai
Bangkok
Lagos
Mt. Kenya
Kilimanjaro ice cap
Jakarta
Quelccaya ice cap
Rio de Janeiro
Buenos Aires

Global Warming

Habitat loss due to global warming
(risk over next 100 years)

- ■ Critical
- ■ High
- ■ Low
- • City vulnerable to sea-level rise
- △ Melting glaciers

WARNING ON WARMING

Scientists say Earth is heating up. That means changes all over the world. This list tells you a bit of what's happening. Use National Geographic's online MapMachine at **maps.nationalgeographic.com** to find maps of these hot spots.

Antarctic Peninsula, Antarctica
Winter temperatures are 11 degrees (Fahrenheit) higher than 50 years ago. Sea ice has shrunk by a fifth, making it tougher for Adélie penguins to survive. Bird populations are shrinking.

Argentina, South America
Rising temperatures and water shortages have sparked massive wildfires in recent years.

Great Barrier Reef, Pacific Ocean near Australia
Ocean water is slowly growing warmer. The heat is hurting and even killing big pieces of the world's largest coral reef.

Hudson Bay, Canada
Winter ice melts two to three weeks earlier than before. That makes it harder for polar bears to find food.

Utah, United States
The last ten years have been very dry in the western United States. As a result, Lake Powell is about half full.

Virgin Islands, Caribbean Sea
Warmer weather is causing problems for sea turtles. The warmer temps make more females hatch than males. Scientists don't know how that will affect the sea turtle populations.

ARCTIC RESEARCH

Scientists wearing cold weather survival suits prepare to measure salt content, nutrients, and plant and animal life in ice and meltwater. They also monitor changes related to global warming, such as the shrinking of the polar ice cap.

World Energy & Minerals

Almost everything people do—from cooking to powering a space shuttle—requires energy. But energy comes in different forms. Traditional energy sources, still used by many people in the developing world, include burning dried animal dung and wood. Industrialized countries and urban centers around the world rely on coal, oil, and natural gas—called fossil fuels because they formed from decayed plant and animal material accumulated from long ago. Fossil fuel deposits, either in the ground or under the ocean floor, are unevenly distributed on Earth, and only some countries can afford to buy them. Fossil fuels are also not renewable, meaning they will run out one day. And unless we find other ways to create energy, we'll be stuck. Without energy we won't be able to drive cars, use lights, or send emails to your friends!

TAKING A TOLL

Environmentally speaking, burning fossil fuels isn't necessarily the best choice either—carbon dioxide from the burning of fossil fuels, as well as other emissions, are contributing to global warming. Concerned scientists are looking at new ways to harness renewable, alternative sources of energy, such as water, wind, and sun.

COOL CLICK To learn more about global trends, go online. www.national geographic.com/ earthpulse

OIL, GAS, AND COAL

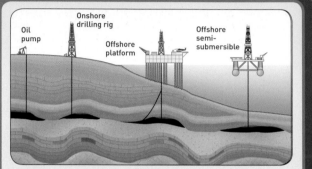

This illustration shows some of the different kinds of onshore and offshore drilling equipment. The type of drilling equipment depends on whether oil or natural gas is in the ground or under the ocean.

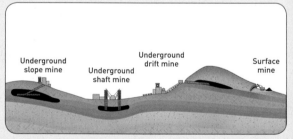

The mining of coal made the industrial revolution possible, and coal still provides a major energy source. Work that was once done by people using picks and shovels now relies heavily on mechanized equipment. This diagram shows some of the various kinds currently in use.

WORLD TOTAL PRIMARY ENERGY SUPPLY

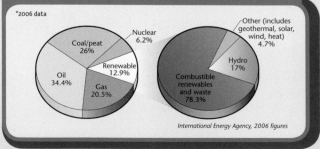

*2006 data

Coal/peat 26%
Nuclear 6.2%
Renewable 12.9%
Oil 34.4%
Gas 20.5%

Other (includes geothermal, solar, wind, heat) 4.7%
Hydro 17%
Combustible renewables and waste 78.3%

International Energy Agency, 2006 figures

230

Alternative Power

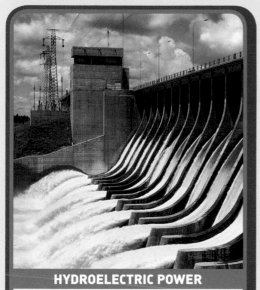

HYDROELECTRIC POWER

Hydroelectric plants, such as Santiago del Estero in Argentina (above), use dams to harness running water to generate clean, renewable energy.

SOLAR POWER

Solar panels on Samso Island in Denmark capture and store energy from the sun, an environmentally friendly alternative to the use of fossil fuels.

GEOTHERMAL POWER

Geothermal power, originating from groundwater heated by magma, provides energy for this power plant in Iceland. Swimmers enjoy the warm, mineral-rich waters of a lake created by the power plant.

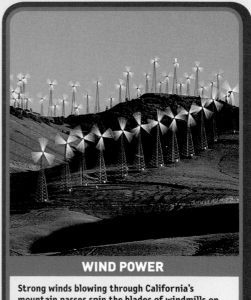

WIND POWER

Strong winds blowing through California's mountain passes spin the blades of windmills on an energy farm, powering giant turbines that generate electricity for the state.

Try This!

Save energy.
Think about what you need
before opening the refrigerator!

The average family opens the fridge 22 times a day. Every time it is opened, cold air whooshes out and warm air takes its place (even more if you have a curious baby brother). This makes the fridge use extra electricity to cool back down.

Don't stand with the fridge door open while you decide what you want. Decide first, *then* open, grab, and shut—quickly. Reduce the cold air you let out and the warm air you let in to lower your use of electricity. Also ask your parents to make sure the fridge is set at the proper temperature, and increase your refrigerator's efficiency by keeping its coils clean.

weird but true

SOME CARS CAN RUN ON USED FRENCH-FRY OIL.

GREEN ENERGY

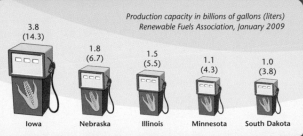

Production capacity in billions of gallons (liters)
Renewable Fuels Association, January 2009

3.8 (14.3)	1.8 (6.7)	1.5 (5.5)	1.1 (4.3)	1.0 (3.8)
Iowa	Nebraska	Illinois	Minnesota	South Dakota

In the United States, Iowa is the leading producer of ethanol, a clean-burning, renewable, non-fossil fuel energy source made from corn.

ENERGY FROM WATER

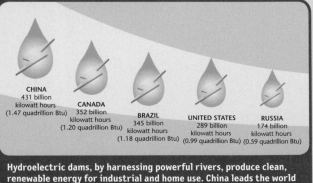

CHINA 431 billion kilowatt hours (1.47 quadrillion Btu)
CANADA 352 billion kilowatt hours (1.20 quadrillion Btu)
BRAZIL 345 billion kilowatt hours (1.18 quadrillion Btu)
UNITED STATES 289 billion kilowatt hours (0.99 quadrillion Btu)
RUSSIA 174 billion kilowatt hours (0.59 quadrillion Btu)

Hydroelectric dams, by harnessing powerful rivers, produce clean, renewable energy for industrial and home use. China leads the world in hydropower production.

Turning GREEN

Every day the media is filled with stories about global warming, pollution, and dwindling resources. Headlines warn of environmental risks that may threaten our way of life. The United States is the source of a quarter of the world's greenhouse gas emissions, and Americans generate more than 250 million tons of trash each year and only recycle about 33 percent of their waste. The average American also uses 32 times more resources than a person in the African country of Kenya. But there's a bright side to these grim statistics. We can make a positive difference to the environment by making simple lifestyle changes, such as using cars that run on alternative fuels. It is up to each of us to make changes that take advantage of these environmentally friendly developments.

SHARE THE ROAD

Biking to work or school reduces the use of gasoline, a source of greenhouse gases, and it is healthy, too.

COOL CLICK

Zipper has green tips for you. Check them out online.
kids.nationalgeographic.com/Stories/SpaceScience/Green-tips

A GREEN RIDE

Can a motorcycle be both superfast and eco-friendly?

The Die Moto bike (left) clocks in at more than 130 miles an hour and holds a world land speed record for diesel motorcycles. Even better, the speedster does so on biodiesel. Unlike diesel or regular fuel, which are produced from oil from the earth, biodiesel is made mainly from vegetable oil—the same stuff that's used for cooking! Biodiesel is cleaner and emits fewer pollutants into the air.

Volunteering

Not sure how you can make a difference in the world? One great way to help out is to volunteer. There are tons of places and organizations looking for volunteers to help them with their efforts. You can also design and organize your own project for your community.

Think about what interests you. Do you like to cook? Maybe you can organize a bake sale to raise money for a charity. Perhaps you love animals. Volunteer at a zoo. There are tons of options.

> A volunteer is a **PERSON** who freely **GIVES** of their **TIME** and **EFFORTS** to **HELP OTHERS** or the community.

Here are some other fun ways to volunteer:

- **Renew a park,** school, or community area by planting flowers or trees.
- **Help deliver food** to seniors and others who may be house-bound.
- **Distribute food** at local homeless shelters or soup kitchens.
- **Offer to walk the pets** of a senior citizen.
- **Donate toys** and goods to organizations for needy children.
- **Tutor children or adults** in reading and other subjects.
- **Sponsor a food drive** for an area food bank or shelter.
- **Recycle old clothing** by donating to shelters or orphanages.
- **Clean up your community** by picking up trash.

Grab a friend, gather your family, or volunteer on your own to help make your world a better place. Volunteering will not only help others and the world around you, it will be a fantastic experience for you, too.

COOL CLICK

If you're still not sure how to volunteer, go online for lots of opportunities and ideas.
www.hud.gov/kids/kidsvlta.html

Take the Plunge

Help this scuba diver clean up the coral reef. Find the following items that don't belong under the sea.

- toy car
- in-line skate
- wristwatch
- peanut butter
- beach ball
- sneaker
- sunglasses
- bananas
- suntan lotion
- scooter
- boat oar

ANSWERS ON PAGE 339

235

It's easy to protect the planet! These 30 tips help save limited resources such as water, energy, and animals; prevent landfill waste; or decrease harmful gases, such as CO_2, which contribute to global warming. So get green and give the tips a try.

EARTH'S FIRST-AID KIT

MAKE SURE TO ASK YOUR PARENTS BEFORE TRYING ANY OF THESE TIPS!

1 BUY METAL OR CERAMIC BOWLS FOR YOUR PET.

PLASTIC BOWLS ARE MADE FROM OIL, A LIMITED RESOURCE.

Check out the website link below for more green tips.

www.kids.nationalgeographic.com

2 SET THE THERMOSTAT TO NO LOWER THAN 78°F (26°C) IN THE SUMMER AND NO HIGHER THAN 68°F (20°) IN THE WINTER.

3 SET OUT CANS AND BOTTLES FOR NEIGHBORHOOD PICKUP, OR EXCHANGE THEM FOR CASH AT A RECYCLING CENTER.

4 TAKE A REUSABLE BAG (SUCH AS ONE MADE OUT OF CLOTH) TO THE STORE INSTEAD OF USING PAPER OR PLASTIC.

5 CHOOSE LOCALLY GROWN FOOD. TRANSPORTING FOOD LONG DISTANCES WASTES FUEL AND CREATES EXTRA CO_2.

6 TURN OFF THE TV OR VIDEO GAME CONSOLE AND PLAY OUTSIDE.

7 REPLACE INCANDESCENT LIGHTBULBS WITH COMPACT FLUORESCENT ONES. THEY LAST UP TO TEN TIMES LONGER AND CAN USE A QUARTER OF THE ENERGY.

8 SCRAPE LEFTOVERS OFF THE DISHES INSTEAD OF RINSING THEM. (WASH THE DISHES SOON AFTER.)

9 KEEP THOSE FANS BUZZING IN SUMMER INSTEAD OF TURNING ON THE AIR CONDITIONER.

10 BUY A LITTLE BIT LESS. DO YOU REALLY NEED IT? CAN YOU RENT OR BORROW IT? CAN YOU FIND IT USED?

11 CARPOOL.

12 TURN OVER USED PAPER AND USE IT FOR ARTWORK OR SCRAP PAPER.

13 CHOOSE RECHARGEABLE BATTERIES. THEN RECYCLE THEM WHEN THEY DIE.

14 RIDE A BIKE OR WALK INSTEAD OF USING THE CAR.

15 CLOSE YOUR CURTAINS TO KEEP OUT DAYTIME SUMMER HEAT OR KEEP IN NIGHTTIME WINTER WARMTH.

16

PARTICIPATE IN CLEANUP DAYS AT A BEACH OR PARK.

17 ASK MOM OR DAD TO TURN OFF THE CAR INSTEAD OF LETTING IT IDLE WHILE YOU'RE WAITING.

18 PLANT A DECIDUOUS (LEAFY) TREE THAT LOSES ITS LEAVES IN FALL ON THE SOUTH SIDE OF YOUR HOME. ITS SHADE WILL COOL YOUR HOUSE IN THE SUMMER. AFTER THE TREE'S LEAVES FALL, SUNLIGHT WILL HELP WARM YOUR HOUSE IN WINTER.

19 PLUG ELECTRONICS INTO A POWER STRIP AND FLIP OFF THE SWITCH WHEN THE GADGETS AREN'T IN USE. (MAKE SURE THIS WON'T MESS UP CLOCKS AND RECORDINGS.)

20 REUSE CREATIVELY! FOR INSTANCE, USE EMPTY YOGURT CONTAINERS AS PAINT CUPS OR PLANT POTS.

21 PLACE YOUR DESK NEXT TO A WINDOW AND USE NATURAL LIGHT INSTEAD OF A LAMP.

22

USE THOSE OUTDOOR TRASH CANS! NEVER LITTER.

EARTH'S FIRST-AID KIT

23 SHARE THESE GREEN TIPS WITH YOUR FAMILY AND FRIENDS.

24 TURN OFF THE WATER WHILE BRUSHING YOUR TEETH.

25 TAKE SHORT SHOWERS INSTEAD OF BATHS. AIM FOR FIVE MINUTES— BUT STILL GET CLEAN!

26 CREATE A LENDING LIBRARY. SHARE ITEMS SUCH AS BOOKS, DVDS, OR VIDEO GAMES WITH YOUR FRIENDS AND NEIGHBORS.

30 "ADOPT" AN ENDANGERED ANIMAL THROUGH A CHARITY.

27 SEND AN E-CARD INSTEAD OF A PAPER CARD.

28 SWITCH OFF THE LIGHT EVERY TIME YOU LEAVE A ROOM.

29 PACK YOUR LUNCH WITH REUSABLE UTENSILS, A CLOTH NAPKIN, AND A CUP. CARRY LUNCH IN A METAL OR FABRIC LUNCH CONTAINER FOR A ZERO-WASTE LUNCH.

WRITE A LETTER THAT GETS RESULTS

KNOWING HOW TO WRITE a good letter is a useful skill. It will come in handy anytime you want to persuade someone to understand your point of view. Whether you're writing to your congressman over email or to grandma by snail mail, knowing the proper form and content of a letter will help you get what you want. Most importantly, a well-written letter leaves a good impression.

Check out the sample letter below for all the elements of a good letter.

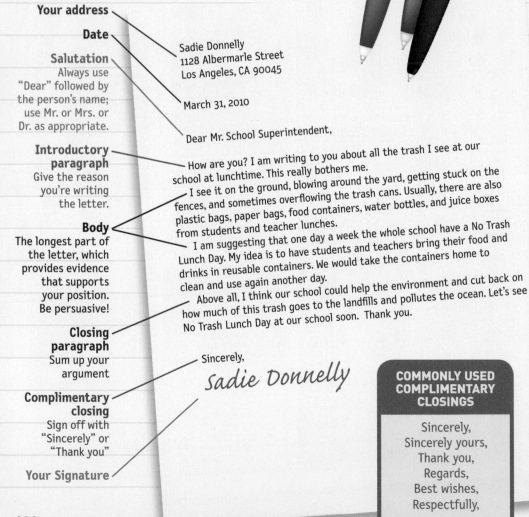

Your address

Date

Salutation
Always use "Dear" followed by the person's name; use Mr. or Mrs. or Dr. as appropriate.

Introductory paragraph
Give the reason you're writing the letter.

Body
The longest part of the letter, which provides evidence that supports your position. Be persuasive!

Closing paragraph
Sum up your argument

Complimentary closing
Sign off with "Sincerely" or "Thank you"

Your Signature

Sadie Donnelly
1128 Albermarle Street
Los Angeles, CA 90045

March 31, 2010

Dear Mr. School Superintendent,

How are you? I am writing to you about all the trash I see at our school at lunchtime. This really bothers me.

I see it on the ground, blowing around the yard, getting stuck on the fences, and sometimes overflowing the trash cans. Usually, there are also plastic bags, paper bags, food containers, water bottles, and juice boxes from students and teacher lunches.

I am suggesting that one day a week the whole school have a No Trash Lunch Day. My idea is to have students and teachers bring their food and drinks in reusable containers. We would take the containers home to clean and use again another day.

Above all, I think our school could help the environment and cut back on how much of this trash goes to the landfills and pollutes the ocean. Let's see No Trash Lunch Day at our school soon. Thank you.

Sincerely,

Sadie Donnelly

COMMONLY USED COMPLIMENTARY CLOSINGS

Sincerely,
Sincerely yours,
Thank you,
Regards,
Best wishes,
Respectfully,

YOU CAN MAKE A DIFFERENCE

WANT TO DO MORE to make the world a better place? Have a question or an opinion? Do something about it. Turn your passion for a cause into meaningful action.

DIG DEEPER! Look to newspaper or magazine articles, books, the Internet, and anything else you can get your hands on. Learn about the issue or organization that most inspires you, intrigues you.

GET INVOLVED! The following organizations can connect you to opportunities to make a difference.
www.dosomething.org
www.volunteermatch.org
www.globalvolunteers.org

MAKE YOUR VOICE HEARD! Email, call, or write to the President, Congress, or state or local government officials.
www.congress.org

GO ONLINE TO HELP CARE FOR THE EARTH
Learn more about environmental issues.
www.earthday.net
www.ecokids.ca/pub/kids_home.cfm
www.treepeople.org
www.meetthegreens.org
www.kidsplanet.org/defendit/new/

Collect pennies to help save wild species and wild places.
www.togethergreen.org/p4p

Start an environmental club at your school.
www.greenguideforkids.blogspot.com/search/label/activities

Learn how to start a kitchen compost bin.
www.meetthegreens.org/episode4/kitchen-composting.html

Reduce paper waste by receiving fewer catalogs.
www.catalogchoice.org

Learn how to green your school.
www.nrdc.org/greensquad

TEST-TAKING TIPS

Getting Ready

- Start reviewing material early.
- Make a consistent study schedule. Don't cram the night before the test.
- Study in a quiet place without distraction.
- Set a goal for each study session.
- Use study guides to review material.
- Be creative. Use outlines, timelines, flash cards, good notes, and charts to help you study and remember test material.
- Take study breaks to refresh yourself.
- Get plenty of rest, and have a nutritious snack before the test for more brainpower!

Test Day

- Remember to relax and breathe during the test to stay calm and focused.
- Read directions and questions carefully.
- For a multiple-choice question, eliminate the answers that you know are wrong.
- Don't spend too much time on any one question. If permitted, skip hard questions and go back to them at the end.
- Review your answers one last time.

TIP: GO GREEN! Save paper and send your letter by email. If you have to print, try to use recycled paper.

Want to find out more about how to help look after the planet? See these websites.
COOL CLICKS
www.meetthegreens.org
www.kidsplanet.org/defendit/new/writeit.html

History
Happens

Morning sunlight hits Mount Rushmore National Memorial in South Dakota. Mount Rushmore features four of America's greatest Presidents: (left to right) George Washington, Thomas Jefferson, Theodore Roosevelt, and Abraham Lincoln.

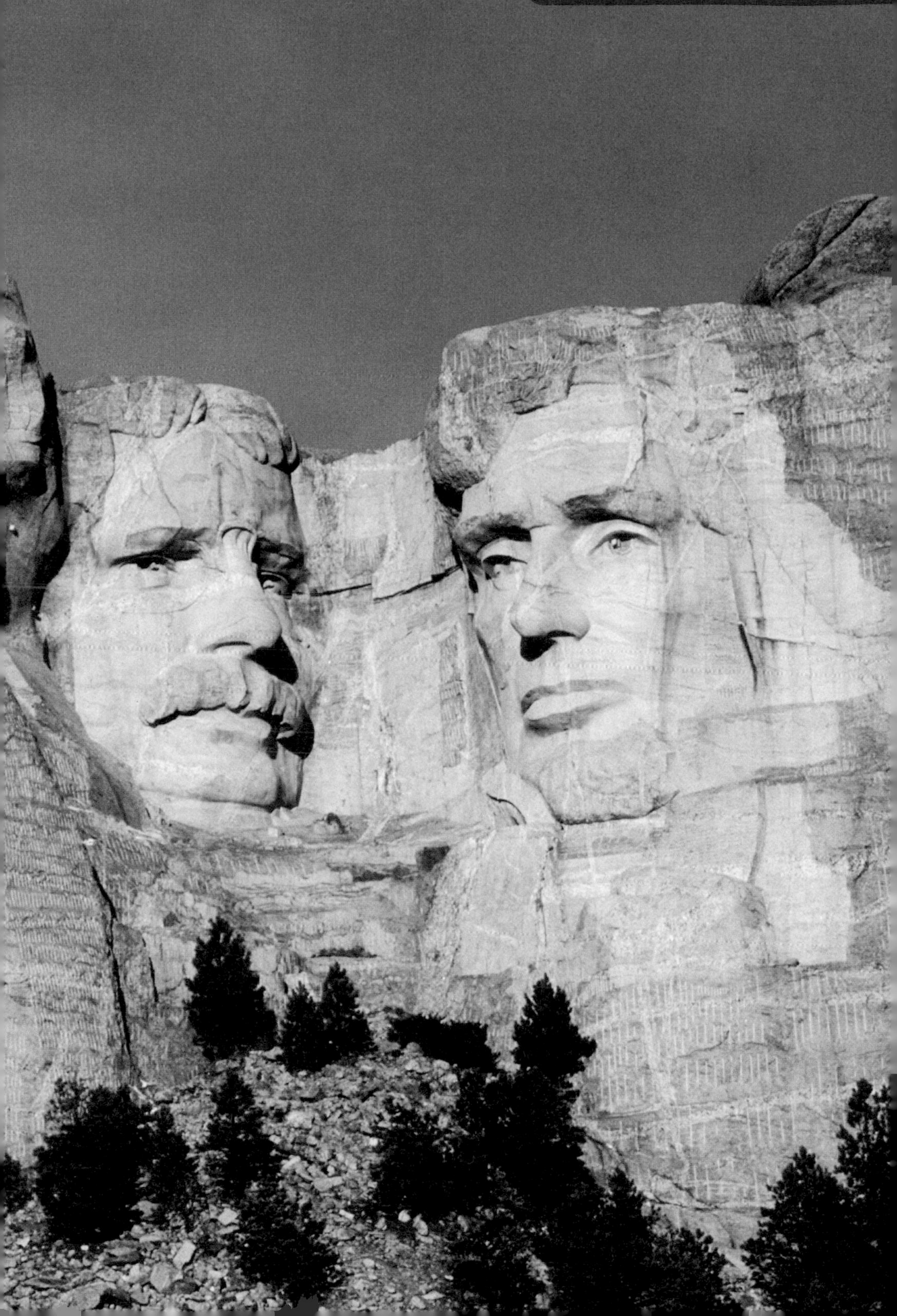

The Constitution & Bill of Rights

The United States Constitution was written in 1787 by a group of political leaders from the 13 states that made up the U.S. at the time. Thirty-nine men, including Benjamin Franklin and James Madison, signed the document to create a national government. While some feared the creation of a strong federal government, all 13 states eventually ratified, or approved, the Constitution, making it the law of the land. The Constitution has three major parts: the preamble, the articles, and the amendments.

The preamble outlines the basic purposes of the government:

We the People of the United States, in order to form a more perfect Union, establish justice, insure domestic tranquility, provide for the common defense, promote the general welfare, and secure the blessings of liberty to ourselves and our posterity, do ordain and establish this Constitution for the United States of America.

Seven articles outline the powers of Congress, the President, and the court system:

Article I outlines the legislative branch—the Senate and the House of Representatives—and its powers and responsibilities.

Article II outlines the executive branch—the presidency—and its powers and responsibilities.

Article III outlines the judicial branch—the court system—and its powers and responsibilities.

Article IV describes the individual states' rights and powers.

Article V outlines the amendment process.

Article VI establishes the Constitution as the law of the land.

Article VII gives the requirements for the Constitution to be approved.

The amendments, or additions to the Constitution, were put in later when needed. In 1791, the first ten amendments, known as the **Bill of Rights**, were added. Since then another 17 amendments have been added. This is the Bill of Rights:

1st Amendment: freedom of religion, speech, the press, assembly, and petition

2nd Amendment: discusses the militia and right of people to bear arms

3rd Amendment: prohibits the military or troops from using private homes without consent

4th Amendment: protects people and their homes from search, arrest, or seizure without probable cause or a warrant

5th Amendment: grants people the right to have a trial and prevents punishment before prosecution; protects private property from being taken without compensation

6th Amendment: guarantees a right to a speedy and public trial

7th Amendment: guarantees a trial by jury in certain cases

8th Amendment: forbids "cruel and unusual punishments"

9th Amendment: states that the Constitution is not all encompassing and does not deny people other rights, as well

10th Amendment: grants the powers not covered by the Constitution to the states and the people

HIDDEN TREASURE

In CONGRESS, JULY 4, 1776.
A DECLARATION
BY THE REPRESENTATIVES OF THE
UNITED STATES OF AMERICA,
IN GENERAL CONGRESS ASSEMBLED.

THE TREASURE: DECLARATION OF INDEPENDENCE

FOUND: IN A FOUR-DOLLAR PICTURE FRAME

NOW WORTH: 8.14 MILLION DOLLARS

The painting was ugly and torn, but its frame seemed worth paying four dollars for. When the buyer took home his flea market find, he found a copy of the Declaration of Independence behind the painting! Convinced it must be a fake, the buyer took the document to experts at Sotheby's auction house. Not only was it real, it also had real value: it sold for 8.14 million dollars!

The **UNITED STATES GOVERNMENT** is divided into three branches: **executive**, **legislative** (see p. 244), and **judicial** (see p. 244). The system of checks and balances is a way to control power and to make sure one branch can't take the reins of government. For example, most of the President's actions require the approval of Congress. Likewise, the laws passed in Congress must be signed by the President before they can take effect. This system prevents one area of government from becoming so powerful as to overly influence the business of the nation.

The White House

Executive Branch

The Constitution lists the central powers of the President: to serve as Commander in Chief of the armed forces; make treaties with other nations; grant pardons; inform Congress on the state of the union; and appoint ambassadors, officials, and judges. The executive branch includes the President and the governmental departments. Originally there were three departments—State, War, and Treasury. Today there are 15 departments (see chart below).

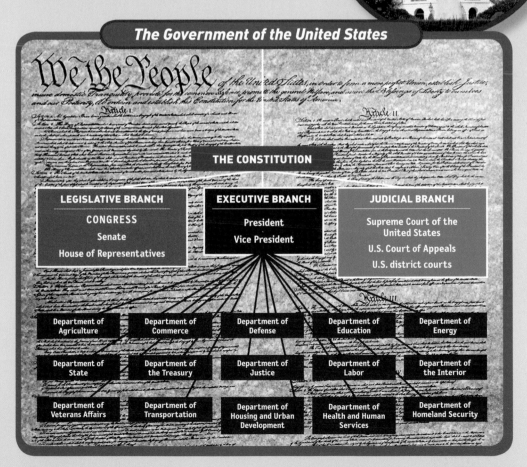

The Government of the United States

THE CONSTITUTION

LEGISLATIVE BRANCH	EXECUTIVE BRANCH	JUDICIAL BRANCH
CONGRESS	President	Supreme Court of the United States
Senate	Vice President	U.S. Court of Appeals
House of Representatives		U.S. district courts

Department of Agriculture • Department of Commerce • Department of Defense • Department of Education • Department of Energy • Department of State • Department of the Treasury • Department of Justice • Department of Labor • Department of the Interior • Department of Veterans Affairs • Department of Transportation • Department of Housing and Urban Development • Department of Health and Human Services • Department of Homeland Security

Legislative Branch

This branch is made up of Congress—the Senate and the House of Representatives. The Constitution grants Congress the power to make laws. Congress is made up of elected representatives from each state. Each state has two representatives in the Senate, while the number of representatives in the House is determined by the size of the state's population. Washington, D.C. and the territories elect non-voting representatives to the House of Representatives. The Founding Fathers set up this system, and the entire system of checks and balances, as a compromise between states' rights.

The U.S. Capitol in Washington, D.C.

Judicial Branch

The judicial branch is composed of the federal court system—the U.S. Supreme Court, the Courts of Appeals, and the district courts. The Supreme Court is the most powerful court. Its motto is "Equal Justice Under Law." This powerful court is responsible for interpreting the Constitution and applying it to the cases that it hears. The decisions of the Supreme Court are absolute—they're the final word on any legal question.

The U.S. Supreme Court building in Washington, D.C.

There are nine justices in the Supreme Court. They are appointed by the President of the United States and confirmed by the Senate.

Bet you didn't know

It's Against the Law to:

WALK A PIG along Miami Beach, in Florida.	THROW STONES in city parks in Fresno, California.
RIDE A SLED that's pulled by a car in Portland, Oregon.	THROW BANANA PEELS on the sidewalks of Mobile, Alabama.
KEEP A PET SKUNK in Virginia.	HOOT LOUDLY after 11 p.m. on weekdays in Athens, Georgia.
RIDE A BIKE with your hands off the handle-bars in Sun Prairie, Wisconsin.	RIDE A HORSE faster than ten miles per hour in the streets of Indianapolis, Indiana.
SPRAY SILLY STRING on Halloween in Hollywood, California.	PREDICT THE FUTURE in Yamhill, Oregon.

Based on 2005 and 2009 research.

How a Bill Becomes a Law

PROPOSAL

After an idea for a bill is formulated, the text of the bill is written. The bill must be sponsored by at least one member of the United States Congress. Most bills originate in either the Senate or the House of Representatives.

INTRODUCTION

A bill can be introduced whenever the House or Senate is in session. It is assigned a number, read on the floor, and then given to a committee for review. A copy of the bill also goes to the Library of Congress, so that it is available to the public.

CONSIDERATION

When the bill is ready, a report is created, and the bill is added to the Senate or House calendar. The bill goes to the floor for consideration, and members debate its merits and problems. Amendments may be made, and the bill can be changed again. After all amendments have been made, the chamber takes a vote.

COMMITTEE REVIEW

A committee that deals with the corresponding policy area debates the bill and may make changes (amendments). After the bill has been amended, the committee votes on the bill, at which point it can table it (stop it), or send it to a subcommittee (for further review) or back to the Senate or House floor.

VOTE

Members in attendance vote to pass or not to pass the bill. They can vote "Yea" for approval, "Nay" for disapproval, or "Present" if they choose not to take either side. If the bill receives a majority (over 50 percent), it then goes to the Senate or House (wherever it did *not* originate) for a similar process.

NAY stops here   **YEA** goes on ▶

2nd CHAMBER REVIEW

The receiving chamber may send the bill to a committee for further review, can vote on it right away, or it can ignore the bill. If the chamber wants to make changes in the bill's language, the bill must go for review to a committee that has members from both the Senate and the House. After agreement, the bill becomes "enrolled." Alternatively, it can be defeated in either chamber, and the bill dies.

VETO OVERRIDE

If a bill is vetoed by the President, it goes back to the chamber where it originated. Congress can drop the bill completely, or the bill can become law if objections to the veto are reviewed and debated, and a two-thirds majority overrides the veto.

PRESIDENTIAL REVIEW

When a bill passes the House and the Senate, it is sent to the President for a signature. The President has three choices: ignore the bill, veto the bill, or sign it to make it law. If the President ignores the bill and Congress is in session, it will become law after ten days. If Congress is not in session, the bill dies.

Bill Becomes a Law!

HAPPENS

...he United States
...tive branch, the
...he U.S. armed forces,
...government.
...ars, the President is
... in the land. The 22nd
...term of office so that a
President cannot serve more than twice. There
have been 44 presidencies and 43 Presidents.

JAMES MONROE
5th President of the United States ★ 1817–1825
BORN April 28, 1758, in
Westmoreland County, VA
POLITICAL PARTY Democratic-Republican
NO. OF TERMS two
VICE PRESIDENT Daniel D. Tompkins
DIED July 4, 1831, in New York, NY

GEORGE WASHINGTON
1st President of the United States ★ 1789–1797
BORN Feb. 22, 1732
Pope's Creek, Westmoreland
County, VA
POLITICAL PARTY Federalist
NO. OF TERMS two
VICE PRESIDENT John Adams
DIED Dec. 14, 1799, at Mount Vernon, VA

JOHN QUINCY ADAMS
6th President of the United States ★ 1825–1829
BORN July 11, 1767, in Braintree
(now Quincy), MA
POLITICAL PARTY Democratic-Republican
NO. OF TERMS one
VICE PRESIDENT John Caldwell Calhoun
DIED Feb. 23, 1848, at the U.S. Capitol,
Washington, D.C.

JOHN ADAMS
2nd President of the United States ★ 1797–1801
BORN Oct. 30, 1735, in Braintree
(now Quincy), MA
POLITICAL PARTY Federalist
NO. OF TERMS one
VICE PRESIDENT Thomas Jefferson
DIED July 4, 1826, in Quincy, MA

ANDREW JACKSON
7th President of the United States ★ 1829–1837
BORN March 15, 1767, in the Waxhaw
region of NC and SC
POLITICAL PARTY Democrat
NO. OF TERMS two
VICE PRESIDENTS 1st term: John Caldwell
Calhoun
2nd term: Martin Van Buren
DIED June 8, 1845, in Nashville, TN

THOMAS JEFFERSON
3rd President of the United States ★ 1801–1809
BORN April 13, 1743, at Shadwell,
Goochland (now Albemarle)
County, VA
POLITICAL PARTY Democratic-Republican
NO. OF TERMS two
VICE PRESIDENTS 1st term: Aaron Burr
2nd term: George Clinton
DIED July 4, 1826, at Monticello,
Charlottesville, VA

MARTIN VAN BUREN
8th President of the United States ★ 1837–1841
BORN Dec. 5, 1782,
in Kinderhook, NY
POLITICAL PARTY Democrat
NO. OF TERMS one
VICE PRESIDENT Richard M. Johnson
DIED July 24, 1862, in Kinderhook, NY

JAMES MADISON
4th President of the United States ★ 1809–1817
BORN March 16, 1751, at Belle Grove,
Port Conway, VA
POLITICAL PARTY Democratic-Republican
NO. OF TERMS two
VICE PRESIDENTS 1st term: George Clinton
2nd term: Elbridge Gerry
DIED June 28, 1836, at Montpelier,
Orange County, VA

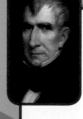

WILLIAM HENRY HARRISON
9th President of the United States ★ 1841
BORN Feb. 9, 1773, in Charles City
County, VA
POLITICAL PARTY Whig
NO. OF TERMS one (cut short by death)
VICE PRESIDENT John Tyler
DIED April 4, 1841, in the White House,
Washington, D.C.

JOHN TYLER

10th President of the United States ★ 1841–1845

BORN March 29, 1790, in Charles City County, VA

POLITICAL PARTY Whig

NO. OF TERMS one (partial)

VICE PRESIDENT none

DIED Jan. 18, 1862, in Richmond, VA

JAMES BUCHANAN

15th President of the United States ★ 1857–1861

BORN April 23, 1791, in Cove Gap, PA

POLITICAL PARTY Democrat

NO. OF TERMS one

VICE PRESIDENT John Cabell Breckinridge

DIED June 1, 1868, in Lancaster, PA

JAMES K. POLK

11th President of the United States ★ 1845–1849

BORN Nov. 2, 1795, near Pineville, Mecklenburg County, NC

POLITICAL PARTY Democrat

NO. OF TERMS one

VICE PRESIDENT George Mifflin Dallas

DIED June 15, 1849, at Nashville, TN

ABRAHAM LINCOLN

16th President of the United States ★ 1861–1865

BORN Feb. 12, 1809, near Hodgenville, KY

POLITICAL PARTY Republican (formerly Whig)

NO. OF TERMS two (cut short by assassination)

VICE PRESIDENTS 1st term: Hannibal Hamlin
2nd term: Andrew Johnson

DIED April 15, 1865, in Washington, D.C.

ZACHARY TAYLOR

12th President of the United States ★ 1849–1850

BORN Nov. 24, 1784, in Orange County, VA

POLITICAL PARTY Whig

NO. OF TERMS one (cut short by death)

VICE PRESIDENT Millard Fillmore

DIED July 9, 1850, in the White House, Washington, D.C.

ANDREW JOHNSON

17th President of the United States ★ 1865–1869

BORN Dec. 29, 1808, in Raleigh, NC

POLITICAL PARTY Democrat

NO. OF TERMS one (partial)

VICE PRESIDENT none

DIED July 31, 1875, in Carter's Station, TN

MILLARD FILLMORE

13th President of the United States ★ 1850–1853

BORN Jan. 7, 1800, in Cayuga County, NY

POLITICAL PARTY Whig

NO. OF TERMS one (partial)

VICE PRESIDENT none

DIED March 8, 1874, in Buffalo, NY

KIDS in the WHITE HOUSE

Although many presidential children are already adults or are away in college by the time their parents move into the White House, some young children have lived there.

In 1861 the Lincolns were the first to bring young children of their own to live in the White House. Among other antics, Tad Lincoln set up a White House refreshment stand and rode through a tea party on a chair pulled by his pet goats!

FRANKLIN PIERCE

14th President of the United States ★ 1853–1857

BORN Nov. 23, 1804, in Hillsborough (now Hillsboro), NH

POLITICAL PARTY Democrat

NO. OF TERMS one

VICE PRESIDENT William Rufus De Vane King

DIED Oct. 8, 1869, in Concord, NH

ULYSSES S. GRANT

18th President of the United States ★ *1869–1877*

BORN April 27, 1822, in Point Pleasant, OH
POLITICAL PARTY Republican
NO. OF TERMS two
VICE PRESIDENTS 1st term: Schuyler Colfax; 2nd term: Henry Wilson
DIED July 23, 1885, in Mount McGregor, NY

RUTHERFORD B. HAYES

19th President of the United States ★ *1877–1881*

BORN Oct. 4, 1822, in Delaware, OH
POLITICAL PARTY Republican
NO. OF TERMS one
VICE PRESIDENT William Almon Wheeler
DIED Jan. 17, 1893, in Fremont, OH

JAMES A. GARFIELD

20th President of the United States ★ *1881*

BORN Nov. 19, 1831, near Orange, OH
POLITICAL PARTY Republican
NO. OF TERMS one (assassinated)
VICE PRESIDENT Chester A. Arthur
DIED Sept. 19, 1881, in Elberon, NJ

CHESTER A. ARTHUR

21st President of the United States ★ *1881–1885*

BORN Oct. 5, 1829, in Fairfield, VT
POLITICAL PARTY Republican
NO. OF TERMS one (partial)
VICE PRESIDENT none
DIED Nov. 18, 1886, in New York, NY

GROVER CLEVELAND

22nd and 24th President of the United States
1885–1889 ★ *1893–1897*

BORN March 18, 1837, in Caldwell, NJ
POLITICAL PARTY Democrat
NO. OF TERMS two (nonconsecutive)
VICE PRESIDENTS 1st administration: Thomas Andrews Hendricks
2nd administration: Adlai Ewing Stevenson
DIED June 24, 1908, in Princeton, NJ

BENJAMIN HARRISON

23rd President of the United States ★ *1889–1893*

BORN Aug. 20, 1833, in North Bend, OH
POLITICAL PARTY Republican
NO. OF TERMS one
VICE PRESIDENT Levi Parsons Morton
DIED March 13, 1901, in Indianapolis, IN

WILLIAM MCKINLEY

25th President of the United States ★ *1897–1901*

BORN Jan. 29, 1843, in Niles, OH
POLITICAL PARTY Republican
NO. OF TERMS two (assassinated)
VICE PRESIDENTS 1st term: Garret Augustus Hobart
2nd term: Theodore Roosevelt
DIED Sept. 14, 1901, in Buffalo, NY

THEODORE ROOSEVELT

26th President of the United States ★ *1901–1909*

BORN Oct. 27, 1858, in New York, NY
POLITICAL PARTY Republican
NO. OF TERMS one, plus balance of McKinley's term
VICE PRESIDENTS 1st term: none
2nd term: Charles Warren Fairbanks
DIED Jan. 6, 1919, in Oyster Bay, NY

WILLIAM HOWARD TAFT

27th President of the United States ★ *1909–1913*

BORN Sept. 15, 1857, in Cincinnati, OH
POLITICAL PARTY Republican
NO. OF TERMS one
VICE PRESIDENT James Schoolcraft Sherman
DIED March 8, 1930, in Washington, D.C.

WOODROW WILSON

28th President of the United States ★ *1913–1921*

BORN Dec. 29, 1856, in Staunton, VA
POLITICAL PARTY Democrat
NO. OF TERMS two
VICE PRESIDENT Thomas Riley Marshall
DIED Feb. 3, 1924, in Washington, D.C.

WARREN G. HARDING
29th President of the United States ★ 1921–1923
BORN Nov. 2, 1865, in Caledonia
(now Blooming Grove), OH
POLITICAL PARTY Republican
NO. OF TERMS one (cut short by death)
VICE PRESIDENT Calvin Coolidge
DIED Aug. 2, 1923, in San Francisco, CA

HARRY S. TRUMAN
33rd President of the United States ★ 1945–1953
BORN May 8, 1884, in Lamar, MO
POLITICAL PARTY Democrat
NO. OF TERMS one, plus balance of
Franklin D. Roosevelt's term
VICE PRESIDENTS 1st term: none
2nd term:
Alben William Barkley
DIED Dec. 26, 1972, in Independence, MO

CALVIN COOLIDGE
30th President of the United States ★ 1923–1929
BORN July 4, 1872, in Plymouth, VT
POLITICAL PARTY Republican
NO. OF TERMS one, plus balance of
Harding's term
VICE PRESIDENTS 1st term: none
2nd term:
Charles Gates Dawes
DIED Jan. 5, 1933, in Northampton, MA

DWIGHT D. EISENHOWER
34th President of the United States ★ 1953–1961
BORN Oct. 14, 1890,
in Denison, TX
POLITICAL PARTY Republican
NO. OF TERMS two
VICE PRESIDENT Richard M. Nixon
DIED March 28, 1969, in Washington, D.C.

HERBERT HOOVER
31st President of the United States ★ 1929–1933
BORN Aug. 10, 1874,
in West Branch, IA
POLITICAL PARTY Republican
NO. OF TERMS one
VICE PRESIDENT Charles Curtis
DIED Oct. 20, 1964, in New York, NY

JOHN F. KENNEDY
35th President of the United States ★ 1961–1963
BORN May 29, 1917, in Brookline, MA
POLITICAL PARTY Democrat
NO. OF TERMS one (assassinated)
VICE PRESIDENT Lyndon B. Johnson
DIED Nov. 22, 1963, in Dallas, TX

FRANKLIN D. ROOSEVELT
32nd President of the United States ★ 1933–1945
BORN Jan. 30, 1882, in Hyde Park, NY
POLITICAL PARTY Democrat
NO. OF TERMS four (cut short by death)
VICE PRESIDENTS 1st & 2nd terms: John
Nance Garner; 3rd term:
Henry Agard Wallace; 4th
term: Harry S. Truman
DIED April 12, 1945,
in Warm Springs, GA

LYNDON B. JOHNSON
36th President of the United States ★ 1963–1969
BORN Aug. 27, 1908,
near Stonewall, TX
POLITICAL PARTY Democrat
NO. OF TERMS one, plus balance of
Kennedy's term
VICE PRESIDENTS 1st term: none
2nd term: Hubert
Horatio Humphrey
DIED Jan. 22, 1973, near San Antonio, TX

PRESIDENTIAL PETS

The first **SIAMESE KITTEN** in the United States lived in the White House with **Rutherford B. Hayes.**

William Taft owned the last **COW** to live in the White House.

Theodore Roosevelt's more than 40 pets included 12 **HORSES**, 5 **GUINEA PIGS**, 5 **BEARS**, a **ZEBRA**, and a **LION.**

President Franklin Roosevelt and his dog Fala

RICHARD NIXON

37th President of the United States ★ 1969–1974
BORN Jan. 9, 1913, in Yorba Linda, CA
POLITICAL PARTY Republican
NO. OF TERMS two (resigned)
VICE PRESIDENTS 1st term and 2nd term (partial): Spiro Theodore Agnew; 2nd term (balance): Gerald R. Ford
DIED April 22, 1994, in New York, NY

GERALD R. FORD

38th President of the United States ★ 1974–1977
BORN July 14, 1913, in Omaha, NE
POLITICAL PARTY Republican
NO. OF TERMS one (partial)
VICE PRESIDENT Nelson Aldrich Rockefeller
DIED Dec. 26, 2006, in Rancho Mirage, CA

JIMMY CARTER

39th President of the United States ★ 1977–1981
BORN Oct. 1, 1924, in Plains, GA
POLITICAL PARTY Democrat
NO. OF TERMS one
VICE PRESIDENT Walter Frederick (Fritz) Mondale

Bet you didn't know

Many Presidents had unusual careers before entering the White House. Harry Truman was a haberdasher—someone who deals in men's clothing and accessories, particularly hats. Jimmy Carter was a peanut farmer, and Ronald Reagan was a movie actor.

There have been many interesting presidential firsts. Barack Obama is our first African-American President, while John Kennedy was the first (and only) non-Protestant President. James Polk was the first to have his photograph taken. And Theodore Roosevelt was the first President to ride in a car while in office. His fifth cousin, Franklin D. Roosevelt, was the first to ride in an airplane.

What will be the next big presidential first? First to ride in a spaceship?

RONALD REAGAN

40th President of the United States ★ 1981–1989
BORN Feb. 6, 1911, in Tampico, IL
POLITICAL PARTY Republican
NO. OF TERMS two
VICE PRESIDENT George Bush
DIED June 5, 2004, in Los Angeles, CA

GEORGE BUSH

41st President of the United States ★ 1989–1993
BORN June 12, 1924, in Milton, MA
POLITICAL PARTY Republican
NO. OF TERMS one
VICE PRESIDENT James Danforth (Dan) Quayle III

BILL CLINTON

42nd President of the United States ★ 1993–2001
BORN Aug. 19, 1946, in Hope, AR
POLITICAL PARTY Democrat
NO. OF TERMS two
VICE PRESIDENT Albert Gore, Jr.

GEORGE W. BUSH

43rd President of the United States ★ 2001–2009
BORN July 6, 1946, in New Haven, CT
POLITICAL PARTY Republican
NO. OF TERMS two
VICE PRESIDENT Richard Bruce Cheney

BARACK OBAMA

44th President of the United States ★ 2009–present
BORN August 4, 1961, in Honolulu, HI
POLITICAL PARTY Democrat
VICE PRESIDENT Joseph Biden

FAST FACTS

At 6 feet, 4 inches (1.9 meters), Abraham Lincoln was the tallest U.S. President.

James Garfield, the 20th President, was the first left-handed President.

U.S. Political Parties

Some of the Founding Fathers hoped that members of the new United States government would work together in harmony without dividing into opposing groups called parties. Yet, soon after George Washington became President, political parties began to form. Leaders partnered with others who shared their geographic background, foreign policy beliefs, or ideas for governing.

THE TWO-PARTY SYSTEM

Today, as then, the party with the largest number of elected members in the U.S. House of Representatives and the U.S. Senate holds a majority of influence over those chambers. Occasionally the same party will control both chambers of Congress and the presidency, like the Democrats do now. With that much political power, it can significantly influence the nature of government. Usually each party will control only one or two of these three areas. In that case, political parties have to compromise and cooperate with one another in order to enact new laws.

Republican Elephant

A LONG HISTORY

Today's leaders are primarily members of the Democratic and Republican parties. Each group can trace its origins far back into the 19th century.

The Democratic Party evolved from the early groups that opposed a strong federal government. Leaders such as Thomas Jefferson shaped these lawmakers into a collection of politicians known variously as the Democratic-Republicans, the National Republicans, and, eventually, the Democrats.

The modern Republican Party was formed during the 1850s to combat the spread of slavery. Its first successful presidential candidate was Abraham Lincoln. Sometimes it is referred to as the Grand Old Party (GOP).

Democratic Donkey

SHIFTING THE VOTE

Often the presidential ballot will include candidates from third parties, those groups that exist beyond the two major parties. Occasionally a candidate has run for office as an independent—that is, without the support of a political party. No independent or third-party candidate has ever made it to the White House. Even so, these candidates may influence an election by dividing the support of voters or by directing attention to a particular issue or cause. In recent decades, third-party and independent candidates have frequently siphoned support away from Republican and Democratic candidates in ways that helped secure a victory for the opposing major party.

SUCCESSION

If the President of the United States becomes incapacitated, dies, resigns, or is removed from office, there is an order of succession to determine who takes over as President. This order, specified by the Presidential Succession Act of 1947 and later amendments, is as follows:

1. Vice President
2. Speaker of the House of Representatives
3. President pro tempore of the Senate (highest ranking Senator)
4. Secretary of State
5. Secretary of the Treasury
6. Secretary of Defense
7. Attorney General
8. Secretary of the Interior
9. Secretary of Agriculture
10. Secretary of Commerce
11. Secretary of Labor
12. Secretary of Health and Human Services
13. Secretary of Housing and Urban Development
14. Secretary of Transportation
15. Secretary of Energy
16. Secretary of Education
17. Secretary of Veterans' Affairs
18. Secretary of Homeland Security

Women of the White House

FIRST LADY	PRESIDENT	TERM	AGE AS FIRST LADY	NUMBER OF CHILDREN
Martha Dandridge Custis Washington	George Washington	1789–1797	57	none
Abigail Smith Adams	John Adams	1797–1801	52	4
Martha Wayles Skelton Jefferson* *Acting First Ladies: Dolley Madison (friend) and Martha Jefferson Randolph (daughter)	Thomas Jefferson	1801–1809	Deceased	2
Dolley Payne Todd Madison	James Madison	1809–1817	40	1
Elizabeth Kortright Monroe	James Monroe	1817–1825	48	2
Louisa Catherine Johnson Adams	John Quincy Adams	1825–1829	50	3
Rachel Donelson Jackson* *Acting First Ladies: Emily Donelson (niece) and Sarah Yorke Jackson (nephew's wife)	Andrew Jackson	1829–1837	Deceased	none
Hannah Hoes Van Buren *Acting First Lady: Angelica Singleton Van Buren (daughter–in–law)	Martin Van Buren	1837–1841	Deceased	4
Anna Tuthill Symmes Harrison	William Henry Harrison	1841	65	9
Letitia Christian Tyler *Died while Tyler was in office.	John Tyler	1841–1845	50	8
Julia Gardiner Tyler	John Tyler	1841–1845	24	7
Sarah Childress Polk	James K. Polk	1845–1849	41	none
Margaret Mackall Smith Taylor	Zachary Taylor	1849–1850	60	4
Abigail Powers Fillmore	Millard Fillmore	1850–1853	52	2
Jane Means Appleton Pierce	Franklin Pierce	1853–1857	46	2
Harriet Lane (Niece of James Buchanan) *Two children with Henry Elliott Johnston	James Buchanan (not married)	1857–1861	26	2*
Mary Todd Lincoln	Abraham Lincoln	1861–1865	42	3
Eliza McCardle Johnson	Andrew Johnson	1865–1869	54	5
Julia Dent Grant	Ulysses S. Grant	1869–1877	43	4
Lucy Ware Webb Hayes	Rutherford B. Hayes	1877–1881	45	5
Lucretia Rudolph Garfield	James A. Garfield	1881	48	5
Ellen Lewis Herndon Arthur* *Acting First Lady: Mary Arthur McElroy (President's sister)	Chester A. Arthur	1881–1885	Deceased	2

Martha Dandridge Custis marries George Washington, who became President.

Michelle LaVaughn Robinson Obama, the first African-American First Lady.

Former First Ladies (left to right):
Lady Bird Johnson, Barbara Bush, Hillary Rodham Clinton, Betty Ford, and Nancy Reagan

FIRST LADY	PRESIDENT	TERM	AGE AS FIRST LADY	NUMBER OF CHILDREN
Frances Folsom Cleveland *Acting First Lady: Rose Elizabeth Cleveland (President's sister)*	Grover Cleveland	1885–1889 & 1893–1897	21	5
Caroline Lavina Scott Harrison	Benjamin Harrison	1889–1893	56	2
Ida Saxton McKinley	William McKinley	1897–1901	49	2
Edith Kermit Carow Roosevelt	Theodore Roosevelt	1901–1909	40	5
Helen Herron Taft	William Howard Taft	1909–1913	48	3
Ellen Louise Axson Wilson* *Died while Wilson was in office. Acting First Ladies: Margaret Woodrow Wilson (daughter) and Helen Bones (President's cousin)*	Woodrow Wilson	1913–1921	52	3
Edith Bolling Galt Wilson*	Woodrow Wilson	1913–1921	43	none
Florence Kling Harding	Warren G. Harding	1921–1923	60	none
Grace Anna Goodhue Coolidge	Calvin Coolidge	1923–1929	44	2
Lou Henry Hoover	Herbert Hoover	1929–1933	54	2
Anna Eleanor Roosevelt	Franklin D. Roosevelt	1933–1945	48	5
Elizabeth Virginia Wallace Truman	Harry S. Truman	1945–1953	60	1
Mamie Geneva Doud Eisenhower	Dwight D. Eisenhower	1953–1961	56	1
Jacqueline Lee Bouvier Kennedy	John F. Kennedy	1961–1963	31	2
Claudia "Lady Bird" Taylor Johnson	Lyndon B. Johnson	1963–1969	50	2
Patricia Ryan Nixon	Richard Nixon	1969–1974	56	2
Elizabeth "Betty" Bloomer Ford	Gerald R. Ford	1974–1977	56	4
Rosalynn Smith Carter	Jimmy Carter	1977–1981	49	4
Nancy Davis Reagan	Ronald Reagan	1981–1989	59	2
Barbara Pierce Bush	George Bush	1989–1993	63	6
Hillary Rodham Clinton	Bill Clinton	1993–2001	45	1
Laura Welch Bush	George W. Bush	2001–2009	55	2
Michelle LaVaughn Robinson Obama	Barack Obama	2009–present	44	2

merican Heroes

Pocahontas circa 1595 (Virginia, U.S.)–1617 (Gravesend, England)

About 400 years ago, the young Indian princess Pocahontas became the first heroine in American history. As the story goes, she was about 12 years old when she saved the life of Captain John Smith, one of the leaders of Virginia's Jamestown Colony. This story won Pocahontas a place in history for her kindheartedness and bravery, but it may be more legend than fact. Today she is celebrated as a symbol of peace and friendship. **Did you know? The word** *pocahontas* **means "playful one."**

Wright Brothers
Wilbur: 1867 (Indiana, U.S.)–1912 (Ohio, U.S.)
Orville: 1871 (Ohio, U.S.)–1948 (Ohio, U.S.)

In December 1903, Wilbur and Orville Wright did what no human being had done before: They flew in a plane powered by an engine. This stunning feat ushered in the age of powered flight and made the Wright brothers the first American heroes of the 20th century. The secrets of flight had baffled great minds for centuries. Wilbur and Orville Wright focused all their intellectual and engineering skills on finding the answers. When they did, it changed the world. Did you know? Wilbur and Orville owned a cat named Old Mom when they were children.

Martin Luther King, Jr. 1929 (Georgia, U.S.)–1968 (Tennessee, U.S.)

Civil rights leader Martin Luther King, Jr., never backed down in his stand against racism. He dedicated his life to achieving equality and justice for all Americans of all colors. From a family of preachers, King experienced racial prejudice early in life. As an adult fighting for civil rights, his speeches, marches, and mere presence motivated people to fight for justice for all people. His March on Washington in 1963 was one of the largest activist gatherings in our nation's history. King's impact on the nation and the world is incalculable. **Did you know? King's original name was Michael, but his parents changed it to Martin after a trip to Germany in 1934.**

John Glenn 1921 (Ohio, U.S.)–

Half a century ago, the United States and the nation then known as the Soviet Union (now Russia) began competing to see which country would be first to explore outer space. The Soviets captured the lead when they sent the first person into orbit around Earth. Ten months later, the United States closed the gap in the space race when American astronaut John Glenn blasted off on February 20, 1962, and circled Earth three times. Glenn became an overnight hero for his brave voyage into the unknown. Did you know? John Glenn served as a U.S. Senator (Dem–OH) from 1974 to 1999.

Albert Einstein 1879 (Ulm, Germany)–1955 (New Jersey, U.S.)

This German-born physicist made his first visit to the U.S. in 1921, and he later became a U.S. citizen. His mind-boggling theories dazzled the public even though very few people understood the science behind them. What everyone did know was that Einstein was the most extraordinary genius of their time—and perhaps of all time. Merely by thinking about it, he came up with a totally new explanation for time and space and the way the universe works. His revolutionary theory of relativity made him a hero. Einstein's passion for science lasted a lifetime. **Did you know? Einstein was offered the position of Israel's second president, a job he refused.**

American Wars

From before the formation of the United States to the present, there have been hundreds of military encounters, both at home and abroad. Major conflicts include the following wars.

1754–63 French and Indian War A nine-year war between the British and the French for control of eastern North America.

1775–83 Revolutionary War The 13 British colonies united to reject the rule of the British monarchy and form their own government.

1812–15 War of 1812 The U.S. declared war against the United Kingdom, who had imposed trade restrictions.

1846–48 Mexican-American War Mexico refused to accept the annexation of Texas by the U.S., and the two went to war over the boundary dispute.

1861–65 Civil War The Civil War was one of the most devastating wars in American history. It occurred when the northern states (the Union) went to war with the southern states, which had seceded to form the Confederate States of America. Slavery was the central issue in the Civil War.

1898 Spanish-American War The U.S. declared war with Spain over control of Cuba.

1914–18 World War I Fought mostly in Europe. The U.S. entered the war after Germany sunk the British ship *Lusitania*, killing over 120 Americans. (See p. 266 for "World Wars".)

An artillery unit on Morris Island, South Carolina during the Civil War

1941–45 (American involvement) **World War II** This massive conflict in Europe, Asia, and North Africa involved many countries on two sides: the Allies and the Axis. After the bombing of Pearl Harbor, the U.S. entered the war on the side of the Allies. Over 50 million people died during the war. (See p. 266 for "World Wars".)

1950–53 Korean War During a military conflict between North and South Korea, the U.S. joined forces with the South while China supported the North.

1950s–75 In the **Vietnam War,** America's longest, the U.S. fought on the side of South Vietnam against North Vietnam, which was supported by China.

1991 Persian Gulf War Following the invasion of Kuwait by Iraq, the U.S. joined a coalition of nations to expel Iraq from the occupied area.

2001–present War in Afghanistan The U.S. invaded Afghanistan in response to the September 11th, 2001, terrorist attacks, which were planned there.

2003–present War in Iraq A coalition led by the U.S., and including Britain, Australia, and Spain, invaded Iraq over worries about weapons of mass destruction.

A World War II American army tank

CIVIL RIGHTS

In March 1965, Dr. Martin Luther King, Jr., joined marchers on a 50-mile march to Montgomery, Alabama.

The Little Rock Nine study during the weeks when they were blocked from school.

Fighting for Your Rights:

The Civil Rights Movement of the 1950s–1964

Although the Constitution protects the civil rights of American citizens, it has not always been able to protect all Americans from persecution or discrimination. During the first half of the 20th century, many Americans, particularly African Americans, were the subject of widespread discrimination and racism. By the mid-1950s, many people were eager to end the bonds of racism and restore freedom to all men and women.

The Civil Rights Movement of the 1950s and 1960s sought to end the racial discrimination against African Americans, especially in the southern states. The movement wanted to restore the fundamentals of economic and social equality to those who had been oppressed. The Civil Rights Movement benefited from powerful leaders, such as Martin Luther King, Jr., Rosa Parks, John F. Kennedy, and Malcolm X.

The Little Rock Nine

As a group of nine African-American teenagers entered an all-white high school in Little Rock, Arkansas, the world changed. In 1957, these young students became civil rights icons by challenging a racist system— and winning. For more on segregation and the Little Rock Nine, go online. nps.gov/history/nr/travel/civilrights/ar1.htm

Important Moments in the Civil Rights Movement

1954 The Supreme Court case *Brown v. Board of Education* declares school segregation illegal.

1955 Rosa Parks refuses to give up her bus seat to a white passenger and spurs a bus boycott.

1957 The Little Rock Nine help integrate schools.

1961 Freedom Rides begin into southern states to protest segregation in transportation.

1963 Martin Luther King, Jr., leads the pivotal March on Washington.

1964 The Civil Rights Act, prohibiting discrimination based on race, color, religion, sex, and national origin, is passed.

The Indian Experience

American Indians are indigenous to North and South America—they are the people who were here before Columbus and other European explorers came to this land. They live (and lived) in nations, tribes, and bands across both continents. For decades following the arrival of Europeans, American Indians clashed with the newcomers who had ruptured the Indians' way of living. For centuries to come, Indians were often displaced, became assimilated, or even worse, killed.

Tribal Land

During the nineteenth century, both United States legislation and military action restricted the movement of American Indians, forcing them to live on reservations and attempting to dismantle tribal structures. In 1924, the Indian Citizenship Act granted citizenship to all American Indians. Unfortunately, this was not enough to end the social discrimination and mistreatment that many Indians have faced. Today, with over two million American Indians living in the U.S., this group still faces challenges.

Healing the Past

Many of the more than 560 recognized tribes in the United States live primarily on reservations. Some tribes have more than one reservation, while others have none. Together these reservations make up less than 3 percent of the nation's land area. The tribes have the right to form their own governments and enforce laws, similar to individual states. Many feel that this sovereignty is still not enough to right the wrongs of the past and hope for a change in the U.S. government's relationship with American Indians.

A young Cherokee man dressed in traditional costume

INDIAN NATIONS

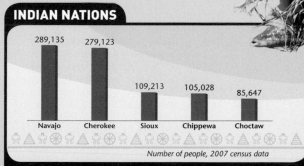

Navajo	Cherokee	Sioux	Chippewa	Choctaw
289,135	279,123	109,213	105,028	85,647

Number of people, 2007 census data

Today, there are more than 2 million American Indians living in the United States. One of the most populous is the Navajo nation, which is concentrated mainly in Arizona, Utah, and New Mexico.

Today there are 2.3 million American Indians in the U.S. and more than a million in Canada.

257

GIRLS RULE!

Two Queens of Egypt Who Rocked the Ancient World

Girls of ancient Egypt had it a lot better than most people. By age 12, they could wear makeup. They walked their pet geese and played ball for fun. As women, they had rights that women didn't have elsewhere. They could buy and sell property, inherit stuff—even sue someone!

Still, men were usually in charge. But that didn't stop some women from defying tradition and taking over. Cleopatra and Hatshepsut were two outrageous queens who showed the ancient world what girl power was all about.

CLEOPATRA: *Political Party Girl*
(Reign: 51 B.C. to 30 B.C.)

Mark Antony was fuming. The ruler of half the Roman Empire waited impatiently for the queen of Egypt to arrive. She was late—on purpose. And when she finally glittered up the Cydnus River on a ship with silver oars, Cleopatra had the nerve to make him board her ship. How dare she?

Antony shouldn't have been surprised at the queen's bold behavior. Cleopatra had star power with the brains to match. Queen by 18, she had her hands full: bad harvests, a forced marriage to her brother, and plots to overthrow her.

Forced to flee her capital of Alexandria, she convinced powerful Roman leader Julius Caesar to help her regain control. But four years later Caesar was assassinated. Cleopatra was back to square one.

Enter Mark Antony. She needed his political support. He needed money. Rich girl Cleopatra tempted him with excess by betting that she could blow a fortune on dinner. Intrigued, Antony watched as she crushed a pearl earring into her now-priceless drink. That's all it took for the charmed yet greedy Antony to become hopelessly devoted to the queen.

With his help, Cleopatra battled to keep Egypt out of the hands of her enemies. She lost. But instead of surrendering, she took her life—probably with the help of a poisonous snake.

Cleopatra left few words. But Egyptologists think they have found an order signed by the queen. On it, the busy ruler had scribbled, "Make it so."

HATSHEPSUT: *Built to Last*
(Reign: 1479 B.C. to 1458 B.C.)

Wearing the royal headdress, with a pharaoh's traditional fake beard on her chin, Hatshepsut was officially the "female king" of Egypt. Not bad for a girl who was forced to wed her 8-year-old half brother at 13.

Now for action! Hatshepsut waged successful warfare against fierce invaders. She created a magnificent temple to the sun god, Amun. Organizing a five-ship expedition to faraway lands, she brought ivory, ebony, gold, and trees to Egypt. Trees? Egypt needed them to grow fragrant incense, burned by the ton in ceremonies.

To celebrate her 15th year of rule, Hatshepsut had two 100-foot obelisks erected. Getting the granite for the structures down the Nile River took a long barge, 27 boats, and 850 rowers!

Hatshepsut was an excellent ruler—so good that she kept the pharaoh-to-be on the sidelines until she died. And she lives on in spirit. In modern Egypt, Hatshepsut's wonders, from an obelisk to an incense tree, are still standing after nearly 3,500 years.

Bet you didn't know

THE ANCIENT EGYPTIANS TRAINED MONKEYS TO DANCE AND PLAY MUSIC.

Greek Gods & Goddesses

MYTHOLOGY: The ancient Greeks believed that many gods and goddesses ruled the universe. According to this mythology, 12 of these gods and goddesses, **the Olympians,** lived high atop Greece's Mount Olympus. Each god or goddess had a unique personality and corresponded to particular aspects of life, such as love or death. Many of these gods and goddesses were also heralded by the Romans, but usually with different names (shown in parentheses).

THE OLYMPIANS

Aphrodite (Venus), was the goddess of love, beauty, and fertility. She also protected sailors.

Apollo (same Roman name), Zeus's son, was god of the sun, music, and healing. Artemis was his twin.

Ares (Mars), Zeus's son (see Zeus below), was the god of war and, in Roman tradition, agriculture. Distrusted and disliked by most, Ares was both handsome and cruel.

Artemis (Diana), Zeus's daughter and Apollo's twin, was goddess of the hunt. She also helped women in childbirth.

Athena (Minerva), for whom Athens, Greece, was named, was the goddess of wisdom and crafts.

According to legend, she was born from the forehead of Zeus.

Hades (Pluto), Zeus's brother, was the god of the underworld and the dead. A gruesome guy, Hades got a wife, Persephone, through trickery.

Hephaestus (Vulcan), Zeus's son, was god of fire and crafts and the husband of Aphrodite. He is known for creating the first woman, Pandora.

Hera (Juno), the wife and older sister of Zeus, was the goddess of women and marriage.

Hestia (Vesta), Zeus's sister, was the goddess of hearth and home.

Hermes (Mercury), Zeus's son, was a messenger of the gods who guided the dead to the underworld. In his winged hat and shoes, he often played pranks and was known for his speed.

Poseidon (Neptune), the brother of Zeus, was god of the sea and earthquakes. He lived under the sea and is often depicted driving a chariot that could ride on the sea.

Zeus (Jupiter), was the most powerful of the gods and the top Olympian. He wielded a thunderbolt and was god of the sky and thunder.

THE ROMAN EMPIRE

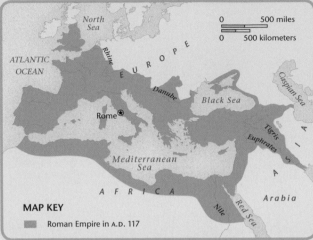

THE ANCIENT ROMANS CONQUERED first the whole of Italy and then a vast empire. At its greatest extent, in A.D. 117, the Roman Empire covered some 2.3 million square miles (5.9 million sq. km)—roughly two-thirds the size of the United States—and had an estimated population of 120 million people. These people were ruled by an emperor, the most famous of which was Julius Caesar.

The Roman Empire had a very successful government and was a leader in war. Its people made significant developments in technology and architecture, and it remains one of the bases for western civilization.

Daily Life in Tudor England

The history of England is broad and diverse. The Tudor period, from 1485 to 1603 (118 years), saw the reign of five powerful monarchs, and was a very smelly time.

Some of these colorful monarchs were kind; others were tyrannical. From the first Tudor monarch, Henry VII, to the last queen of the period, Elizabeth I, the Tudor times were romantic and turbulent at the same time.

The Tudor period was the time of Shakespeare, frilly fashions, and exploring heroes. But it wasn't all great feasts and beautiful music. For most, living in Tudor England was hard—to say the least.

Social classes, or groups of people organized by power, were important in Tudor England, where there were four main classes. Nobility, like dukes, barons, and the royal family, made up the smallest and richest class. Just below them was the gentry, knights, and wealthy landowners who lived in mansions with hundreds of servants. The next class was made up of professionals like merchants and lawyers. The largest and lowest class included farmhands, servants, and people living in poverty.

Cities were smaller than they are now, more like big towns, and most people lived in the countryside. There were no sewers, so sewage and polluted water ran right down the streets. Pests like rats were everywhere. The lack of sanitation led to many outbreaks of plague and smallpox, and the lack of medical knowledge meant that many households had to face illness and death.

To sum up, be very happy you didn't live in Tudor England, where having a bath was a rarity!

BUILD A TIME CAPSULE.

Fill a shoe box with reminders of the current year: ticket stubs, cool music, favorite books, photographs, and small treasures. Put it away until you're ready for a trip down memory lane.

SPIES who changed the world

DOSSIER 001: OPERATION MISDIRECTION | YEAR: 1944 | SPY: JUAN PUJOL GARCIA | AKA: "THE ACTOR"

It's the most powerful collection of planes, ships, armor, and troops Earth has ever seen. American, British, Canadian, and French forces are preparing for one lethal D-Day strike at the German-occupied Normandy beaches, in France. Victory equals a free Europe. Defeat means, well, bad stuff.

To know where the allies will strike, the Germans turn to their secret weapon, Juan Pujol Garcia, who is leading a network of spies against Britain. Wrong! There's no network. Garcia is really working against Germany for Britain!

As the Allies prepare to bring it on, the Germans ask Garcia where American and British soldiers will land. He tells them to move to Calais, France—about 15 miles from where the Allies will actually strike.

So while most of the German army waits near Calais, the Allies battle to victory at Normandy. The defeat leads to the German surrender. When the smoke clears, Britain presents "The Actor" with a medal for heroism. And so do the Germans, never suspecting that the double agent has fooled them all along.

DOSSIER 002: OPERATION RED BLUFF | YEAR: 1962 | SPY: OLEG PENKOVSKY | AKA: "THE SPY WHO SAVED THE WORLD"

In the blue corner, hailing from the United States, President John F. Kennedy. In the red corner, his challenger from the Soviet Union (now Russia), Premier Nikita S. Khrushchev.

As the bell clangs, the two enemy superpowers begin their grudge match. Biff! Bam! Kapow!

At ringside is double agent Oleg Penkovsky. Khrushchev believes that the spy is on his team. In reality, he's Kennedy's go-to spy guy. And luckily for the President, Penkovsky knows Khrushchev's footwork inside and out.

Round 1: Penkovsky warns Kennedy's people of Khrushchev's punch: nuclear missile launch sites he's building in Cuba, 90 miles off Florida's shore.

Round 2: Kennedy counters with a naval blockade of Cuba.

Round 3: Khrushchev and Kennedy are at a standoff. The U.S. and Cuba fear a nuclear attack.

Round 4: Penkovsky tells Kennedy the Soviet threat is trash talk. Kennedy agrees to remove missiles from Turkey.

Khrushchev throws in the towel. Launch site construction is halted, and the Soviets dump their missile plans in Cuba. Nuclear holocaust is averted.

Harriet Tubman: CIVIL WAR SPY

Harriet Tubman is well known for risking her life as a "conductor" in the Underground Railroad, which led escaped slaves to freedom during the United States Civil War. But did you know that the former slave also served as a spy for the Union? And that she was the first woman in American history to lead a military expedition? It's true!

Tubman decided to help the Union Army because she wanted freedom for all of the people who were forced into slavery. Tubman was five feet two inches tall, born a slave, had a debilitating illness, and was unable to read or write. Yet here was this tough crusader who could take charge and lead men. Quite a gal!

SPYSPEAK

Talk like a spy with these terms.

BLACK BAG JOB: secret entry into a place to steal or copy materials

EARS ONLY: material too secret to put in writing

GHOUL: an agent who finds the names of dead people so that spies can use them as aliases

UNCLE: the headquarters of any spy service

Atlantis

HOW IN THE BIG, WIDE, WACKY WORLD DO YOU FIND A SUNKEN CITY?

Not easily! But that hasn't stopped explorers from trying to locate Atlantis anyway.

Think something sounds a little fishy? Many experts say Atlantis is about as real as SpongeBob's pineapple. But we want you to slap on your flippers, dive into the controversy, and judge for yourself.

LIVING LARGE IN ATLANTIS. Atlantis was an ancient paradise island—or so the story goes. When Greek philosopher Plato first wrote the tale of Atlantis around 360 B.C., he described an idyllic island that may have been located near the Straits of Gibraltar—a waterway that separates Europe and Africa (see map).

The Atlanteans were supposedly real fat cats, ruling the richest empire in the world. Three sparkling moats of water encircled a metropolis of posh palaces, with a silver-and-gold temple towering above the city's center.

Elephants and other wild animals roamed the island, and food was so plentiful that every night was like an all-you-can-eat buffet.

SHAKE, RATTLE, AND ROLL. Legend has it that Atlanteans soon grew so spoiled and lazy that the Greek gods literally blew their tops! They set off earthquakes, raised the seas, and sank the city faster than you can say *blub, blub, blub*. But did Atlantis ever really exist?

YES! Explorers claim to have discovered Atlantis everywhere from Ireland to Brazil to Antarctica. Explorer Robert Sarmast disagrees. He says images of an underwater island near Cyprus (see map) show evidence of walls, canals, and a temple hill that fit Plato's description perfectly. "Atlantis matches the maps of this island so closely," Sarmast says. "It just can't be a coincidence."

Still, some critics think Sarmast's theory is all wet. They believe the story of Atlantis was inspired by a Greek island called Santorini, where a volcanic eruption buried an ancient civilization around 1500 B.C.

NO! You'd have to have seaweed for brains to believe Atlantis was real, according to some historians. "So far not a single piece of solid evidence has emerged," says Atlantis expert Richard Ellis. Others point out that Plato dated the island in the Stone Age—long before a sophisticated city could have existed. To these doubters, Atlantis is just a fable, reminding people not to be greedy and selfish—or else!

Did Atlantis really get swallowed by the sea? Who knows? But one thing's for sure: The mystery of this famous city will stay afloat for years to come.

An artist's rendering of what Atlantis might have looked like

Atlantis allegedly found near Cyprus

Plato may have placed Atlantis here

NORTH AMERICA · EUROPE · ASIA · Atlantic Ocean · Pacific Ocean · AFRICA · Pacific Ocean · SOUTH AMERICA · Indian Ocean · AUSTRALIA · ANTARCTICA

Who Killed the
Iceman?

Discoveries raise questions about Europe's oldest mummy

THE CRIME SCENE: In 1991 hikers found the body of a man encased in the ice of a melting glacier. Nicknamed the Iceman or Ötzi (OOTS-ee) for the Ötztal Alps where he was discovered, he was thought to have frozen to death in a snowstorm while tending sheep some 5,300 years ago. His body was mummified in the ice.

THE CRIME: Ten years later, closer study revealed that Ötzi did not die of exposure to the cold. X-rays show an arrowhead buried deep in his left shoulder. He had been shot in the back. But whodunnit? And why?

ONE DETECTIVE'S THEORY: Archaeologist Johan Reinhard, a National Geographic Society explorer-in-residence, was one of the detectives trying to solve the crime.

SUSPECTS AND MOTIVE: Reinhard believes that Ötzi may have been a victim of ritual sacrifice, killed by people to pacify mountain gods.

THE CLUES: "The place where the body was found is the kind of place where sacrifices happened in many other cultures around the world," Reinhard says. "It's a hard location to get to. I don't think a body would end up there by coincidence." And the placement of Ötzi's possessions—a bow, a backpack, and the oldest prehistoric copper ax ever found in Europe—indicates that a ceremony may have taken place there, Reinhard believes.

ANOTHER DETECTIVE'S THEORY: At the South Tyrol Museum of Archaeology, in Bolzano, Italy, where Ötzi is now kept frozen, Dr. Eduard Egarter Vigl is also working on the case. He believes that Ötzi was ambushed.

SUSPECTS AND MOTIVE: Egarter Vigl thinks Ötzi was involved in a fight—perhaps surprised while walking. He managed to escape, but later died of his wounds and exposure to the cold.

THE CLUES: A knife wound in Ötzi's hand proves that he struggled with someone before he died, Vigl says. He also points out that there is no evidence that sacrifices ever occurred in Europe during that time. And besides, most sacrifice victims aren't shot by arrows—especially in the back.

SO WHO KILLED THE ICEMAN?

Reinhard agrees that the clues are confusing. With no witnesses to tell what actually took place, there's no way to know exactly what happened. So this 5,300-year-old case may forever remain an unsolved mystery.

Johan Reinhard believes an explanation for the Iceman's well-preserved body is that he was buried by the person who killed him.

Women on the High Seas

True adventures of girl pirates

For as long as there have been pirates, some of those pirates have been girls and women. Piracy offered women freedoms that were denied them on land. Plus there was no household to run, no family to support, no chamber pots to empty. At sea a female pirate kept her own hours and spent them drinking, gambling, sailing, killing, and plundering. Some pirate women followed their boyfriends into piracy; others tried it out after spending time in the military (disguised as men); still others carried on a family tradition.

Mary Read and Anne Bonny

Reign of terror: The Caribbean, early 1700s

After Mary Read's husband died, she needed money. So she signed up as a sailor on a merchant ship heading to the West Indies. When the ship reached the Caribbean, English pirates took it over. They gave Mary a choice: Join up or be killed. Mary officially turned pirate.

Mary soon had a chance to show off her dueling skills. Fearing that her boyfriend on the ship would be killed in a duel, Mary picked a fight with the challenger and scheduled a duel herself—two hours before her beau's. Mary killed the other pirate without suffering a single scratch.

Mary met Anne Bonny, who ran away to sea with a flashy pirate named Calico Jack, when both women ended up on Jack's ship. Together they attacked other boats, mostly stealing small items like fishing gear and food. Despite the minor nature of their plundering, the English authorities issued a proclamation declaring Jack and the gals "Enemies to the Crown of Great Britain."

Rachel Wall

Reign of terror: New England, late 1700s

Rachel Wall worked the islands off the coast of Maine with her husband, George, and their crew. After storms they'd moor their sloop and raise a distress flag. When passersby responded to Rachel's screams for help, they were murdered for their trouble. In two summers of piracy, Rachel and George killed 24 men, maybe more—and raked in $6,000 cash, plus an unknown amount of valuable stuff. They later sold their loot, pretending to have found it washed up on a beach.

Cheng I Sao

Reign of terror: South China Sea, 1801–1810

The greatest pirate of all time (by the numbers, anyway) was Cheng I Sao, who ruled a terrifying fleet of 2,000 ships in the South China Sea. Cheng I Sao, sometimes called Madame Cheng, turned to crime when she married a famous pirate. More than 80,000 pirates—men, women, and even children—did Madame Cheng's bidding. They seized loot in all sorts of ways—selling "protection" from pirate attacks, raiding ships, and kidnapping. Madame Cheng paid her pirates cash for each head they brought back from their assaults. Her raiders could be seen fighting with five or six bloody heads hanging over their shoulders tied together by the hair.

Crime doesn't pay, even on the high seas—or does it? Mary Read and Anne Bonny were captured in 1720. Mary died of fever while she was in prison; what happened to Anne is a mystery. Eventually the law caught up with Rachel Wall, too. In 1789 she made history when she was the last woman to be hanged in Massachusetts. Government attempts to stop Madame Cheng, however, all met with failure. Rumor has it that after she retired from piracy, she embarked on a second career as a smuggler. She died peacefully at age 69.

MEET THE NAT GEO EXPLORER

FREDRIK HIEBERT

Archaeologist and explorer, Hiebert has traced ancient trade routes over land and across the seas for more than 20 years.

What was your most exciting discovery?
My most memorable find is from my first dig when I was a student. I was digging an 800-year-old house of an Egyptian merchant. On the last day I pulled up an ancient reed mat from in front of the door ... and there, under the mat was the key to the door, left behind by the merchant for when he came back. I will never forget that connection with the last person who had been in that house hundreds of years earlier.

How would you suggest kids follow in your footsteps?
Keep exploring. If you love what you are doing, that's the best life you can have.

What is one place or thing you'd still like to explore?
I'm always eager to explore ancient cultures. I'm really looking forward to visiting Mongolia next ... hope to see you there!

Fearless Fliers

Charles Lindbergh

On May 20, 1927, he took off on the flight that made him world-famous. Six men had died trying to make the 3,600-mile nonstop trip from New York to Paris, France, but Charles Lindbergh was going to do it. He flew alone in a small, single-engine plane. To avoid extra weight, he didn't take a radio or a parachute. The cockpit didn't have a front window, so Lindbergh used a homemade periscope to look out the side for dangers. He used charts, compasses, and the stars to guide his way. At 10,000 feet, it became so cold that he wore mittens and a wool-lined helmet. For two hours, he flew in total darkness. Lindbergh's flight lasted 33½ hours. Once, he even fell asleep with his eyes wide open! At 10:22 p.m. on May 21, he landed safely in Paris.

Amelia Earhart

In 1937 her plane disappeared mysteriously over the Pacific Ocean—that's how most people remember her. But by then Amelia Earhart was already the world's most famous female pilot. Her dream was to follow Lindbergh's example and cross the Atlantic alone. She wanted to prove that a woman could do it. Earhart began her solo flight on May 20, 1932. For several hours she flew at 12,000 feet, watching the sun set and the moon come up. But a key instrument failed and she ran into a severe storm that battered her plane. Ice formed on the wings, sending Earhart into a dangerous spin. Later, flames shot out of the engine. A fuel leak dripped gas down the back of her neck. Nearly 15 hours after starting, Earhart landed her plane in a meadow in Northern Ireland.

WORLD WARS

Since the beginning of time, people have been fighting each other over land, religion, money, politics, and pretty much anything else you can think of. At any given time, there are numerous armed conflicts occurring around the globe.

A world war is one that involves the world's most powerful nations, yet spans several continents and lasts for a long time. There have only been two wars in history that have earned the name "World War"— both of which were in the 20th century.

World War I (1914–1918)

Often referred to as the Great War, this was the largest war in human history. It was also one of the deadliest wars in history, with over 15 million people killed. There were two sides to the war: the Allied Powers (United States, Britain, France, Russia, Belgium, Italy, Japan, and more) and the Central Powers (Austria-Hungary, Germany, Bulgaria, and the Ottoman Empire).

World War II (1939–1945)

World War II began with the German invasion of Poland, causing England and France to declare war on Nazi Germany. There were two sides to the war: the Allies (led by England, the U.S., the Soviet Union, and France) and the Axis (Germany, Italy, Japan, Hungary, Romania, and Bulgaria). World War II was the deadliest war in history, with more than 50 million people killed. Many of those killed were Jews and other groups being persecuted by the Nazis. At the end of the war, the Axis powers were defeated, leaving the United States and the Soviet Union to emerge as the world's superpowers.

For more information on the world wars and other wars in history, check out the wide range of books from National Geographic Children's Books. shop.nationalgeographic.com

Bet you **didn't know**

The **GERMAN** submarine **U-120** was **SUNK** by a broken **TOILET.**

THE OLYMPICS

A LEGEND TELLS THAT the Olympic Games were founded by Heracles, the son of the Greek god Zeus, in ancient times. Unfortunately, that can't really be proven. The first Olympic Games for which there are still written records took place in 776 B.C. There was only one event, a running race called the stade. From then on, the Olympics were played every four years until they were abolished in A.D. 393.

It wasn't until more than 1,500 years later that the Olympics were resurrected. The modern Olympic Games were held for the first time in 1896. They have continued to be held around the world ever since.

Summer Olympic Games Sites

1896	Athens, Greece
1900	Paris, France
1904	St. Louis, MO, United States
1906	Athens, Greece
1908	London, England
1912	Stockholm, Sweden
1920	Antwerp, Belgium
1924	Paris, France
1928	Amsterdam, Netherlands
1932	Los Angeles, CA, United States
1936	Berlin, Germany
1948	London, England
1952	Helsinki, Finland
1956	Melbourne, Australia
1960	Rome, Italy
1964	Tokyo, Japan
1968	Mexico City, Mexico
1972	Munich, West Germany (now Germany)
1976	Montreal, Canada
1980	Moscow, USSR (now Russia)
1984	Los Angeles, CA, United States
1988	Seoul, South Korea
1992	Barcelona, Spain
1996	Atlanta, GA, United States
2000	Sydney, Australia
2004	Athens, Greece
2008	Beijing, China
2012	London, England

Winter Olympic Games Sites

1924	Chamonix, France
1928	St. Moritz, Switzerland
1932	Lake Placid, NY, United States
1936	Garmisch-Partenkirchen, Germany
1948	St. Moritz, Switzerland
1952	Oslo, Norway
1956	Cortina d'Ampezzo, Italy
1960	Squaw Valley, CA, United States
1964	Innsbruck, Austria
1968	Grenoble, France
1972	Sapporo, Japan
1976	Innsbruck, Austria
1980	Lake Placid, NY, United States
1984	Sarajevo, Yugoslavia
1988	Calgary, Alberta, Canada
1992	Albertville, France
1994	Lillehammer, Norway
1998	Nagano, Japan
2002	Salt Lake City, Utah, United States
2006	Torino (Turin), Italy
2010	Vancouver, Canada
2014	Sochi, Russia

Note: Due to World Wars I and II, the 1916 Summer Olympics, and both the summer and winter games of 1940 and 1944 were not held.

Strange Olympic Sports of the Past & Future

There are a bunch of sports, some rather odd, that were once played in the Olympics but no longer get to make an appearance. Here are a few: Tug-of-War • Croquet • Lacrosse • Golf • Power Boating

Recognized as International Sports Federations by the Olympic Committee, the following are among a long list of sports that aren't currently played at the games. Who knows, maybe one day you'll win a gold medal in chess: Billiards • Bridge • Chess • Lifesaving • Netball • Orienteering • Roller Sports • Water Skiing

RICAL APHIES ROCK

A BIOGRAPHY IS THE STORY OF A PERSON'S LIFE. A biography can be a brief summary or a super-long book. Biographers—those who write biographies—use many different sources to learn about their subject. You can write your own biography of a famous person you find interesting or inspiring.

How to Get Started

Want to write an interesting biography? Start by choosing a subject you find interesting. If you think Amelia Earhart is cool, you have a good chance of getting your reader interested, too. If you're bored by aviation, your reader will be snoring after your first paragraph.

Your subject can be almost anyone: an inventor, an author, a celebrity, a President, or a member of your family. To find someone to write about, ask yourself these simple questions:

1. Whom do I want to know more about?
2. What did this person do that was special?
3. How did this person change the world?

Do Your Research

- Find out as much about your subject as possible. Read books, newspaper articles, and encyclopedia entries. Watch video clips and movies, and search the Internet. Conduct interviews, if possible.
- Take notes, writing down important facts and interesting stories about your subject.

Writing the Biography

- Come up with a title. Include the person's name.
- Write an introduction. Consider asking a probing question about your subject.
- Include information about the person's child-hood. When was this person born? Where did he or she grow up? Whom did he or she admire?
- Highlight the person's talents, accomplishments, and his or her personal attributes.
- Describe the specific events that helped to shape this person's life. Has this person ever had a problem and overcome it?

- Write a conclusion. Include your thoughts about why it is important to learn about this person.
- Once you have finished your first draft, proofread and then revise.

Here's a SAMPLE BIOGRAPHY for President Barack Obama.
Of course, there is so much more for you to research, uncover, and reveal!

Barack Obama—Number 44

Barack Obama is the 44th President of the United States and the first African-American to hold the office. But what did he want to be when he was younger?

Obama was born on August 4, 1961, in Honolulu, Hawai'i. As a child he lived in Indonesia. In elementary school he once wrote an essay titled "I want to become President"—some dreams start early! Later, Obama graduated from Columbia University and earned a degree in law from Harvard Law School.

Obama was the Democratic Illinois state senator from 1997 to 2004. He gave the keynote address at the 2004 Democratic National Convention, an honor that helped him on the path to his successful presidential candidacy.

He married Michelle Robinson Obama and has two daughters, Malia and Sasha. Obama is a good example for them—and kids everywhere!—that if you work hard, your dreams can come true.

REVEAL YOUR SOURCES

A BIBLIOGRAPHY IS A LIST of all the sources you used to get information for your essay, such as books, magazine articles, interviews, and websites. It is included at the end of your essay or report.

The bibliography should list sources in alphabetical order by author's last name. If a source doesn't have an author, then it should be alphabetized by title.

BOOK

Author (last name, first name). *Title*. City of publisher: publisher, date of publication.

Ex: Allen, Thomas B. *George Washington, Spymaster*. Washington, D.C.: National Geographic, 2004.

ENCYCLOPEDIA

Author (last name, first name) (if given). "Article title." *Name of Encyclopedia*. Edition. Volume. City of publisher: publisher, date of publication.

Ex: "Gerbil." *The Encyclopedia Britannica*. 15th ed. Vol. 5. Chicago: Encyclopedia Britannica, 2007.

MAGAZINE/NEWSPAPER ARTICLE

Author (last name, first name). "Article title." *Name of magazine*. Date: page numbers.

Ex: Kassinger, Ruth. "Gold Fever." *NATIONAL GEOGRAPHIC KIDS*. Jan–Feb 2009: p. 8–11.

DVD/FILM

Title of film. Director's name. Year of original film's release. Format. Name of distributor, year, video/DVD/etc. produced.

Ex: *Lewis & Clark: Great Journey West*. Dir. Bruce Neibaur. 2002. Large-format film. National Geographic, 2002.

INTERVIEW

Person interviewed (last name, first name). Type of interview (personal, telephone, email, etc.). Date of interview.

Ex: Hiebert, Fredrik. Personal interview with *NATIONAL GEOGRAPHIC KIDS*. April 28, 2008.

WEBSITE

Author (last name, first name) (if given). *Title of the site*. Editor, Date and/or version number. Name of sponsoring institution. Date of access <URL>.

Ex: *Animals*. 2006. National Geographic. January 12, 2009. <http://kids.national geographic.com/Animals>.

TIP:

If you keep track of all the sources as you use them, you will find that compiling the information to create your bibliography will be done in a snap. It's merely the task of typing up the information into a list.

COOL CLICK

Want to find out more about sources and books? The Library of Congress has a great website where you can discover tons of new stuff, including more about America's past. www.loc.gov/families

Wonders of
Nature

Night-blooming water lilies
in Botswana

World Climate

Weather is the condition of the atmosphere—temperature, precipitation, humidity, wind—at a given place at a given time. Climate, however, is the average weather for a particular place over a long period of time. Different places on Earth have different climates, but climate is not a random occurrence. There is a pattern that is controlled by factors such as latitude, elevation, prevailing winds, temperature of ocean currents, and location on land relative to water. Climate is generally constant, but human activity is causing a change in the patterns of climate.

CLIMATE FACTS

Data collected by satellites suggests that the Sahara, Earth's largest hot desert, had a wet climate that supported vast forests some 12,000 years ago. Extremely dry conditions did not begin until about 5,000 years ago.

According to climatologists, Earth had what is called the Little Ice Age, which lasted from the 17th century to the late 19th century. During that time, temperatures were cold enough to cause glaciers to advance.

Ice cores taken from Antarctica and Greenland have enabled scientists to gain detailed information about the history of Earth's climate and its atmosphere—especially the presence of greenhouse gases—dating back thousands of years.

According to the National Oceanic and Atmospheric Administration (NOAA), 2008 tied with 2001 as the eighth warmest year on record for the Earth. All of the top ten hottest years have occured since 1997.

3 DAY FORECAST

TUE   WED   THU

80°   83°   8

CHANNEL 10

GLOBAL CLIMATE ZONES

Climatologists, people who study climate, have created different systems for classifying climates. An often-used system is called the Köppen system, which classifies climate zones according to precipitation, temperature, and vegetation. It has five major categories—Tropical, Dry, Mild, Continental, and Polar—with a sixth category for locations where high elevations override other factors. Climate zones can shift over time, but the changes are accelerated by human activity.

Learn all about weather and other forms of nature in this chapter. Then go online for more fun weather information.
COOL CLICK   kids.nationalgeographic.com/Games/PuzzlesQuizzes/Weather-word-search

Bet you didn't know

WEATHER REPORT

The hottest temperature ever recorded in the United States is 134°F (57°C), and the lowest is −80°F (−62°C).

Severe thunderstorm clouds can be more than 11 miles (17.7 km) high.

The biggest snowflake ever recorded was 15 inches (38.1 cm) wide.

In 1816 a summer snow-storm left 20-inch (50.8 cm) snowdrifts in Vermont.

Every minute about 600 bolts of lightning strike the Earth.

In February 1899, ice flowed down the Mississippi River into the warm waters of the Gulf of Mexico.

An estimated 600 tornadoes struck the U.S. in May 2003, setting a new record.

The longest-lasting rainbow reportedly shone for six hours over England.

Temperature

There are two types of temperature scales in the world, **Fahrenheit** (used in the U.S.) and **Celsius** (used in most countries of the world). Although they both measure temperature, the numbers are different. For example, **water freezes at 32°F or 0°C.**

To convert from Fahrenheit to Celsius, subtract 32, then multiply by 5, and divide by 9.

To convert from Celsius to Fahrenheit, multiply by 9, divide by 5, and then add 32.

Example: If water boils at 100°C and we want to know what temperature that is in Fahrenheit, we'd use the second formula:
100°C x 9 = 900
900 ÷ 5 = 180
180 + 32 = 212°F

CLIMATE CHANGE

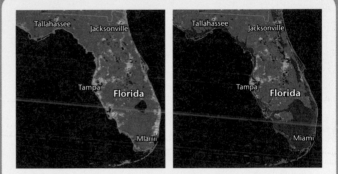

Earth's climate history has been a story of ups and downs, with warm periods followed by periods of bitter cold. The early part of the 20th century was marked by colder than average temperatures (see graph below), followed by a period of gradual and then steady increase. Scientists are concerned that the current warming trend is more than a natural cycle. Evidence indicates that human activity is adding to the warming. One sign of change is melting glaciers in Greenland and Antarctica. If glaciers continue to melt, areas of Florida (shown above in red) and other coastal land will be underwater.

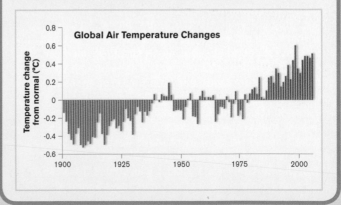

Global Air Temperature Changes

273

Lightning!

Lightning hits the United States at least 22 million times a year.

Clouds suddenly appeared on the horizon, the sky turned dark, and it started to rain as Sabrina was hiking through the Grand Canyon with her parents.

As lightning flashed around them, Sabrina and her parents ran for cover. "When it stopped raining, we thought it was safe," says Sabrina. They started to hike back to their car along the trail. Then zap! A lightning bolt struck nearby. It happened so fast that the family didn't know what it hit. A jolt of electricity shot through their bodies. "It felt like a strong tingling over my whole body," says Sabrina. "It really hurt."

Sabrina and her family were lucky. The lightning didn't zap them directly, and they recovered within minutes. Some people aren't so lucky. Lightning kills about 100 people in the United States each year. It injures hundreds more.

Lightning is a giant electric spark similar to the small spark you get when you walk across a carpet and touch a metal doorknob—but much stronger. One flash can contain a billion volts of electricity—enough to light a 100-watt incandescent bulb for three months. Lightning crackles through the air at a temperature five times hotter than the surface of the sun. The intense heat makes the surrounding air expand rapidly, creating a sound we know as thunder. Getting hit by lightning is rare, but everyone must be careful.

"For the first few years after I was struck, I was so scared every time there was a storm," says Sabrina. "Now I'm not scared. But I'm always cautious."

LIGHTNING SAFETY TIPS

INSIDE

Stay inside for 30 minutes after the last lightning or thunder.

Don't take baths or showers or wash dishes.

Avoid the use of landline phones (cell phones are OK), computers, TVs, and other electrical equipment.

OUTSIDE

Get into an enclosed structure or vehicle and shut the windows.

Stay away from bodies of water.

Avoid tall objects such as trees.

If you're in the open, crouch down (but do not lie flat) in the lowest place you can find.

Bet you didn't **know**

7 frosty facts about **snow**

1 **Snirt** is slang for snow combined with **dirt.**

2 **Ten** inches of snow **equals one inch of water** on average.

3 Some **avalanches** can travel more than **100** miles per hour.

4 **The tallest snowman ever built was higher than a ten-story building.**

5 Almost **90** percent of **snow** is **air.**

6 Snowflakes get smaller as the **TEMPERATURE DROPS.**

7 The word **Himalaya** means "**house of snow.**"

Natural Disasters

Every world region has its share of natural disasters—the menacing mix just varies from place to place. The Ring of Fire—grinding tectonic plate boundaries that follow the coasts of the Pacific Ocean—shakes with volcanic eruptions and earthquakes. Coastal lives and livelihoods here and along other oceans can be swept away by quake-caused tsunamis. The U.S. heartland endures blizzards in winter and dangerous tornadoes that can strike in spring, summer, or fall. Tropical cyclones batter many coastal areas with ripping winds, torrents of rain, and huge storm surges along their deadly paths.

KINDS OF DISASTERS

EARTHQUAKE
A shaking of Earth's crust caused by a volcanic eruption or by the release of energy along a fault in the crust

TORNADO
A violently rotating column of air that touches Earth's surface during intense thunderstorm activity

HURRICANE
A large weather system, fueled by warm water, that can become a rotating storm packing winds of at least 74 miles per hour (119 kph). The storms are called hurricanes in the Atlantic Ocean and eastern Pacific, cyclones in the Indian Ocean, and typhoons in the western Pacific.

TSUNAMI
Huge ocean waves caused by an undersea earthquake or by a volcanic eruption

VOLCANIC ERUPTION
The upward movement and usually forceful release of molten material and gases from Earth's interior onto the surface

Tsunami!

The day after Christmas 2004, a tsunami—a series of massive waves—hit coastlines around the Indian Ocean. In minutes, buildings were destroyed and people lost their families. Rina Kamal, then five years old, was one of them. She was found on the shore; her mother and sisters had been swept away.

This tsunami began with a powerful undersea earthquake. Waves began to roll across the ocean in a series. They traveled behind each other very fast—at about the speed of a jet plane.

Closer to shore, the waves slowed. The ones at the back got closer to the waves in the front. One after another they crashed ashore. Some were as tall as a four-story building. The devastating tsunami killed more than 225,000 people.

All over the world people rushed to help the tsunami's survivors. Some sent blankets, school supplies, and canned goods. Others found unique ways to raise funds. Kids helped, too; in Benson, North Carolina, first grade students collected pennies—158,451 of them!

Meanwhile, Rina's father never stopped looking for his wife and daughters. A month after the tsunami, he found Rina's name on a list of survivors. Volunteers brought him to where Rina was living. At last father and daughter were reunited and could begin to rebuild their lives together.

Scale of Hurricane Intensity

CATEGORY	ONE	TWO	THREE	FOUR	FIVE
DAMAGE	Minimal	Moderate	Extensive	Extreme	Catastrophic
WINDS	74–95 mph	96–110 mph	111–130 mph	131–155 mph	Over 155 mph

(DAMAGE refers to wind and water damage combined.)

Avalanche!

A million tons of snow rumble eight miles downhill, kicking up a cloud of snow dust visible a hundred miles away.

This is not a scene from a disaster movie—this describes reality one day in April 1981. The mountain was Mount Sanford in Alaska, and the event was one of history's bigger avalanches. Amazingly no one was hurt, and luckily avalanches this big are rare.

An avalanche is a moving mass of snow that may contain ice, soil, rocks, and uprooted trees. The height of a mountain, the steepness of its slope, and the type of snow lying on it all help determine the likelihood of an avalanche. Avalanches begin when an unstable mass of snow breaks away from a mountainside and moves downhill. The growing river of snow picks up speed as it rushes down the mountain. Avalanches have been known to reach speeds of 155 miles per hour (249 km/hr)—about the same as the record for downhill skiing.

This winter in the western United States alone, thousands upon thousands of avalanches will tumble down mountainsides. In the United States and Canada crashing walls of white will bowl over about 300 people. Most will be skiers, snowboarders, or snowmobilers who set out to have fun. Many will be buried by snow. Most will survive; some will not. Follow the safety tips below to help stay safe when you play in the mountains.

France has had the greatest number of avalanche fatalities.

Safety Tips

SAFETY FIRST
Before heading out, check for avalanche warnings.

EQUIPMENT
Carry safety equipment, including a long probe, a small shovel, and an emergency avalanche rescue beacon that signals your location.

NEVER GO IT ALONE
Don't hike in the mountain wilderness without a companion. Keep plenty of distance between party members, so if there is an avalanche not everyone is swept away.

CAUGHT
If caught in the path of an avalanche, try to get to the side of it. If you can't, grab a tree as an anchor. If swept into an avalanche, "swim" with the slide to stay as close to the surface as you can.

277

Tornado

STORM SYSTEM

Tornado

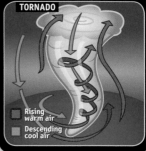

TORNADO

Rising warm air
Descending cool air

"One time a tornado we were filming was coming right at us," says filmmaker Sean Casey. "As it moved closer, the wind picked up, and we felt as if the wind were pulling us into the tornado." Casey wants to film the perfect tornado. So when he sees one, he plants himself nearby with his cameras. That's not the safest thing to do. "The trick is knowing when to get out of there," says Casey.

With swirling winds that can top 300 miles per hour, twisters can rip up trees, turn houses into piles of twisted wood, and toss cars around like toys. They're nature's most violent storms.

People like Casey chase tornadoes to make large-format films. But to find the storms, Casey tags along with a group of meteorologists, or weather scientists, who chase storms to find out why tornadoes form in some thunderstorms but not in others. The data that these meteorologists collect could make it easier to predict tornadoes.

Casey's team of filmmakers and scientists have had close calls. "We were following a storm one day and the wind pushed our 13-ton radar truck backward," remembers Casey.

The chase has its exciting moments. But it can also be long and tedious. Seeing a tornado up close is exciting. But what's even more important is that storm chasers gain insight about twisters that could one day save lives.

Earthquake

The people of Northridge, California, will never forget the morning the ground started to shake, rattle, and roll. It was 4:30 a.m. when a huge block of rock 11 miles under the city suddenly jolted upward several inches. As the ground above it bounced and buckled, thousands of buildings cracked and crumbled. Bridges snapped like toothpicks, and cracks opened in the ground. Gas lines broke, starting fires. The 1994 earthquake lasted only 30 seconds but caused 57 deaths, 9,000 injuries, and left thousands of people homeless.

Earthquakes are common; thousands occur each day. But unlike the Northridge quake, most are too weak to feel. Even some strong quakes are harmless because they happen in isolated, unpopulated areas. "Earthquakes don't kill people, falling buildings do," says Lucy Jones, a seismologist, or scientist who studies earthquakes. "You can't stop an earthquake," says Jones, who works for the U.S. Geological Survey in California. "The best thing you can do is prepare."

SURVIVE! A quake in Japan caused this damage. If you're in an earthquake, follow these tips. Outside, find an open space away from heavy structures and utility poles. Inside, avoid windows. Get under a sturdy table and stay there, or move into a hallway and press yourself against an inside wall.

Volcanic Eruption

So you're climbing your favorite mountain, just minding your own business, when *ba-da-bing, ba-da-boom!* It explodes! But don't blow your top. Just stay cool and follow these VOLCANO SURVIVAL TIPS.

SHAKE YOUR BOOTIES
Volcanic eruptions are often preceded by earth tremors. So if you feel the mountain start to mambo, make like Scooby-Doo and—*zoinks!*—get outta there!

CARRY A DISGUISE
Volcanoes may not erupt for hundreds of years, but you might want to bring a breathing mask and goggles just in case. They'll protect your eyes and lungs from harmful ash and noxious gases. (Plus they make a really cool Halloween costume!)

DON'T WADE AROUND
Ooey-gooey lava can reach temperatures of 2,200°F (1204°C). That'll turn your toenails into toast! So don't go with the (lava) flow. Hotfoot it to safety before your shoes scorch!

ROCKS 'N' ROLL
Question: How do red-hot rocks flying toward you feel? Answer: Don't find out! Run up the closest nonexploding, 100-foot (30-m) hill, the "safety zone" outside the spew range.

HANG 10, DUDE
A volcanic blast can trigger a huge tidal wave, so even after you're off the volcano, you still could be all washed up. If you see a towering wall of water crashing your way, hightail it to high ground.

Signs That "It's Gonna Blow!"

1 In and around a volcano, the frequency and intensity of earthquakes increase.

2 The ground at the eruption site deforms or bulges.

3 The amount of gas released by the volcano increases.

A volcano's "fireworks" begin deep underground.

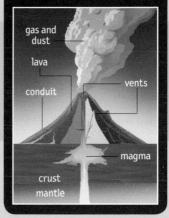

gas and dust

lava

vents

conduit

magma

crust

mantle

weird but true

ABOUT 75 PERCENT OF ALL VOLCANOES ARE UNDERWATER.

World Vegetation

TEMPERATE BROADLEAF FOREST

Broadleaf trees that grow in mid-latitude areas with mild temperatures, such as this one in Shenandoah National Park, are deciduous, meaning they lose their leaves in winter. Many such forests have been cleared for cropland.

DESERT AND DRY SHRUB

Deserts, areas that receive less than 10 inches (25 cm) of rainfall a year, have vegetation that is specially adapted to survive under dry conditions, such as these dry shrubs and cacti growing in the Sonoran Desert in Arizona.

TUNDRA

With only two to three months of temperatures above freezing, tundra plants are mostly dwarf shrubs, grasslike sedges, mosses, and lichens. Much of Canada's Yukon has tundra vegetation, which turns red as winter approaches.

CONIFEROUS FOREST

Needleleaf trees with cones to protect their seeds from bitter winters grow in cold climates with short summers, such as British Columbia, Canada. These trees are important in lumber and paper-making industries.

NATURAL VEGETATION—

plants that would grow under ideal circumstances at a particular place—depends on several factors. The climate is very important, as are the quality and type of soil available. Therefore, vegetation often reflects patterns of climate. Forests thrive in places with ample precipitation; grasses are found in places with less precipitation or with only seasonal rainfall; and xerophytes—plants able to survive lengthy periods with little or no water—are found in arid areas that receive little precipitation. Grasses and shrubs cover almost half of Earth's land. Here is a sampling of some of the world's vegetation zones and cropland.

TEMPERATE GRASSLANDS

Grasslands, such as this tall-grass prairie in southwestern Missouri, are sometimes found in areas where precipitation is too low to support forests. Many temperate grasslands have been converted to cropland for grain production.

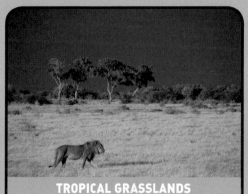

TROPICAL GRASSLANDS

Tall grasses and scattered trees that can survive a hot, dry season dominate low-latitude grasslands, also called savannas. Africa's grasslands are home to many large animals, such as this male lion crossing the savanna in Botswana.

RAIN FOREST

A waterfall tumbles over a cliff in the Costa Rican rain forest. Rain forest trees can grow as tall as 200 feet (61 m) above the forest floor. The overlapping branches of the tallest trees keep sunlight from reaching the forest floor.

CROPLAND

People remove natural vegetation in many places to create fields for growing crops to feed both people and animals. Here, a farmer in the Catskill Mountains of New York uses a mechanized harvester to cut corn that feeds his dairy cows.

Countries Around the World
Where Crystals and Gems Are Mined

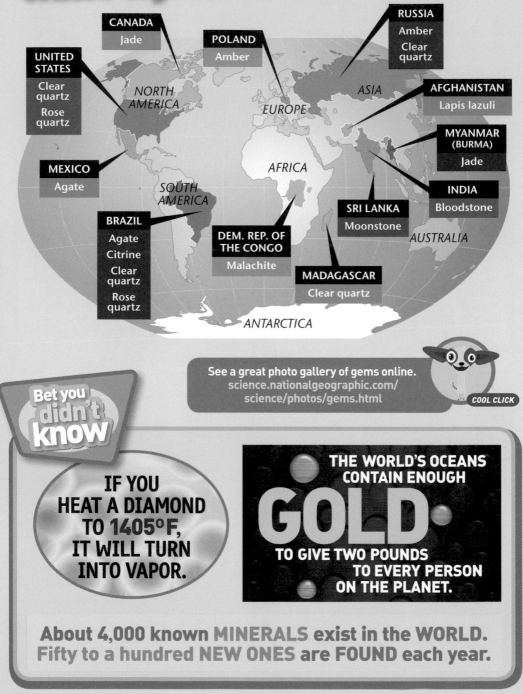

CANADA
Jade

POLAND
Amber

RUSSIA
Amber
Clear quartz

UNITED STATES
Clear quartz
Rose quartz

NORTH AMERICA

EUROPE

ASIA

AFGHANISTAN
Lapis lazuli

MYANMAR (BURMA)
Jade

MEXICO
Agate

AFRICA

INDIA
Bloodstone

SOUTH AMERICA

SRI LANKA
Moonstone

AUSTRALIA

BRAZIL
Agate
Citrine
Clear quartz
Rose quartz

DEM. REP. OF THE CONGO
Malachite

MADAGASCAR
Clear quartz

ANTARCTICA

See a great photo gallery of gems online.
science.nationalgeographic.com/
science/photos/gems.html

COOL CLICK

Bet you didn't know

IF YOU HEAT A DIAMOND TO 1405°F, IT WILL TURN INTO VAPOR.

THE WORLD'S OCEANS CONTAIN ENOUGH
GOLD
TO GIVE TWO POUNDS TO EVERY PERSON ON THE PLANET.

About 4,000 known MINERALS exist in the WORLD.
Fifty to a hundred NEW ONES are FOUND each year.

BIRTHST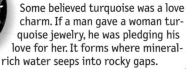NES

GARNET LOYALTY

January — Garnets were once thought to hold medicinal value and protect against poisons, wounds, and bad dreams! They come in red, black, green, or are colorless.

RUBY CONTENTMENT

July — A ruby supposedly brought good health, cured bleeding, guarded against wickedness, and foretold misfortune. Rubies are a red form of the mineral corundum.

AMETHYST SINCERITY

February — Amethysts were believed to help people stay awake and think clearly. They are found in geodes and range in color from light mauve to deep purple.

PERIDOT HAPPINESS

August — People felt that peridots could ward off anxiety, help one speak better, and improve relationships. Peridot is the only gem ever found in meteorites.

AQUAMARINE COURAGE

March — This gem was thought to heal illnesses of the stomach, liver, jaws, and throat. They range from deep blue to blue-green. The most valued and rare are the deep blue gems.

SAPPHIRE CLEAR THINKING

September — Once a source of protection for travelers, sapphires brought peace and wisdom. Some are pale; others are brilliant blue. They also come in orange, green, yellow, and pink.

DIAMOND ENDURING LOVE

April — People associate them with romance, mystery, power, greed, and magic. The hardest natural substance on Earth, diamonds are a form of carbon.

OPAL HOPE

October — An opal was believed to bring beauty, success, and happiness, as well as to ward off heart and kidney failure, and prevent fainting. Opals form over a long, long time.

EMERALD PURE LOVE

May — Emeralds were thought to prevent epilepsy, stop bleeding, cure fevers and diarrhea, and keep the wearer from panicking. These gems are light to deep green.

TOPAZ FAITHFULNESS

November — Legends proclaimed that a topaz made one clear-sighted, increased strength, and warned of poison. Topazes come in a range of colors: gold, pink, green, or colorless.

PEARL INNOCENCE

June — Thought to possess magical powers, there used to be laws about who could own and wear pearls (powerful, rich people). No two pearls are exactly alike.

TURQUOISE SUCCESS

December — Some believed turquoise was a love charm. If a man gave a woman turquoise jewelry, he was pledging his love for her. It forms where mineral-rich water seeps into rocky gaps.

HOW DOES Your Garden GROW?

Over 275,000 organisms strong, the plant kingdom is growing wild! Plants can be found all over the world—on top of mountains, in the sea, in frigid temperatures—everywhere. Without plants, life on Earth would not be able to survive. Plants provide food and oxygen for animals and humans on the planet.

There are three characteristics that make plants distinct:

1 Most have chlorophyll (a green pigment that makes photosynthesis work and turns sunlight into glucose), while some are parasitic.

2 They cannot change their location on their own.

3 Their cell walls are made from cellulose.

Photosynthesis

light

oxygen

carbon dioxide

water

Plants are lucky—they don't have to hunt or shop for food. Most produce their own food—and they do it using the sun! In a process called photosynthesis, the plant's chloroplast (the part of the plant where the chemical chlorophyll is located) captures the sun's energy and combines it with carbon dioxide from the air and nutrient-rich water from the ground to produce glucose, a sugar. Plants use the glucose to help them grow. As a waste product, plants emit oxygen, which humans need to breathe. When we breathe, we exhale carbon dioxide, which the plants then use for more photosynthesis—it's all a big, finely tuned system. So the next time you pass a lonely houseplant, give it thanks for helping you live.

Try This! MAKE A COOL TERRARIUM!

YOU WILL NEED

- **Fishbowl or glass jar of any size** • **Small stones**
- **Horticultural charcoal from a garden store**
- **Potting soil** • **Plants of your choice** (see ideas at right)
- **Scissors** • **Water** • **Decorative rocks and figurines**

WHAT TO DO

1. Wash the glass container in hot, soapy water. Rinse and dry completely.

2. Create a one-inch layer of stones on the bottom of the jar.

3. Add a half-inch layer of charcoal.

4. Spoon in a two- to three-inch layer of potting soil. (Pile soil higher on one side to make plants visible from a side view.) Dig small holes for the roots.

5. Take plants out of their pots, remove extra soil from the roots, and trim damaged leaves.

6. While the roots are still moist, place the plants in the holes and pat soil over the roots. Put tall plants in back.

7. Dampen the soil. Do not overwater.

8. Decorate with pretty rocks, animal figurines, or a garden gnome.

9. Place in indirect sunlight. Add water when your terrarium gets dry.

PICK THE RIGHT PLANTS

Almost any houseplant will grow inside a terrarium. For best results, use plants that need about the same amount of water and sunlight, such as:

Moss and lichens	Wintergreens
Begonias	African violets
Spider plants	Baby tears
Small palms	Hepaticas
Miniature orchids	Gloxinias
Miniature ferns	Coleuses

Green Invaders

They're taking over America. No, not invaders from space. Plants from other countries! Ever since people started to arrive on American shores, they've carried along trees, flowers, and vegetables from other places. Now there are so many, they're crowding out the native plants that lived there long before the settlers.

And that's a problem, says Dr. Doug Tallamy, an entomologist at the University of Delaware. He explains that almost all the plant-eating insects in the United States—90 percent of them—are specialized. That means they eat only certain plants. Orange-and-black monarch caterpillars, for example, can only dine on one plant: milkweed. If people cut down milkweed and replace it with something else, the caterpillars would starve. And the trouble goes across the food web.

Fewer of the right plants mean fewer bugs, and fewer bugs mean fewer birds. And that's bad for Earth, because we need a variety of living things to keep the planet healthy. The good news is, gardeners are working hard to protect native plants and get rid of invaders.

"Adopt a bird species in trouble and plant some things that will attract the insects they need," Tallamy suggests. "It will happen—insects move around a lot, and they will find the plants you put out there for them!"

WORLD WATER

Earth's most precious resource

More than two-thirds of Earth is covered by water, but freshwater, which is needed by plants and animals—including humans—makes up less than 3 percent of all the water on Earth. Much of this freshwater is trapped deep underground or frozen in ice sheets and glaciers. Of the small amount of water that is fresh, less than one percent is available for human use.

Unfortunately, human activity often puts great stress on vital watersheds. For example, in Brazil, plans are being made to build large dams on the Amazon River. This will alter the natural flow of water in this giant watershed. In the United States, heavy use of chemical fertilizers and pesticides has created toxic runoff that threatens the health of the Mississippi River watershed.

Access to clean freshwater is critical for human health. But in many places, safe water is scarce due to population pressure and pollution.

Water Facts

Rivers that have been dammed to generate electricity are the source of almost 90 percent of Earth's renewable energy resources.

If all the glaciers and ice sheets on Earth's surface melted, they would raise the level of Earth's oceans by about 230 feet (70 m). It is estimated that during the last ice age, when glaciers covered about one-third of the land, the sea level was 400 feet (122 m) lower than it is today.

Desalination is the process of removing salt from ocean water so that it can be used for irrigation and for people and livestock to drink. Most of the world's desalination plants are in the arid countries of the Arabian Peninsula.

Without food, a person can live for weeks, but without water you can expect to live only a few days.

If all the world's water were placed in a gallon jug, the freshwater available for humans to use would equal only about one tablespoon.

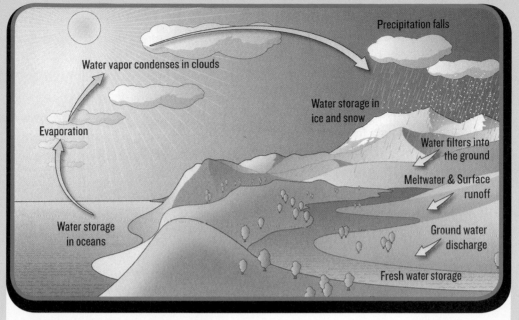

Precipitation falls

Water vapor condenses in clouds

Water storage in ice and snow

Evaporation

Water filters into the ground

Meltwater & Surface runoff

Water storage in oceans

Ground water discharge

Fresh water storage

WATER CYCLE

The amount of water on Earth is more or less constant—only the form changes. As the sun warms Earth's surface, liquid water is changed to water vapor in a process called **evaporation.** Plants lose water from the surface of leaves in a process called **transpiration.** As water vapor rises into the air, it cools and changes form again. This time it becomes clouds in a process called **condensation.** Water droplets fall from the clouds as **precipitation,** which then travels as groundwater or runoff back to the lakes, rivers, and oceans, where the cycle (shown above) starts all over again.

The **LARGEST ICEBERG** in the Northern Hemisphere contained enough water for **EVERY PERSON IN THE WORLD** to drink about **THREE GLASSES A DAY FOR FOUR YEARS.**

Bet you **didn't know**

As a result of wind, a waterfall in **Hawai'i** sometimes **GOES UP** instead of **DOWN.**

EARTH HAS THE SAME AMOUNT OF **WATER TODAY** AS IT DID **100 MILLION YEARS AGO.**

We're Parched!

We live in a thirsty world, and water is our drink of necessity. Our world would not survive without water—plants would not grow, and animals would not live.

Drought is when there is a prolonged period of lack of rainfall. If the amount of rain lessens too much, particularly if it's combined with unpredictable wind patterns and high temperatures, we can end up in a severe drought. When droughts persist, water often has to be rationed, or given out in limited amounts. Crops and animals won't get the water that they need to survive, which can lead to food shortages. Droughts can also cause dust storms and fires.

Since drought is related to weather, it may seem like there is nothing we can do to help prevent it, but that is wrong. As humans, the activities we engage in, like burning fossil fuels, contribute to the process of global warming, which is gradually changing the climate of our planet. To help prevent devastating droughts and slow global warming, we need to burn less fossil fuel, conserve water, change farming methods, and treat our planet with love. Because if the water runs out, we just might, too.

Drought Drives Them Out

A lost world lies hidden in the rain forests of the Americas. Hundreds of cities and towns stand among the trees. Once they were home to millions of Native Americans known as the Maya.

The Maya have lived in the jungles of the Americas for 3,000 years. They built an incredible civilization. It was at its peak for about 750 years. The peak ended about 1,000 years ago.

Today the Mayan cities are empty. Trees and vines embrace the old buildings. Many once proud temples and palaces are now ruins.

Tikal was one of the greatest Mayan cities. Some 55,000 people lived there 1,300 years ago. The city boasted roughly 3,000 major buildings.

Yet, one day, its people were all gone. Why?

Archaeologists think Tikal suffered a drought that made it hard to grow corn, beans, squash, and other foods. Warfare may also have weakened Tikal.

That's not all. Drought and war probably shook the people's faith in their king. The Maya thought of their rulers as gods. When the king couldn't bring rain or victory, though, people may have stopped listening to him. Their community fell apart.

They left behind a great city and a great mystery.

Ruins of a temple in Palenque, an ancient Mayan city

WAYS YOU CAN PRESERVE FRESHWATER SUPPLIES

- Don't clean sidewalks by blasting them with a hose. Use a broom instead.

- Turn off the tap while brushing your teeth. Letting the faucet run wastes a gallon of water each time. If you brush your teeth twice a day, that's 730 gallons of water a year!

- Keeping the lawn green can be tough on the environment. Fertilizers wash into neighborhood storm drains, creating unhealthy algae growth in rivers and streams.

Every living thing depends on water.

Water Isn't Everywhere

Lake Itasca, Minnesota

Freshwater is always a fresh subject for photographer Jim Richardson, who has been taking pictures for NATIONAL GEOGRAPHIC since 1984. Many of his photographs, including the one here, deal with freshwater. "The world's supply of freshwater is dwindling," he says. "In some places, entire suburbs are being built where the supply of freshwater will run out in a matter of years." Cleanliness is just as important as supply, according to Richardson. "But good water isn't always crystal clear," he says. "Healthy freshwater can also be muddy and full of nutrients for the animals that depend on it."

COOL CLICKS

There is a lot to know about water and water conservation, so check out some of these great websites to learn more.

National Integrated Drought Information System
www.drought.gov

Water Conservation Tips
www.monolake.org/waterconservation

Water Conservation Game
www.ecokidsonline.com/pub/eco_info/topics/water/water/index.cfm

Bet you didn't know

The longest drought in recorded history lasted 400 years! It took place in the Atacama Desert in Chile, the driest place on Earth.

THE OC

PACIFIC OCEAN

STATS

Surface area
65,436,200 sq mi (169,479,000 sq km)

Percent of Earth's water area
47 percent

Greatest depth
Challenger Deep
(in the Mariana Trench)
-35,827 ft (-10,920 m)

Surface temperatures
Summer high: 90°F (32°C)
Winter low: 28°F (−2°C)

Tides
Highest: 30 ft (9 m)
near Korean peninsula
Lowest: 1 ft (0.3 m)
near Midway Islands

GEO WHIZ

The Pacific Ocean has more islands—tens of thousands of them—than any other ocean.

The ocean's name comes from the Latin *Mare Pacificum,* meaning "peaceful sea," but earthquakes and volcanic activity along its coasts generate powerful waves called tsunamis, which cause death and destruction when they slam ashore.

With the greatest area of tropical waters, the Pacific is also home to the largest number of coral reefs, including Earth's longest: Australia's 1,429-mile- (2,300-km-) long Great Barrier Reef.

The Hawaiian monk seal, the most endangered marine mammal in U.S. waters, lives only on a few islands in the remote northwestern end of the Hawaiian archipelago.

ATLANTIC OCEAN

STATS

Surface area
35,338,500 sq mi (91,526,400 sq km)

Percent of Earth's water area
25 percent

Greatest depth
Puerto Rico Trench
-28,232 ft (-8,605 m)

Surface temperatures
Summer high: 90°F (32°C)
Winter low: 28°F (-2°C)

Tides
Highest: 52 ft (16 m)
Bay of Fundy, Canada
Lowest: 1.5 ft (0.5 m)
Gulf of Mexico and Mediterranean Sea

GEO WHIZ

In 2005, the Atlantic Ocean produced a record-setting 15 hurricanes. For the first time in a single season, four hurricanes—Emily, Katrina, Rita, and Wilma—reached category 5 level, with sustained winds of at least 155 miles per hour (249 kph).

The Atlantic Ocean is about half the size of the Pacific, but it's growing. Spreading along the Mid-Atlantic Ridge allows molten rock from Earth's interior to escape and form new ocean floor.

Fishermen in the North Atlantic were eyewitnesses to the volcanic eruption that created the island of Surtsey, off the southeastern coast of Iceland, in November 1963.

Each year, the amount of water that flows into the Atlantic Ocean from the Amazon River in South America is equal to 20 percent of Earth's available freshwater.

EANS

INDIAN OCEAN

STATS

Surface area
28,839,800 sq mi (74,694,800 sq km)

Percent of Earth's water area
21 percent

Greatest depth
Java Trench
-23,376 ft (-7,125 m)

Surface temperatures
Summer high: 93°F (34°C)
Winter low: 28°F (-2°C)

Tides
Highest: 36 ft (11 m)
Lowest: 2 ft (0.6 m)
Both along Australia's west coast

GEO WHIZ

Each day tankers carrying 17 million barrels of crude oil from the Persian Gulf enter the waters of the Indian Ocean, transporting their cargo for distribution around the world.

Some of the world's largest breeding grounds for humpback whales are in the Indian Ocean, the Arabian Sea, and off the east coast of Africa.

The Bay of Bengal, off the coast of India, is sometimes called Cyclone Alley because of the large number of tropical storms that occur each year between May and November.

Sailors from what is now Indonesia used seasonal winds called monsoons to reach Africa's east coast. They arrived on the continent long before Europeans did.

The earthquake that caused the tsunami that killed more than 225,000 people in countries bordering the Indian Ocean in December 2004 created waves as high as 49 feet (15 m).

ARCTIC OCEAN

STATS

Surface area
5,390,000 sq mi (13,960,100 sq km)

Percent of Earth's water area
4 percent

Greatest depth
Molloy Deep
-18,599 ft (-5,669 m)

Surface temperatures
Summer high: 41°F (5°C)
Winter low: 28°F (-2°C)

Tides
Less than a 1 ft (0.3 m) variation throughout the ocean

GEO WHIZ

Satellite monitoring of Arctic sea ice, which began in the late 1970s, shows that the extent of the sea ice is shrinking by approximately 11 percent every 10 years. Scientists think this is caused by global warming.

The geographic North Pole lies roughly in the middle of the Arctic Ocean under 13,000 feet (3,962 m) of water.

Many of the features on the Arctic Ocean floor are named for early Arctic explorers and bordering landmasses.

Mapping of the Arctic Ocean floor did not begin until 2001. The initial research was by a joint U.S.-German operation called AMORE (Arctic Mid-Ocean Ridge Expedition). Surprising discoveries included 12 volcanoes, hydrothermal vents, and a vast, gently sloping, shallow sea bed (continental shelf) off Siberia. This shelf, called the Siberian Shelf, is the largest on Earth.

To see the major oceans and bays, look at the map on pages 148–149.

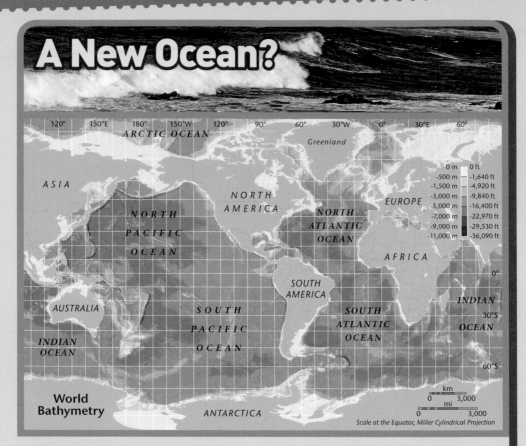

A New Ocean?

ARCTIC OCEAN

Greenland

ASIA

NORTH AMERICA

NORTH PACIFIC OCEAN

NORTH ATLANTIC OCEAN

EUROPE

AFRICA

SOUTH AMERICA

SOUTH ATLANTIC OCEAN

INDIAN OCEAN

SOUTH PACIFIC OCEAN

AUSTRALIA

INDIAN OCEAN

ANTARCTICA

0 m	0 ft
-500 m	-1,640 ft
-1,500 m	-4,920 ft
-3,000 m	-9,840 ft
-5,000 m	-16,400 ft
-7,000 m	-22,970 ft
-9,000 m	-29,530 ft
-11,000 m	-36,090 ft

World Bathymetry

km
0   3,000
mi
0   3,000

Scale at the Equator, Miller Cylindrical Projection

The map above shows that more than 70 percent of Earth's surface is underwater, mainly covered by four great oceans. There is growing support for a fifth ocean, called the Southern Ocean, in the area from Antarctica to 60°S latitude. The oceans are really interconnected bodies of water that together form one global ocean. The ocean floor is as varied as the surface of the continents, but mapping the oceans is challenging. Past explorers cut their way through jungles of the Amazon and conquered icy heights of the Himalaya, but explorers could not march across the floor of the Pacific Ocean, which in places descends to more than 35,000 feet (10,668 m) below the surface of the water.

Bet you didn't know

IT WOULD TAKE A STACK OF MORE THAN NINE EMPIRE STATE BUILDINGS TO EQUAL THE AVERAGE DEPTH OF THE OCEAN.

THE WORLD'S LONGEST mountain range is under the sea.

MEET THE NAT GEO EXPLORER

ROBERT BALLARD

Among the most accomplished of the world's deep-sea explorers, Robert Ballard is best known for his historic discovery of the sunken R.M.S. *Titanic*. During his long career he has conducted more than 120 deep-sea expeditions, and he is a trailblazer in the use of deep-diving submarines.

How did you become an explorer?
I became an explorer the moment I could walk.

What was your closest call in the field?
I have had several, a fire in a bathyscaphe (a kind of submersible) in the rift valley of the Mid-Atlantic Ridge at 9,000 feet, crashing into the side of a volcano in the Cayman Trough in 20,000 feet of water, and almost getting entangled in the cables of a World War II Australian heavy cruiser in Iron Bottom Sound in the Solomon Islands.

How would you suggest kids follow in your footsteps?
Follow your own dreams wherever they take you—your passion to do something, to become someone, is the driving energy you will need to overcome setbacks in your life.

What is one place or thing you'd still like to explore?
I want to go where no one has ever gone on planet Earth—a quest that will keep me busy for the rest of my life.

UNDERWATER LANDSCAPES

The landscape of the ocean floor is varied and constantly changing. A continental edge that slopes gently beneath the water is called a continental shelf. Mountain ranges, called mid-ocean ridges, rise where ocean plates are spreading and magma flows out to create new land. Other plates plunge into trenches more than six miles (ten km) deep. And magma, rising through vents called hot spots, pushes through ocean plates, creating seamounts and volcanoes.

Continents on the Move

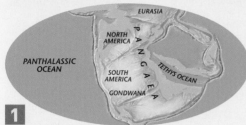

1

PANGAEA. About 240 million years ago, Earth's landmasses were joined together in one supercontinent that extended from pole to pole.

3

EXTINCTION. About 65 million years ago, an asteroid smashed into Earth, creating the Gulf of Mexico. This impact may have resulted in the extinction of half the world's species, including the dinosaurs. This was one of several major mass extinctions.

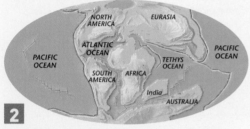

2

BREAKUP. By 94 million years ago, Pangaea had broken apart into landmasses that would become today's continents. Dinosaurs roamed Earth during a period of warmer climates.

4

ICE AGE. By 18,000 years ago, the continents had drifted close to their present positions, but most far northern and far southern lands were buried beneath huge glaciers.

A LOOK WITHIN

The distance from Earth's surface to its center is 3,963 miles (6,378 km). There are four layers: a thin, rigid crust; the rocky mantle; the outer core, which is a layer of molten iron; and finally the inner core, which is solid iron.

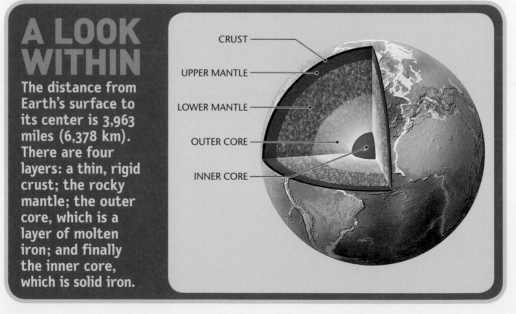

CRUST
UPPER MANTLE
LOWER MANTLE
OUTER CORE
INNER CORE

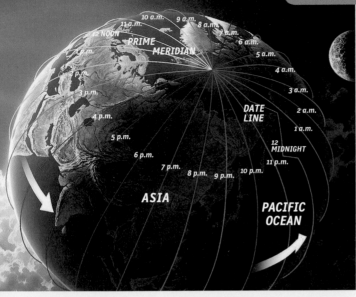

TIME ZO

Long ago, when people liv
in relative isolation, they
measured time by the position
of the sun overhead. That
meant that noon in one place
was not the same as noon in a
place 100 miles (160 km) to
the west. Later, with the
development of long-distance
railroads, people needed to
coordinate time. In 1884, a
system of 24 standard time
zones was adopted. Each time
zone reflects the fact that
Earth rotates west to east
15 degrees each hour.
Time is counted from the
prime meridian, which runs
through Greenwich, England.

Earth Shapers

Earth's features are constantly undergoing change—being built
up, destroyed, or just rearranged. Plates are in constant, very
slow motion. Some plates collide, others pull apart, and still others
slowly grind past each other. As the plates move, mountains are
uplifted, volcanoes erupt, and new land is created.

◀ FAULTING happens when two
plates grind past each other,
creating large cracks along
the edges of the plates.

▲ VOLCANOES form when molten rock,
called magma, rises to Earth's surface.
Some volcanoes occur as one plate
pushes beneath another plate. Other
volcanoes result when a plate passes
over a column of magma, called a hot
spot, rising from the mantle.

▶ COLLISION of two continental
plates causes plate edges to
break and fold, creating
mountains, Earth's highest
landforms.

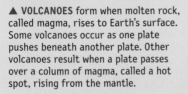

◀ SPREADING
results when
oceanic plates
move apart. The
ocean floor cracks,
magma rises, and new crust is
created. The Mid-Atlantic Ridge spreads
a few centimeters—about an inch—a year,
pushing Europe and North America farther apart.

◀ SUBDUCTION
occurs when an
oceanic plate
dives under a
continental plate.
This often results
in volcanoes and
earthquakes, as well
as mountain building.

NATURALLY
rts Made Easy

…ught of public speaking start your stomach churning like a tornado? Does your mouth feel like a desert when making a speech? Would you rather get caught in an avalanche than give an oral report?

Giving an oral report does not have to be a natural disaster. The basic format is very similar to a written essay. There are two main elements that make up a good oral report—the writing and the presentation. As you write your oral report, remember that your audience will be hearing the information as opposed to reading it. Follow the guidelines below, and the process will be as smooth as glass.

Writing Your Material

1 Choose a subject that is interesting to you.
This is important for all writing, but even more for a report to be delivered orally. Your interest and enthusiasm will come through to your audience, making your presentation more engaging and lively. If you're not all that jazzed about your subject, your audience will sense it and probably tune out.

2 Be clear about the purpose of your presentation.
Do you want to inform your audience, entertain them, or persuade them to take your point of view? Depending on what you want to accomplish, your oral report will follow the general guidelines for a narrative, expository, descriptive, or persuasive essay (see p. 36 for "How To Write an Awesome Essay").

3 Research it, and then organize it.
As with any report or essay, do research so you know your subject inside and out. Then organize your information and ideas thoughtfully.

Need a good subject? Go online. kidsblogs.national geographic.com/kidsnews

COOL CLICK

An oral report has three basic parts:

• **Introduction**—This is your chance to engage your audience and really capture their interest in the subject you are presenting. Use a funny personal experience, a dramatic story, or start with an intriguing question.

• **Body**—This is the longest part of your report. Here you elaborate on the facts and ideas you want to convey. Give information that supports your main idea and expand on it with specific examples or details. In other words, structure your oral report in the same way you would a written essay so that your thoughts are presented in a clear and organized manner.

• **Conclusion**—This is the time to summarize the information and emphasize your most important points to the audience one last time.

4 Write it to be spoken.
Try to keep your sentences short and simple. Long, complex sentences are harder to follow. Limit yourself to just a few key points. You don't want to overwhelm your audience with too much information. To be most effective, hit your key points in the introduction, elaborate on them in the body, and then repeat them once again in your conclusion.

Preparing Your Delivery

1 Practice makes perfect.

Practice! Practice! Practice! Confidence, enthusiasm, and energy are key to delivering an effective oral report, and they can best be achieved through rehearsal. Ask family and friends to be your practice audience, and ask them for feedback when you're done. Were they able to follow your ideas? Did you seem knowledgeable and confident? Did you speak too slow or too fast, too soft or too loud? The more times you practice giving your report, the more you'll master the material. Then you won't have to rely so heavily on your notes or papers and can give your report in a relaxed and confident manner.

2 Present with everything you've got.

Be as creative as you can. Incorporate videos, sound clips, slide presentations, charts, diagrams, and photos. Visual aids help stimulate your audience's senses and keep them intrigued and engaged. They can also help to reinforce your key points. And remember that when you're giving an oral report, you're a performer. Take charge of the spotlight and be as animated and entertaining as you can. Have fun with it.

3 Keep your nerves under control.

Everyone gets a little nervous when speaking in front of a group. That's normal. But the better prepared you are—including good research, well-organized material, and plenty of rehearsal—the more confident you'll be. Preparation is the key. And if you make a mistake or stumble over your words, just regroup and keep going. Nobody's perfect, and nobody expects you to be.

Connecting Words

Effective use of connecting words will make your oral report go smoothly. Connecting words help the listener understand as you transition from one idea to the next.

Here are some words you can use to make your oral report flow:

also	meanwhile
anyway	moreover
consequently	nevertheless
finally	next
furthermore	nonetheless
hence	otherwise
however	still
incidentally	then
indeed	therefore
instead	thus
likewise	

Presentation checklist:

✓ Get a good night's sleep before your presentation.

✓ Have a healthy meal or nutritious snack beforehand.

✓ When you think you're fully prepared, practice it one more time.

✓ Maintain eye contact with your audience throughout your report.

✓ Use your voice and your presence to communicate effectively.

✓ Take a deep breath, relax, and have fun with it.

297

Super Science

Humanoid robots perform a synchronized dance. These 23-inch- (58-cm-) tall robots can remember people's faces, dance, and even sing in harmony!

The Three Domains of Life

Biologists divide all living organisms into three domains: Bacteria, Archaea, and Eukarya. Archaean and Bacteria cells do not have a nuclei; they are so different from each other that they belong to different domains. Since human cells have a nuclei, humans belong to the Eukarya domain, which is divided into fungi, protists, plants, and animals.

1 BACTERIA

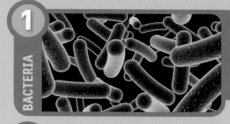

Domain Bacteria: These single-celled micro-organisms are found almost everywhere in the world. Bacteria are small and do not have nuclei or organelles. They can be rod-shaped, spiral, or spherical. Some bacteria are helpful to humans, and some are harmful.

2 ARCHAEA

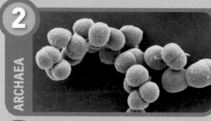

Domain Archaea: These single-celled micro-organisms are often found growing in extremely hostile environments. For this reason, scientists think that the archaea living today most closely resemble the earliest forms of life on Earth.

3 EUKARYA

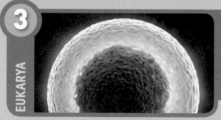

Domain Eukarya: This diverse group of life-forms is more complicated than Bacteria and Archaea, as eukarya have one or more cells with nuclei. All organisms, except for bacteria and archaea, are Eukarya. They are divided into four groups: fungi, protists, plants, and animals.

FYI

What is a domain? Scientifically-speaking, a domain is a major taxonomic division into which natural objects are classified (see p. 40 for "what is Taxonomy?").

FUNGI

Kingdom Fungi (about 100,000 species): Mainly multicellular organisms, fungi cannot make their own food. Mushrooms and yeast are Fungi.

PROTISTS

Protists: Once considered a kingdom, this group is a veritable "grab bag" that includes unicellular and multicellular organisms of great variety, including algae.

PLANTS

Kingdom Plantae (about 275,000 species): Plants are multicellular, and many can make their own food using photosynthesis (see p. 284 for "Photosynthesis").

ANIMALS

Kingdom Animalia (about 1,000,000 species): Most animals, which are multicellular, have their own organ systems. Animals do not make their own food.

WHAT IS LIFE?

This seems like such an easy question to answer. Everybody knows singing birds are alive and rocks are not. But when we start studying bacteria and other microscopic creatures, things get more complicated.

SO WHAT EXACTLY IS LIFE?

Most scientists agree that something is alive if it has the following characteristics: it can reproduce, grows in size to become more complex in structure, takes in nutrients to survive, gives off waste products, and responds to external stimuli, such as increased sunlight or changes in temperature.

KINDS OF LIFE

Biologists classify living organisms by how they get their energy. Organisms such as algae, green plants, and some bacteria use sunlight as an energy source. Human beings, fungi, and other archaea, use chemicals to provide energy. When we eat food, chemical reactions within our digestive system turn our food into fuel.

Living things inhabit land, sea, and air. In fact, life also thrives deep beneath the oceans, embedded in rocks miles below the Earth's crust, in ice, and in other extreme environments. The life-forms that thrive in these challenging environments are called extremophiles. Some of these draw directly upon the chemicals surrounding them for energy. Since these are very different forms of life than what we're used to, we may not think of them as alive, but they are alive just the same.

HOW IT ALL WORKS

To try and understand how a living organism works, it helps to look at one example of its simplest form—the single-celled bacterium called *Streptococcus*. There are many kinds of these tiny organisms, and some are responsible for human illnesses. What makes us sick or uncomfortable are the toxins the bacteria give off in our bodies.

A single *Streptococcus* bacterium is so small that at least 500 of them could fit on the dot above the letter *i* in this sentence. These bacteria are some of the simplest forms of life we know. They have no moving parts, no lungs, no brain, no heart, no liver, no leaves or fruit. And yet this life-form reproduces, grows in size by producing long chain structures, takes in nutrients, and gives off waste products. This tiny life-form is "alive," just as you are alive.

Just what makes something alive is a question scientists grapple with when they study viruses. Viruses, such as the ones that cause the common cold and smallpox, can make you sick, but they can only grow within host cells, like your body. Since viruses lack cells and cannot metabolize nutrients for energy or reproduce without a host, scientists ask whether they are even alive. And don't go looking for them without a strong microscope—viruses are a hundred times smaller than bacteria!

Scientists think life began on Earth some 4.1 to 3.9 billion years ago, but no fossils exist from that time. The earliest fossils ever found are from the primitive life that existed 3.6 billion years ago. Other life-forms soon followed, and some of these are shown below. Scientists continue to study how life evolved on Earth, and whether or not it is possible that life exists on other planets.

MICROSCOPIC ORGANISMS

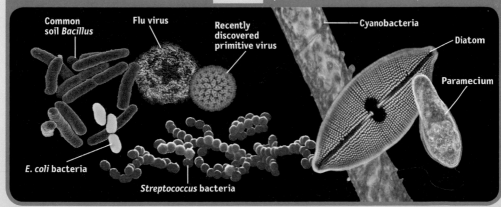

Common soil *Bacillus*
Flu virus
Recently discovered primitive virus
Cyanobacteria
Diatom
Paramecium
E. coli bacteria
Streptococcus bacteria

THE UNIVERSE BEGAN WITH A BIG BANG

Clear your mind for a minute and try to imagine this: All the things you see in the universe today—all the stars, galaxies, and planets floating around out there—are not out there. Everything that now exists is concentrated in a single, incredibly dense point scientists call a singularity. Then, suddenly, the elements that make up the universe flash into existence. That actually happened about 13.7 billion years ago, in the moment we call the big bang.

For centuries scientists, religious scholars, poets, and philosophers wondered how the universe came to be. Was it always there? Will it always be the same, or will it change? If it had a beginning, will it someday end or will it go on forever?

These were huge questions. But today, because of recent observations of space and what it's made of, we think we may have answers to some of them. We know the big bang created not only matter but also space itself. And scientists think that in the very distant future, stars will run out of fuel and blink out. Once again the universe will become dark.

Everything we can see or detect around us in the universe began with the big bang. After the big bang, the universe expanded.

COOL CLICK

Go online for more information on the origins of the universe.
science.nationalgeographic.com/
science/space/universe/origins-
universe-article.html

PROGRESS OF LIFE ON EARTH

About 3.5 billion years ago Earth was covered by one gigantic reddish ocean. The color came from hydrocarbons.

The first life-forms on Earth were archaea that were able to live without oxygen. They released large amounts of methane gas into an atmosphere that would have been poisonous to us.

About 3 billion years ago something new appeared in the global ocean. Erupting volcanoes linked together to form larger landmasses. And a new form of life appeared—blue-green algae, the first living thing that used energy from the sun.

Some 2 billion years ago these algae filled the air with oxygen, killing off the methane-producing archaea. Colored pools of greenish-brown plant life floated on the oceans. The oxygen revolution that would someday make human life possible was now under way.

About 530 million years ago, the Cambrian explosion occurred. It's called an explosion because it's the time when most major animal groups first appeared in our fossil records. Back then, Earth was made up of swamps, seas, a few active volcanoes, and oceans teeming with strange life.

More than 450 million years ago, life began moving from the oceans onto dry land. About 200 million years later dinosaurs first appeared. They would dominate life on Earth for more than 150 million years.

Our New Solar System

JUST THE FACTS

- The solar system is made up of planets, dwarf planets, asteroids, and comets orbiting around a star we call the sun.

- Our star system formed 4.5 billion years ago from a nebular cloud, a large, spinning cloud of gas and dust.

- The solar system is divided into three different categories of planets, based on size and density: terrestrial, dwarf, and Jovian.

- The terrestrial planets—Mercury, Venus, Earth, and Mars—orbit closest to the sun and are small, dense, and rocky.

- Ceres, a dwarf planet, lies in the asteroid belt, beyond the terrestrial planets.

- The gas giants—Jupiter, Saturn, Uranus, and Neptune—are large, surrounded by rings and multiple moons, and made out of gases. These are called the Jovian planets.

- The Kuiper Belt, an area filled with comets and other solar system debris, lies past the gas planets.

- In the Kuiper Belt are more dwarf planets, including Pluto, Eris, Haumea, and Makemake.

DAYS ARE LONGER THAN YEARS ON THE PLANET MERCURY

Solar System Glossary

ASTEROID
A rocky body, measuring from less than 1 mile to 600 miles in diameter, in orbit around a sun. Most asteroids in our solar system are found between the orbits of Mars and Jupiter.

DWARF PLANET
Generally smaller than Mercury, a dwarf planet orbits the sun along with other objects near it. Its gravity has pulled it into a round (or nearly round) shape.

ECLIPSE
An event caused by the passage of one astronomical body in front of another astronomical body, briefly blocking light from the farther astronomical body.

COMET
A body of rock, dust, and gaseous ice in an elongated orbit around the sun. Near the sun, heat diffuses gas and dust to form a streaming "tail" from the comet's nucleus.

PLANET
A planet orbits a star. Gravity has pulled it into a round (or nearly round) shape, and it has cleared its neighborhood of other objects.

THE SUN

The sun is a star that is about 4.6 billion years old. As the anchor that holds our solar system together, it provides the energy necessary for life to flourish on Earth. It accounts for 99 percent of the matter in the solar system. The rest of the planets, moons, asteroids, and comets added together amount to the remaining one percent.

Even though a million Earths could fit inside the sun, it is still considered an average-size star. Betelgeuse (BET-el-jooz), the star on the shoulder of the constellation known as Orion, is almost 400 times larger.

ALL THE SAME

Like other stars, the sun is a giant ball of hydrogen gas radiating heat and light through nuclear fusion—a process by which the sun converts about four million tons of matter to energy every second.

Also like other stars, the sun revolves around its galaxy. Located halfway out in one of the arms of the Milky Way Galaxy, the sun takes 225 to 250 million years to complete one revolution around the galaxy.

The sun is composed of about 74 percent hydrogen, 25 percent helium, and 1 percent trace elements like iron, carbon, lead, and uranium. These trace elements provide us with amazing insight into the history of our star. They're the heavier elements that are produced when stars explode. Since these elements are relatively abundant in the sun, scientists know it was forged from materials that came together in two previous star explosions. All of the elements found in the sun, on Earth, and in our bodies were recycled from those two exploding stars.

OUR AMAZING SUN

When viewed from space by astronauts, the sun burns white in color. But when we see it from Earth, through our atmosphere, it looks like a yellow star.

Solar flares, explosions of charged particles, sometimes erupt from the sun's surface. They create beautiful aurora displays on Earth, Jupiter, Saturn, and even distant Uranus and Neptune.

We know the sun makes life possible here on Earth. We couldn't survive without it.

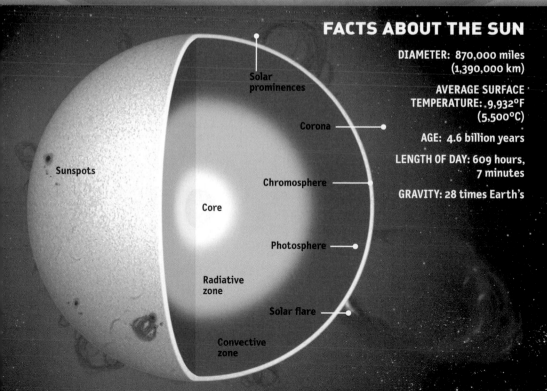

FACTS ABOUT THE SUN

Solar prominences

Corona

Chromosphere

Photosphere

Solar flare

Core

Radiative zone

Convective zone

Sunspots

DIAMETER: 870,000 miles (1,390,000 km)

AVERAGE SURFACE TEMPERATURE: 9,932°F (5,500°C)

AGE: 4.6 billion years

LENGTH OF DAY: 609 hours, 7 minutes

GRAVITY: 28 times Earth's

PLANETS

Ceres

Mars

Earth

Venus

Mercury

Jupiter

Sun

MERCURY
Average distance from the sun:
35,980,000 miles (57,900,000 km)
Position from the sun in orbit: first
Equatorial diameter: 3,030 miles (4,878 km)
Mass (Earth = 1): 0.055   Density (Water = 1): 5.43
Length of day: 176 Earth days
Length of year: 88 Earth days
Surface temperatures: -300°F (-183°C) to 800°F (427°C)
Known moons: 0

VENUS
Average distance from the sun:
67,230,000 miles (108,200,000 km)
Position from the sun in orbit: second
Equatorial diameter: 7,520 miles (12,100 km)
Mass (Earth = 1): 0.815   Density (Water = 1): 5.25
Length of day: 243 Earth days
Length of year: 225 Earth days
Average surface temperature: 864°F (462°C)
Known moons: 0

EARTH
Average distance from the sun:
93,000,000 miles (149,600,000 km)
Position from the sun in orbit: third
Equatorial diameter: 7,900 miles (12,750 km)
Mass (Earth = 1): 1   Density (Water = 1): 5.52
Length of day: 24 hours
Length of year: 365 days
Surface temperatures: -126°F (-88°C) to 136°F (58°C)
Known moons: 1

MARS
Average distance from the sun:
141,633,000 miles (227,936,000 km)
Position from the sun in orbit: fourth
Equatorial diameter: 4,333 miles (6,794 km)
Mass (Earth = 1): 0.107   Density (Water = 1): 3.93
Length of day: 26 Earth hours
Length of year: 1.88 Earth years
Surface temperatures: -270°F (-133°C) to 80°F (27°C)
Known moons: 2

CERES (DWARF PLANET)
Position from the sun in orbit: fifth
Length of day: 9.1 Earth hours
Length of year: 4.60 Earth years
Known moons: 0

JUPITER
Average distance from the sun:
483,682,000 miles (778,412,000 km)
Position from the sun in orbit: sixth
Equatorial diameter: 86,880 miles (139,800 km)
Mass (Earth = 1): 318   Density (Water = 1): 1.3
Length of day: 9.9 Earth hours
Length of year: 11.9 Earth years
Average surface temperature: -235°F (-150°C)
Known moons: At least 63

WINTER
lasts for
21
years on
URANUS.

This artwork shows the 13 planets that astronomers now recognize in our solar system. The relative sizes and positions of the planets are shown but not the relative distances between them. Many of the planets closest to Earth can be seen without a telescope in the night sky.

Saturn

Uranus

Neptune

Pluto

Haumea

Makemake

Eris

SATURN
Average distance from the sun:
886,526,000 miles (1,426,725,000 km)
Position from the sun in orbit: seventh
Equatorial diameter: 72,370 miles (116,460 km)
Mass (Earth = 1): 95   Density (Water = 1): 0.71
Length of day: 10 Earth hours
Length of year: 29.46 Earth years
Average surface temperature: -218°F (-170°C)
Known moons: At least 60

URANUS
Average distance from the sun:
1,784,000,000 miles (2,870,970,000 km)
Position from the sun in orbit: eighth
Equatorial diameter: 31,500 miles (50,724 km)
Mass (Earth = 1): 15   Density (Water = 1): 1.24
Length of day: 17.9 Earth hours
Length of year: 84 Earth years
Average surface temperature: -323°F (-200°C)
Known moons: 27

NEPTUNE
Average distance from the sun:
2,795,000,000 miles (4,498,250,000 km)
Position from the sun in orbit: ninth
Equatorial diameter: 30,775 miles (49,528 km)
Mass (Earth = 1): 17   Density (Water = 1): 1.67
Length of day: 19 Earth hours
Length of year: 164.8 Earth years
Average surface temperature: -353°F (-210°C)
Known moons: 13

PLUTO (DWARF PLANET)
Position from the sun in orbit: tenth
Length of day: 6.4 Earth days
Length of year: 248 Earth years
Known moons: 3

HAUMEA (DWARF PLANET)
Position from the sun in orbit: eleventh
Length of day: 4 Earth hours
Length of year: 284 Earth years
Known moons: 2

MAKEMAKE (DWARF PLANET)
Position from sun in orbit: twelfth
Length of day: unknown
Length of year: 307 Earth years
Known Moons: 0

ERIS (DWARF PLANET)
Position from the sun in orbit: thirteenth
Length of day: less than 8 Earth hours
Length of year: 557 Earth years
Known moons: 1

FOR THE DEFINITIONS OF *PLANET* AND *DWARF PLANET* SEE P. 304.

HOW PLANETS FORM

Planets arise as a natural result of the star-formation process. Stars are born from large clouds of gas and dust. That gas and dust spins in space, flattening into a disk the way pizza dough does when a baker tosses it. The center of the disk becomes a star, while the rest of the disk may form planets.

Within the disk, dusty bits of carbon and silicon begin to clump together. Those clumps eventually get bigger and become rocky objects called protoplanets, which smack into each other and stick together to make planets.

The asteroids in our solar system are leftover planetesimals, or small planets from the early solar system. Jupiter's gravity stirred them up and prevented them from sticking together. Astronomers have found evidence of asteroids in other star systems.

If a rocky planet grows large enough, it can collect and hold on to surrounding hydrogen gas. That's how the gas giants of our outer solar system grew so big.

Time Line of Earth

IF THE AGE OF THE EARTH AND SOLAR SYSTEM was compared to the length of time in a year, here's how long things would take to form and develop.

JANUARY 1
On New Year's Day, the solar system begins condensing out of a swirling cloud of stardust.

JANUARY 7
The nuclear fires of the sun ignite.

JANUARY 28
A truly memorable day— Earth forms.

FEBRUARY
Through the month of February, Earth continues to shrink and cool.

MARCH 10
Escaped water vapor returns to Earth as rain, and oceans form.

APRIL 15
Somewhere in Earth's warm blue-green waters, life begins.

MAY 22
Oxygen starts to form in the atmosphere.

JULY TO AUGUST
Life continues to develop.

SEPTEMBER 14
Somewhere in the oceanic depths, single-cell plants begin sexual reproduction.

OCTOBER
Multicell creatures and plants burst onto the scene.

DECEMBER 2
Some animals and plants begin to live on land.

DECEMBER 13
Dinosaurs appear.

DECEMBER 25
Dinosaurs disappear.

DECEMBER 31
At 5:00 in the evening, Lucy, one of the earliest known ancestors of the human tree, is born in Africa.

Bet you didn't know

The term **ASTRONAUT** comes from **Greek** words that mean "STAR SAILOR."

Since nothing is pulled down by gravity IN OUTER SPACE, **blood from a cut** doesn't trickle down your body. It just forms A GOOEY BLOB.

AT TAKEOFF, the space shuttle moves MORE SLOWLY THAN A CAR on a local street. One minute later, it's flying faster than the SPEED OF SOUND.

When astronauts are **confined to their space suits,** they wear **undergarments** similar to DISPOSABLE DIAPERS.

The Life Cycle of a Star

Poets might say that the stars are forever, but scientists know that's not true. All stars eventually die when they run out of fuel.

You might think a more massive star would live longer because it has more fuel to burn. But the heavier a star is, the faster it burns through its fuel, and the shorter its lifetime is. The most massive stars will live for only a few million years, while the smallest can live for trillions of years.

All stars spend most of their lives fusing hydrogen and turning it into helium in their cores. This nuclear fusion creates the energy we see as starlight. Eventually, the star's core runs out of hydrogen. This is the end for low-mass stars like the sun.

When higher-mass stars run out of hydrogen, they can start fusing the helium in their cores, creating carbon and oxygen. The largest stars can keep fusing heavier and heavier elements until their core is full of hot, dense iron. That's when the star dies, because no energy comes from fusing iron.

Black Holes

A black hole really seems like a hole in space. Most black holes form when the core of a massive star collapses, falling into oblivion. A black hole has a stronger gravitational pull than anything else in the universe. It's like a bottomless pit, swallowing anything that gets near enough to it to be pulled in. It's black because it pulls in light.

Black holes come in different sizes. The smallest has a mass about three times that of the sun. The biggest one scientists have found so far has a mass about three billion times greater than the sun's. Really big black holes at the centers of galaxies probably form by swallowing enormous amounts of gas over time. One of NASA's spacecraft has found thousands of possible black holes in the Milky Way, but there are probably more. The nearest one to Earth is about 1,600 light-years away.

What is the Milky Way?

Our galaxy, the Milky Way, appears to be a band of stars in the sky, but it's actually a disk. Its 400 billion stars are clumped into lines called spiral arms because they spiral outward. When we look up at the night sky, we're seeing the edge of the disk, like the side of a Frisbee. It appears to us as a hazy band of white light.

Earth is located about halfway between the center of the Milky Way and its outer edge, in one of the spiral arms. Light from the galaxy's center takes 25,000 years to reach us.

Our solar system orbits the galactic center once every 250 million years. The last time we were on this side of the Milky Way, the earliest dinosaurs were just starting to emerge.

At the galaxy's center, frequent star explosions fry huge sections of space. Those explosions would wipe out any life on nearby planets. We're lucky that Earth is located where it is, far away from the center.

Constellations—Sky Dreams

Long ago, people looking at the sky noticed that some stars made shapes and patterns. By playing connect-the-dots, they imagined people and animals in the sky. Their legendary heroes and monsters were pictured in the stars.

Today, we call the star patterns identified by the Ancient Greeks and Romans, constellations. There are 88 constellations in all. Some are only visible when you're north of the Equator, and some only south of it.

European ocean voyagers named the constellations that are visible in the Southern Hemisphere, such as the Southern Cross. In the 16th-century Age of Exploration, their ships began visiting southern lands. Astronomers used the star observations of these navigators to fill in the blank spots on their celestial maps.

Constellations aren't fixed in the sky. The star arrangement that makes up each one would look different from another location in the universe. Constellations also change over time because every star we see is moving through space. Over thousands of years, the stars in the Big Dipper (right), which is part of the larger constellation Ursa Major (the Great Bear), will move so far apart that the dipper pattern will disappear.

A constellation wheel depicting imagined people and animals in star patterns.

MAJOR CONSTELLATIONS

The Big Dipper, or Ursa Major, is also commonly known as the Great Bear.

Some Major Constellations	When to See Them in the Northern Hemisphere
The Big Dipper, The Great Bear	Always
Cassiopeia, The Queen	Always
Perseus, Medusa's Killer	Always
Cepheus, The King	Always
Cygnus, The Swan	Autumn
Lyra, The Lyre	Autumn
Pegasus, The Winged Horse	Autumn
Aquila, The Eagle	Autumn
Orion, The Hunter	Winter
Andromeda, The Chained Maiden	Winter
Taurus, The Bull	Winter
Canis Major, The Great Dog	Winter
Gemini, The Twins	Spring
Leo, The Lion	Spring
Virgo, The Virgin	Spring
Bootes, The Herdsman	Summer
Sagittarius, The Archer	Summer
Scorpio, The Scorpion	Summer

THE SIGNS AND CONSTELLATIONS OF THE ZODIAC

Capricorn Sagittarius Aquarius Scorpio Pisces Libra Aries Virgo Taurus Leo Gemini Cancer

9 Cool Things IN YOUR FUTURE

1 Wireless technology is everywhere. You can call your friends using your jacket sleeve and have your shoe email someone else's shoe. Often nano-size, **"smart technology"** is in fabrics and other materials. Your whole body will become part of the same network. People rely on smart technology for nearly everything yet barely notice it exists— much as people have lived with electricity since it became widespread.

2 Presto-chango, your stained, torn shirt cleans and mends itself. Paint, cement, and fabrics self-repair and self-clean, making them nearly indestructible. Spilled grape juice on the couch? No problem. **Nanomaterials** will basically shake off the stains, not allowing them to stick. What if an earthquake causes a crack in the wall of your house? Inside the cement, nanomaterials recognize the problem and repair it by rearranging matter molecule by molecule to fill in the damage.

3 The kitchen is your personal shopper. All food packaging contains a **radio frequency identification** (RFID) tag, a tiny electronic version of today's bar code. Your kitchen reads RFIDs, so it knows whether last week's milk is about to go sour and when you ate the last cookie. It automatically adds them to your grocery list and even e-shops to have your favorite foods delivered.

4 **Robots** make your life easier, often taking over tasks you find boring. They come in various forms and sizes. "Many will seem invisible because they're hidden within already known technology," explains robotics expert Reid Simmons. "Smart household appliances are examples." He envisions tiny dust-eating bugs that will work together to keep things clean. Other robots will slurp up spills, mow the lawn, or feed the dog. Will robots do your homework? Maybe, but the teacher's grouchy robot may not accept it!

5 Play **video games** that blend reality with virtual reality for amazing action and adventure. When you are wearing the game glasses, three-dimensional characters become part of your world. The blending of the digital world and the real world is so flawless that you actually see a pterodactyl swooping toward you on the climbing wall, a monster creeping up the bridge in town, or aliens zooming alongside the car!

6 Thanks to **holographic technology,** you can have a face-to-face discussion with a virtual Elvis about rock-and-roll or ask Einstein to help you solve a tough math problem. Or maybe you'd like to swim and hunt with a great white shark without becoming lunch. Museums in the future will be accessible from your home and will bring music, history, science, and other subjects alive (almost!) using holograms.

7 Forget carryout! Have sushi at your favorite Japanese restaurant—in Japan. Travel from New York City to Tokyo in only 60 minutes. You fly at speeds of 15,000 miles per hour in a **rocketplane** that skims just beyond Earth's atmosphere, at the edge of space. Why fly so high? No air means no friction to slow the plane down, allowing it to travel faster and more efficiently. People might live in one hemisphere and commute to another for work, to find entertainment, or to have dinner with friends.

8 It's easy and painless to stay healthy and live longer. Hate those vaccine shots? **Genetically altered fruits and veggies** contain vaccinations for such things as flu, measles, and cholera. Instead of poking you with a needle, the doctor will have a robot give you a handful of strawberries. The doc's prescription? "Eat two banana splits and call me in the morning."

9 If you need something—just about anything—**"print" it in 3-D.** Cracked hoverboard after an accident involving a tree? No big deal: Just print a new one with a desktop object printer. Simply scan the object or download plans from the Internet. Click the print button and right before your eyes the printer creates a three-dimensional item. Instead of ink, the object printer uses liquid plastic or metal.

You've **got** to be **joking** . . .

Q Why did **the robot eat a lightbulb?**

A Because he was in need of a light snack.

ROBOT REVOLUTION

CUTTING-EDGE TECHNOLOGY IS COMING YOUR WAY.

SNAKES ON A SPACESHIP

It's well known that snakes aren't very good at kickball or the long jump. But when it comes to slithering, snakes are the world champs. That's why NASA has tested robot snakes to help explore the surface of Mars. On Mars, snake-bots could enter tiny holes or cracks in the planet's surface and burrow under loose dirt. They could snake their way over boulders and up steep hills where wheeled robots would get stuck. Scientists are also designing snake robots for uses here on Earth, such as searching collapsed buildings for survivors after an earthquake.

A ROBOT ZOO

To accomplish a variety of tasks, scientists have created a wide range of robots that mimic animals. Frog-bots jump over large obstacles. Fly-bots and slug-bots walk upside down on the ceiling. (The secret to the slug-bot is to get the slime just right.) Spider-bots (right) and scorpion-bots travel over rough terrain, and lobster-bots hold their ground in rapidly moving water. Scientists patterned some robots after flying insects to copy their amazing ability to hover in place and then quickly dart off in any direction. They've even made a robot that mimics the cockroach. Perhaps they'll call this the yuck-bot.

FRIENDLY BOTS

A smile, a frown, a look of surprise—all these expressions communicate important information. Robots don't have emotions, but they would get along better with people if they behaved as if they did. Scientists are trying to find ways to make robots friendlier and more human. George the chat-bot, a computer-controlled face on a screen, uses facial expressions, learns from every conversation, and can fool people into thinking he's human. A robot named Kismet (left) has lips and big blue eyes, and can mimic and respond to human emotions. What's next? The truly impossible—getting a robot to laugh at your brother's dumb jokes.

SPACE HOTEL

The space taxi is waiting. Mars-bound astronauts climb into the little craft, buckle up, and lift off from Earth. Soon they see their next stop: a huge spaceship soaring past in the dark. Their pilot pulls along-side, carefully bringing the taxi's speed to 13,000 miles per hour (21,000 kph) to match the big craft's. With a few more delicate maneuvers, the pilot docks the taxi, and the astronauts enter their new home away from home: the moving Mars hotel.

Traveling to Mars on a regular spacecraft has some serious problems: The journey would require a huge amount of expensive fuel, and being weightless for a long time can badly weaken human bones and muscles. But "space hotels," also called cyclers, would ride the solar system's gravitational forces in a never-ending loop between Mars and Earth. They wouldn't require much fuel, and each one would spin to create a kind of artificial gravity for the travelers inside. Cycler hotels could be the healthiest, cheapest, and most comfortable way to visit our planetary neighbor—if they ever actually happen!

Solar Sailing

One day, travelers in the solar system may see a glorious sight: a craft pulled through space by a huge, delicate, mirrorlike sail. The force pushing the sail forward would be nothing more than light from the sun.

The idea behind solar sailing is pretty simple. Light is made of extremely tiny particles called photons. When photons bounce off objects, they push on those objects just a little bit. On Earth we don't notice this because other forces, like friction in the air, are so much stronger. But in space, where there is no air to get in the way, the gentle pressure of photons from the sun is enough to move a lightweight object.

Sunlight bouncing off a solar sail would move it—and the spacecraft attached to it—very slowly at first. Over time, the solar sailer would pick up speed, moving faster and faster. By the time the sailer passed the outer planets, it could be traveling at 200,000 miles per hour (324,000 kph), ten times as fast as today's space shuttle.

Although it's not luxurious, this imagined space hotel has comfortable little cabins, exercise machines, and games to play. A space taxi would take the astronauts to the Martian surface to start their work.

315

COOL inventions

SPINNING LIGHT
FROM AIR

Inspired by the windmills of the Netherlands, the Light Wind, a giant outdoor lamp taller than an adult, features a propeller on top that twirls in the wind. The spinning creates electricity that is stored in a battery, which in turn powers the lamp. After a day of gusts, the battery is fully charged and will last for about a week when used four hours a day. The Light Wind is a cool way to illuminate backyard sleepovers, especially because it gets its power from nature.

FLYING
WITH WINGS

Ever wonder what it's like to fly like Superman? With a pair of FusionMan wings strapped to your back, you no longer have to just imagine. You take flight by launching yourself from a plane. At about 10,000 feet high, start the wing's engines and step out into the sky. Push a switch to unfurl the wings to their full ten-foot span. Fly with your legs straight back, arms at your sides. To fly lower, bend downward; to go higher, arch your body and increase the engine power. Fuel runs low after about five minutes of soaring, so open your parachute and start a gentle descent. As you float back to the ground, you're already planning your next flight.

PERSONAL
SUBMARINE

Leave the scuba gear behind: The C-Quester underwater boat dives so deep that you can "swim" with the fishes and sea turtles. A see-through dome shields you from the elements, and a joystick lets you steer the boat. (Move it right or left, push forward to dive down, and pull back to go up.) You can dive deeper than you usually could scuba diving, and you can stay there longer—for six hours. Because the cabin is pressurized, you can rise to the surface quickly (unlike scuba, which requires a slow ascent so that your body can adjust to the pressure of changing depths). Best of all, there's no need to freak if you come face to face with a shark!

SELECT OUTFIT HERE.

TALK TO THE
MIRROR

You're at the mall when you spot the perfect dress in a store window. But does it look good on you? With Social Retailing, you can try it on in a flash. Bonus: You don't even have to shimmy out of what you're wearing to see how it looks. A full-size image of the dress flashes on a special mirror. You step in the right position to see the dress on your mirror image. Still not sure? Get your best friend—who's at home—to weigh in over the Internet. Beam contact info from your cell phone to the mirror. Your pal can then click on a special website to see a live video of you modeling the outfit. She can send you a text message that appears on the mirror, like "Looks awesome." Sold!

NOW TRY IT ON.

317

MEET THE NAT GEO EXPLORER

ENRIC SALA

A marine ecologist who studies underwater systems, Sala doesn't mind making waves to make sure oceans are protected. Sala's focus is unlike traditional marine scientists who generally study individual species. "It's the only way to understand the full impact humans have on these places," says Sala.

How did you become an explorer?
I think the first time I got in the water of the Mediterranean when I was a kid, I wanted to emulate my heroes, famous undersea explorer Jacques Cousteau and his divers on the *Calypso*. When I grew up and became a marine biologist, I led expeditions to many wild places around the world, but one only needs curiosity to become an explorer.

What was your closest call in the field?
I was once diving deep in the Mediterranean and the hose of my oxygen tank exploded. Air came out of the hose violently, making a very loud noise, and the tank was being emptied very fast. Fortunately, I was diving with a good buddy, and we were trained for such emergencies. I turned the air valve on my tank off, and we shared the air from his tank as we came back to the surface calmly and safely.

How would you suggest kids follow in your footsteps?
I urge kids to go out to nature (a forest, the seashore) and find out about the wonderful animals and plants that live there. There are natural wonders in every square inch of our planet! If they like nature, kids should ask their parents to take them camping, climbing, walking in the woods, and snorkeling.... And if you want to turn your life into an explorer's, choose what you like, study hard, and don't stop until you make it.

THE **FIRST** TELEPHONE ANSWERING MACHINE WAS **3** FEET TALL.

What kind of scientist would you be?

Here's a list of some of the types of scientists who help our world.

PHYSICAL SCIENCE
Physicists study matter and energy, and how they are related.
Chemists study the composition, properties, reactions, and structure of matter.
Astronomers study stars, planets, and galaxies.

EARTH SCIENCE
Geologists specialize in the history of Earth.
Oceanographers study and explore the ocean.
Paleontologists specialize in fossils.

Meteorologists study weather and climate.
Geographers study Earth's surface.

LIFE SCIENCE
Botanists specialize in plants.
Microbiologists study microscopic forms of life.
Zoologists study animals and animal life.
Geneticists study heredity and variations in organisms.
Medical doctors diagnose, treat, and prevent injury, illness, and disease.

Science Pioneers

Isaac Newton (1642–1727)

One of the most influential scientists ever, Newton developed the three laws of motion and defined how gravity works.

Benjamin Franklin (1706–1790)

A pioneer in the study of electricity, this Founding Father of the United States was a creator of numerous inventions, including bifocal lenses, the Franklin stove (heat circulating stove), the odometer (measures speed), and the lightning rod.

Eli Whitney (1765–1825)

This inventor created the cotton gin, which made cotton a profitable crop and helped revolutionize agriculture.

Michael Faraday (1791–1867)

Inventor of the generator in 1831, Faraday's accomplishments changed the use of electricity.

Florence Nightingale (1820–1910)

Known as the "lady with the lamp," Nightingale's changes to battlefield hospitals revolutionized the modern nursing field.

Alexander Graham Bell (1847–1922)

Considered the inventor of the telephone, Bell was also one of the founding members of the National Geographic Society.

Thomas Alva Edison (1847–1931)

Edison was the inventor of the phonograph, the incandescent lightbulb, the kinetoscope (peephole viewer), and more than a thousand other things. His success with the lightbulb helped bring electricity to the masses.

Marie Curie (1867–1934)

Nobel Prize winner Marie Curie is best known for her theory of radioactivity and her discovery of two new elements, radium and polonium.

Albert Einstein (1879–1955)

A German-born physicist, Einstein is best known for his theory of relativity and his most popular equation, $E=mc^2$, which relates energy, mass, and the speed of light.

BACK-TO-SCHOOL SCIENTIFIC DISCOVERY

2.5 MONTHS IS THE APPROXIMATE LENGTH OF TIME IT TAKES FOR JELL-O TO RETURN TO EARTH AFTER BEING TOSSED ONTO THE CEILING.

FUTURE HOUSE
THE LATEST ECO-TECHNOLOGY FOR YOUR HOME

You just moved into the coolest house on the block. From top to bottom, inside and out, your green house cuts natural resource use and decreases CO_2 emissions by using smart design and construction that emphasize renewable resources. Your house is all about recycling, which significantly decreases waste that would otherwise go to landfills. Check out some of the sustainable and biodegradable items in your unique eco-friendly home.

(1) A ROOFTOP GARDEN provides insulation for the house, makes oxygen, and absorbs CO_2.

(2) SOLAR PANELS, facing south, use sunlight to generate electricity for the whole house.

(3) DOUBLE-PANED WINDOWS reduce the need for mechanical heat and air-conditioning systems, keeping your house comfortable year-round.

(4) The TALL DESIGN OF THE HOUSE uses less land.

(5) BRICKS for the exterior walls are made from recycled materials.

(6) You have CHAIRS made from recycled seat belts and LAMPS made of RECYCLED CHOPSTICKS.

(7) STRATEGICALLY PLACED TREES provide indoor climate control by shading out summer heat and letting in light and warmth when the leaves fall in autumn.

(8) The DECK is made from recycled plastic.

(9) A PASSIVE SOLAR SYSTEM uses concrete, brick, stone, and tile to absorb and maintain heat from the sun.

(10) WOOD for the stairways and furniture comes from trees grown specifically for harvest, not from old-growth forests.

(11) SOFT, NATURAL FIBER BEDDING is made from bamboo, a renewable resource.

(12) CEILING FANS circulate air and help keep rooms cooler in warm weather.

(13) In the bathrooms, you use BIODEGRADABLE SOAPS AND SHAMPOOS that won't add chemicals to streams, rivers, and oceans. DUAL-FLUSH TOILETS choose the amount of water you need for flushing. BIODEGRADABLE TOILET PAPER is made from recycled paper. Your shower curtain is made of HEMP, a renewable resource.

(14) Energy-saving light switches called OCCUPANT SENSORS automatically turn lights on when you enter the room and off when you leave. COMPACT FLUORESCENT BULBS in all the light fixtures use 75% less energy and last ten times longer than standard bulbs.

(15) To water your garden, you use the rainwater that collects in OUTDOOR HOLDING TANKS.

(16) The FRONT-LOADING WASHING MACHINE uses less water than a top-loading one.

(17) The kitchen COUNTERTOP is made of reclaimed granite, salvaged from discarded granite products. The APPLIANCES are certified energy savers. AERATORS conserve water by reducing faucet flow.

(18) Your whole family's stylish clothing is made from RENEWABLE, NATURAL FIBERS, such as organically grown cotton.

(19) The dog and cat eat ORGANIC PET FOOD. The pets use HEMP collars, beds, and toys. The KITTY LITTER comes from recycled paper.

(20) SOLAR GARDEN LIGHTS store energy for nighttime use.

(21) Your family's new HYBRID CAR emits very little CO_2.

(22) RECYCLING BINS make it easy for you to sort glass, plastic, aluminum, and paper.

Is THIS Bill FAKE?

A hundred-dollar bill buys a lot of video games. No wonder sneaky thieves try to pass off fake, or counterfeit, money to unsuspecting stores.

But the government is sneakier. They've hidden security features such as those shown below to make it easier to spot counterfeit cash.

"Counterfeiters want to produce bills that will easily fool people," says Agent Brian Marr of the United States Secret Service, which investigates counterfeiting cases. Computers, color printers, and color copiers have made fooling people with fake money a lot easier.

Now, the most secure bill ever produced in the U.S. is in wallets everywhere—a $20 bill that's green, peach, and blue. The Bureau of Engraving and Printing, which prints all U.S. paper money, says the color change makes the note more difficult to reproduce.

You can find other security features in paper money—if you know what to look for. Check out some from the current hundred-dollar bill, then find similarities in your own money (printed from 1996 on). At least you'd better *hope* you can find them!

NICE THREAD!
A thin security thread to the left of the portrait reads "USA 100" and shows a picture of a flag in regular light. The strip glows red under ultraviolet light.

STRAIGHT AND NARROW
Fine lines behind Franklin's portrait make the bill difficult to copy.

HAUNTED BILL
A ghostly Benjamin Franklin appears in the space to the right of his portrait when the bill is held up to light. Called a watermark, the image is created from different thicknesses of paper.

JUST YOUR TYPE
"USA 100" (above, left) is repeated within the number 100 in the lower left corner. "The United States of America" appears as a line in the left collar of Franklin's coat (above, right).

INK STAINS
The number 100 on the lower right of the bill looks green when viewed straight on. Tilt it back, though, and color-shifting ink turns the number black.

5 WAYS
You Use Satellites

Psst! Want in on a secret? Spaceships control our world! Well, not exactly. But much of the high-tech stuff you use—TVs, telephones, email—relies on tons of satellites whizzing around Earth. Here's a look at five ways you use satellites.

1 TELEVISION If you've watched TV, then you've used a satellite. Broadcast stations send images from Earth up to satellites as radio waves. The satellite bounces those signals, which can only travel straight, back down to a satellite dish at a point on Earth closer to your house. Satellite transmission works sort of like a shot in a game of pool when you ricochet your ball off the side of the pool table at an angle that sinks it into the right pocket.

2 WEATHER News flash! A severe thunderstorm with dangerous lightning is approaching your town. How do weather forecasters know what's coming so they can warn the public? They use satellites equipped with cameras and infrared sensors to watch clouds. Computers use constantly changing satellite images to track the storm.

3 TELEPHONE As you talk back and forth with a relative overseas on a landline, you might experience a delay of a quarter second—the time it takes for your voices to be relayed by a satellite bounce.

4 EMAIL Satellites also bridge long distances over the Internet by transmitting emails. Communications satellites, for phones and the Internet, use a geostationary orbit. That means that a satellite's speed matches Earth's rotation exactly, keeping the satellite in the same spot above Earth.

5 GPS Driving you to a party at a friend's house, your dad turns down the wrong street. You're lost. No problem if the car has a global positioning system (GPS) receiver. GPS is a network of satellites. The receiver collects information from the satellites and plots its distance from at least three of them. It can show where you are on a digital map. Thanks to satellites, you will make it to the party on time!

HOW A BASIC CELL CALL REACHES A FRIEND

You punch in a phone number and press SEND.

Your cell phone sends a coded message—a radio signal—to a tall cellular tower. The tower transfers the radio signal to a landline wire, and the signal travels underground.

The underground signal reaches a switching center where a computer figures out where the call needs to go next.

Through landlines, the message reaches the cell tower nearest the call's destination.

Switched back to a radio signal, the call reaches the person you dialed. Let the talking begin!

WHAT IS THE "CELL" IN CELL PHONE?

Each cellular tower serves a small area—about ten square miles (16 sq km). That area is called a cell. Whichever cell you are in when you make your call is the cell that picks up your data and sends it on.

IM Lingo

WANT A QUICK WAY TO chat with your friends and family when instant messaging? Use IM lingo for a fun and quick way to communicate. IM lingo is all based on making common phrases as short as possible so you can communicate as quickly as possible. **GTG! GL!** (Got to go! Good luck!)

AFK Away from keyboard	**IM** Instant message	**OTP** On the phone
ATM At the moment	**IMO** In my opinion	**PLS** Please
ASAP As soon as possible	**IMS** I am sorry	**PPL** People
B4 Before	**JIC** Just in case	**QT** Cutie
BBS Be back soon	**JIT** Just in time	**SRY** Sorry
BC Because	**JK** Just kidding	**SYL** See you later
BG Big grin	**JMS** Just making sure	**TAFN** That's all for now
BRB Be right back	**JTLYK** Just to let you know	**TBH** To be honest
BTW By the way	**K** Okay	**THX** Thanks
CUL8R See you later	**L8R** Later	**TIA** Thanks in advance
FYI For your information	**LOL** Laughing out loud	**TMI** Too much information
G2G Got to go	**NVM** Never mind	**TTYL** Talk to you later
GL Good luck	**NM** Not much	**TY** Thank you
GR8 Great	**MSG** Message	**WB** Welcome back
HAND Have a nice day	**NP** No problem	**WFM** Works for me
HT Hi there	**NW** No way	**WU?** What's up?
HTH Hope this helps	**OIC** Oh I see	**YT?** You there?
HW Homework	**OMG** Oh my gosh	**YTB** You're the best
IDK I don't know	**OTOH** On the other hand	**YW** You're welcome

EMOTICONS
These keyboard symbols represent faces and express your mood.

:) Smile **:(** Sad **;)** Wink **:D** Big Smile **:p** Sticking your tongue out
:—* Kiss **:O** Gasp **:|** Straight-faced/emotionless **:X** Denotes something bad
:'D Laughing so hard you're crying **:'(** Crying **:S** Confused

5 TIPS for Staying Safe on the Internet

1 Always get your parents' permission before posting messages or pictures on the Internet.

2 Make sure you know who you are "chatting" with. Sometimes people pretend to be different from who they really are. And definitely do not give out personal details.

3 Don't reply to emails from people you don't know.

4 Make sure to mind your manners. Just because you are online doesn't mean that you can be rude or mean.

5 If something makes you feel scared, uncomfortable, or confused while online, make sure you tell your parent or a trusted adult. Don't be scared to ask for help.

Common Conversions

TO CHANGE	TO	MULTIPLY BY	TO CHANGE	TO	MULTIPLY BY
acres	hectares	0.40	metric tons	tons (short)	1.10
centimeters	inches	0.39	miles	kilometers	1.61
cubic inches	milliliters	16.39	millimeters	inches	0.04
cubic feet	cubic meters	0.03	millimeters	cubic inches	0.06
cubic meters	cubic feet	35.31	millimeters	ounces (liquid)	0.03
cubic meters	cubic yards	1.31	ounces	grams	28.35
cubic yards	cubic meters	0.76	ounces (liquid)	milliliters	29.57
feet	meters	0.30	pints (dry)	liters	0.55
gallons (U.S.)	liters	3.79	pints (liquid)	liters	0.47
grams	ounces	0.04	pounds	kilograms	0.45
hectares	acres	2.47	quarts (dry)	liters	1.10
inches	millimeters	25.40	quarts (liquid)	liters	0.95
inches	centimeters	2.54	square inches	square centimeters	6.45
kilograms	pounds	2.20	square feet	square meters	0.09
kilometers	miles	0.62	square centimeters	square inches	0.16
liters	gallons	0.26	square kilometers	square miles	0.39
liters	pints (dry)	1.812	square meters	square feet	10.76
liters	pints (liquid)	2.11	square meters	square yards	1.20
liters	quarts (dry)	0.91	square miles	square kilometers	2.59
liters	quarts (liquid)	1.06	square yards	square meters	0.86
meters	feet	3.28	tons (short)	metric tons	0.91
meters	yards	1.09	yards	meters	0.91

The Periodic Table of Elements

Body Systems

60,000 miles of **blood vessels** *run through* your body.

The human body is a complicated mass of systems—

nine systems, to be exact. Each system has a unique and critical purpose in the body, and we wouldn't be able to survive without any of them.

The **NERVOUS** system controls the body.

The **MUSCULAR** system makes movement possible.

The **SKELETAL** system supports the body.

The **CIRCULATORY** system moves blood throughout the body.

The **RESPIRATORY** system provides the body with oxygen.

The **DIGESTIVE** system breaks down food into nutrients and gets rid of waste.

The **IMMUNE** system protects the body against disease and infection.

The **ENDOCRINE** system regulates the body's functions.

The **REPRODUCTIVE** system enables people to produce offspring.

Is it bedtime?

Most people think we yawn because we are tired. But that may not be true. We don't know for certain why we yawn, but there are many theories. Some scientists believe that we yawn when there is a change in activity. Other research has shown that we might yawn to cool off our brain by breathing in cool air. We also seem to yawn when we are bored or stressed, or even because we see someone else yawning! So you might be yawning for many reasons—not necessarily because it's time for bed!

Bet you didn't know

9 wacky facts about the human body

1 Your *hair* grows faster IN **WARM** WEATHER.

2 YOU CAN'T MOVE **YOUR BODY** when you **dream.**

3 People's **TONGUE PRINTS** are as unique as their **FINGERPRINTS.**

4 IF YOU **EAT** TOO MANY CARROTS, YOUR SKIN CAN TURN ORANGE.

5 THE AVERAGE AMERICAN'S **heart** beats about **three billion** TIMES IN A LIFETIME.

6 YOUR EYES CAN SEE ABOUT **TEN MILLION** DIFFERENT COLORS.

7 ABOUT ONE-QUARTER OF THE **body's bones are in the feet** —that's 52 out of more than 200!

8 YOUR THUMB is the same **LENGTH** as your **NOSE.**

9 DURING YOUR **LIFETIME,** YOU WILL PRODUCE ENOUGH SALIVA TO **FILL TWO** BACKYARD POOLS.

Your Amazing
eyes

Discover the magic of your body's built-in cameras.

You carry around a pair of cameras in your head so incredible they can work in bright sunshine or at night. Only about an inch in diameter, they can bring you the image of a tiny ant or a twinkling star trillions of miles away. They can change focus almost instantly and stay focused even when you're shaking your head or jumping up and down. These cameras are your eyes.

A CRUCIAL PART OF YOUR EYE IS AS FLIMSY AS A WET TISSUE.

A dragonfly darts toward your head! Light bounces off the insect, enters your eye, passes through your pupil (the black circle in the middle of your iris), and goes to the lens. The lens focuses the light onto your retina—a thin lining on the back of your eye that is vital but as flimsy as a wet tissue. Your retina acts like film in a camera, capturing the picture of this dragonfly. The picture is sent to your brain, which instantly sends you a single command—*duck!*

YOU BLINK MORE THAN 10,000 TIMES A DAY.

Your body has many ways to protect and care for your eyes. Each eye sits on a cushion of fat, almost completely surrounded by protective bone. Your eyebrows help prevent sweat from dripping into your eyes. Your eyelashes help keep dust and other small particles out. Your eyelids act as built-in windshield wipers, spreading tear fluid with every blink to keep your eyes moist and wash away bacteria and other particles. And if anything ever gets too close to your eyes, your eyelids slam shut with incredible speed—2/5 of a second—to protect them!

YOUR EYES SEE EVERYTHING UPSIDE DOWN AND BACKWARD!

As amazing as your eyes are, the images they send your brain are a little quirky: they're upside down, backward, and two-dimensional! Your brain automatically flips the images from your retinas right side up and combines the images from each eye into a three-dimensional picture. There is a small area of each retina, called a blind spot, that can't record what you're seeing. Luckily your brain makes adjustments for this too!

YOUR PUPILS CHANGE SIZE WHENEVER THE LIGHT CHANGES.

Your black pupils may be small, but they have an important job—they grow or shrink to let just the right amount of light enter your eyes to let you see.

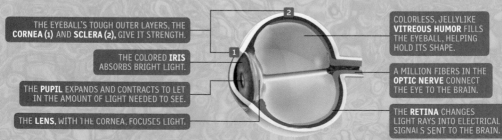

THE EYEBALL'S TOUGH OUTER LAYERS, THE **CORNEA (1)** AND **SCLERA (2),** GIVE IT STRENGTH.

THE COLORED **IRIS** ABSORBS BRIGHT LIGHT.

THE **PUPIL** EXPANDS AND CONTRACTS TO LET IN THE AMOUNT OF LIGHT NEEDED TO SEE.

THE **LENS,** WITH THE CORNEA, FOCUSES LIGHT.

COLORLESS, JELLYLIKE **VITREOUS HUMOR** FILLS THE EYEBALL, HELPING HOLD ITS SHAPE.

A MILLION FIBERS IN THE **OPTIC NERVE** CONNECT THE EYE TO THE BRAIN.

THE **RETINA** CHANGES LIGHT RAYS INTO ELECTRICAL SIGNALS SENT TO THE BRAIN.

The FIVE Senses

Do you love the feel of your favorite stuffed animal? Or the smell and taste of your favorite food? Maybe you love to look at beautiful flowers or listen to the latest band. If you enjoy doing any of these things, then you better thank your senses, all five of them! The five senses and their related organs help you to experience the world around you. Using our sense organs, we take in information from the world. This information is then sent to our brain, which tells us how to respond. These five senses are:

3 TASTE
Tongues taste sweet, sour, salty, and bitter.

1 SIGHT
Eyes see color, light, and depth.

4 HEARING
Ears hear sounds and vibrations.

2 SMELL
Noses smell scents.

5 TOUCH
Skin feels pain, temperature, and pressure.

Your eyes produce a teaspoon of tears every hour.

Scents smell better through your

right nostril   than your left.

Your Amazing
brain

Inside your body's supercomputer

Y ou carry around a three-pound mass of wrinkly material in your head that controls every single thing you will ever do. From enabling you to think, learn, create, and feel emotions to controlling every blink, breath, and heartbeat—this fantastic control center is your brain. It is a structure so amazing that a famous scientist once called it "the most complex thing we have yet discovered in our universe."

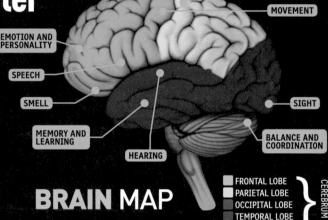

TOUCH

MOVEMENT

EMOTION AND PERSONALITY

SPEECH

SMELL

SIGHT

MEMORY AND LEARNING

BALANCE AND COORDINATION

HEARING

BRAIN MAP

FRONTAL LOBE
PARIETAL LOBE
OCCIPITAL LOBE } CEREBRUM
TEMPORAL LOBE

CEREBELLUM
BRAIN STEM

Your brain determines if you are left-handed or right-handed, but what does it say about you?

LEFTIES

Several studies suggest that lefties are highly creative and artistic. In fact, many performers—including Mary-Kate Olsen, Jim Carrey, and Paul McCartney of the Beatles—are left-handed. Lefties also seem to have an edge in tennis, fencing, and other individual sports. And they may learn better visually. For instance, if someone draws them a map, they understand exactly how to get where they're going.

AMBIDEXTROUS

Surprise! Most scientists think that no one is truly ambidextrous, or able to use both hands equally well. But if you have a dominant hand and can still write or throw accurately with the other, you're what scientists call mixed-handed. Studies show mixed-handers tend to have better memories of everyday experiences, such as what they had for lunch a week ago. Mixed-handers also may be more open-minded.

RIGHTIES

Some studies show that right-handers are more talkative and outgoing than lefties. Other research has revealed that righties are more coordinated. They also tend to learn better verbally— they can listen to directions to a friend's house and understand how to get there. Right-handers also may be better pitchers and basketball guards. Just ask righty Michael Jordan.

How to Decode Your Dreams

YOUR BRAIN MAY BE TELLING YOU SOMETHING

How many times have you told someone, "I had the craziest dream last night"? Lots of times, huh? You can have up to six dreams a night. Some of them are sure to be wild!

Dreams are created by the part of your brain that stores memories, emotions, and thoughts. At night your brain blends what's stored in your mind with what you've been thinking about lately. The result can be wild but realistic dreams.

Dreams hardly ever become reality, but they may contain hints about what's going on in your life. "Dreams help us get in touch with our deeper feelings," says dream researcher Alan Siegel. "They can tell us a lot about ourselves and may even help us figure out problems."

Scientists have discovered that many dreams contain common themes that have meaning. Here are eight types of dreams that may tell you a lot about you and what's happening in your life!

THE THEME Being chased

WHAT IT MEANS The scary thing that's chasing you is probably a symbol of a real-life problem you don't want to deal with. But this dream is telling you it's time to stop running from the problem and start facing it.

THE THEME Showing up in pajamas

WHAT IT MEANS Your brain may be helping you recover from a real-life embarrassing moment. If no one's making a big deal about the pj's, chances are your friends think you're cool no matter what. If they *are* laughing? It may be time for some new friends!

THE THEME Flying

WHAT IT MEANS It's likely you're flying high in real life as well. Maybe your friends see you as a leader, or your parents have given you more freedom.

THE THEME Being lost

WHAT IT MEANS You're probably feeling a little lost in life. Are you currently facing a tough decision? You might be afraid of making the wrong choice. Think carefully about your options to find your way out of this dilemma.

THE THEME Falling

WHAT IT MEANS You might have too much going on. It's time to slow down and take a break from whatever is stressing you out. And the soft landing? A sign that you'll soon get over this tough time.

THE THEME Not being able to move

WHAT IT MEANS You're probably feeling "stuck" in life. (Maybe your parents just grounded you.) You need to think about how you got into this sticky situation and then try to make smarter choices in the future.

THE THEME Losing something

WHAT IT MEANS You may be looking for an ego boost. Perhaps you want to try out a new sport or hobby, and you're not sure if you can do it. Search deep inside yourself for that confidence. It's there—you just have to find it!

THE THEME Being unprepared or late

WHAT IT MEANS You're worrying big-time about an upcoming event or project. If you're prepared, it's just a sign that you're nervous. That's normal. But if you've been slacking, take this dream as a hint and get to work!

ZZzz!

A dream usually lasts from 10 to 40 minutes.

Your brain waves can be more active when you're dreaming than when you're awake.

You'll spend about six years of your life dreaming.

Exercise for Health

Why should you exercise? You will ...
- be stronger.
- be less likely to be overweight.
- decrease chances of getting sick.
- feel happier.

Exercise without even knowing it!

STAY OUT OF THE CAR—Walk or bike short distances instead of driving.

GET OUT THERE—Help with yard work and housework; they're great calorie burners.

STEP IT UP—Take the stairs instead of elevators or escalators.

STICK TOGETHER—Gather your family and go for a run, walk, or bike ride.

Warm Up
Spend about five minutes before exercising doing light activity, such as walking or stretching.

Exercise
Try to do about 15 to 45 minutes of exercise each day. Some great ideas for exercise include walking, running, swimming, biking, skateboarding, or group sports, like basketball, soccer, baseball, volleyball, or football.

Cool Down
Don't hurt yourself—make sure you cool down after vigorous exercise by doing five minutes of light activity.

Eat healthy and try new foods.

COOL CLICK

To learn more about nutrition and the food pyramid, go online to the U.S. Department of Agriculture's website. www.mypyramid.gov

Grains	Vegetables	Fruits	Milk	Meat & Beans
Make half your grains whole	Vary your veggies	Focus on fruits	Get your calcium-rich foods	Go lean with protein

Oils Oils are not a food group, but you need some for good health. Get your oils from fish, nuts, and liquid oils such as corn oil, soybean oil, and canola oil.

★ Find your balance between food and fun ★ Fats and sugars — know your limits

FunStuff

Healthy Choices

You might think you'd like to eat everything in this candy store. But there are a few things that most candy stores don't sell hidden among all the mouthwatering treats. Can you find the good-for-you items listed at right?

HIDDEN ITEMS

- apple
- banana
- bowl of soup
- broccoli
- carrot
- carton of milk
- drumstick
- fish
- grapefruit
- jar of vitamins
- lima bean
- sandwich
- toothbrush

ANSWERS ON PAGE 339

What Your FAVORITE COLOR Says About YOU

Your favorite color can say a lot about you.

Researchers say that we have two basic responses to color: physical (red can make you hot) and emotional (yellow can make you happy). These responses, as well as what some colors represent historically, mean fave colors may reflect your personality. Just for fun, see how colors may affect your mood. Feeling blue? Maybe grab some yellow!

ORANGE
can represent energy and warmth. It can also make you hungry and boost your health.

IF YOU LIKE ORANGE, YOU ... are a nice person who's rarely sick. When you're not cooking or eating, you're outside enjoying the sun.

PINK
can represent health and love.

IF YOU LIKE PINK, YOU ... are cheerful and always look out for your friends. You have no problem speaking your mind, and you express your feelings well.

RED
can represent danger. It can also excite the senses and activate blood circulation.

IF YOU LIKE RED, YOU ... are energetic and like taking risks. Very aware of what's going on around you, you are a leader who's not afraid to speak up.

YELLOW
can represent victory. It can also help you be more organized and optimistic.

IF YOU LIKE YELLOW, YOU ... are a positive person who likes cheering people up. Your competitiveness and organizational skills help you succeed.

PURPLE
can represent wealth or royalty. It's also associated with art and music.

IF YOU LIKE PURPLE, YOU ... have great taste in anything from clothes to music to food, which you always share with your friends. You are also very creative.

BLUE
can represent peace and loyalty. It's also a universally popular color.

IF YOU LIKE BLUE, YOU ... are well liked by everyone. People come to you with their problems, and you do what you can to make sure everyone gets along.

GREEN
can represent nature and growth. It may also calm people down.

IF YOU LIKE GREEN, YOU ... spend a lot of time outside and like doing new things. You're very mellow and easygoing, never taking things too seriously.

COLOR-CODE YOUR LIFE!

Some people think colors can help influence your life. Decorate your room with colors based on what you want to achieve.

RED daring

ORANGE power

YELLOW/ GOLD happiness

GREEN growth

BLUE calm

PURPLE wealth

PINK love

BLACK wisdom

BROWN stability

The Straight Scoop

3 TRICKS THAT WILL PUT YOU IN A GREAT MOOD

Make your own decisions.
WHY IT WORKS
You'll feel confident and in control when you make thoughtful, individual choices.
HOW TO DO IT
• Decide your family's dinner menu for a week. Go through cookbooks and select your favorite recipes.
• Redecorate your room (with permission). Make it scream "you" by choosing a theme and your favorite colors.

Chill out.
WHY IT WORKS
Relaxing can zap stress and put you in a positive mood.
HOW TO DO IT
• Turn off the TV and pick up a book, letting the story launch you into another world.
• Do at least one quiet activity a week, such as listening to music or stargazing.

Laugh.
WHY IT WORKS
Laughter releases endorphins, chemicals in your brain that make you feel good.
HOW TO DO IT
• Tell a new joke every day. For ideas, go online. **kids.nationalgeographic.com/ Activities/JustJoking**
• Make a hilarious video with your friends.

STOP! Freeze right there! Now, without moving a muscle, check out your posture. If you're like a lot of people, you are sitting sort of slumped over.

Ergonomics refers to the study of the relationship between people and their surroundings. For example, if you are slumping at the computer or are hunched over carrying a really heavy backpack, you have poor ergonomics. When you don't practice good ergonomics, that's when the pain sets in, so be sure to take good care of yourself and your ergonomics. Follow these tips to good health.

Good Ideas for Gaming and Computer Use
• Sit up straight with your shoulders back.
• Make sure your feet are on the ground.
• Take frequent breaks; walk around and stretch.

Better Backpack Strategies
• Carry less. Buying an extra set of books to keep at home is less expensive than doctor visits.
• Tighten straps so the weight is close to your body, and don't let the backpack ride below the waist.
• Put the heaviest items closest to your back, and the pack will be less likely to pull you out of balance.
• Kids should not carry backpacks that weigh more than 10 to 15 percent of their body weight. So students weighing 100 pounds (45 kilograms) should not carry more than 10 to 15 pounds (4.5 to 6.8 kilograms) in their packs.

SENSATIONAL SCIENCE PROJECTS

YOU CAN LEARN A LOT ABOUT SCIENCE from books, but to really experience it firsthand, you need to get into the lab and "do" some science. Whether you're entering a science fair or just want to learn more on your own, there are many scientific projects you can do. So put on your goggles and lab coat and start experimenting!

Most likely, the topic of the project will be up to you. So remember to choose something that is interesting to you.

THE BASIS OF ALL SCIENTIFIC INVESTIGATION AND DISCOVERY IS THE SCIENTIFIC METHOD. CONDUCT THE EXPERIMENT USING ITS STEPS:

1 **Observation/Research**—Ask a question or identify a problem.

2 **Hypothesis**—Once you've asked a question, do some thinking and come up with some possible answers.

3 **Experimentation**—How can you determine if your hypothesis is correct? You test it. You perform an experiment. Make sure the experiment you design will produce an answer to your question.

4 **Analysis**—Gather your results and use a consistent process to carefully measure the results.

5 **Conclusion**—Do the results support your hypothesis?

6 **Report Your Findings**—Communicate your results in the form of a paper that summarizes your entire experiment.

Bonus Hint
Take your project one step farther. Your school may have an annual science fair, but there are also local, state, regional, and national science fair competitions. Compete with other students for awards, prizes, and scholarships!

EXPERIMENT DESIGN
There are three types of experiments you can do.

A Model Kit—a display, such as an "erupting volcano" model. Simple and to the point.

The Demonstration—shows the scientific principles in action, such as a tornado in a wind tunnel.

The Investigation—the home run of science projects, and just the type of project for science fairs because it demonstrates proper scientific experimentation, this uses the scientific method to reveal answers to questions.

SURFING THE INTERNET

ALMOST ANY AND ALL INFORMATION can be found on the Internet (also known as the World Wide Web). The Internet is used for many reasons—work, study, and, fun!

Be Specific
To come up with the most effective keywords, write down what you're looking for in the form of a question and then circle the most important words in that sentence. Those are the keywords to use in your search! And for best results, use words that are specific rather than general.

Research
Research on the Internet involves "looking up" information using a search engine (see list below). Type one or two keywords—words that describe what you're looking to know more about—and the search engine will provide a list of websites that contain information pertinent to your topic.

Trustworthy Sources
When conducting Internet research, be sure the website you use is reliable and the information it provides can be trusted. Sites produced by well-known, established organizations, companies, publications, educational institutions, or the United States government are your best bet.

Don't Copy
Avoid Internet plagiarism. Take careful notes and cite the websites you use to conduct research (see p.37 for "No Copying!").

Here are some HELPFUL and SAFE search engines for kids:

Google Safe Search **www.squirrelnet.com/search/Google_SafeSearch.asp**

Yahooligans **www.yahooligans.com**

Superkids **www.super-kids.com**

Ask Jeeves Kids **www.ajkids.com**

Kids Click **www.kidsclick.org**

COOL CLICKS

Looking for a good science fair project idea? Go online. **www.sciencebuddies.org.** Or read about a science fair success. **kids.nationalgeographic.com/Stories/SpaceScience/Snowfences**

ANSWERS

Safari Search
ANSWERS (from page 51):

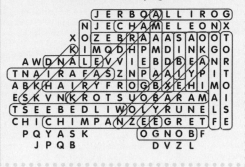

Yipes! Stripes!
ANSWER (from page 61): **E**

Go Fish!
ANSWERS (from page 73):

What in the World?
ANSWERS (from page 89):
top row: **spider, moth, horsefly.**
middle row: **millipede, grasshopper.**
bottom row: **beetle, caterpillar, dragonfly.**

Take the Plunge
ANSWERS (from page 235):

Fun Stuff
ANSWERS (from page 333):

Stump Your Parents
ANSWERS
(from inside front cover):
1. C;   2. A;   3. C;
4. C;   5. C;   6. B

ABBREVIATIONS:

AA: Animals Animals
AP: Associated Press
AWS: Archivo White Star
AA: Animals Animals - Earth Scenes
BAL: The Bridgeman Art Library
CB: Corbis
DA: David Aguilar
GI: Getty Images
IS: iStockphoto.com
JI: Jupiter Images
MW: Martin Walz
NGS: NationalGeographicStock.com
PF: Pieter A. Folkens
PR: Photo Researchers, Inc
SS: Shutterstock
WHHA: White House Historical Association
ZSD: Zoological Society of San Diego

All Maps
by NGS unless otherwise noted

All illustrations & charts
by Stuart Armstrong unless otherwise noted

Zipper artwork
by Nathan Jurevicius

Front Cover
Dolphin, Stephen Frink/The Image Bank/GI; Snowboarder, Michael Reusse/JI; Frog, Mark Kostich/IS; Tut, Michael Melford/The Image Bank/GI

Back Cover
Gecko, Cre8tive Images/SS; Earth, Alex Staroseltsev/SS; Spider, Eric Isselée/SS; Shark, Michele Westmorland/Photodisc/GI; Sushi, Patricia Brabant/Cole Group/PhotoDisc/GI; Gorilla, Michael Nichols/NGS; Chichén Itzá pyramid, Hannamariah/SS; Light bulb, Radius Images/JI; Horn, Ingram Premiere Edition

Spine
Snowboarder, Michael Reusse/JI; Frog, Mark Kostich/IS; Tut, Michael Melford/The Image Bank/GI

Inside Front Cover
Moon, Steve Satushek/Stone/GI; Lion, Thomas Mangelsen/Minden Pictures; Dinosaur, Gary Ombler/Dorling Kindersley/GI

Front Matter (2–7)
2–3, Tom Brakefield/PhotoDisc/GI; 5 up, Damien Meyer/AFP/GI; 5 center, Colin Monteath/Minden Pictures/NGS; 5 lo, Suzi Eszterhas/Minden Pictures; 6 up, Celia Peterson/Arabian Eye/GI; 6 center, Michael & Patricia Fogden/Minden Pictures; 6 lo, Jonathan Kirn/Stone/GI; 7 up, Paul A. Souders/CB; 7 center, Frans Lanting/CB; 7 lo, Katsumi Kasahara/AP

Your World 2010 (8–17)
8–9, Brad Wrobleski/Masterfile; 10 up, Chuck Kennedy/Pool/Newscom; 10 lo, Charles Dharapak/AP; 11 up, Julie NG/NGS; 11 lo, Wang Changshan/AP; 12, A. L. Stanzani/Ardea; 13 up, Michael A. King/www.Kasbah-Cattery.com; 13 lo A, Ervin Monn/SS; 13 lo B,

Hagit Berkovich/SS; 13 lo C, Bryan Bedder/GI; 13 lo D, Dreamworks LLC/The Kobal Collection; 13 lo E, Lauren Greenfield/VII/AP; 14 A, Bettmann/CB; 14 B, Lyle Stafford/Reuters; 14 C, Mihai Simonia/SS; 14 D, Gary Braasch/CB; 14 E, Kyodo/AP; 14 F, Scott Neville/AP; 14 G, Emory Kristoff/NGS; 14 H, Earl Quenzel; 14 I, David W. Kelley/SS; 15 up, Toby Kroner; 15 center, map, MW; 15 lo, F. Latreille©IMC; 16, Robert Clark/NGS; 16 up, Cre8tive Images/SS; 17 up, Doug Perrine/naturepl.com; 17 lo A, Michael Zysman/SS; 17 lo B, Michael Woodruff/SS; 17 lo C, Mark Bonham/SS

Awesome Adventure (18–37)
18-19, Colin Monteath/Hedgehog House/Minden Pictures; 20-21, illustrations, Tom Richmond; 20-21, maps, MW; 22 up, Radius Images/JI; 22 far left, John Birdsall/Age Fotostock; 22 left, Philip Kaake/Photonica/GI; 22 right, Foodfolio/ImageState/JI; 22 far right, Martin Jacobs/FoodPix/JI; 23, Ian Austin/Aurora; 23 up, map, MW; 24 left, www.macfreefilms.com; 24 right, Jimmy Chin/NGS; 25 up, George Steinmetz/NGS; 25 lo, Rebecca Hale/NGS; 26-27, Araldo De Luca/AWS; 27 up right, Drawings by Elisabetta Ferrero/AWS; 27 lo, ExtrordinAir, Inc; 28 left, Johnson Space Center/NASA; 28 right, Kennedy Space Center/NASA; 28-29, Carsten Peter/NGS; 29 left, Martin Harvey/National Geographic Television; 29 right, Michael Nichols/NGS; 30 up, Stephen Fink/Digital Vision/GI; 30 center, EcoPrint/SS; 30 lo, Annie Griffiths Belt; 30 lo left, map, MW; 31 up, Martin Harvey; 32 up, Eric Gevaert/SS; 32 lo, Ali Pellatt; 33 up, Noah Hamilton/Sipa; 33 center, Fujimoto/Garden Island Newspapers/Sipa; 33 lo, Barbara Kinney; 34 left, Losevsky Pavel/SS; 34 center, Trutta/SS; 34 right, Rebecca Roth; 35 up, 2008 Gregory Guida/Durrell; 35 lo, Mattias Klum/NGS; 36, Killroy Productions/SS

Amazing Animals (38–111)
38-39, Suzi Eszterhas/Minden Pictures; 40 right, EML/SS; 40 left, Eric Isselée/SS; 41 up left, Johan Swanepoel/SS; 41 up right, Michele Westmorland/Photodisc/GI; 41 lo, Eric Isselée/SS; 41 up, mashe/SS; 41 lo right, Dennis Sabo/SS; 42, Joel Sartore/NGS; 43, Tim Davis/CB; 44 up, Johnny Johnson/AA; 44 lo, Paul Nicklen/NGS; 45, Keren Su/Digital Vision/GI; 45 lo, map, MW; 46, Keren Su/CB; 47, Joel Sartore/NGS; 48, Anne Keiser/NGS; 49, Randy Olson; 50 up, Henk Bentlage/SS; 50 lo, WEDA/EPA/Sipa; 51, illustration, Greg Clarke; 52 up, George Grall/NGS; 52 lo all, Chris Collins Studio; 53 up left, Michael Gadomski/AA; 53 up right, Joe McDonald/Bruce Coleman, Inc.; 53 lo a, Dr. Paul A. Zahl/PR.; 53 lo b, Martijan Lammertink; 53 lo c, Michael P. Fogden/Bruce Coleman, Inc.; 53 lo d, G. Carleton Ray/PR.; 54 left, Milton Heiberg Studios; 54 right, Bill Bachman; 55, gallimaufry/SS; 56, Howard Noel; 57 up, uri press gmbh/safaripark - Udo Richter; 57 lo, Sergei Karpukhin/Reuters; 58-1, Art Wolfe; 58-2, Gertrud & Helmet Denzau/naturepl.com; 58-3, Renee Lynn/CB; 58-4, Randy Green/Taxi/GI; 59-5, Lynn M. Stone/naturepl.com; 59-6, Peter Blackwell/naturepl.com; 59-7,

William Dow/CB; 59-8, Anup Shah/naturepl.com; 59-a, Lynda Richardson/CB; 59-b, Jonathan & Angie Scott/JI; 59-c, Fritz Polking/Frank Lane Picture Agency/CB; 59-d, Joel Sartore/NGS; 59-e, Philip Perry/Frank Lane Picture Agency/CB; 60, Xinhua, Mao Siqian/AP; 61-a, Andy Rouse; 61-b, Zig Leszczynski/AA; 61-c, VCG/FPG; 61-d, Gerard Lacz/AA; 61-e, Andy Rouse; 61-f, David Boyle/AA; 62, Chris Johns/NGS; 63, Mattias Klum/NGS; 64, Jeff Hunter/Photographer's Choice/GI; 65, Dave King/Dorling Kindersley/GI; 66-67, Illustration, PF; 67 up, Tom Brakefield/Digital Vision/GI; 68 up, Rebecca Hale/NGS; 68 lo, Paul Souders/Photodisc/GI; 69, Tyson Mangelsdorf; 70, Mike Parry/Minden Pictures/NGS; 71, Design Pics Inc/Alamy Ltd; 72 up, Norbert Wu; 72 lo, Sissie Brinberg & Cotton Coulson/NGS; 73, illustration, James Yamasaki; 74 up, SecondShot/SS; 74 lo, maps, MW; 75 up, Fritz Polking/Frank Lane Picture Agency/CB; 75 lo, FloridaStock/SS; 76-1, Ken Bohn/ZSD; 76-2, Newscom.com; 76-3, Ken Bohn/ZSD; 76-4, Ken Bohn/ZSD; 76-5, Tammy Spratt/ZSD; 76-6, Ken Bohn/ZSD; 77 up, Keith Levit/SS; 77 lo, W. Perry Conway; 78 up, Chris Whittier; 78 lo, Kevin Welsh/Oregon Zoo; 79, map, MW; 80 up, David Haring/Duke University Primate Center; 80 lo left, Siede Preis/GI; 80 lo right, The Image Bank/GI; 80 inset, maps, MW; 81 all, Karine Aigner/NGS; 82, A. Witte/C. Mahaney/GI; 83, G.K.& Vikki Hart/GI; 83 center, Susan Crawford; 84 up left, Petra Wegner/Alamy Ltd; 84 up right, Denise Kappa/SS; 84 center, Richard Kolar/AA; 84 lo left, illustration, Alec Longstreth; 84 lo right, Demark/SS; 85 up (dog), Mary Evans Picture Library/Alamy Ltd; 85 up, Hemera Technologies/JI; 85 center, Image 100/JI; 85 lo, Rebecca Hale/NGS; 86 left, Karel Brož/SS; 86 right, Melinda Fawver/SS; 87, Romanchuck Dimitry/SS; 88, Stephen Dalton/Minden Pictures; 89-1, Ingo Arndt/naturepl.com; 89-2, Millard H. Sharp/PR.; 89-3, BIOS Borrell Bartomeu/Peter Arnold, Inc.; 89-4, George Grall/NGS; 89-5, George Grall/NGS; 89-6, George Grall/NGS; 89-7, Mark Moffett/Minden Pictures; 89-8, Tim Fitzharris/Minden Pictures; 90, Tui De Roy/Minden Pictures; 91 up, Karine Aigner/NGS; 91 lo, Nicole Garmston/newspix/AP; 92, Gerry Ellis/Minden Pictures/NGS; 93 up, Anup Shah/naturepl.com; 93 lo, Cyril Ruoso/JH Editorial/Minden Pictures; 94 up, illustration, Scott Matthews; 94, Sebastian Knight/SS; 95, David Lohman/NGS; 96 up, Chris Butler/PR.; 96 center, Publiphoto/PR.; 96 lo, Pixeldust Studios/NGS; 97 up, Laurie O'Keefe/SS; 97 center, Chris Butler/PR.; 97 lo, Publiphoto/PR.; 97 very lo, D. Krentz, courtesy Project Exploration; 98 left, Martha Cooper/NGS; 98-99, Pixeldust Studios/NGS; 99 up, Ira Block/NGS; 99 lo, Ira Block/NGS; 100 left, Paul B. Moore/SS; 100 right, Andreas Meyer/SS; 101-105, Franco Tempesta; 106 up, Michael Ledray/SS; 106 lo, Stock Foundry Images/SS; 107 up, Andrea Danti/SS; 107 lo, Atlantic Digital/Dorling Kindersley RF/GI; 108-109 all, © 2007 NGHT, Inc.; 110, Walter Meayers Edwards/NGS; 111, Gelpi/SS

Culture Connection (112–143)

112-113, Celia Peterson/ Arabian Eye/ GI; 114, Annie Griffiths Belt; 114 lo, illustrations, Graham Smith; 116 up, Madlen/ SS; 116-117 all, Comstock; 118, illustrations, Scott Matthews; 119 up, Brian Stablyk/ Stone/ GI; 119 lo, Scott S. Warren; 120 up, Rebecca Hale/ NGS; 120 center all (food), Comet Photography Inc., Food Styling by Lisa Cherkasky; 120 lo, Jose Fuste Raga/ CB; 121 up, Rebecca Hale/ NGS; 121 center, Rebecca Hale/ NGS; 121 lo, Pavlo Vakhrushev/ IS; 122 up, Bradley-Ireland Productions; 122 lo, Mark Thiessen/ NGS; 123, illustrations, Susan Crawford; 124 up, Randy Olson/ NGS; 124 lo left, Martin Gray/ NGS; 124 lo right, Reuters/ CB; 125 up, Reza/ NGS; 125 lo left, Richard Nowitz/ NGS; 125 lo right, Winfield Parks/ NGS; 127 up, Phillipe Lissac/Godong/CB; 127 lo, Mark Thiessen/ NGS; 128 up, Florida Division of Blind Services; 128 lo, Stephen Coburn/ SS; 130 left, Comet Photography Inc., Food Styling by Lisa Cherkasky; 130 right, Mark Thiessen/ NGS; 131 up left, Sandra Caldwell/ SS; 131 up right, IS; 131 lo left, Patricia Brabant/ Cole Group/ GI; 131 lo right, Richard Nowitz/ NGS; 132 up left, J. Helgason/ SS; 132 lo left, Julián Rovagnati/ SS; 132 right, Maram/ SS; 133 up, Desmond Boylan/ Reuters/ CB; 133 lo, Brad Hoffmann; 135 left, Stephen St. John/ NGS; 135 center, Joel Sartore/ NGS; 135 right, Michael Nichols/ NGS; 136 left, Doug Matthews/ SS; 137 up, Mark Thiessen/ NGS; 137, illustrations, John Montroll; 138, Reproduction by permission of the Buffalo and Erie County Public Library, Buffalo, New York; 139 background, XYZ/ SS; 139 lo, Michelle Harvey/ SS; 140, Visions of America, LLC/ Alamy; 141 up, Ingram Premier Editions; 141 lo, Ingram Premier Editions; 142 up, Joanne van Hoof/ SS; 142 center, Route66/ SS; 142 lo, Joel Blit/ SS

Geography Rocks (144–217)

144-145, Michael & Patricia Fogden/ Minden Pictures; 151-a, Maria Stenzel/ NGS; 151-b, Bill Hatcher/ NGS; 151-c, Carsten Peter/ NGS; 151-d, Carsten Peter/ NGS; 151-e, Gordon Wiltsie/ NGS; 151-f, James P. Blair/ NGS; 151-g, Thomas J. Abercrombie/ NGS; 151-h, Bill Curtsinger/ NGS; 152 up, WilleeCole/ SS; 152 center, SS; 152 lo, Eric Isselée/ SS; 152-153, map, MW; 153 up left, Katja Kreder/ FAN Travelstock/ JI; 153 up right, Yoshio Tomii/ SuperStock; 153 lo left, Comstock/ CB; 153 lo right, Radius Images/ JI; 154, George F. Mobley/ NGS; 155, Keith Levit/ SS; 156-157, Theo Allofs/ Danita Delimont.com; 158 up, Penny Tweedie/ CB; 158 lo, Neale Cousland/ SS; 159, Tim Laman/ NGS; 160, Holger Mette/ SS; 161 up, John Warden/ Riser/ GI; 161 lo, David Evans/ NGS; 162 up, fdimeo/ SS; 162 lo, Jorma Jaemsen/ zefa/ CB; 163, Chet/ SS; 164 lo, Paul Damien/ National Geographic/ GI; 165 inset, Olivier Le Queinec/ SS; 165, Radius Images/ JI; 166, Photos.com; 167 left, Jarno Gonzalez Zarraonandia/ SS; 167 right, Juan Silva/ Iconica/ GI; 175, Phidias/ CB; 177, illustration, Susan Crawford; 180, Charles & Josette Lenars/ CB; 183, Rebecca Hale/ NGS; 184, Bob Krist; 191 up, Alex Staroseltsev/ SS; 196, Carlos Sanchez Pereyra/ SnapVillage.com; 200, Jennifer Lynn Arnold/ SS; 202 up, GI; 202 lo left, PhotoDisc;

202 lo right, PhotoDisc; 204-205, gary718/ SS; 205 left, Glenn Taylor/ IS; 205 right, James Steidl/ SS; 206-207, Layne Kennedy/ CB; 206 up, David Barnes/ Danita Delimont. com; 207 up, Jennay Hitesman/ ManePhoto; 207 center, Joe Oesterle/ Weird US; 207 lo, www.Roadsideamerica.com; 208 up left, Courtesy of Dreamworld; 208 up right, Courtesy of Ocean Park, Hong Kong; 208 lo, Stefan Merkl; 209, illustration, Marty Baumann; 210, Photos.com; 211 up left, Jeremy Woodhouse/ Photodisc Green/ GI; 211 up right, map MW; 211 lo, Mark Thiessen/ NGS; 212-a, David Sutherland/ The Image Bank / GI; 212-b, Ferdinand Knab/ BAL/ GI; 212-c, Ferdinand Knab/BAL/GI; 212-d, Ferdinand Knab/BAL/GI; 212-e, Wilhelm van Ehrenberg/ BAL/ GI; 212-f, Ferdinand Knab/BAL/GI; 212-g, DEA Picture Library/ GI; 212-h, Holger Mette/ SS; 212-i, Holger Mette/ SS; 212-j, Jarno Gonzalez Zarraonandia/ SS; 212-k, David Iliff/ SS; 212-l, ostill/ SS; 212-m, Hannamariah/ SS; 212-n, Jarno Gonzalez Zarraonandia/ SS; 213 up left, Gilmanshin/ SS; 213 up right, Taylor S. Kennedy/ NGS; 213 lo, Iourii Tcheka/ SS; 214, inset, SS; 214-215, illustration, Clayton Hanmer; 217 all, NGS

Going Green (218–239)

218-219, Jonathan Kirn/ Stone/ GI; 220 up left, Andrjuss/ SS; 220 up center, hfng/ SS; 220 up right, Milos Luzanin/ SS; 220 lo left, Kenneth C. Zirkel/ IS; 220 center right, Andrjuss/ SS; 220 lo right, Cristian Lupu/ IS; 221, Rick Barrentine/ CB; 222 inset, UncleGenePhoto/ SS; 222, David T. Gomez/ IS; 223 up, image100/ CB; 223 lo, Michael & Patricia Fogden/ CB; 224 up, Olga Kolos/ SS; 224 lo, Mosista Pambudi/ SS; 225, Joel Sartore/ NGS; 226 up, Paul Marcus/ SS; 226 lo, Rebecca Hale/ NGS; 227, Rebecca Hale/ NGS; 228, Nik Niklz/ SS; 229, Paul Nicklen/ NGS; 231 up left, Walter Rawlings/ Robert Harding World Imagery/ GI; 231 up right, Sarah Leen/ NGS; 231 lo left, Richard Nowitz/ NGS; 231 lo right, Marc Moritsch/ NGS; 232 up, SS; 232 lo, Mikael Damkier/ SS; 233 up, Jim Parkin/ SS; 233 lo, J. Weishaar/ D&W Images; 234, Morgan Lane Photography/ SS; 235, illustration, James Yamasaki; 236 up left, Jim Craigmyle/ CB; 236 up right, Richard Heinzen/ SuperStock; 236 center, Evan Sklar/ FoodPix/ JI; 236 lo left, Big Cheese Photo/ SuperStock; 236 lo right, Lori Adamski/ Sport// JI; 237 up, Tom Stewart/ CB; 237 center, Purestock/ SuperStock; 237 lo left, Brand X Pictures/ JI; 237 lo right, Mitsuaki Iwago/ Minden Pictures; 238, Albo003/ SS

History Happens (240–269)

240-241, Paul A. Souders/ CB; 242 up, Scott Rothstein/ SS; 242 lo, Courtesy of Declaration of Independence Road Trip; 243 up, Cristina Ciochina/ SS; 243 lo, Stephen Coburn/ SS; 244 left, Gary Blakeley/ SS; 244 right, S.Borisov/ SS; 246, WHHA; 247, WHHA; 247 lo right, Charles Dharapak/ AP; 248, WHHA; 249, WHHA; 249 lo right, Bettmann/ CB; 250, WHHA; 250 (Bush), The White House; 250 (Obama), The White House; 251 left, Cory Thoman/ SS; 251 right, SS; 252 right, Ron Edmonds/ AP; 252 left, The Granger Collection, NY; 253, John Mottern/ AFP/ GI; 254

left, Bettmann/ CB; 254 up right, CB; 254 center, AP; 254 lo left, GI; 254 lo right, NASA; 255 up, Ivan Cholakov/ SS; 255 lo, Library of Congress; 256 up, AP; 256 lo, Bettmann/ CB; 257, Aga/ SS; 258, illustration, Kimberly Schumber; 259, images.com; 260, Mark Thiessen/ NGS; 261, illustration, Chip Wass; 262 up, map, MW; 262, illustration, Tyson Mangelsdorf; 263, Eduard E. Vigl/ NGS; 264 all, illustrations, Susan Synarski; 265 up, Rebecca Hale/ NGS; 265 center, Bettmann/ CB; 265 lo, Bettmann/ CB; 266, Bettmann/ CB; 267, Bob Thomas/ Popperfoto/ GI; 268, Pablo Martinez Monsivais/ AP; 269 lo, Bluehill/ SS

Wonders of Nature (270–297)

270-271, Frans Lanting/ CB; 272, Stockbyte/ GI; 273 left, Artem Efimov/ SS; 273 center & right, Weiss and Overpeck, The University of Arizona ; 274, Digital Vision/ GI; 276, Eric Skitzi/ AP; 277, Galen Rowell/ SS; 278 up, illustrations, Johnee Bee; 278 lo, Kimimasa Mayama/ Reuters Newmedia Inc./ CB; 280 up left, Raymond Gehman/ NGS; 280 up right, George F. Mobley/ NGS; 280 lo left, Paul Nicklin/ SS; 280 lo right, Raymond Gehman/ NGS; 281 up left, Annie Griffiths Belt/ NGS; 281 up right, Beverly Joubert/ NGS; 281 lo left, Michael Melford/ NGS; 281 lo right, Maria Stenzel/ NGS; 283 up, SS; 283 lo, JewelryStock/ Alamy Ltd; 284, David Nicholls/ Science Photo Library/ PR; 285, Mark Thiessen/ NGS; 286, Jarvis Gray/ SS; 288 up, Raymond Gehman/ NGS; 288 lo, SS; 289, Jim Richardson, 290-291, Chris Anderson/ SS; 293 up, Mark Thiessen/ NGS; 293 lo, illustration, NGS; 295, illustration, NGS; 295 (volcano), Shusei Nagaoka/ NGS; 295 lo all, Susan Sanford/ NGS; 296, AVAVA/ SS

Super Science (298–337)

298-299, Katsumi Kasahara/ AP; 300-a, Sebastian Kaulitzki/ SS; 300-b, sgame/ SS; 300-c, Arie v.d. Wolde/ SS; 300-d, Hydromet/ SS; 300-e, André Klaassen/ SS; 300-f, SS; 300-g, Benjamin Jessop/ IS; 301, DA; 302-303, all, DA; 304 up, JPL-Caltech/ NASA; 304 lo, JPL-Caltech/G. Helou (Caltech)/ NASA; 305-308 all, DA; 309 up, Neo Edmund/ SS; 309 center, Michael Taylor/ SS; 309 lo, JPL-Caltech/ NASA; 310, BAL; 310 background, Giovanni Benintende/ SS; 311, Maisei Raman/ SS; 312, illustration, Mondolithic Studios; 313, Dan Herrick/ Alamy Ltd; 314 up, Dr. Gavin Miller; 314 center, JPL/ NASA; 314 lo, Sam Ogden/ PR.; 315, DA; 316 up, Ingmar Cramers; 316 lo, Babylon-Freefly.com; 317 up, Courtesy of U-Boat Worx B.V.; 317 center & lo, Yun Rhee; 318, Zafer Kizilkaya; 319, illustration, Michele Romero; 321, illustration, Mondolithic Studios; 322 all, Daniel R. Westergren; 323 up left, Courtesy of Lockheed Martin Missiles & Space; 323 right all, illustrations, Johnee Bee; 324 up, Ian Hooton/ SPL/ Alamy Ltd; 324 background, pakowacz/ SS; 325, Joachim Angeltun/ PhotoDisc/ GI; 326 up, Sebastian Kaulitzki/ SS; 326 lo, Suzanne Tucker/ SS; 328 up, Dennis Cooper/ zefa/ CB; 328 lo, illustration, Linda Nye; 330, illustration, Robert J. Demarest; 331, illustration, Blake Thornton; 332, USDA; 333, illustration, George Bates; 335, Mike Kemp/ Rubberball; 336, Rob Marmion/ SS; 337 up, Fred Sweet/ SS; 337 lo, Rob Marmion/ SS

344

Published by the
National Geographic Society

John M. Fahey, Jr.
President and Chief Executive Officer

Gilbert M. Grosvenor
Chairman of the Board

Tim T. Kelly
President, Global Media Group

John Q. Griffin
President, Publishing

Nina D. Hoffman
Executive Vice President,
President of Book Publishing Group

Melina Gerosa Bellows
Executive Vice President of
Children's Publishing and Editor in Chief,
NATIONAL GEOGRAPHIC KIDS Magazine

Prepared by the Book Division

Nancy Laties Feresten, *Vice President,*
Editor in Chief, Children's Books
Bea Jackson, *Director of Design and Illustrations,*
Children's Books
Jennifer Emmett, *Executive Editor,*
Reference and Solo, Children's Books
Amy Shields, *Executive Editor, Series,*
Children's Books
Carl Mehler, *Director of Maps*

Staff for this Book

Jennifer Emmett, Priyanka Lamichhane,
Project Editors
Susan Kehnemui Donnelly, *Editor*
James Hiscott Jr., *Art Director*
Ruthie Thompson, Dennis Voss, *Designers*
Lori Renda, Rebecca Roth, *Illustrations Editors*
Matt Chwastyk, Steven D. Gardner,
Nicholas P. Rosenbach, *Map Research, Editing,*
and Production
Stuart Armstrong, *Graphics Illustrator*
Nikki Clapper, *Copy Editor*
Connie D. Binder, *Indexer*
Michelle Harris, *Researcher*
Vicki Ariyasu, *Homework Help*
Educational Consultant
Jennifer Thornton, *Managing Editor*
Grace Hill, *Associate Managing Editor*
Kathryn Murphy, *Editorial Intern*
Jamie McCoy, *Photography Intern*
Heidi Vincent, *Vice President,*
Direct Response Sales and Marketing
Jeff Reynolds, *Marketing Director, Children's Books*
R. Gary Colbert, *Production Director*
Lewis R. Bassford, *Production Manager*
Susan Borke, *Legal and Business Affairs*

Manufacturing and Quality Management

Christopher A. Liedel, *Chief Financial Officer*
Phillip L. Schlosser, *Vice President*
Chris Brown, *Technical Director*
Rachel Faulise, Nicole Elliott, Monika Lynde,
Manufacturing Managers

In Partnership with
NATIONAL GEOGRAPHIC KIDS Magazine

Julie Vosburgh Agnone, *Executive Editor*
Jonathan Halling, *Design Director*
Robin Terry, *Senior Editor*
Rachel Buchholz, *Special Projects Editor*
Catherine D. Hughes, *Science Editor*
Photo: Jay Sumner, *Photo Director;* Karine Aigner,
Senior Editor; Kelley Miller, *Editor*
Art: Eva Absher, *Associate Design Director;*
Nicole M. Lazarus, *Associate Art Director;*
Julide Obuz Dengel, *Art Production Assistant*
Erin Taylor Monroney, Eleanor Shannahan, Sharon
Thompson, *Writer-Researchers*
Administration: Jill E. Yaworski, *Editorial Assistant;*
Tammi Colleary, *Business Specialist*
Production: David V. Showers, *Director*

Founded in 1888, the National Geographic Society is
one of the largest nonprofit scientific and educational
organizations in the world. It reaches more than
285 million people worldwide each month through
its official journal, NATIONAL GEOGRAPHIC, and its four
other magazines; the National Geographic Channel;
television documentaries; radio programs; films;
books; videos and DVDs; maps; and interactive media.
National Geographic has funded more than 8,000
scientific research projects and supports an
education program combating geographic illiteracy.

For more information, please call
1-800-NGS LINE (647-5463) or write
to the following address:
NATIONAL GEOGRAPHIC SOCIETY
1145 17th Street NW
Washington, D.C. 20036-4688 U.S.A.

Visit us online at nationalgeographic.com
For information about special discounts for bulk
purchases, please contact National Geographic Books
Special Sales: ngspecsales@ngs.org
For rights or permissions inquiries, please contact
National Geographic Books Subsidiary Rights:
ngbookrights@ngs.org
Teachers and librarians go to ngchildrensbooks.org